PLUTO
URASAWA x TEZUKA

A NEW VISION BASED ON ASTRO BOY – *'THE GREATEST ROBOT ON EARTH'*
BY NAOKI URASAWA AND OSAMU TEZUKA

04

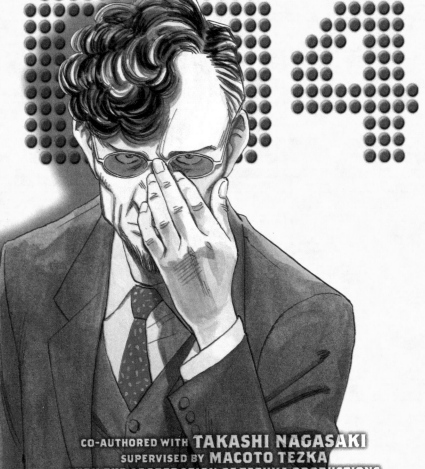

CO-AUTHORED WITH **TAKASHI NAGASAKI**
SUPERVISED BY **MACOTO TEZKA**
WITH THE COOPERATION OF TEZUKA PRODUCTIONS

Act 24 THE PROFESSOR'S DAY OFF

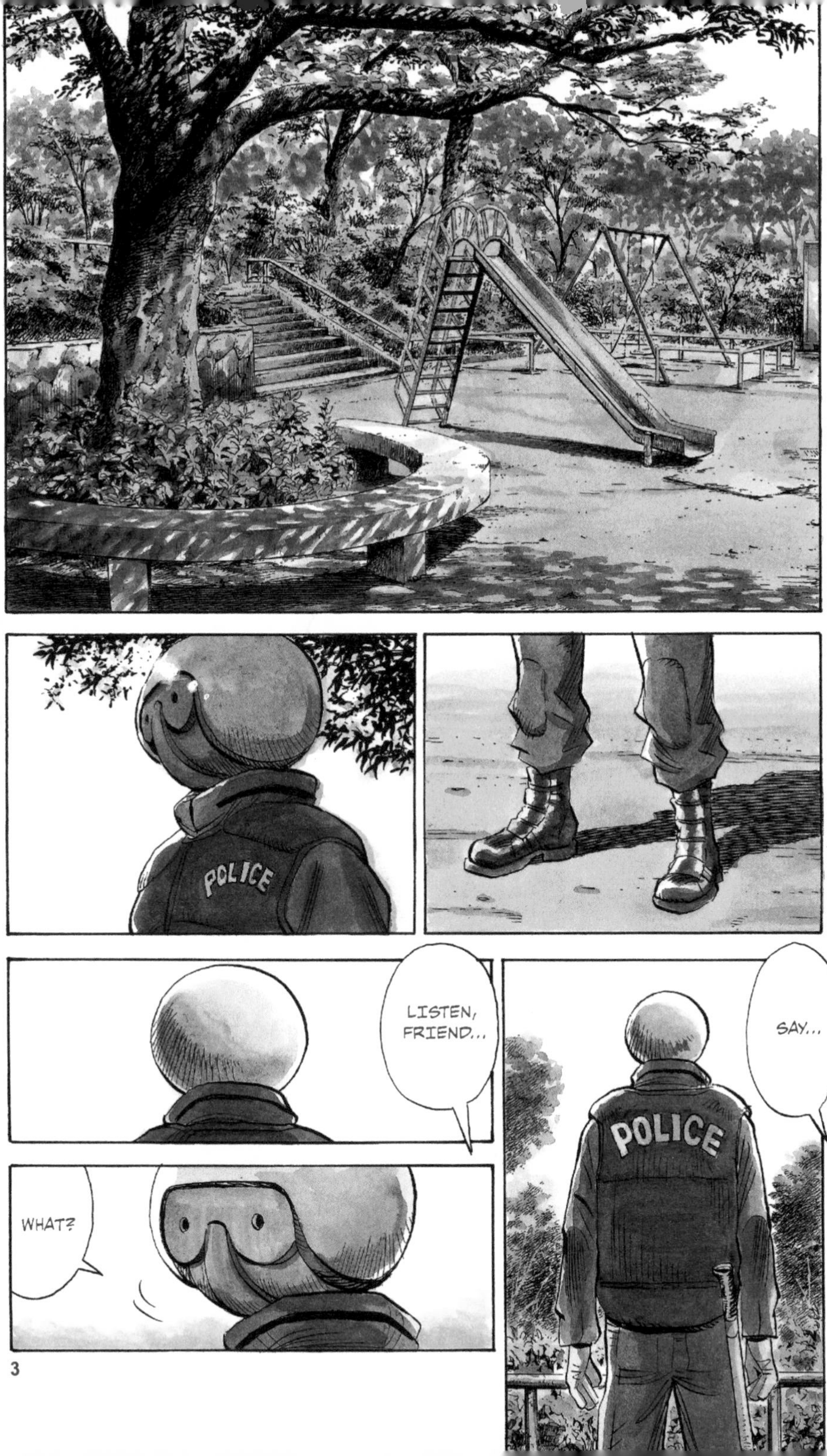
POLICE
POLICE
SAY...
LISTEN, FRIEND...
WHAT?
POLICE

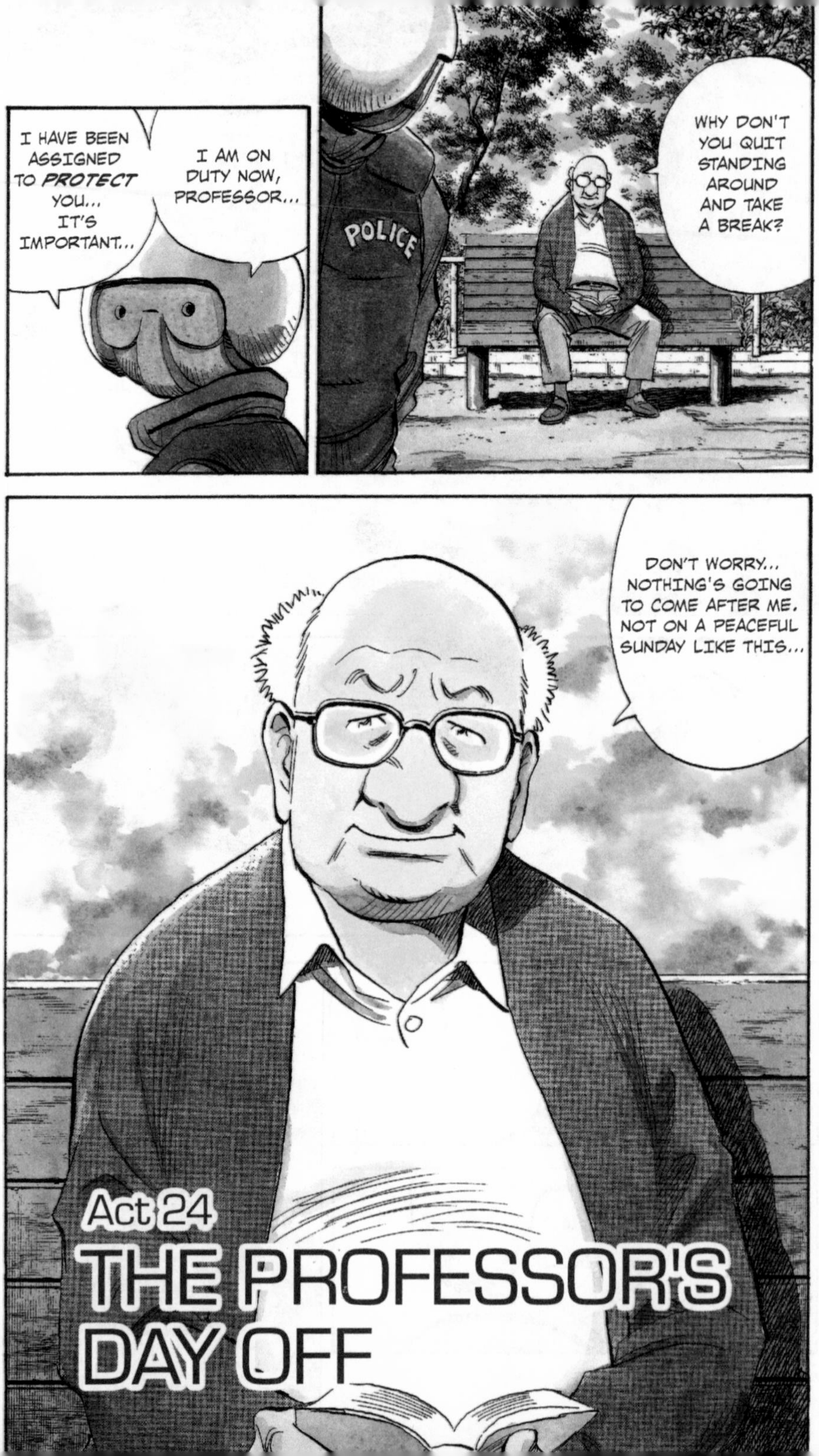
WHY DON'T YOU QUIT STANDING AROUND AND TAKE A BREAK?
I AM ON DUTY NOW, PROFESSOR...
I HAVE BEEN ASSIGNED TO PROTECT YOU... IT'S IMPORTANT...
POLICE
DON'T WORRY... NOTHING'S GOING TO COME AFTER ME. NOT ON A PEACEFUL SUNDAY LIKE THIS...
Act 24
THE PROFESSOR'S DAY OFF

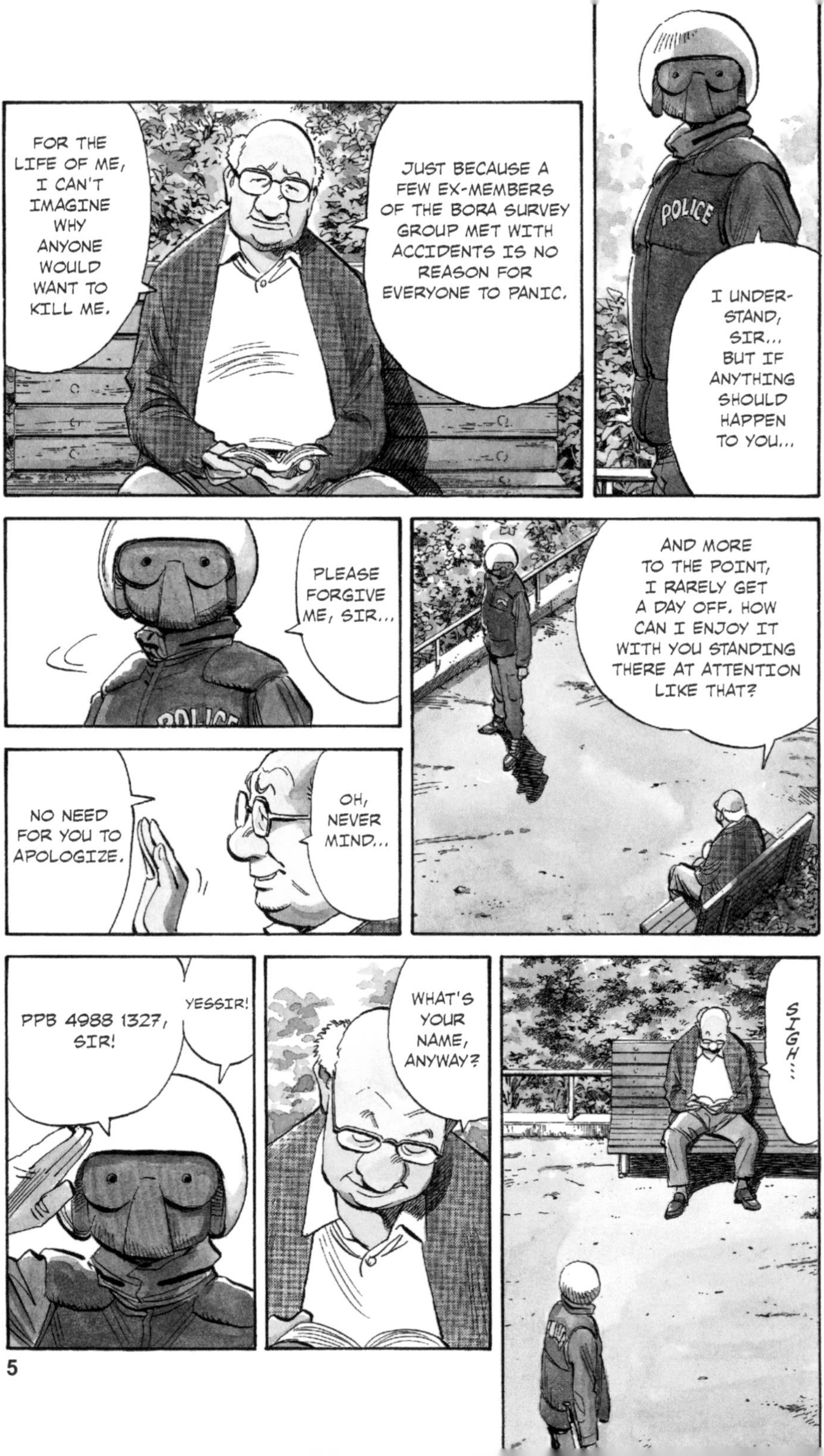
I UNDER-STAND, SIR... BUT IF ANYTHING SHOULD HAPPEN TO YOU...
JUST BECAUSE A FEW EX-MEMBERS OF THE BORA SURVEY GROUP MET WITH ACCIDENTS IS NO REASON FOR EVERYONE TO PANIC.
FOR THE LIFE OF ME, I CAN'T IMAGINE WHY ANYONE WOULD WANT TO KILL ME.
AND MORE TO THE POINT, I RARELY GET A DAY OFF. HOW CAN I ENJOY IT WITH YOU STANDING THERE AT ATTENTION LIKE THAT?
PLEASE FORGIVE ME, SIR...
POLICE
OH, NEVER MIND...
NO NEED FOR YOU TO APOLOGIZE.
SIGH...
WHAT'S YOUR NAME, ANYWAY?
YESSIR!
PPB 4988 1327, SIR!

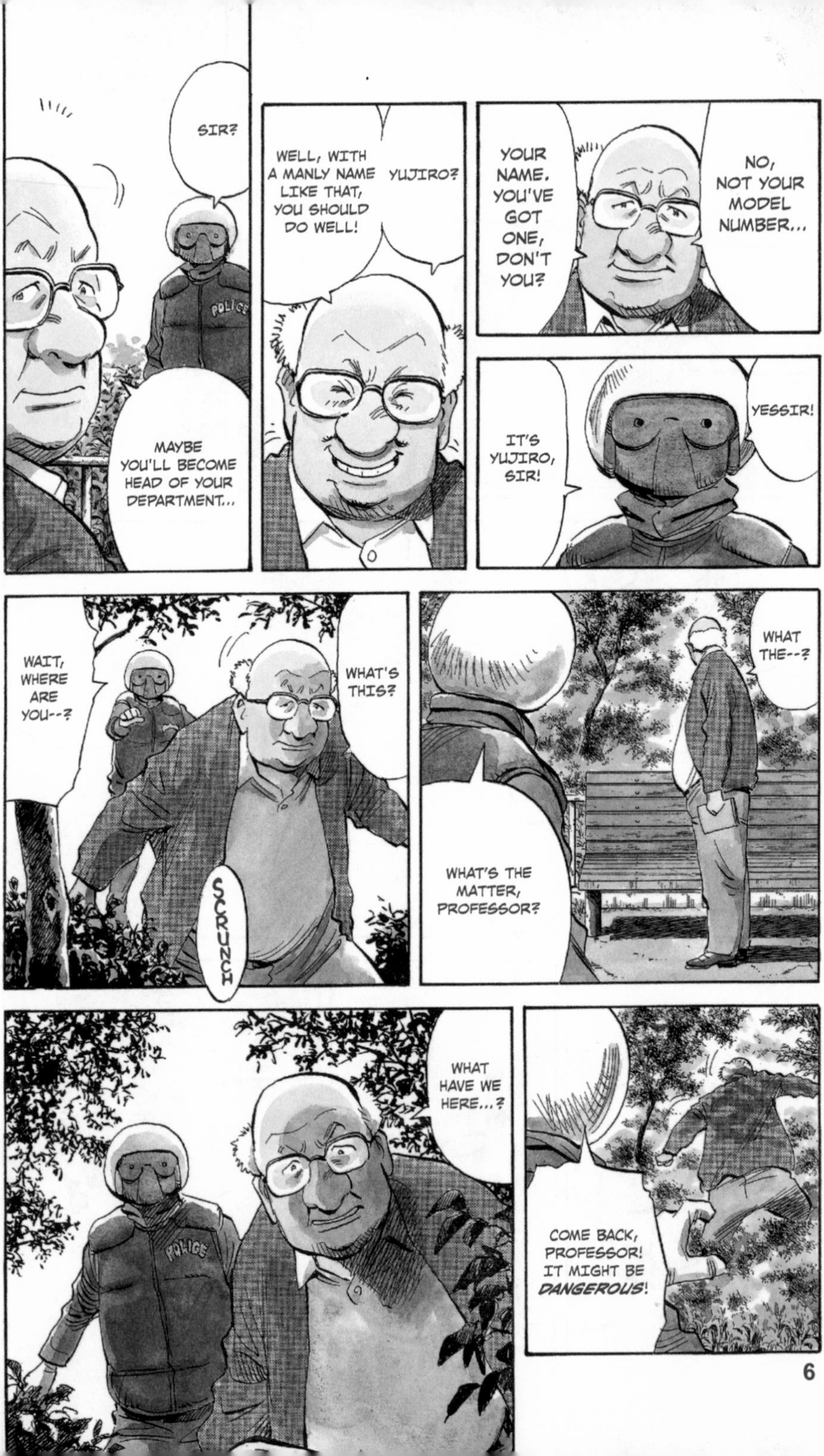
NO, NOT YOUR MODEL NUMBER...
YOUR NAME. YOU'VE GOT ONE, DON'T YOU?
YESSIR!
IT'S YUJIRO, SIR!
YUJIRO?
WELL, WITH A MANLY NAME LIKE THAT, YOU SHOULD DO WELL!
SIR?
MAYBE YOU'LL BECOME HEAD OF YOUR DEPARTMENT...
WHAT THE--?
WHAT'S THE MATTER, PROFESSOR?
WHAT'S THIS?
WAIT, WHERE ARE YOU--?
SCRUNCH
COME BACK, PROFESSOR! IT MIGHT BE ***DANGEROUS***!
WHAT HAVE WE HERE...?

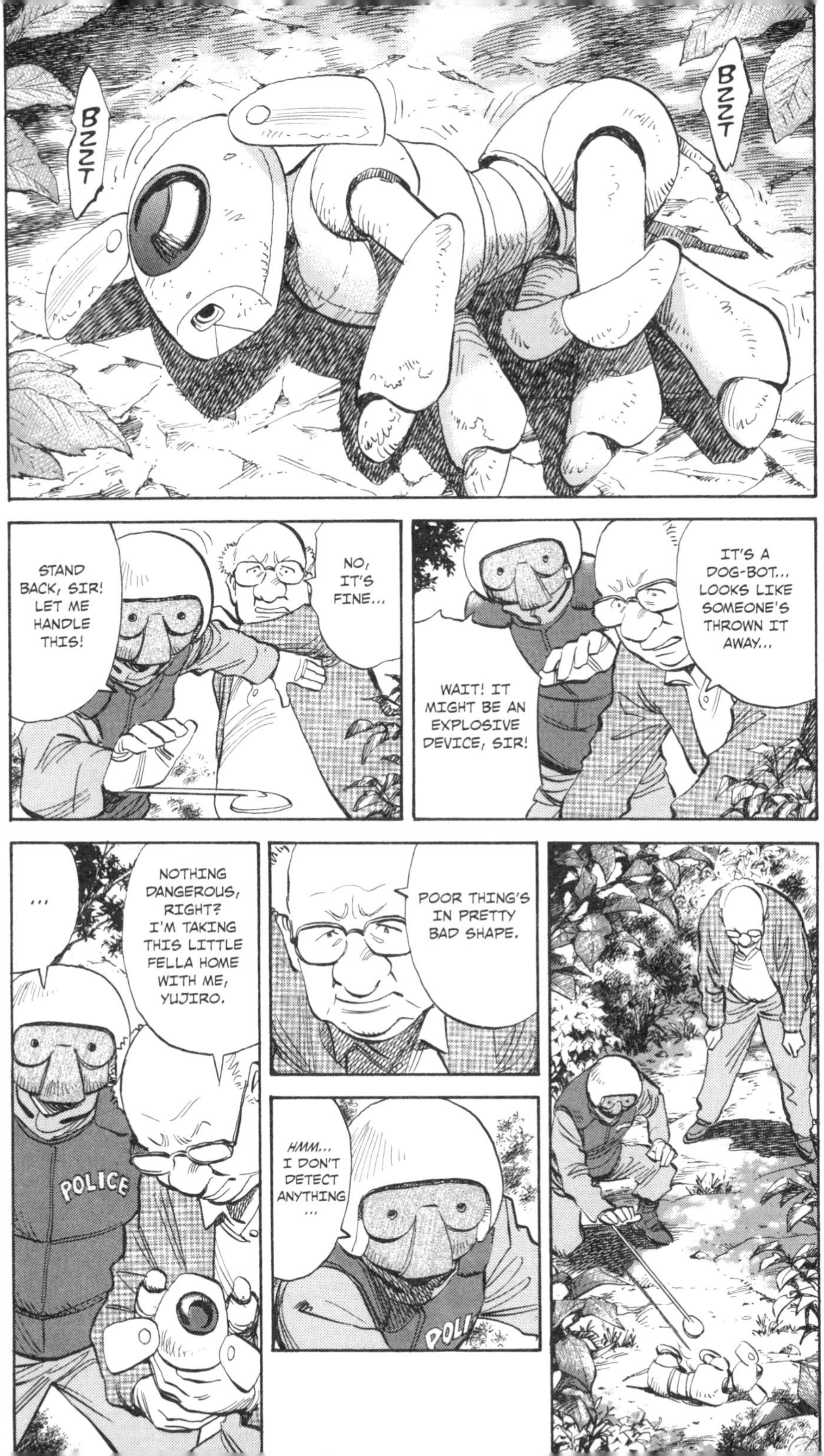
BZZT
BZZT
IT'S A DOG-BOT... LOOKS LIKE SOMEONE'S THROWN IT AWAY...
WAIT! IT MIGHT BE AN EXPLOSIVE DEVICE, SIR!
NO, IT'S FINE...
STAND BACK, SIR! LET ME HANDLE THIS!
POOR THING'S IN PRETTY BAD SHAPE.
HMM... I DON'T DETECT ANYTHING...
NOTHING DANGEROUS, RIGHT? I'M TAKING THIS LITTLE FELLA HOME WITH ME, YUJIRO.
...
POLICE

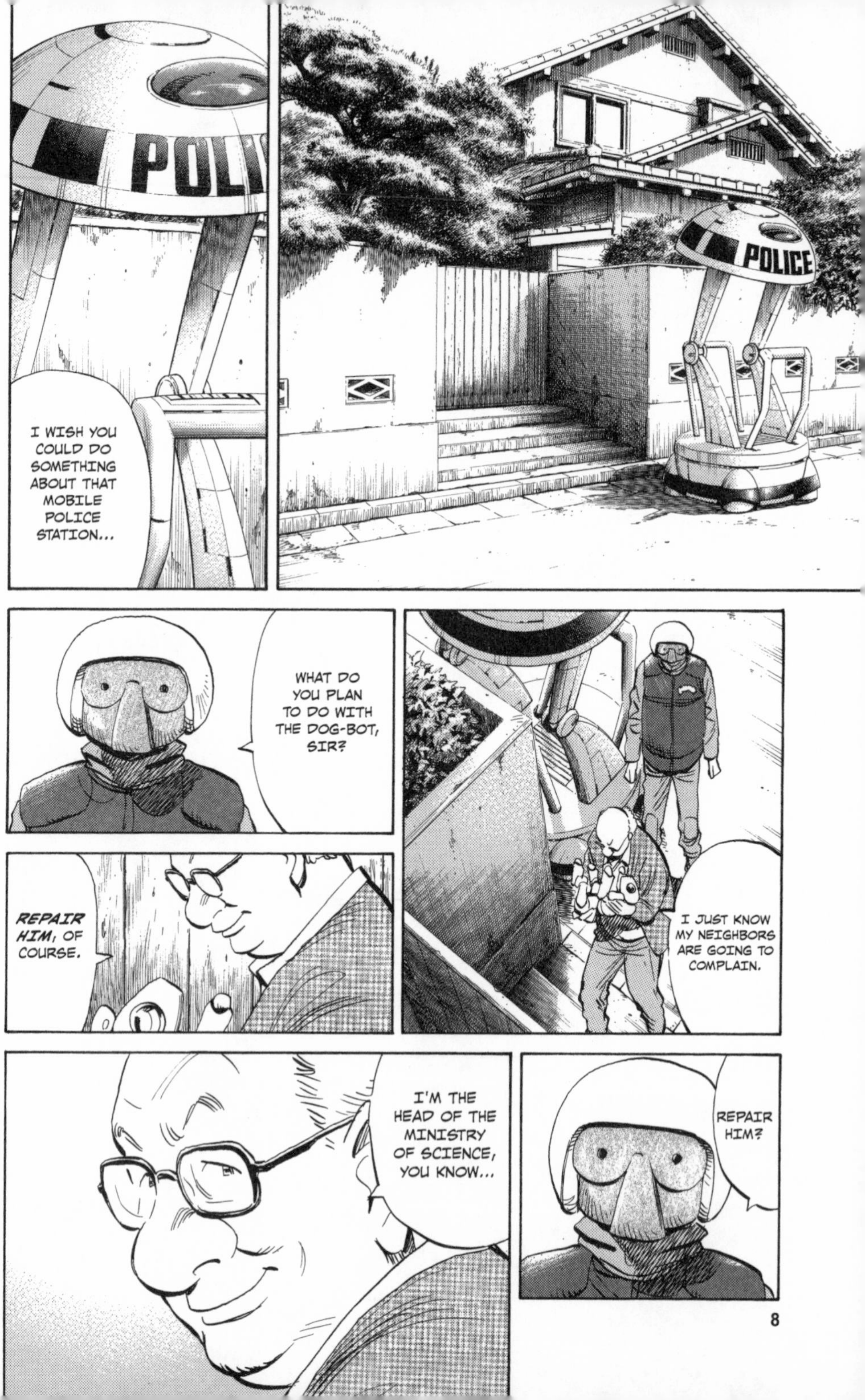
POLICE
I WISH YOU COULD DO SOMETHING ABOUT THAT MOBILE POLICE STATION...
I JUST KNOW MY NEIGHBORS ARE GOING TO COMPLAIN.
WHAT DO YOU PLAN TO DO WITH THE DOG-BOT, SIR?
REPAIR HIM, OF COURSE.
REPAIR HIM?
I'M THE HEAD OF THE MINISTRY OF SCIENCE, YOU KNOW...

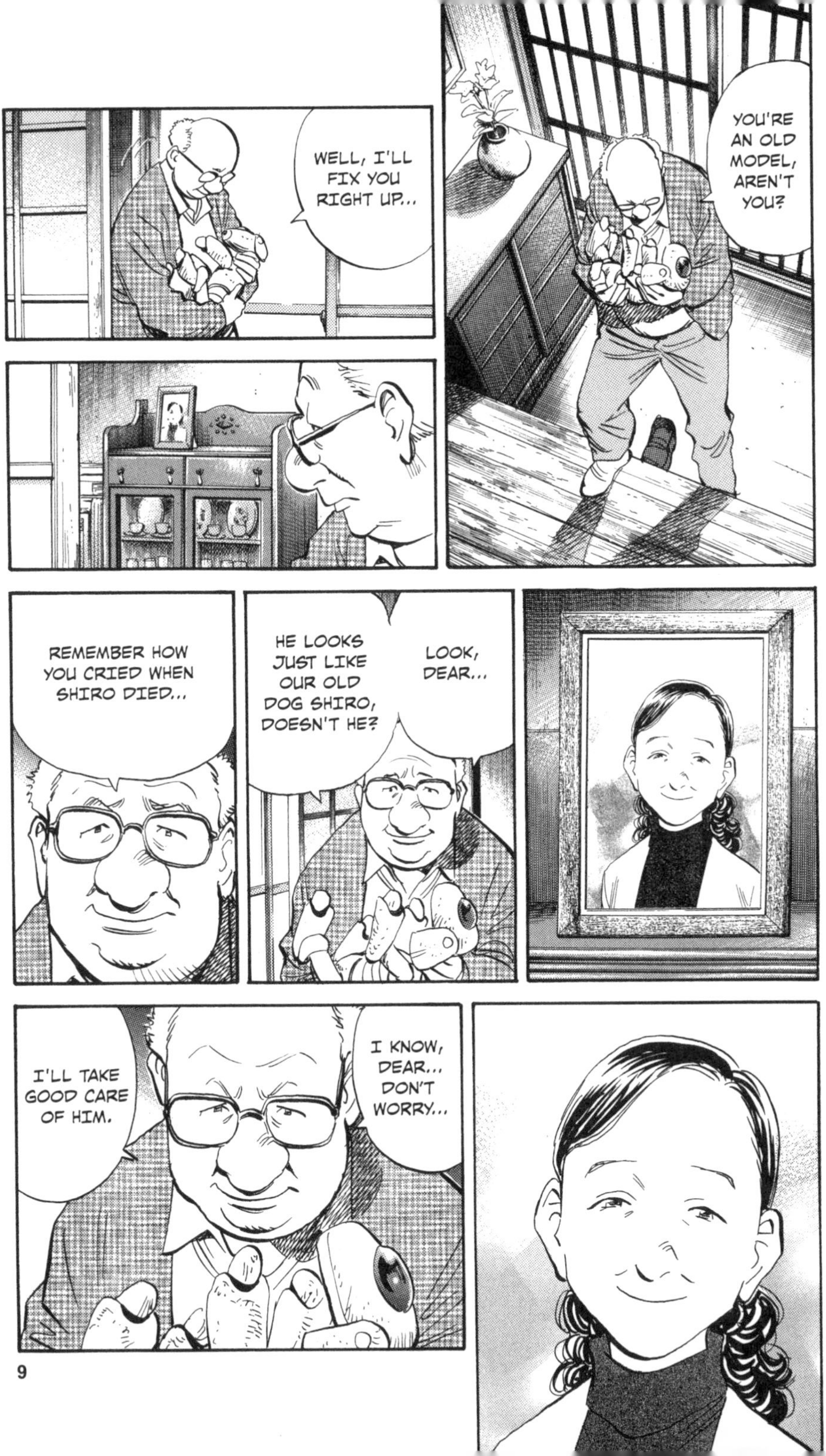
YOU'RE AN OLD MODEL, AREN'T YOU?
WELL, I'LL FIX YOU RIGHT UP...
LOOK, DEAR...
HE LOOKS JUST LIKE OUR OLD DOG SHIRO, DOESN'T HE?
REMEMBER HOW YOU CRIED WHEN SHIRO DIED...
I KNOW, DEAR... DON'T WORRY...
I'LL TAKE GOOD CARE OF HIM.

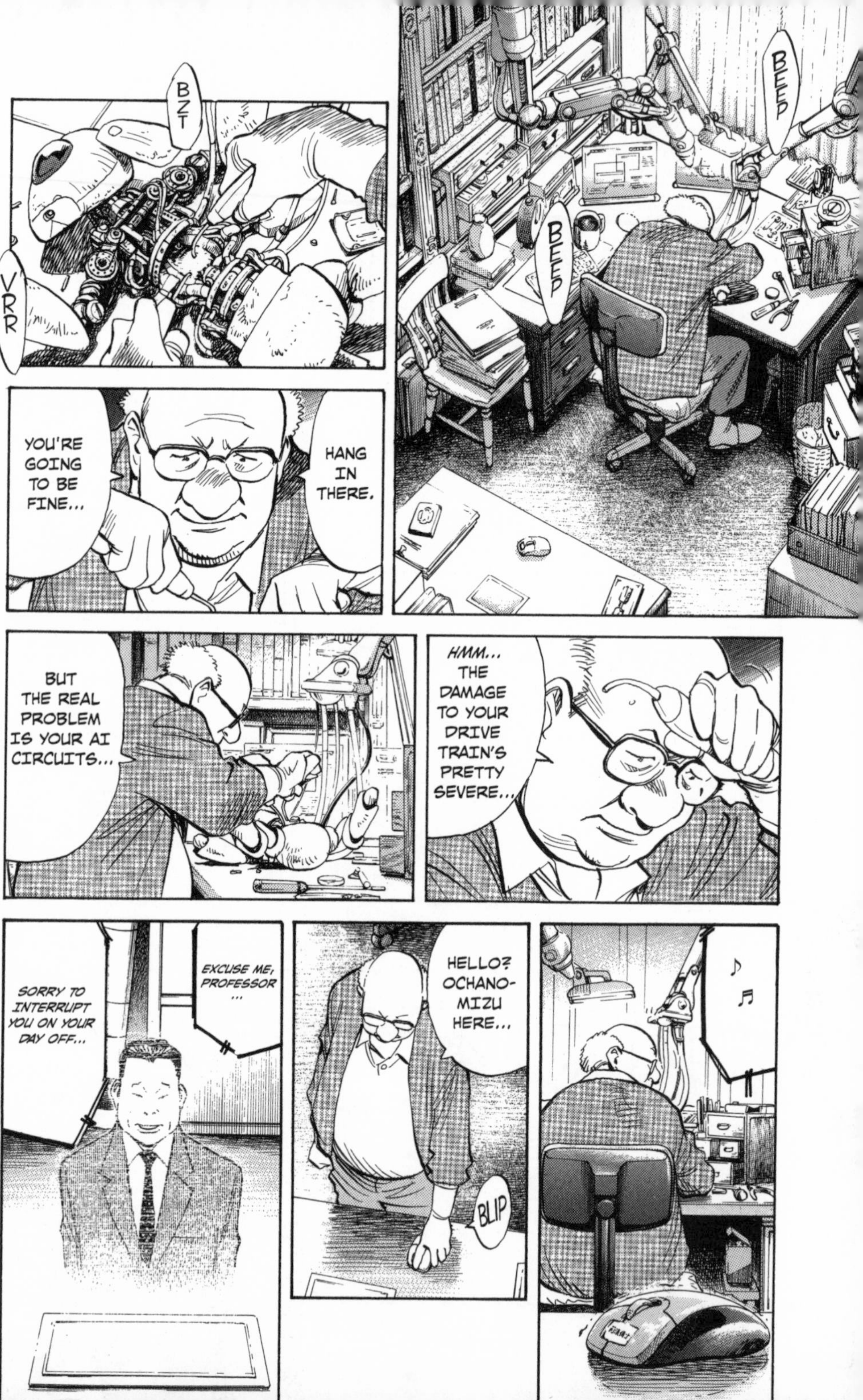
BEEP
BEEP
BZT
VRR
HANG IN THERE.
YOU'RE GOING TO BE FINE...
HMM... THE DAMAGE TO YOUR DRIVE TRAIN'S PRETTY SEVERE...
BUT THE REAL PROBLEM IS YOUR AI CIRCUITS...
♪ ♬
HELLO? OCHANO-MIZU HERE...
BLIP
EXCUSE ME, PROFESSOR...
SORRY TO INTERRUPT YOU ON YOUR DAY OFF...

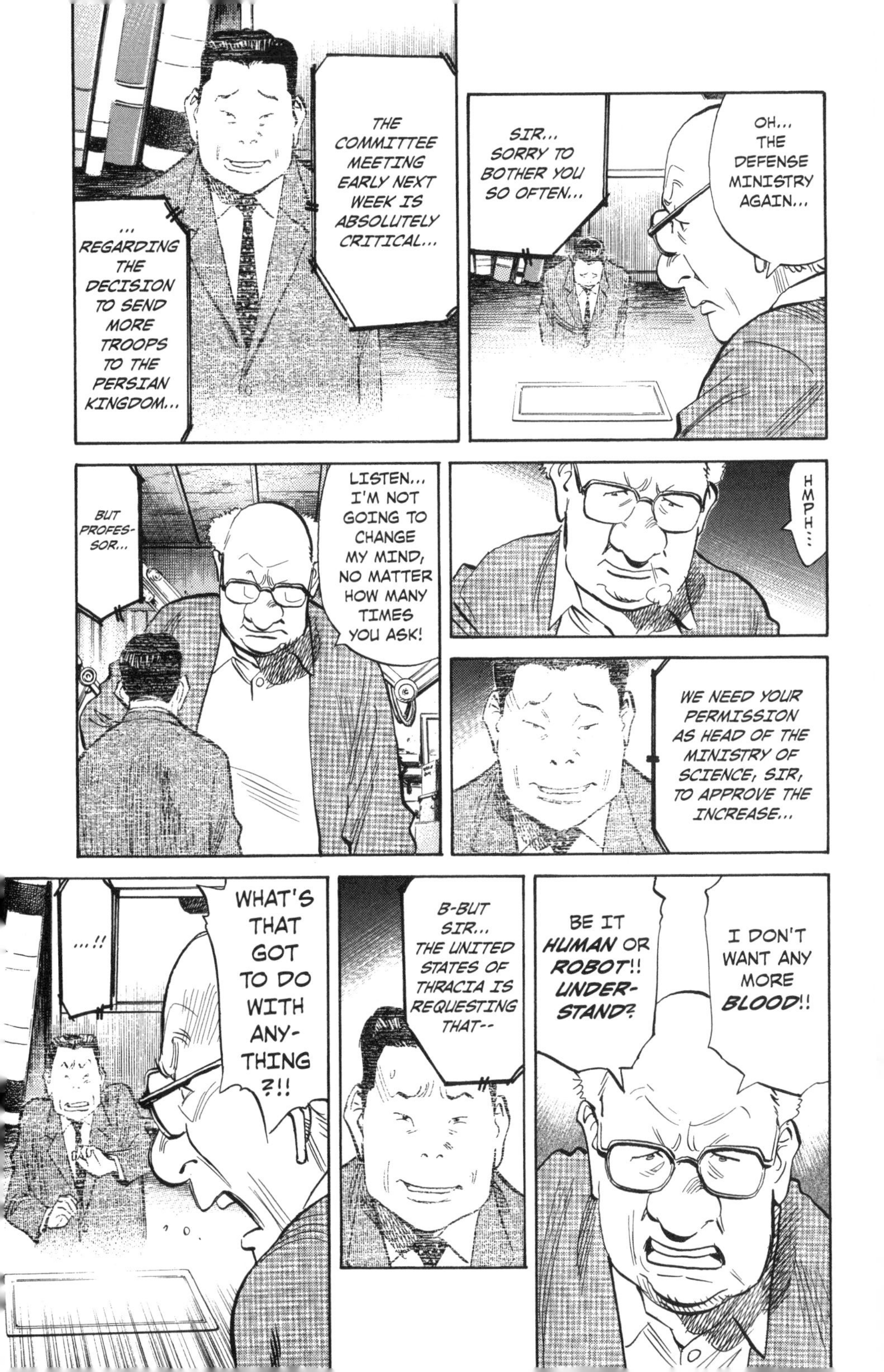

OH... THE DEFENSE MINISTRY AGAIN...
SIR... SORRY TO BOTHER YOU SO OFTEN...
THE COMMITTEE MEETING EARLY NEXT WEEK IS ABSOLUTELY CRITICAL...
...REGARDING THE DECISION TO SEND MORE TROOPS TO THE PERSIAN KINGDOM...
HMPH...
WE NEED YOUR PERMISSION AS HEAD OF THE MINISTRY OF SCIENCE, SIR, TO APPROVE THE INCREASE...
LISTEN... I'M NOT GOING TO CHANGE MY MIND, NO MATTER HOW MANY TIMES YOU ASK!
BUT PROFES-SOR...
I DON'T WANT ANY MORE BLOOD!!
BE IT HUMAN OR ROBOT!! UNDER-STAND?
B-BUT SIR... THE UNITED STATES OF THRACIA IS REQUESTING THAT--
WHAT'S THAT GOT TO DO WITH ANY-THING?!!
...!!

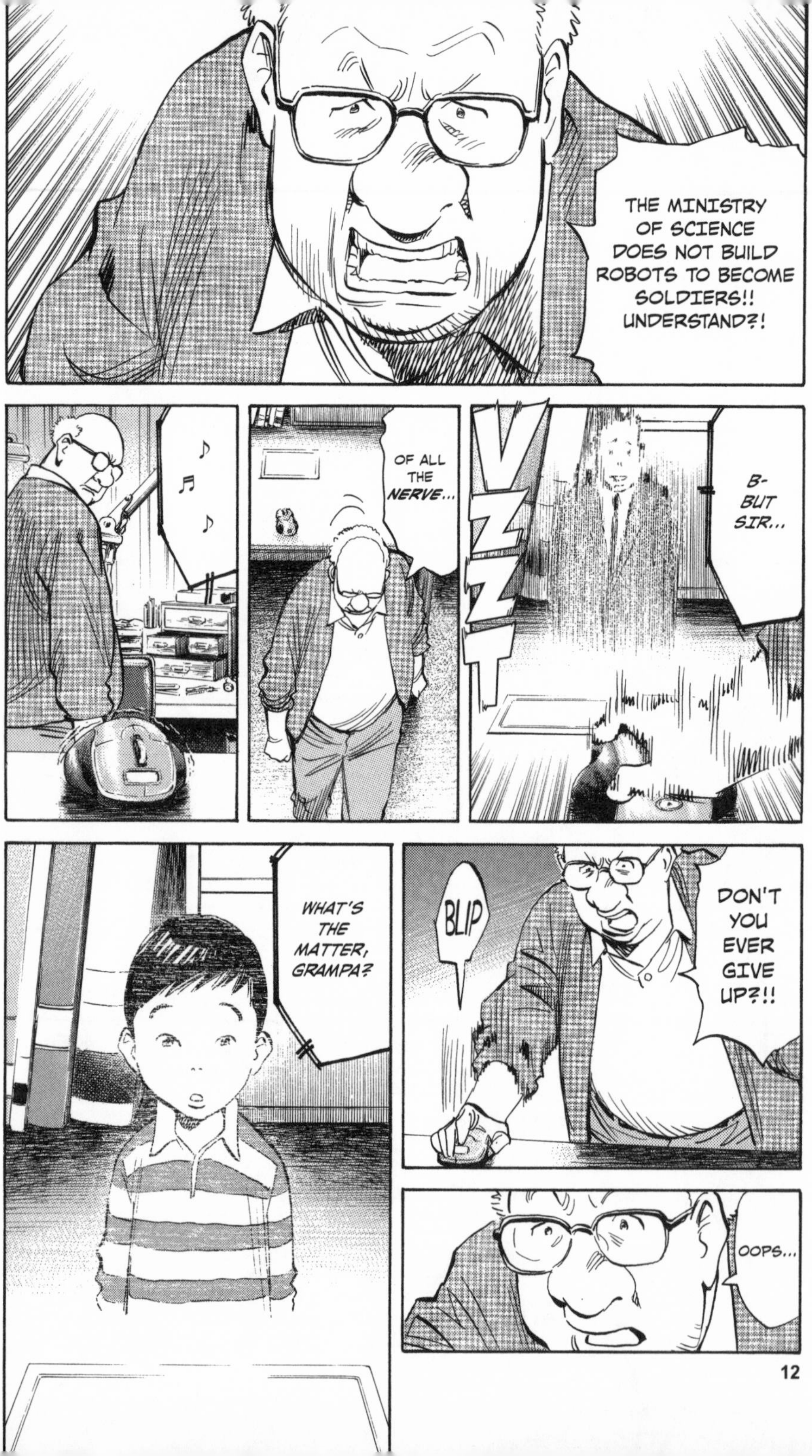
THE MINISTRY OF SCIENCE DOES NOT BUILD ROBOTS TO BECOME SOLDIERS!! UNDERSTAND?!
B-BUT SIR...
VZZT
OF ALL THE *NERVE*...
DON'T YOU EVER GIVE UP?!!
BLIP
OOPS...
WHAT'S THE MATTER, GRAMPA?

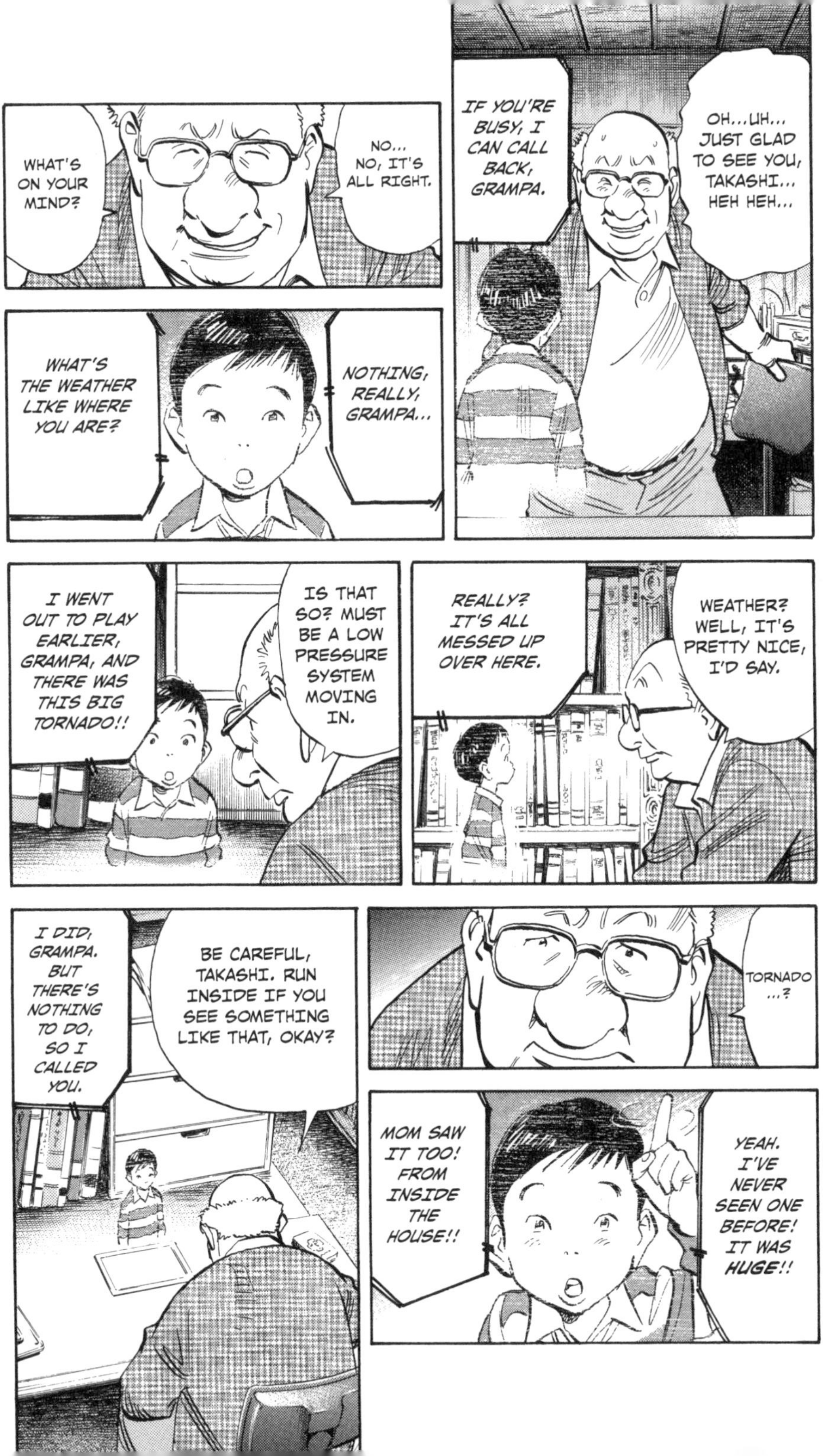
OH...UH... JUST GLAD TO SEE YOU, TAKASHI... HEH HEH...
IF YOU'RE BUSY, I CAN CALL BACK, GRAMPA.
NO... NO, IT'S ALL RIGHT.
WHAT'S ON YOUR MIND?
NOTHING, REALLY, GRAMPA...
WHAT'S THE WEATHER LIKE WHERE YOU ARE?
WEATHER? WELL, IT'S PRETTY NICE, I'D SAY.
REALLY? IT'S ALL MESSED UP OVER HERE.
IS THAT SO? MUST BE A LOW PRESSURE SYSTEM MOVING IN.
I WENT OUT TO PLAY EARLIER, GRAMPA, AND THERE WAS THIS BIG TORNADO!!
TORNADO...?
YEAH. I'VE NEVER SEEN ONE BEFORE! IT WAS **HUGE**!!
MOM SAW IT TOO! FROM INSIDE THE HOUSE!!
BE CAREFUL, TAKASHI. RUN INSIDE IF YOU SEE SOMETHING LIKE THAT, OKAY?
I DID, GRAMPA. BUT THERE'S NOTHING TO DO, SO I CALLED YOU.

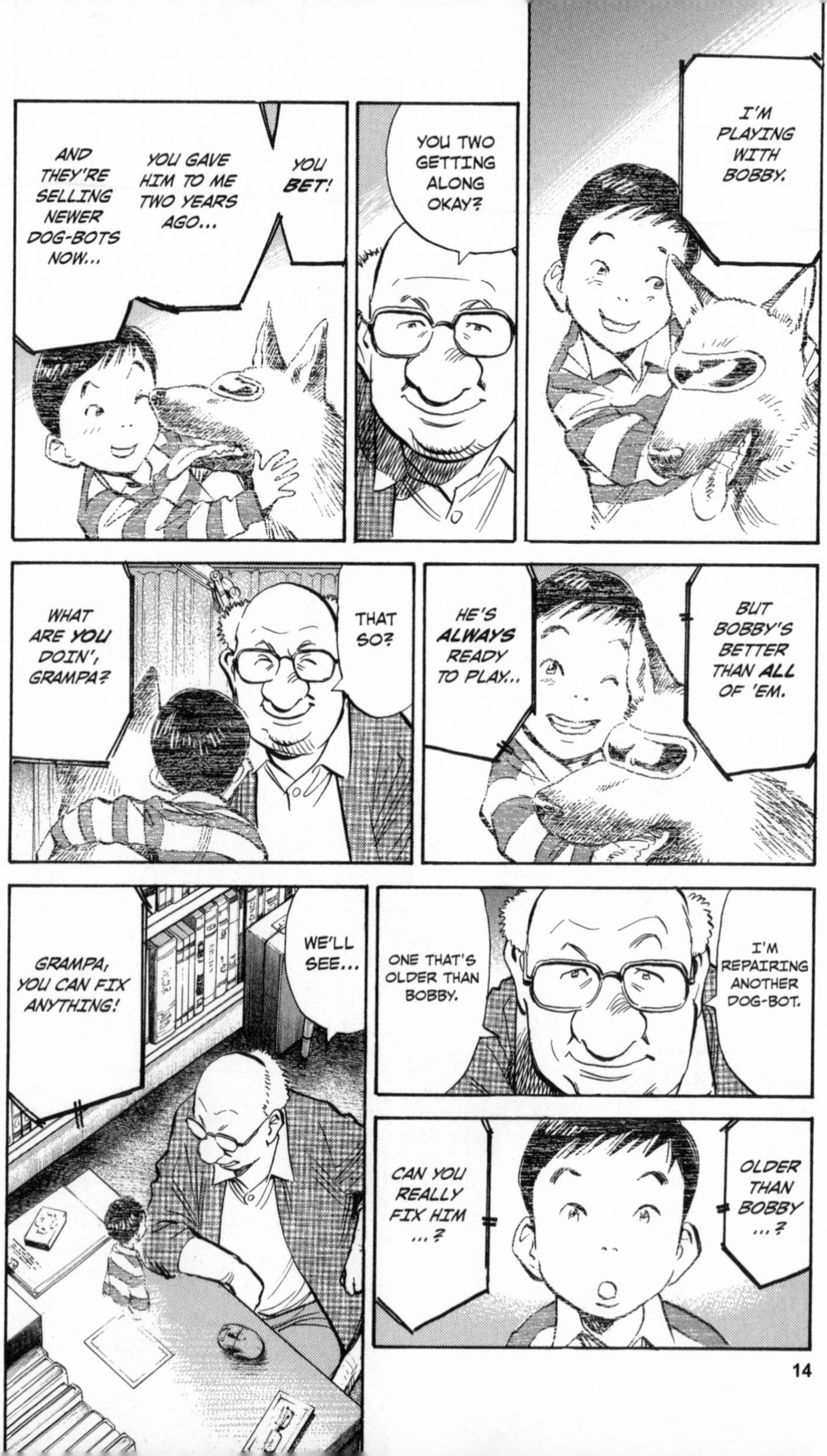
I'M PLAYING WITH BOBBY.
YOU TWO GETTING ALONG OKAY?
YOU BET!
YOU GAVE HIM TO ME TWO YEARS AGO...
AND THEY'RE SELLING NEWER DOG-BOTS NOW...
BUT BOBBY'S BETTER THAN ALL OF 'EM.
HE'S ALWAYS READY TO PLAY...
THAT SO?
WHAT ARE YOU DOIN', GRAMPA?
I'M REPAIRING ANOTHER DOG-BOT.
ONE THAT'S OLDER THAN BOBBY.
OLDER THAN BOBBY ...?
CAN YOU REALLY FIX HIM ...?
WE'LL SEE...
GRAMPA, YOU CAN FIX ANYTHING!

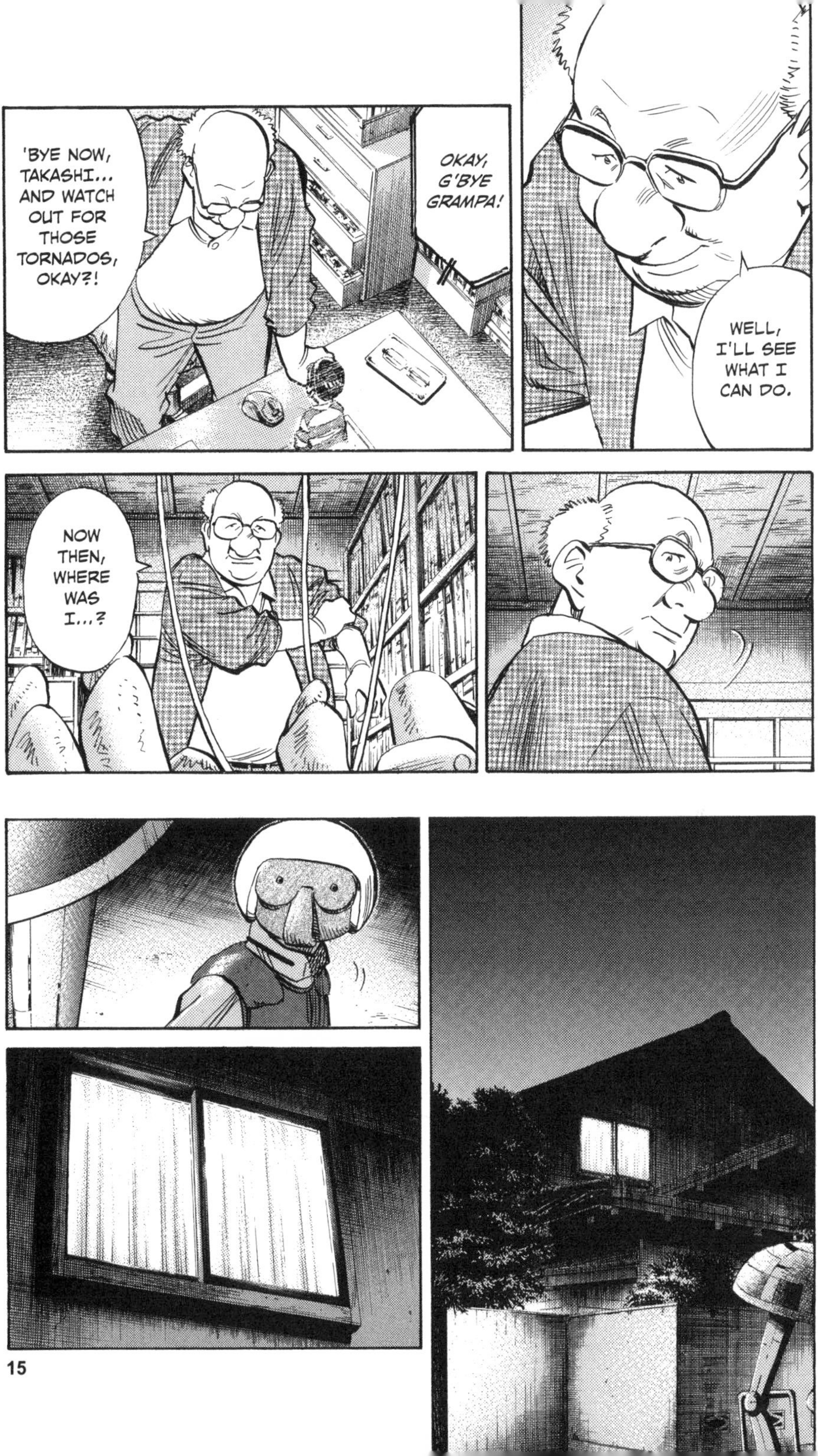
WELL, I'LL SEE WHAT I CAN DO.
'BYE NOW, TAKASHI... AND WATCH OUT FOR THOSE TORNADOS, OKAY?!
OKAY, G'BYE GRAMPA!
NOW THEN, WHERE WAS I...?

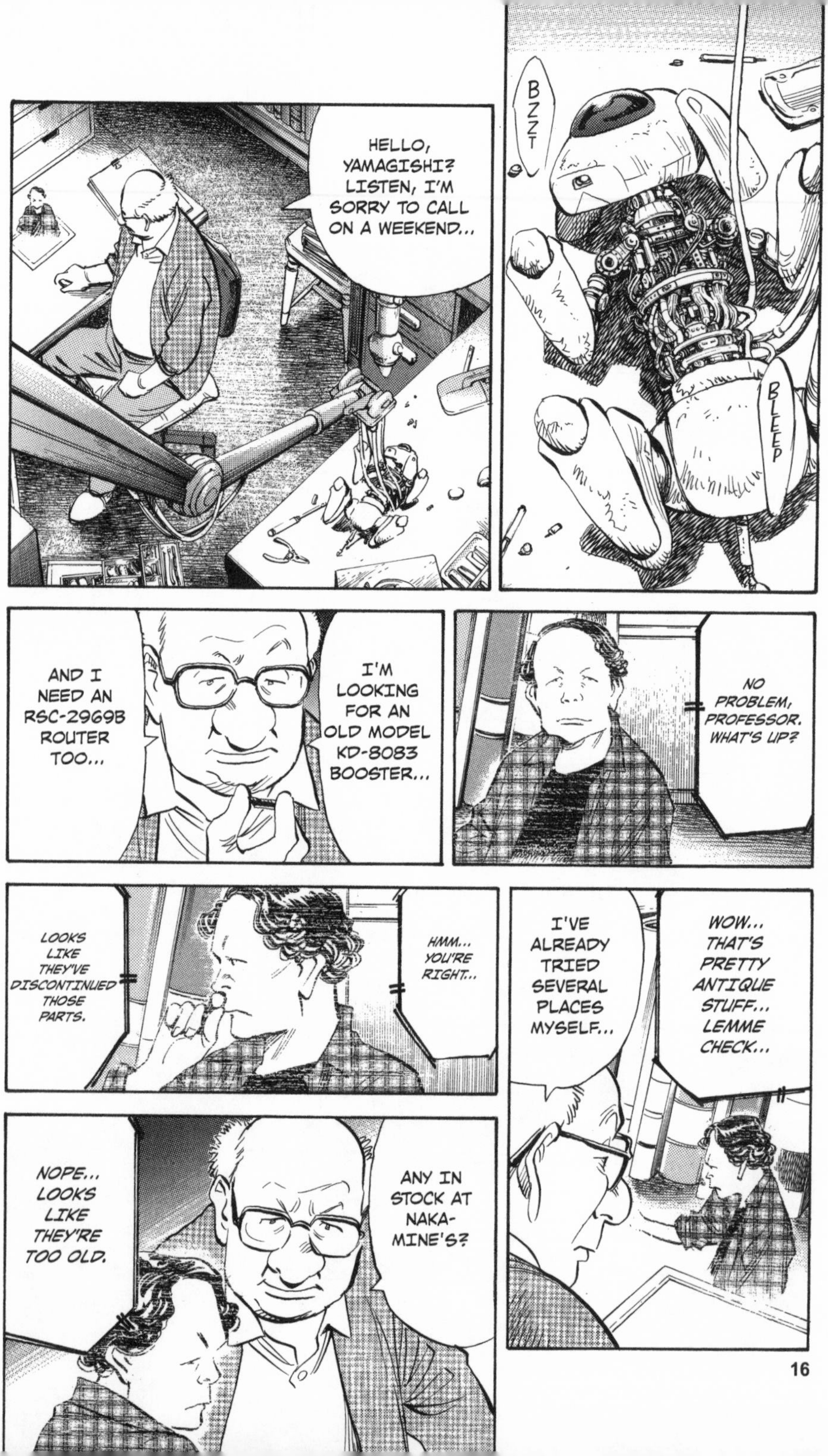

BZZT
BLEEP
HELLO, YAMAGISHI? LISTEN, I'M SORRY TO CALL ON A WEEKEND...
NO PROBLEM, PROFESSOR. WHAT'S UP?
I'M LOOKING FOR AN OLD MODEL KD-8083 BOOSTER...
AND I NEED AN RSC-2969B ROUTER TOO...
WOW... THAT'S PRETTY ANTIQUE STUFF... LEMME CHECK...
I'VE ALREADY TRIED SEVERAL PLACES MYSELF...
HMM... YOU'RE RIGHT...
LOOKS LIKE THEY'VE DISCONTINUED THOSE PARTS.
ANY IN STOCK AT NAKA-MINE'S?
NOPE... LOOKS LIKE THEY'RE TOO OLD.

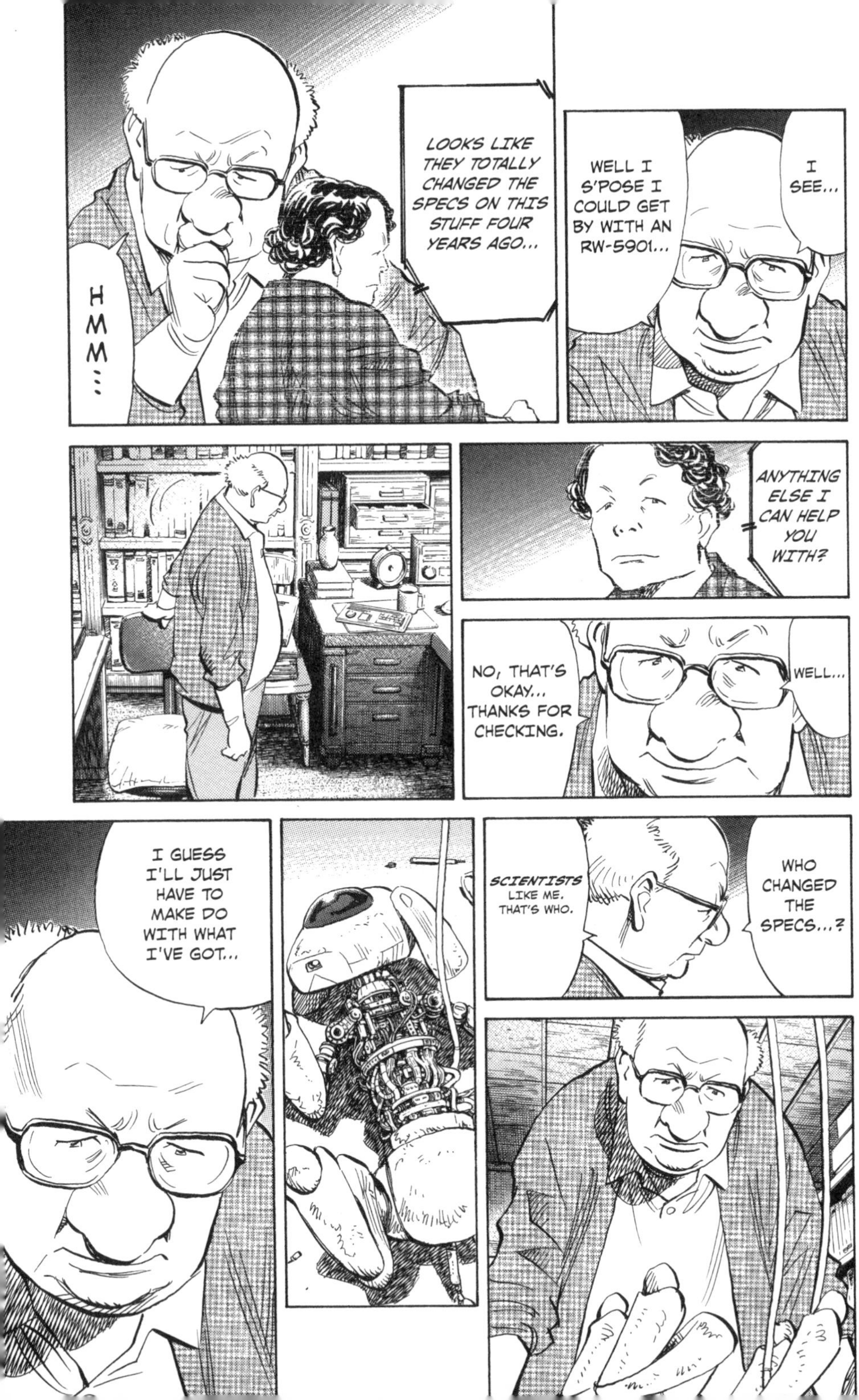
I SEE...
WELL I S'POSE I COULD GET BY WITH AN RW-5901...
LOOKS LIKE THEY TOTALLY CHANGED THE SPECS ON THIS STUFF FOUR YEARS AGO...
HMM...
ANYTHING ELSE I CAN HELP YOU WITH?
WELL...
NO, THAT'S OKAY... THANKS FOR CHECKING.
WHO CHANGED THE SPECS...?
SCIENTISTS LIKE ME. THAT'S WHO.
I GUESS I'LL JUST HAVE TO MAKE DO WITH WHAT I'VE GOT...

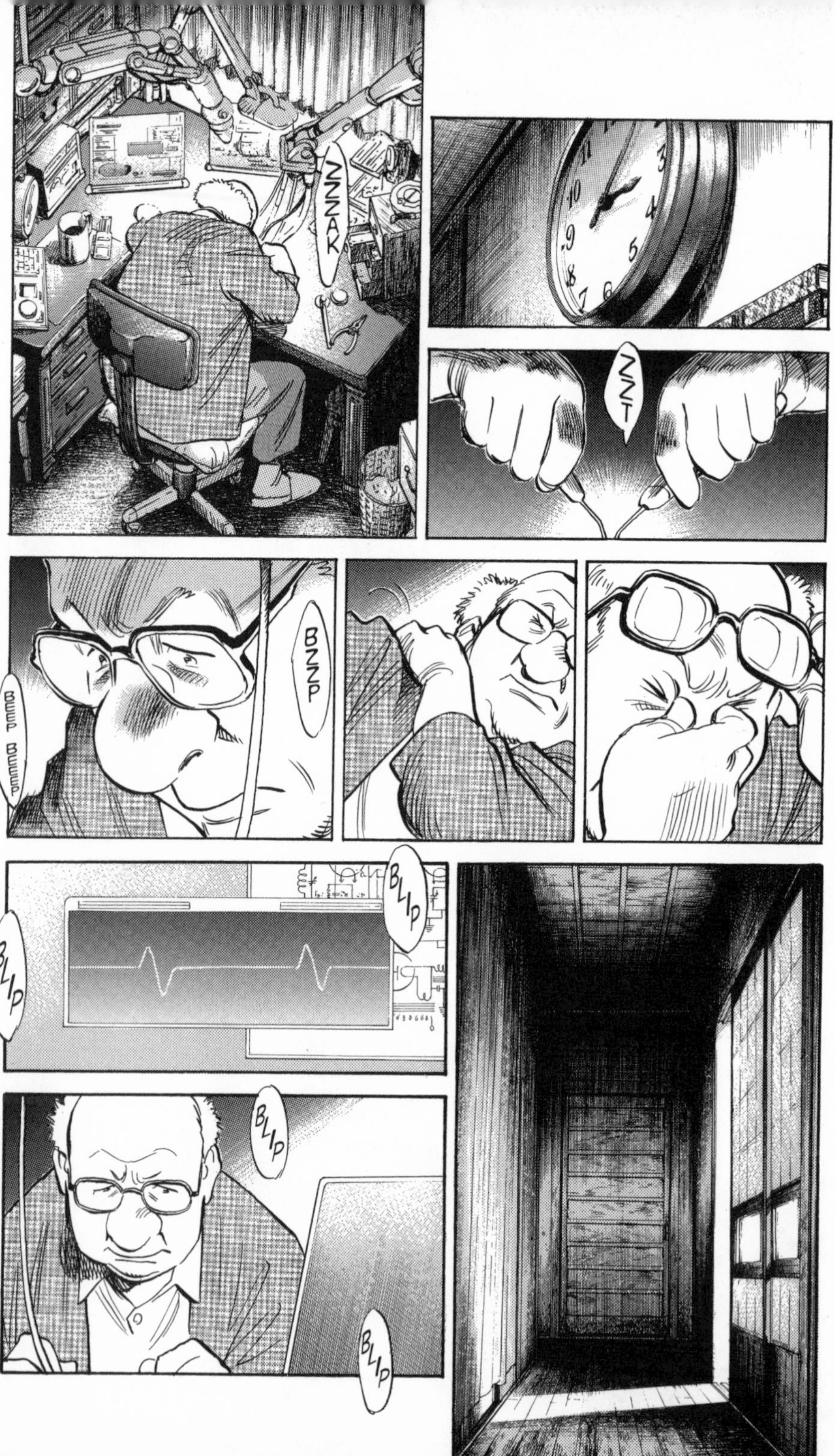
ZZT
ZZZAK
BZZP
BEEP BEEEP
BLIP
BLIP
BLIP
BLIP

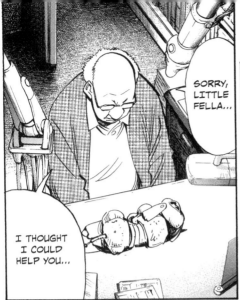

BLIP
SORRY, LITTLE FELLA...
I THOUGHT I COULD HELP YOU...
BZZRT
YOU REALLY HUNG IN THERE...
ZZT ZT
I KNOW...
YOUR OWNER TOOK REAL GOOD CARE OF YOU...
THAT'S WHY YOU'VE LASTED AS LONG AS YOU HAVE...
YOU WERE TRULY LOVED...

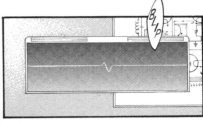

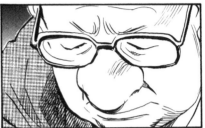

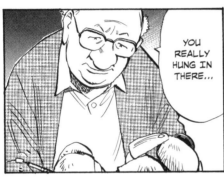

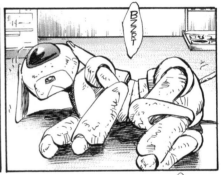

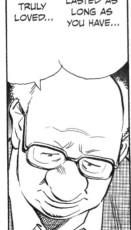

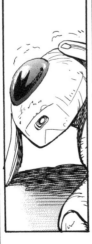

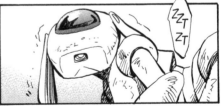

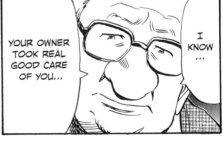

CREAK
THERE, THERE...
WOBBLE WOBBLE
STILL TRYING TO GET UP AND PLAY, AREN'T YOU?
THUNK
IT'S ALL RIGHT...
CREAK
IT'S ALL RIGHT...
YOU'VE DONE ENOUGH...

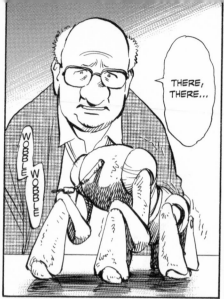

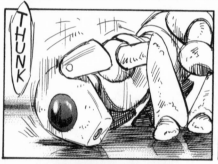

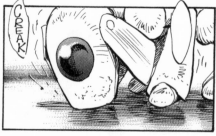

YOU CAN REST NOW...

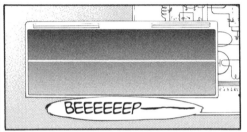

BEEEEEEP

DING DONG!

HUH?

DING DONG!

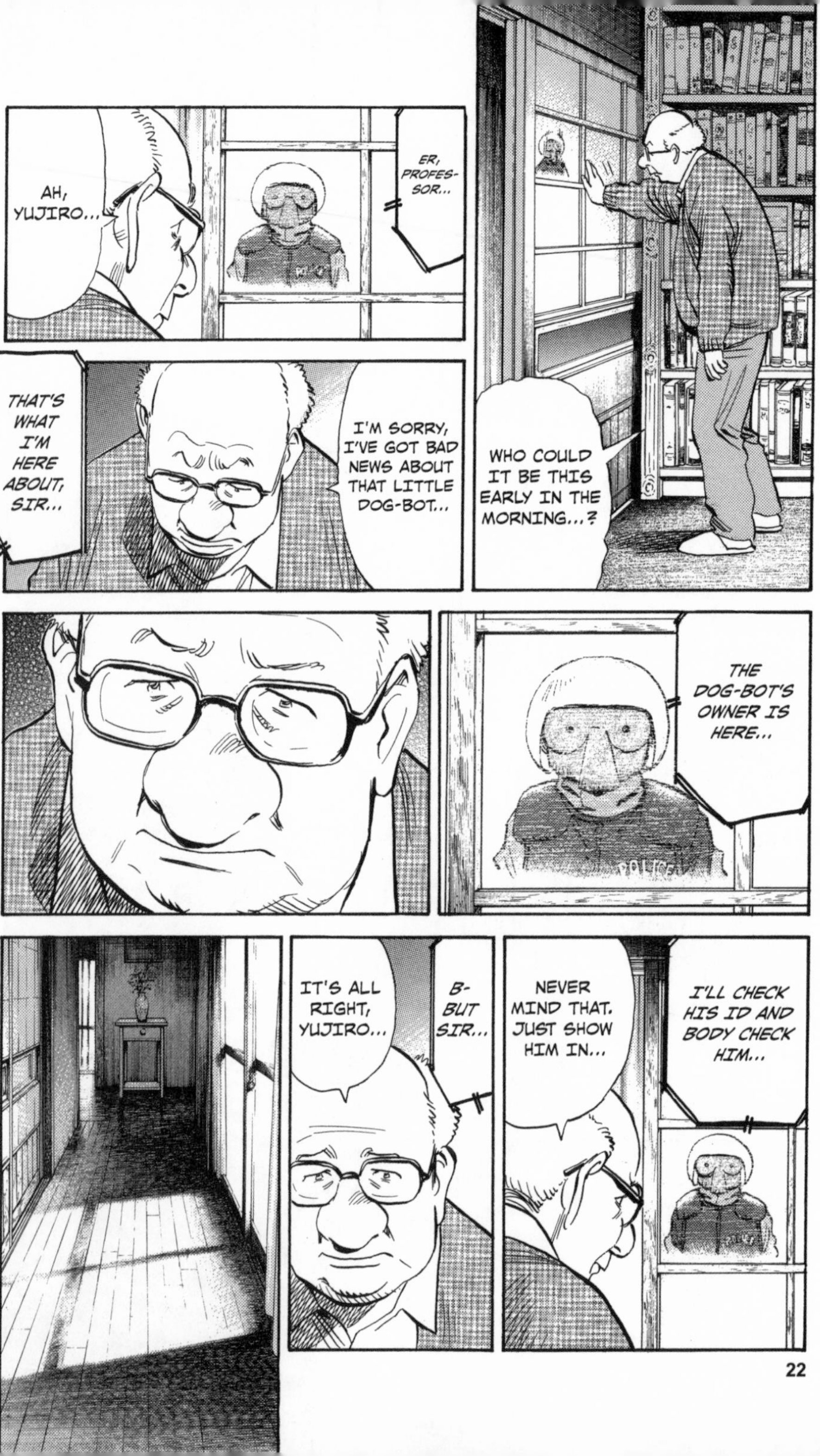
WHO COULD IT BE THIS EARLY IN THE MORNING...?
ER, PROFESSOR...
AH, YUJIRO...
I'M SORRY, I'VE GOT BAD NEWS ABOUT THAT LITTLE DOG-BOT...
THAT'S WHAT I'M HERE ABOUT, SIR...
THE DOG-BOT'S OWNER IS HERE...
I'LL CHECK HIS ID AND BODY CHECK HIM...
NEVER MIND THAT. JUST SHOW HIM IN...
B-BUT SIR...
IT'S ALL RIGHT, YUJIRO...

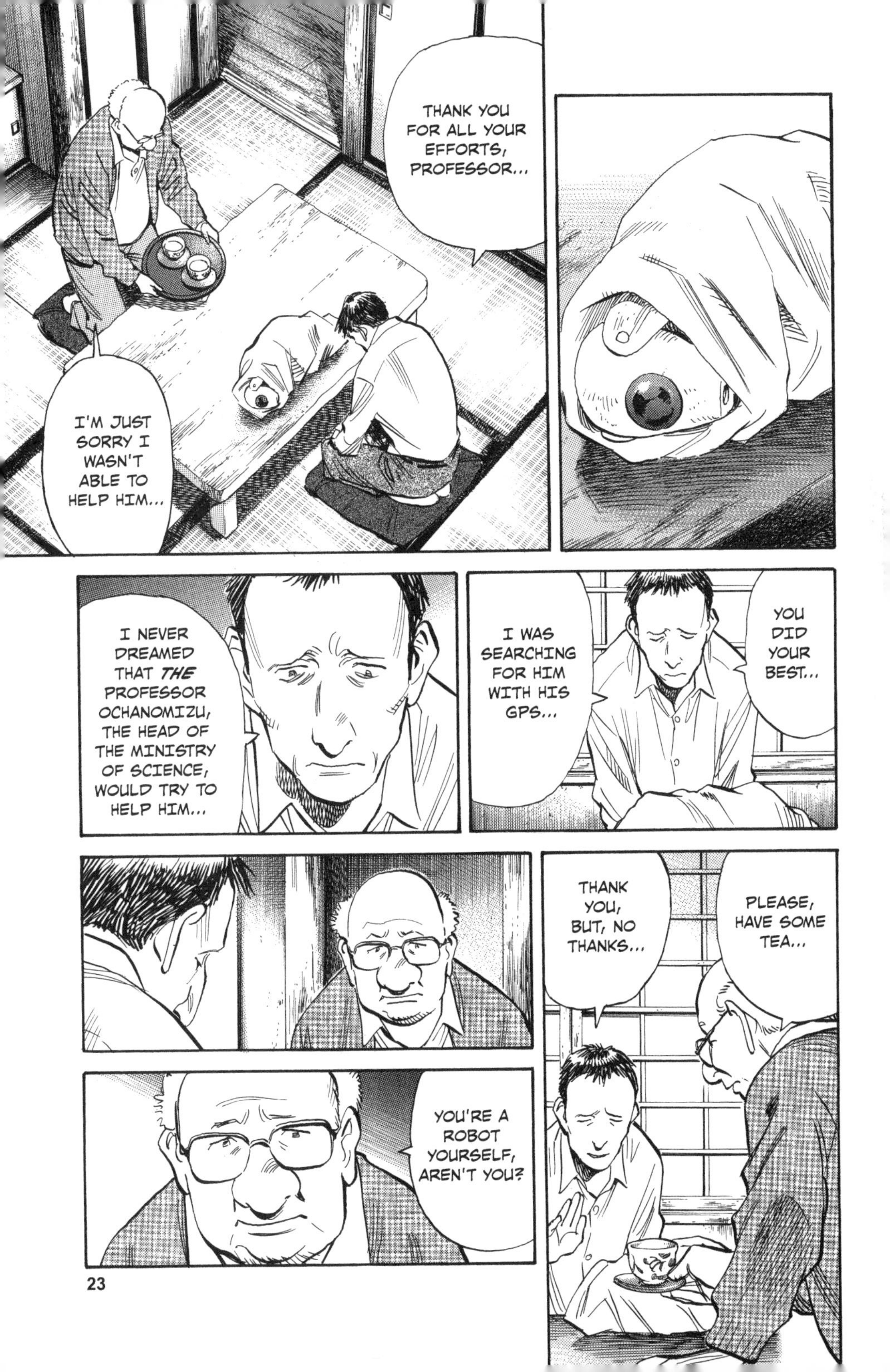
THANK YOU FOR ALL YOUR EFFORTS, PROFESSOR...
I'M JUST SORRY I WASN'T ABLE TO HELP HIM...
YOU DID YOUR BEST...
I WAS SEARCHING FOR HIM WITH HIS GPS...
I NEVER DREAMED THAT *THE* PROFESSOR OCHANOMIZU, THE HEAD OF THE MINISTRY OF SCIENCE, WOULD TRY TO HELP HIM...
PLEASE, HAVE SOME TEA...
THANK YOU, BUT, NO THANKS...
YOU'RE A ROBOT YOURSELF, AREN'T YOU?

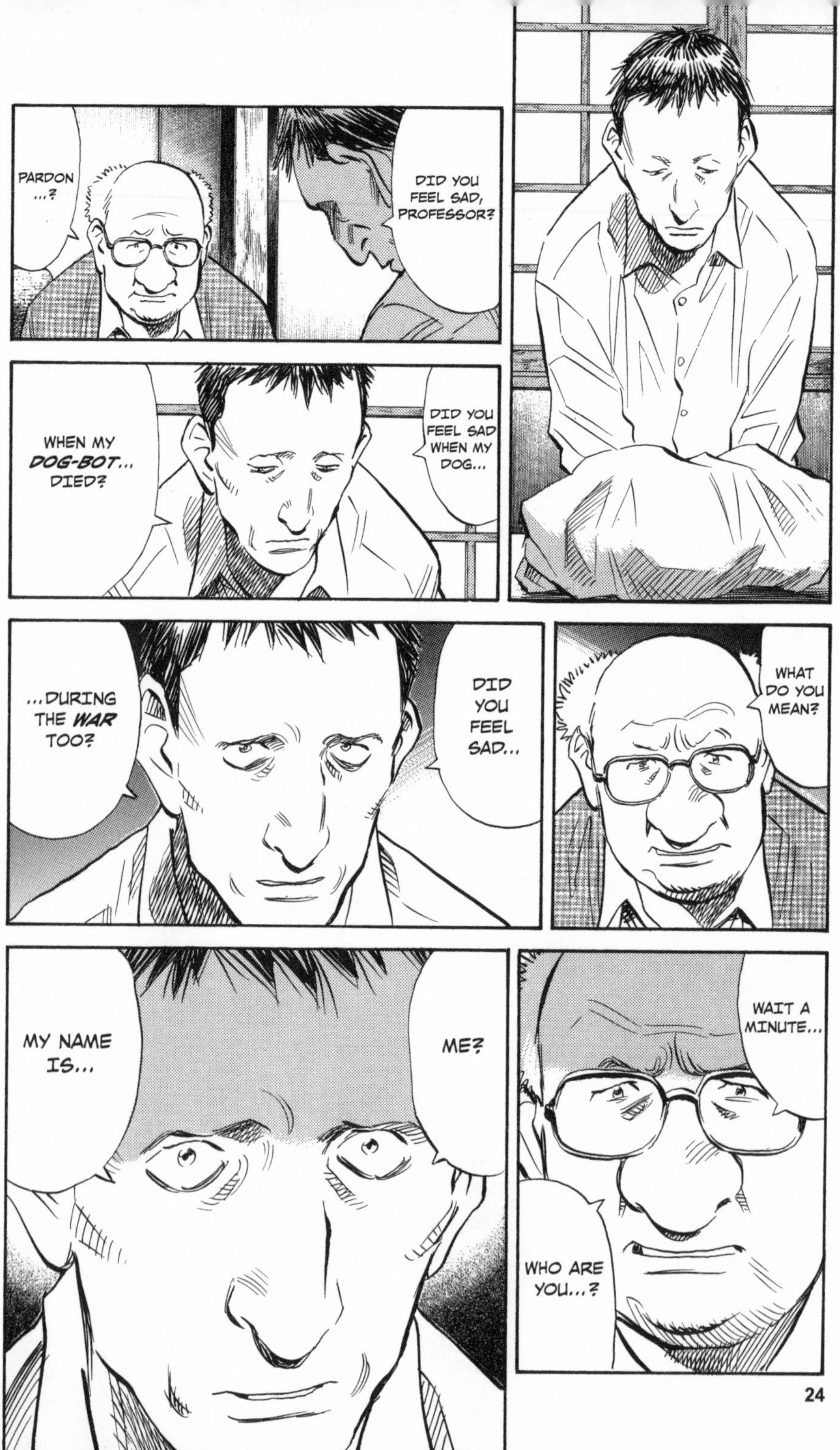
DID YOU FEEL SAD, PROFESSOR?
PARDON ...?
DID YOU FEEL SAD WHEN MY DOG...
WHEN MY DOG-BOT... DIED?
WHAT DO YOU MEAN?
DID YOU FEEL SAD...
...DURING THE WAR TOO?
WAIT A MINUTE...
WHO ARE YOU...?
ME?
MY NAME IS...

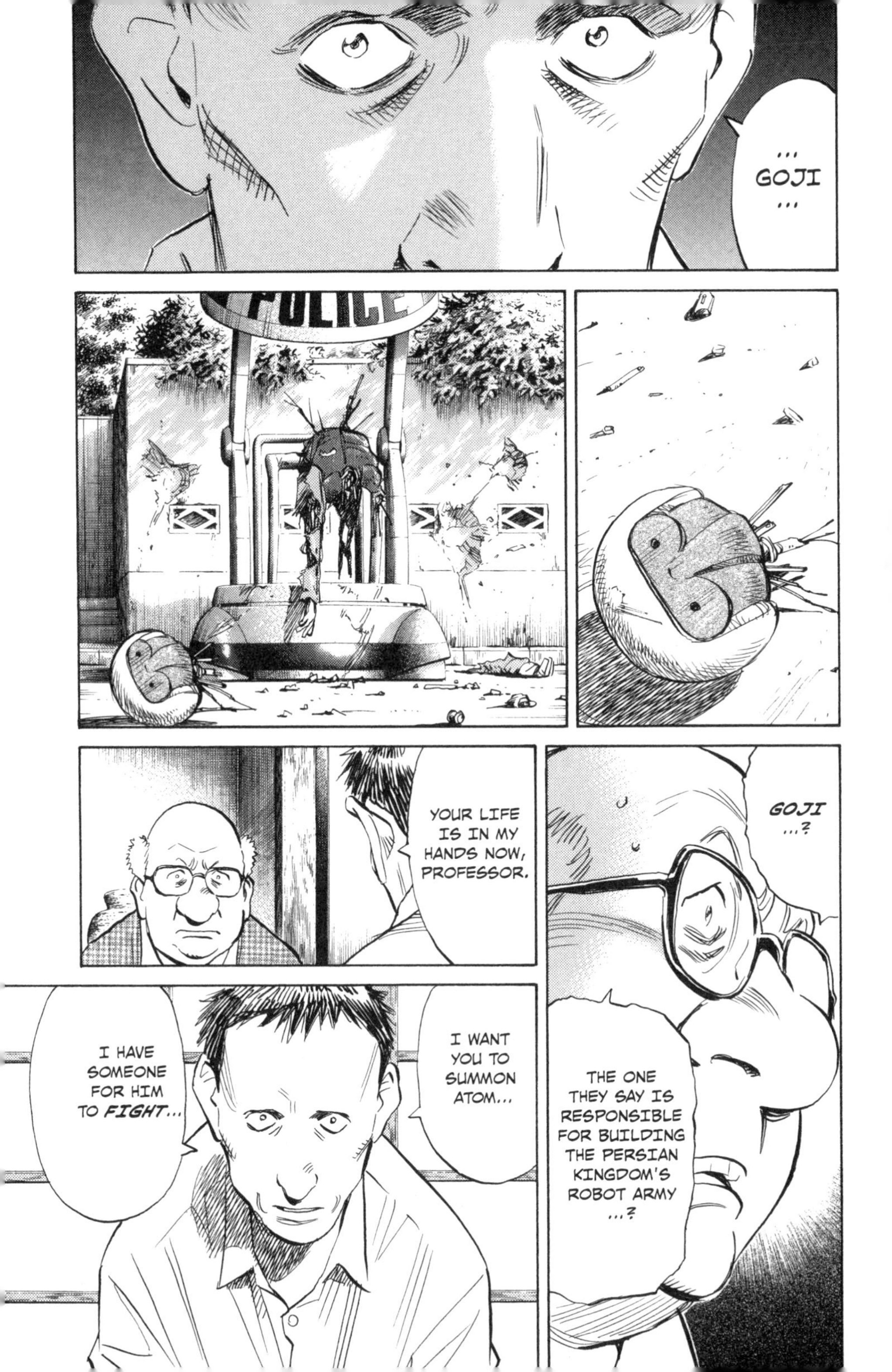

... GOJI ...
GOJI ...?
THE ONE THEY SAY IS RESPONSIBLE FOR BUILDING THE PERSIAN KINGDOM'S ROBOT ARMY ...?
YOUR LIFE IS IN MY HANDS NOW, PROFESSOR.
I WANT YOU TO SUMMON ATOM...
I HAVE SOMEONE FOR HIM TO *FIGHT*...

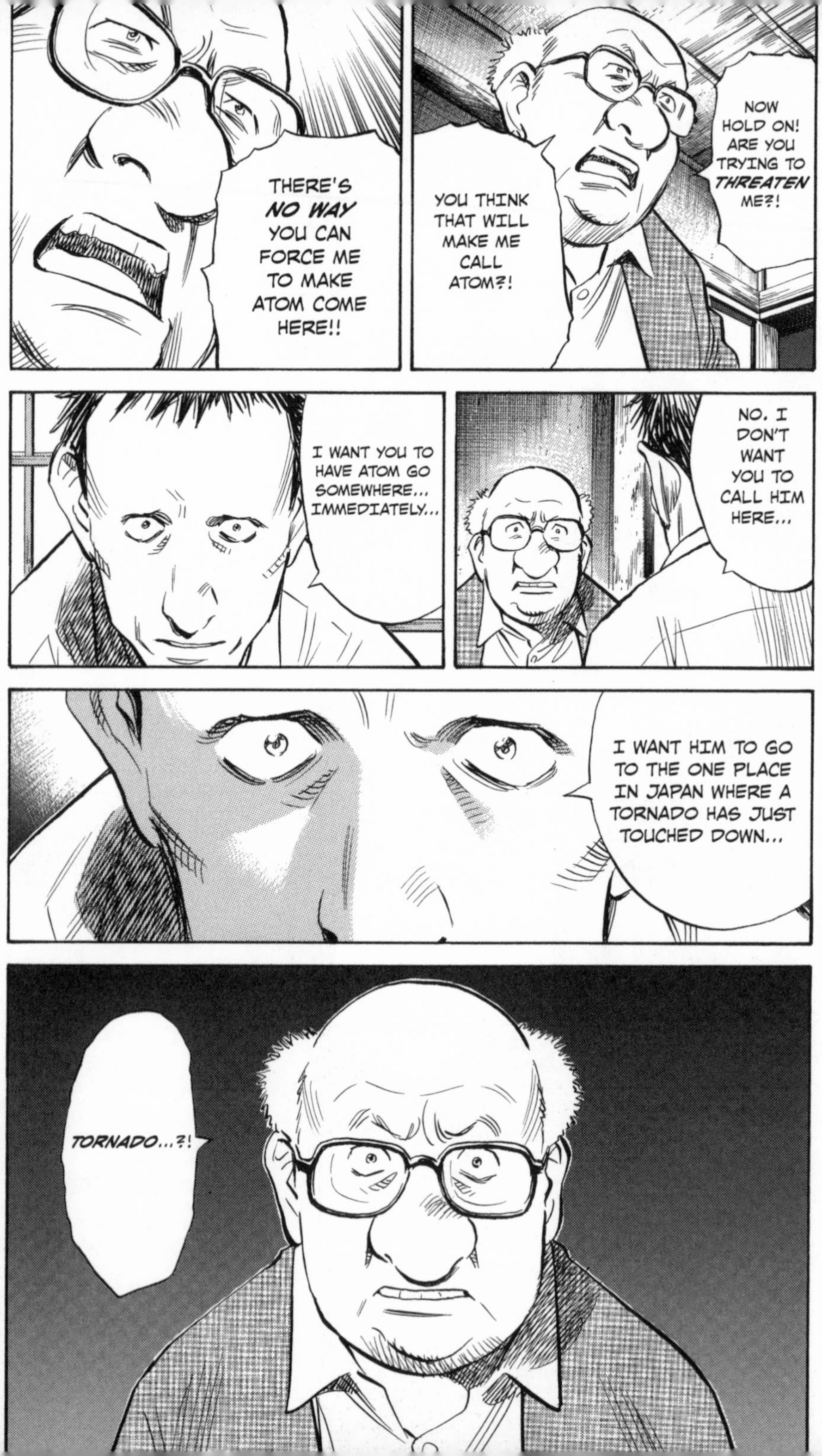
NOW HOLD ON! ARE YOU TRYING TO THREATEN ME?!
YOU THINK THAT WILL MAKE ME CALL ATOM?!
THERE'S NO WAY YOU CAN FORCE ME TO MAKE ATOM COME HERE!!
NO. I DON'T WANT YOU TO CALL HIM HERE...
I WANT YOU TO HAVE ATOM GO SOMEWHERE... IMMEDIATELY...
I WANT HIM TO GO TO THE ONE PLACE IN JAPAN WHERE A TORNADO HAS JUST TOUCHED DOWN...
TORNADO...?!

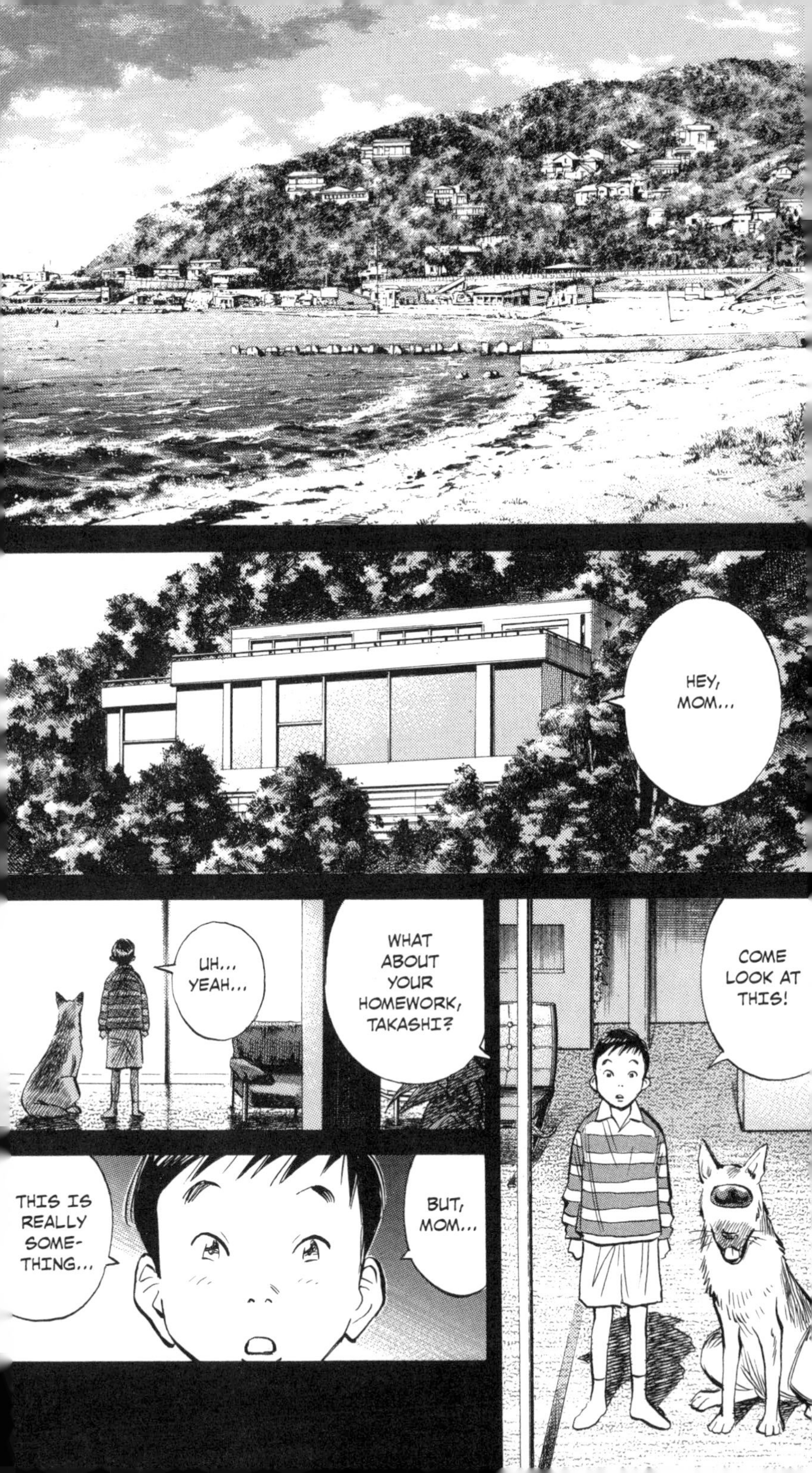
HEY, MOM...
COME LOOK AT THIS!
WHAT ABOUT YOUR HOMEWORK, TAKASHI?
UH... YEAH...
BUT, MOM...
THIS IS REALLY SOME-THING...

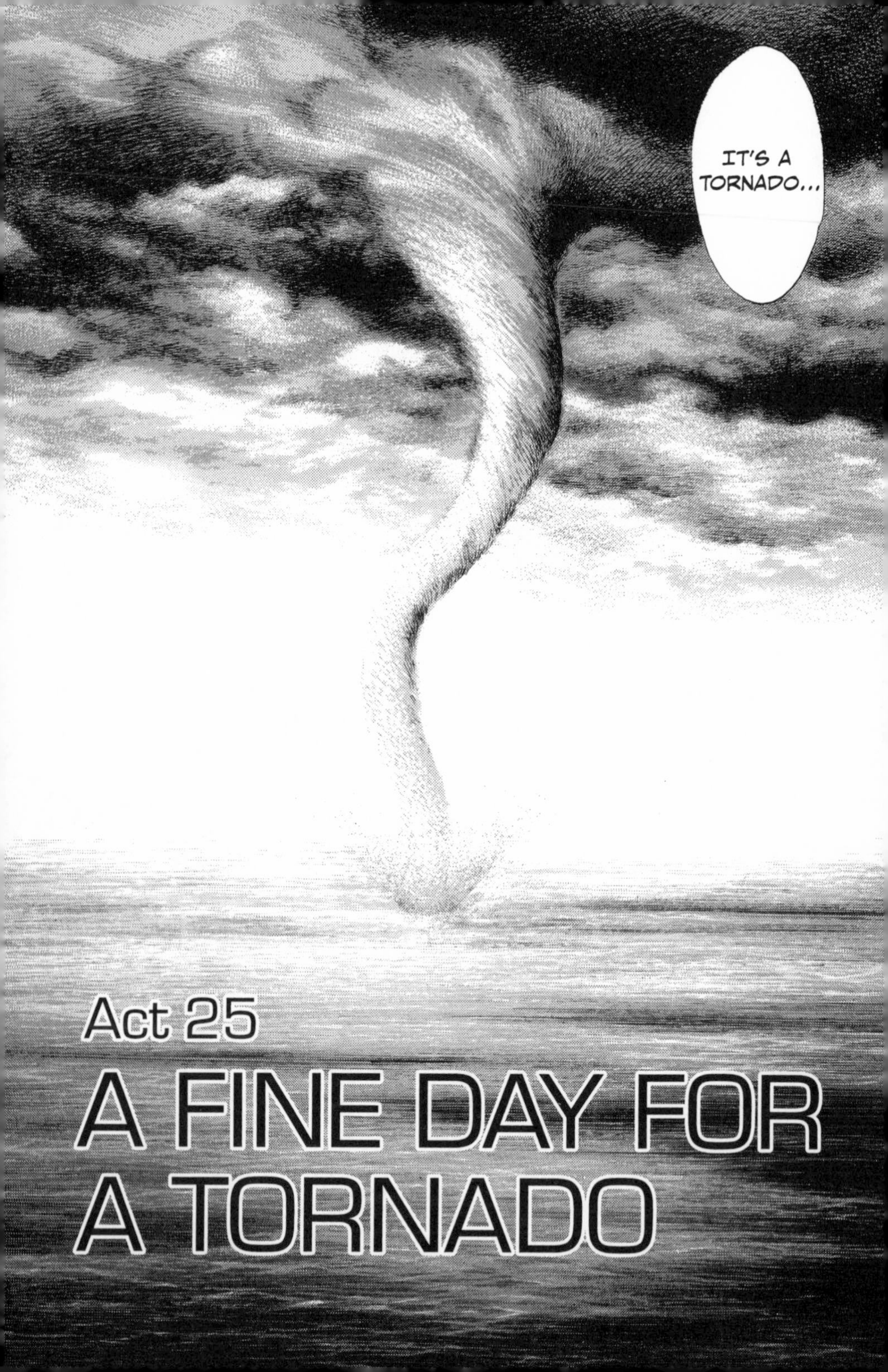

Act 25
A FINE DAY FOR A TORNADO

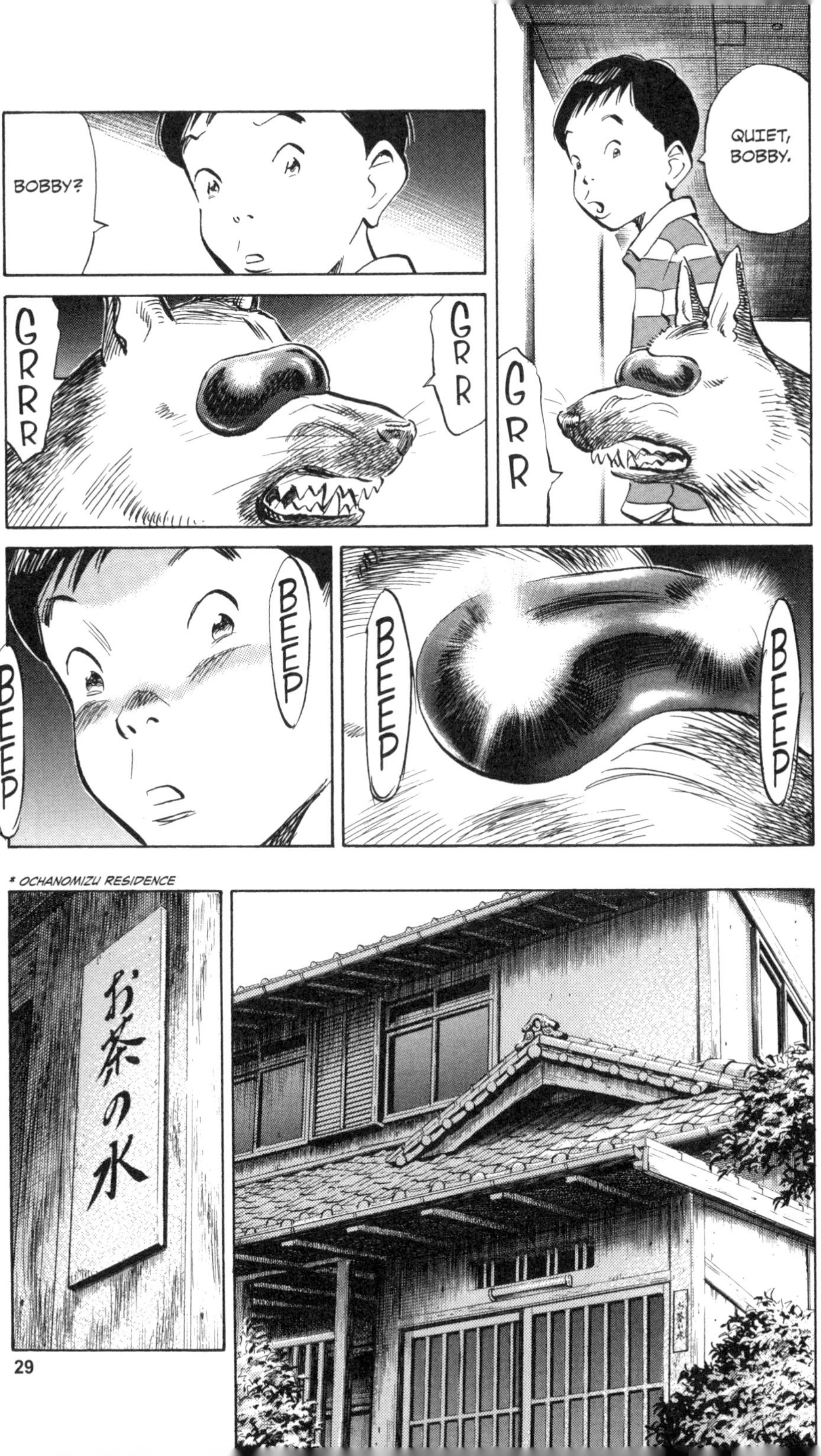
QUIET, BOBBY.
GRR
BOBBY?
GRR
GRRR
BEEP
BEEP
BEEP
BEEP
* OCHANOMIZU RESIDENCE
お茶の水

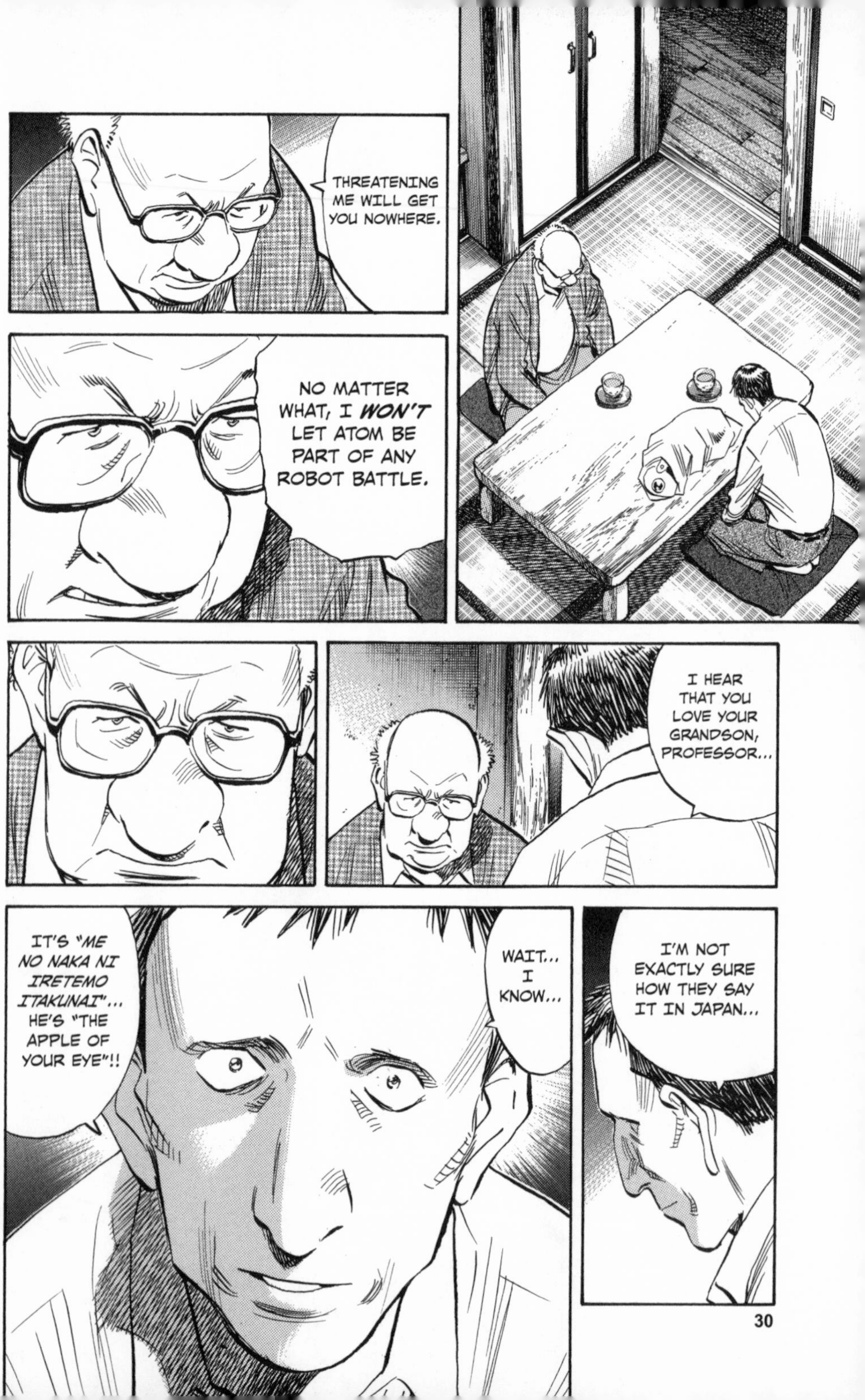
THREATENING ME WILL GET YOU NOWHERE.
NO MATTER WHAT, I **WON'T** LET ATOM BE PART OF ANY ROBOT BATTLE.
I HEAR THAT YOU LOVE YOUR GRANDSON, PROFESSOR...
I'M NOT EXACTLY SURE HOW THEY SAY IT IN JAPAN...
WAIT... I KNOW...
IT'S *"ME NO NAKA NI IRETEMO ITAKUNAI"*... HE'S "THE APPLE OF YOUR EYE"!!

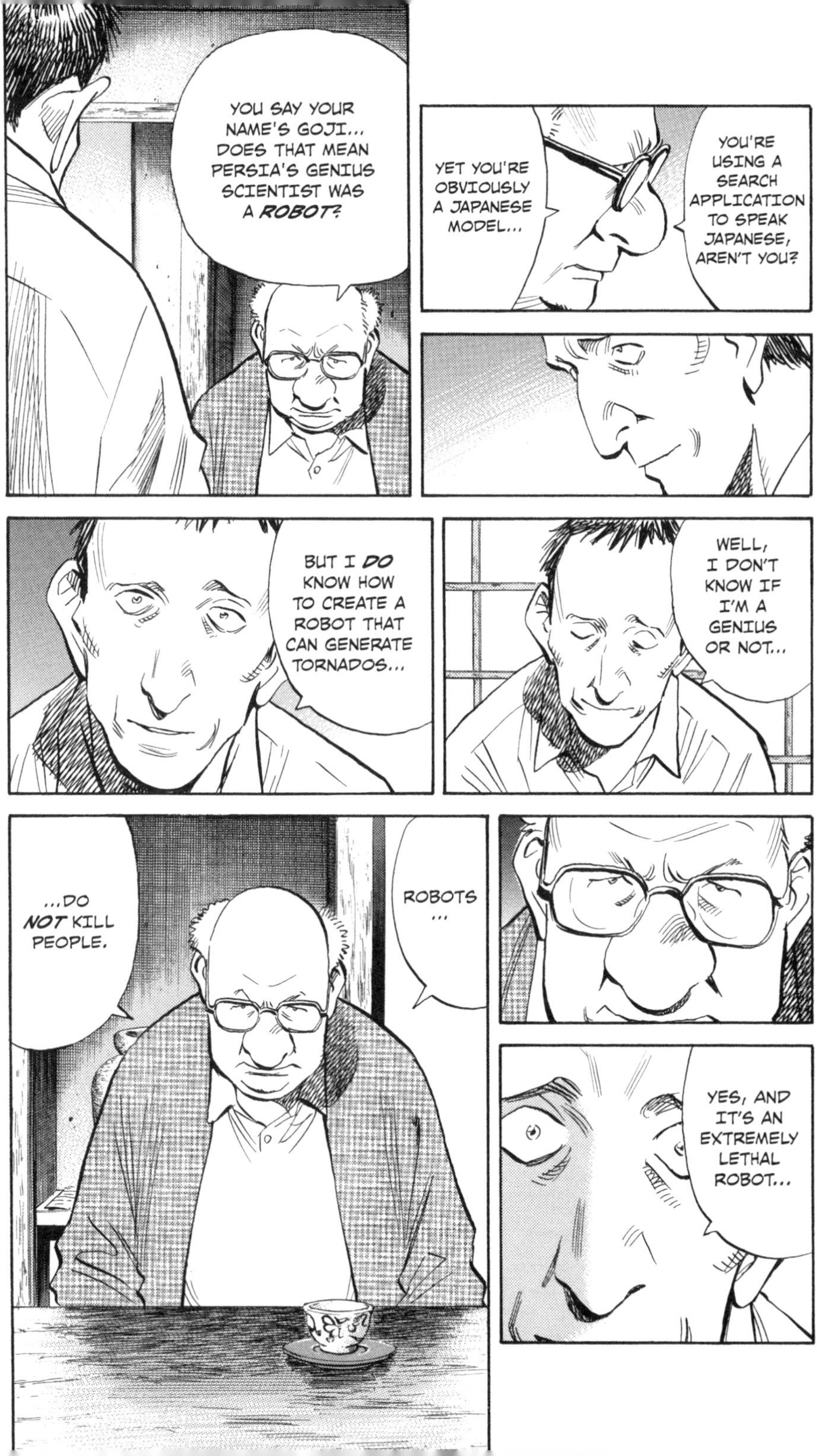
YOU'RE USING A SEARCH APPLICATION TO SPEAK JAPANESE, AREN'T YOU?
YET YOU'RE OBVIOUSLY A JAPANESE MODEL...
YOU SAY YOUR NAME'S GOJI... DOES THAT MEAN PERSIA'S GENIUS SCIENTIST WAS A *ROBOT*?
WELL, I DON'T KNOW IF I'M A GENIUS OR NOT...
BUT I *DO* KNOW HOW TO CREATE A ROBOT THAT CAN GENERATE TORNADOS...
YES, AND IT'S AN EXTREMELY LETHAL ROBOT...
ROBOTS...
...DO *NOT* KILL PEOPLE.

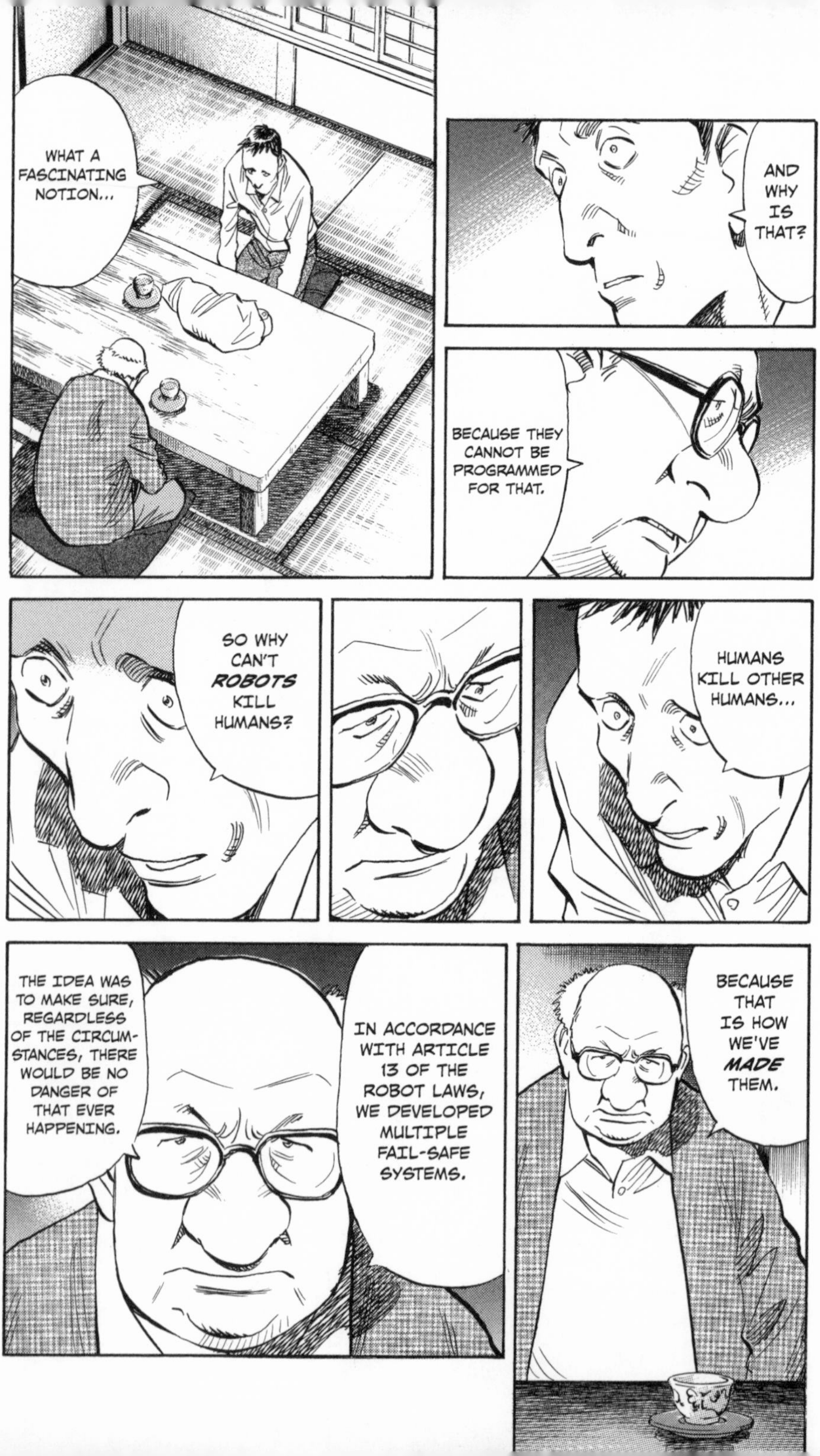
AND WHY IS THAT?
BECAUSE THEY CANNOT BE PROGRAMMED FOR THAT.
WHAT A FASCINATING NOTION...
HUMANS KILL OTHER HUMANS...
SO WHY CAN'T ROBOTS KILL HUMANS?
BECAUSE THAT IS HOW WE'VE MADE THEM.
IN ACCORDANCE WITH ARTICLE 13 OF THE ROBOT LAWS, WE DEVELOPED MULTIPLE FAIL-SAFE SYSTEMS.
THE IDEA WAS TO MAKE SURE, REGARDLESS OF THE CIRCUMSTANCES, THERE WOULD BE NO DANGER OF THAT EVER HAPPENING.

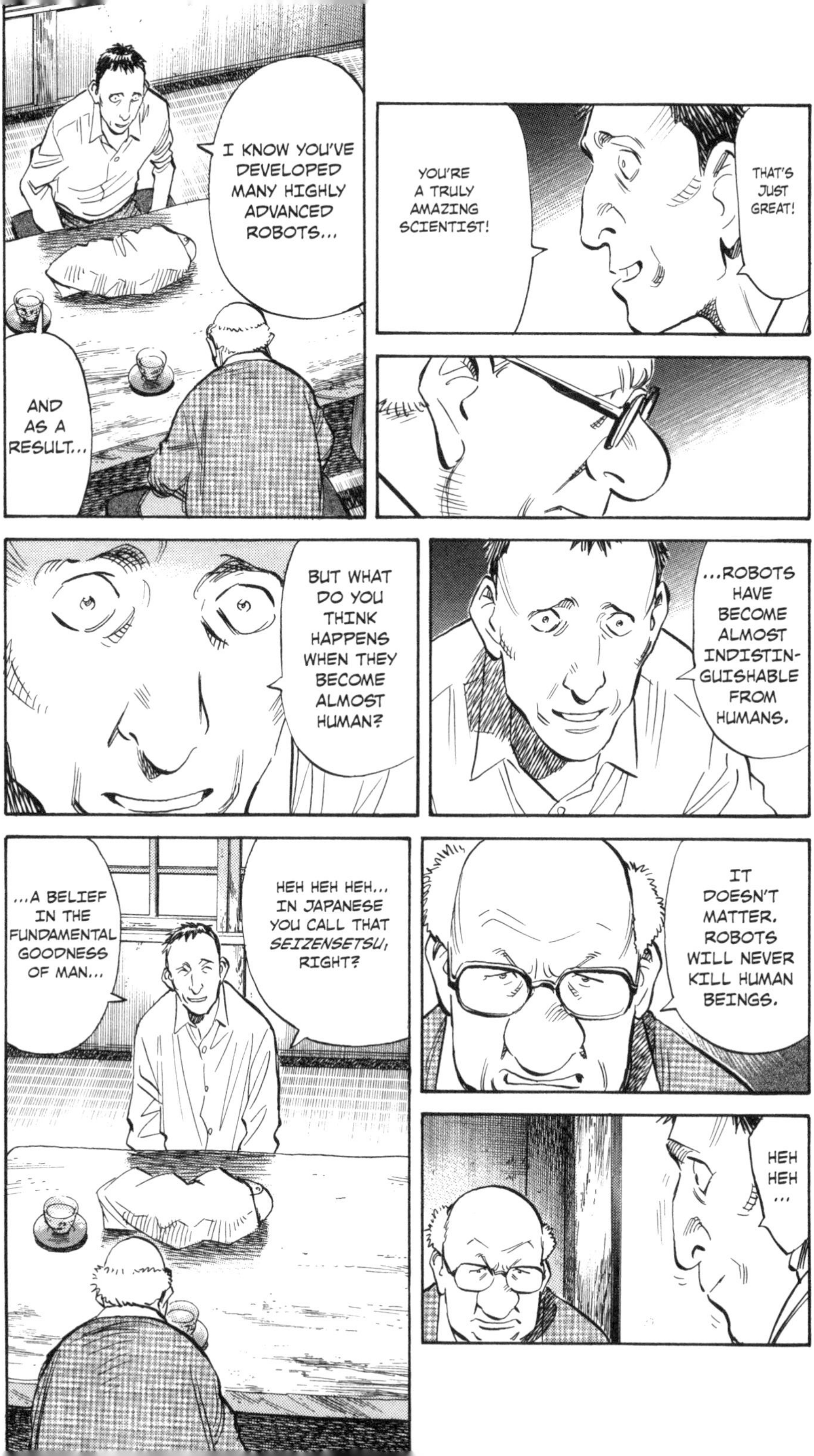
THAT'S JUST GREAT!
YOU'RE A TRULY AMAZING SCIENTIST!
I KNOW YOU'VE DEVELOPED MANY HIGHLY ADVANCED ROBOTS...
AND AS A RESULT...
...ROBOTS HAVE BECOME ALMOST INDISTIN-GUISHABLE FROM HUMANS.
BUT WHAT DO YOU THINK HAPPENS WHEN THEY BECOME ALMOST HUMAN?
IT DOESN'T MATTER. ROBOTS WILL NEVER KILL HUMAN BEINGS.
HEH HEH...
HEH HEH HEH... IN JAPANESE YOU CALL THAT *SEIZENSETSU*, RIGHT?
...A BELIEF IN THE FUNDAMENTAL GOODNESS OF MAN...

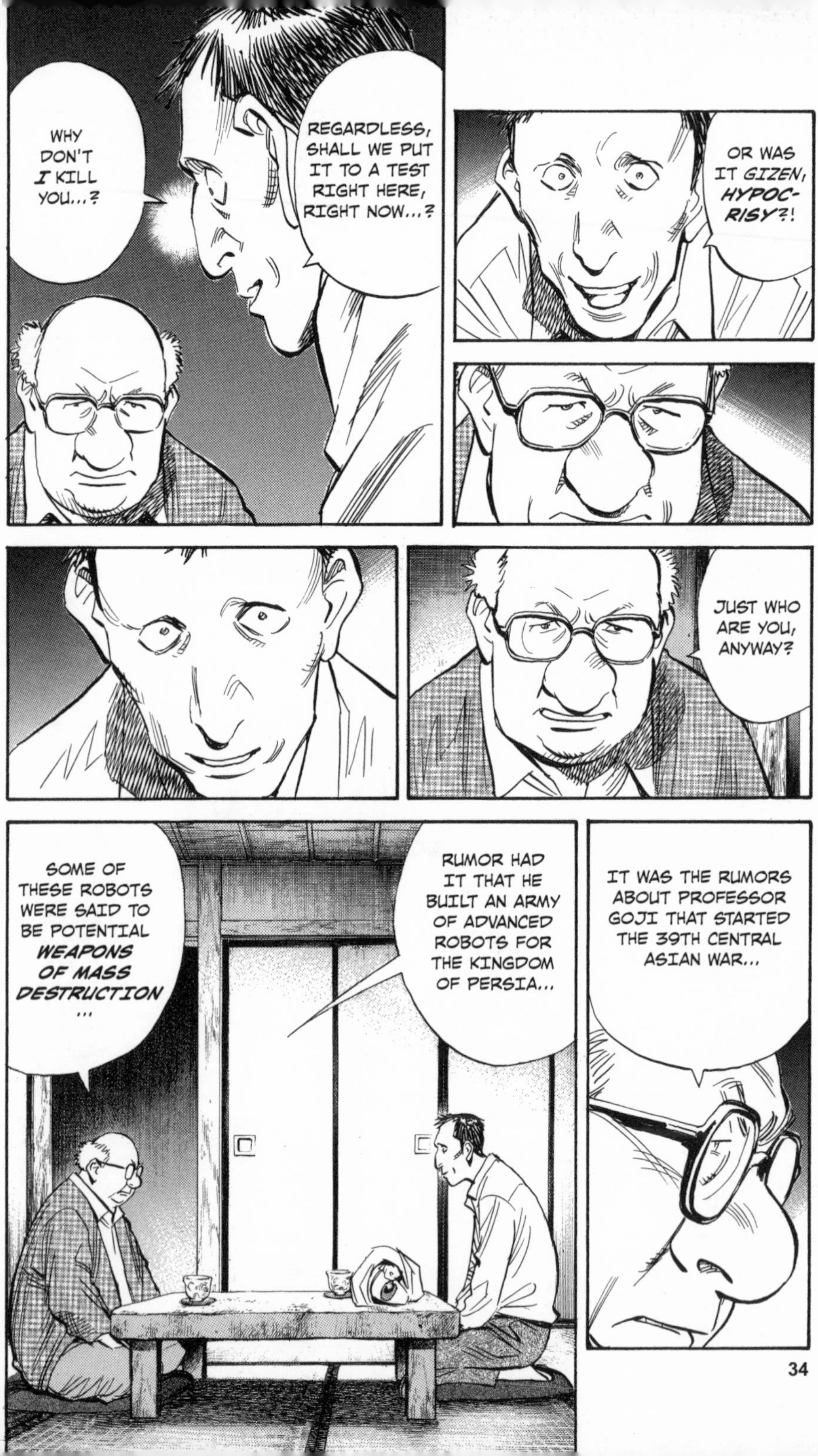
OR WAS IT GIZEN, HYPOCRISY?!
REGARDLESS, SHALL WE PUT IT TO A TEST RIGHT HERE, RIGHT NOW...?
WHY DON'T I KILL YOU...?
JUST WHO ARE YOU, ANYWAY?
IT WAS THE RUMORS ABOUT PROFESSOR GOJI THAT STARTED THE 39TH CENTRAL ASIAN WAR...
RUMOR HAD IT THAT HE BUILT AN ARMY OF ADVANCED ROBOTS FOR THE KINGDOM OF PERSIA...
SOME OF THESE ROBOTS WERE SAID TO BE POTENTIAL WEAPONS OF MASS DESTRUCTION...

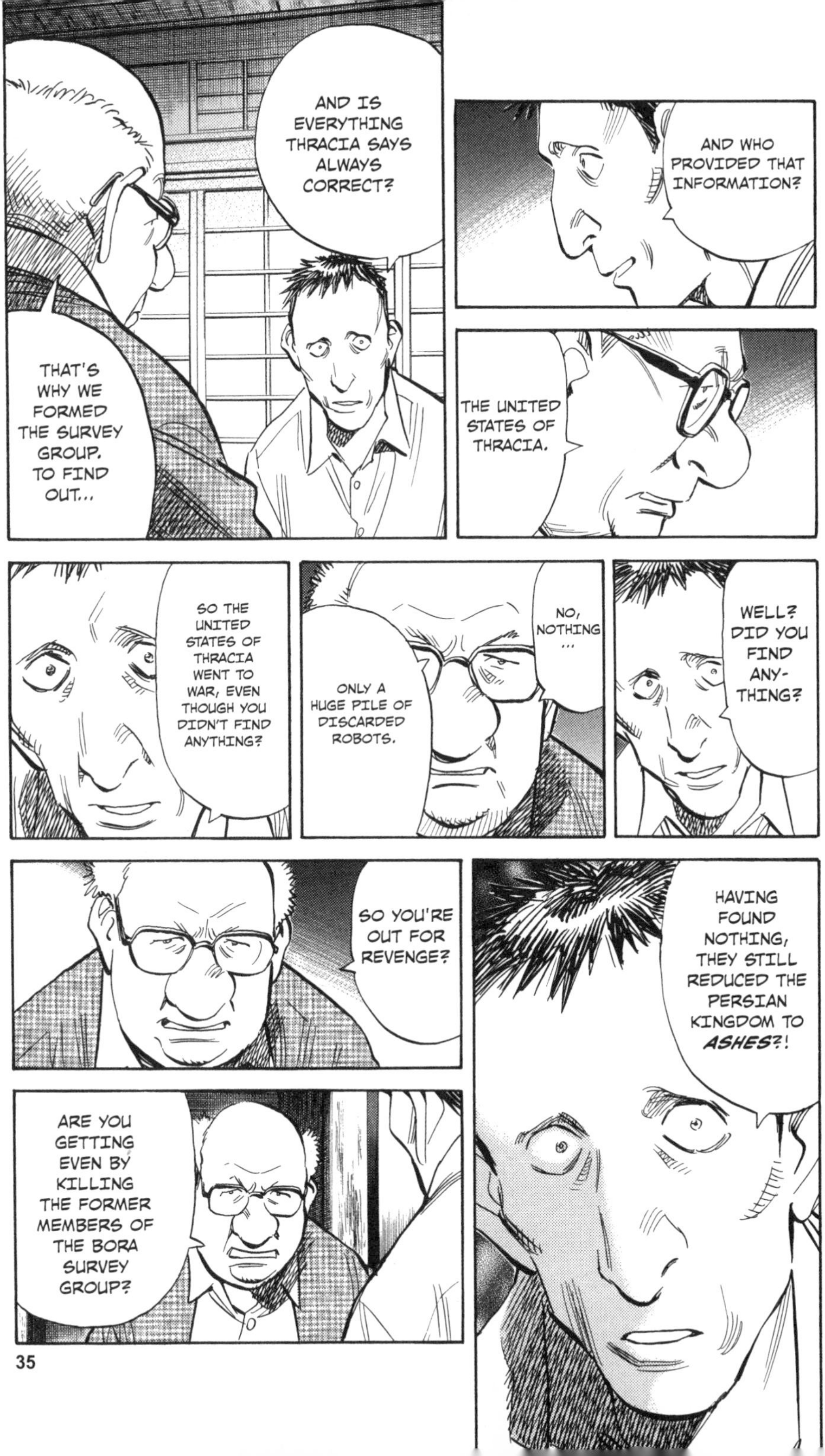
AND WHO PROVIDED THAT INFORMATION?
THE UNITED STATES OF THRACIA.
AND IS EVERYTHING THRACIA SAYS ALWAYS CORRECT?
THAT'S WHY WE FORMED THE SURVEY GROUP. TO FIND OUT...
WELL? DID YOU FIND ANY-THING?
NO, NOTHING ...
ONLY A HUGE PILE OF DISCARDED ROBOTS.
SO THE UNITED STATES OF THRACIA WENT TO WAR, EVEN THOUGH YOU DIDN'T FIND ANYTHING?
HAVING FOUND NOTHING, THEY STILL REDUCED THE PERSIAN KINGDOM TO *ASHES*?!
SO YOU'RE OUT FOR REVENGE?
ARE YOU GETTING EVEN BY KILLING THE FORMER MEMBERS OF THE BORA SURVEY GROUP?

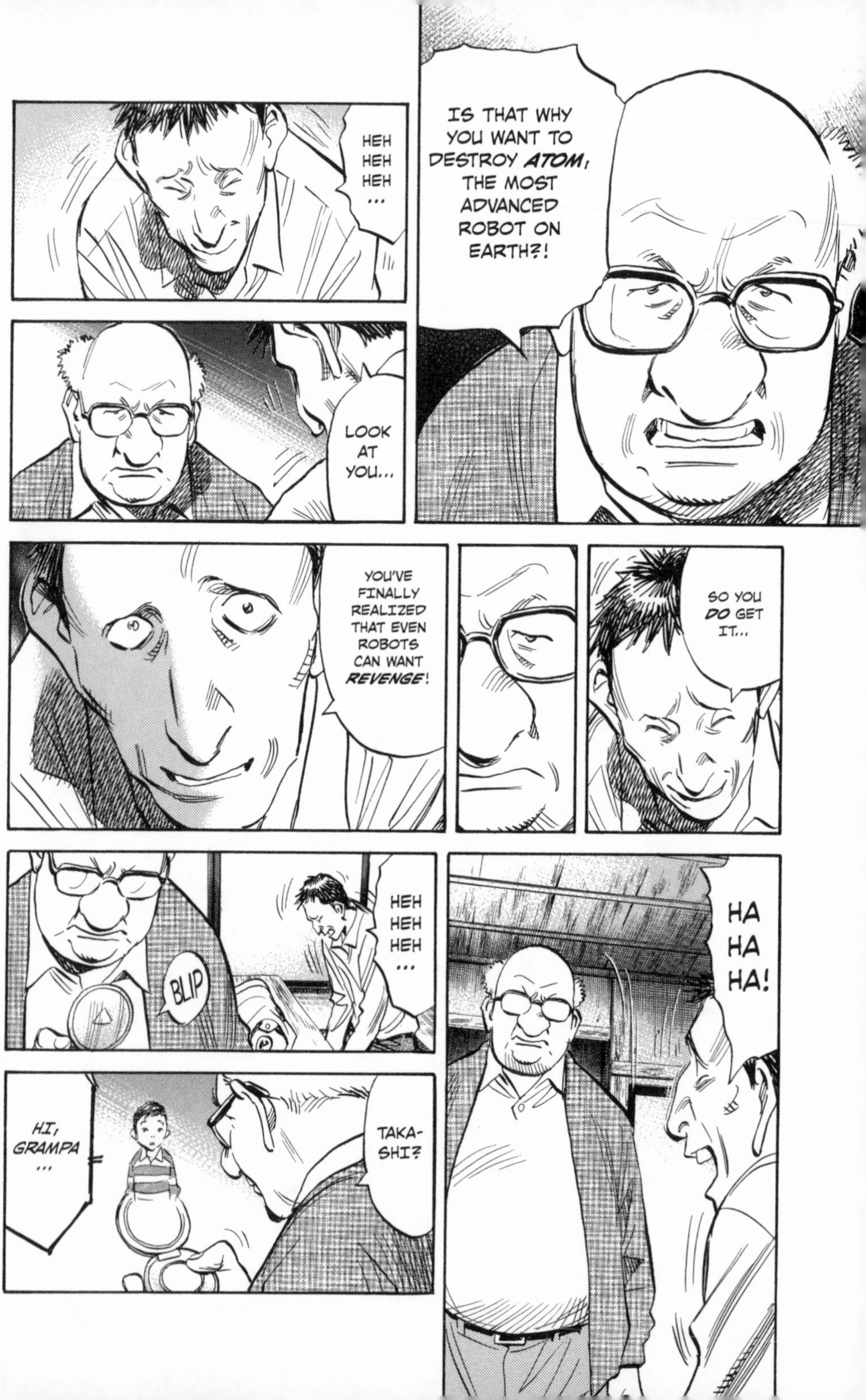
IS THAT WHY YOU WANT TO DESTROY ATOM, THE MOST ADVANCED ROBOT ON EARTH?!
HEH HEH HEH ...
LOOK AT YOU...
SO YOU DO GET IT...
YOU'VE FINALLY REALIZED THAT EVEN ROBOTS CAN WANT REVENGE!
HA HA HA!
HEH HEH HEH ...
BLIP
TAKA-SHI?
HI, GRAMPA ...

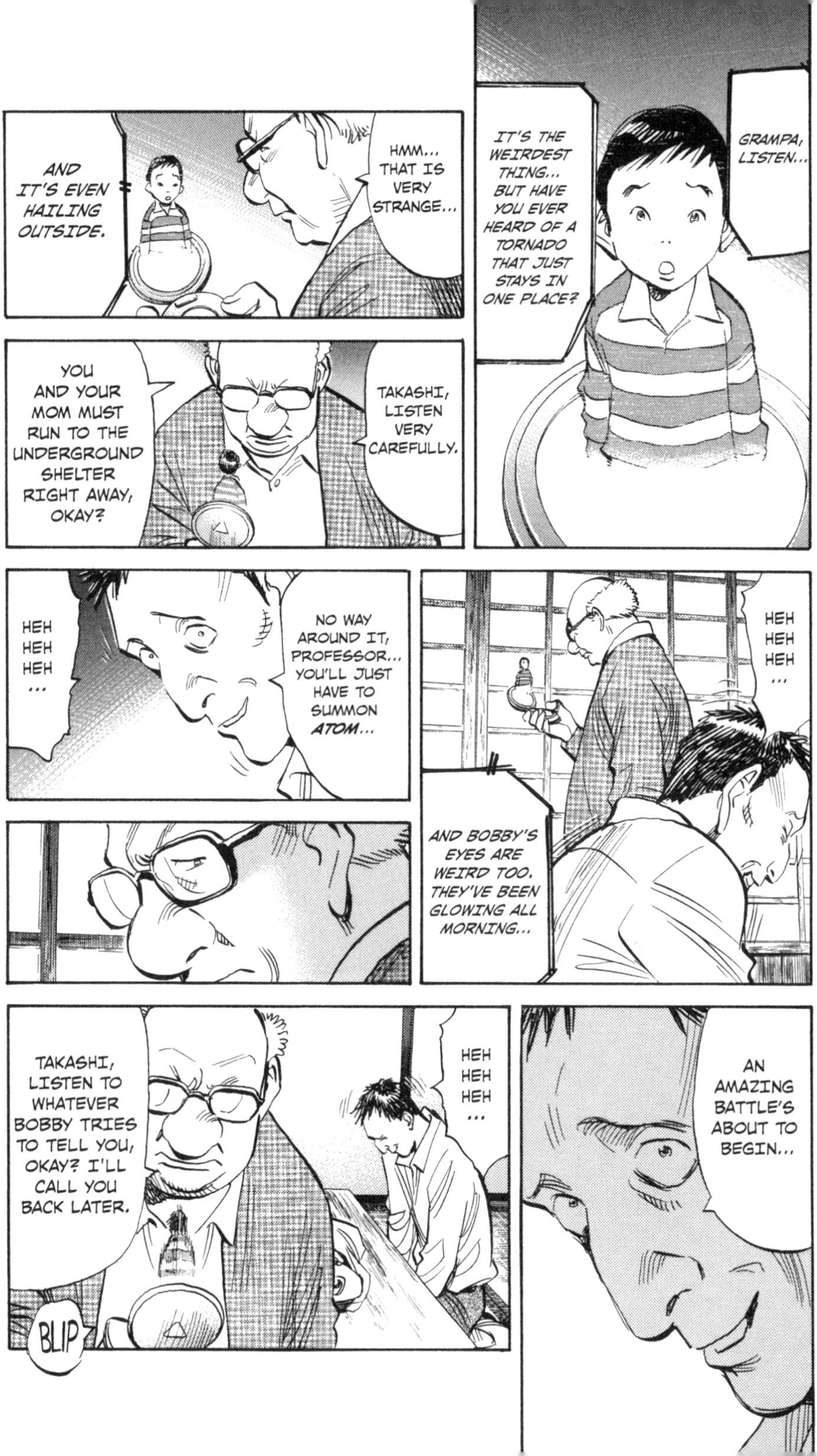
GRAMPA, LISTEN...
IT'S THE WEIRDEST THING... BUT HAVE YOU EVER HEARD OF A TORNADO THAT JUST STAYS IN ONE PLACE?
HMM... THAT IS VERY STRANGE...
AND IT'S EVEN HAILING OUTSIDE.
TAKASHI, LISTEN VERY CAREFULLY.
YOU AND YOUR MOM MUST RUN TO THE UNDERGROUND SHELTER RIGHT AWAY, OKAY?
HEH HEH HEH...
AND BOBBY'S EYES ARE WEIRD TOO. THEY'VE BEEN GLOWING ALL MORNING...
NO WAY AROUND IT, PROFESSOR... YOU'LL JUST HAVE TO SUMMON ATOM...
HEH HEH HEH...
AN AMAZING BATTLE'S ABOUT TO BEGIN...
HEH HEH HEH...
TAKASHI, LISTEN TO WHATEVER BOBBY TRIES TO TELL YOU, OKAY? I'LL CALL YOU BACK LATER.
BLIP

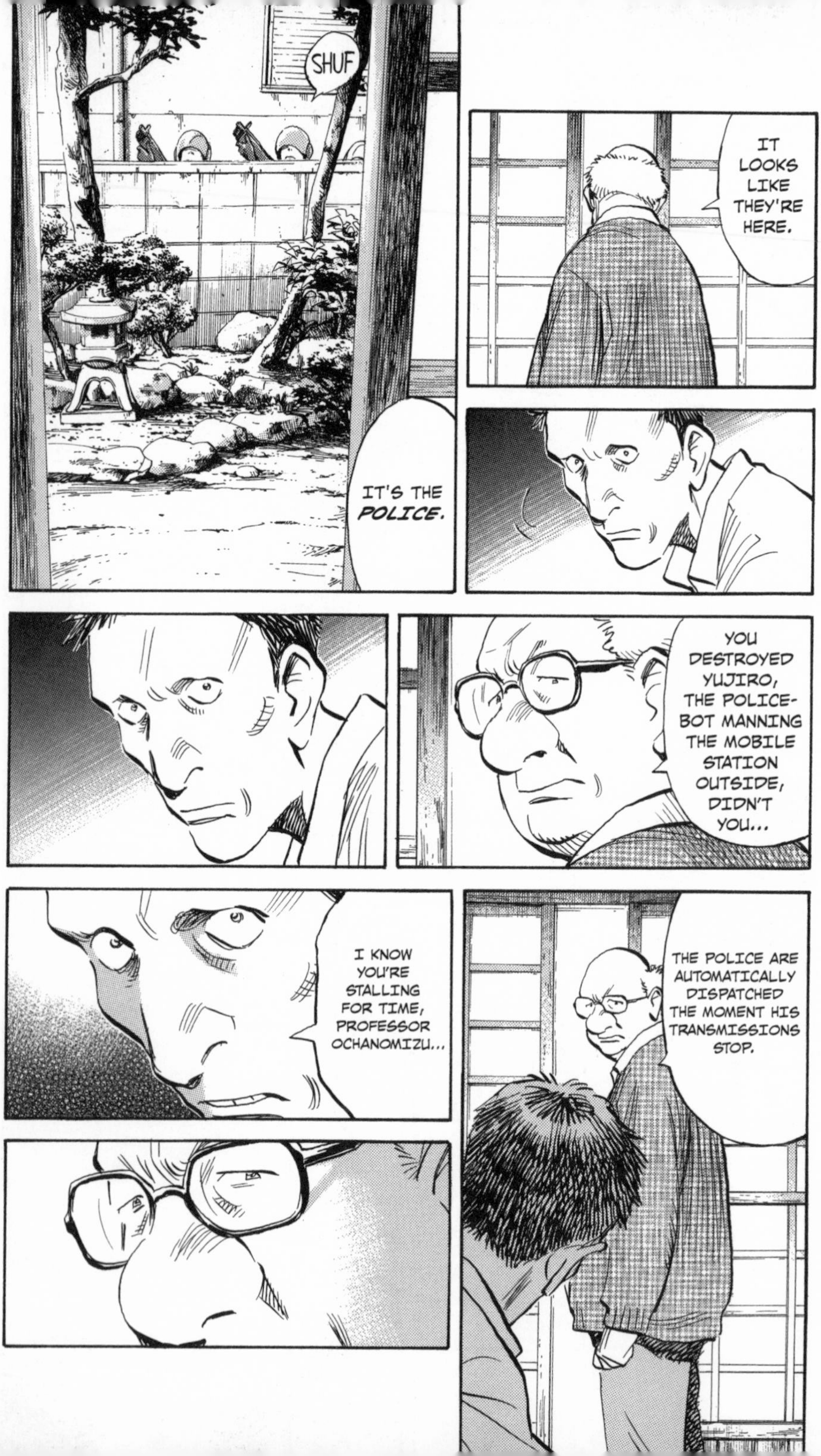
IT LOOKS LIKE THEY'RE HERE.
SHUF
IT'S THE *POLICE*.
YOU DESTROYED YUJIRO, THE POLICE-BOT MANNING THE MOBILE STATION OUTSIDE, DIDN'T YOU...
THE POLICE ARE AUTOMATICALLY DISPATCHED THE MOMENT HIS TRANSMISSIONS STOP.
I KNOW YOU'RE STALLING FOR TIME, PROFESSOR OCHANOMIZU...

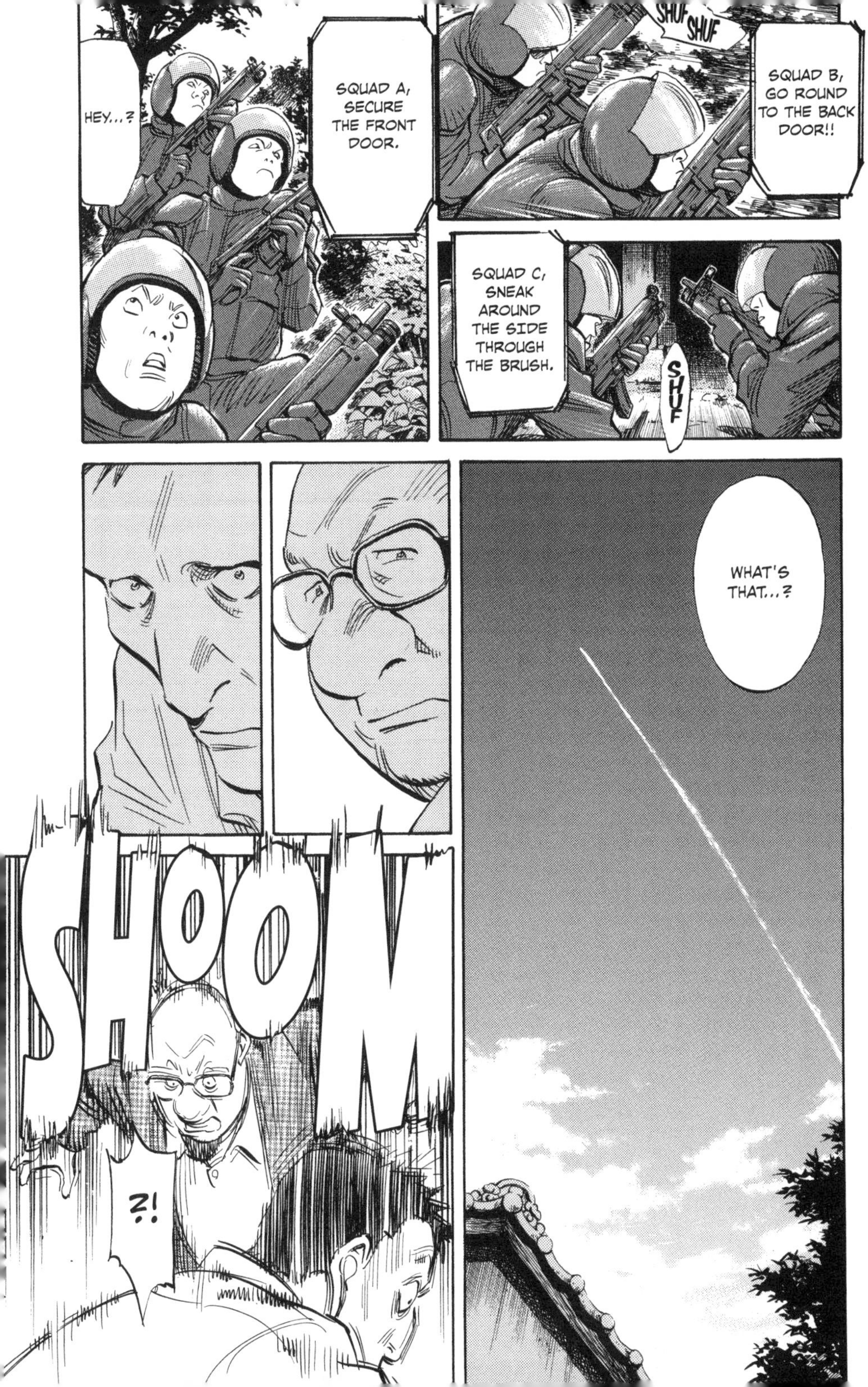
SHUF SHUF
SQUAD B, GO ROUND TO THE BACK DOOR!!
SQUAD C, SNEAK AROUND THE SIDE THROUGH THE BRUSH.
SHUF
SQUAD A, SECURE THE FRONT DOOR.
HEY...?
WHAT'S THAT...?
SHOOM
?!

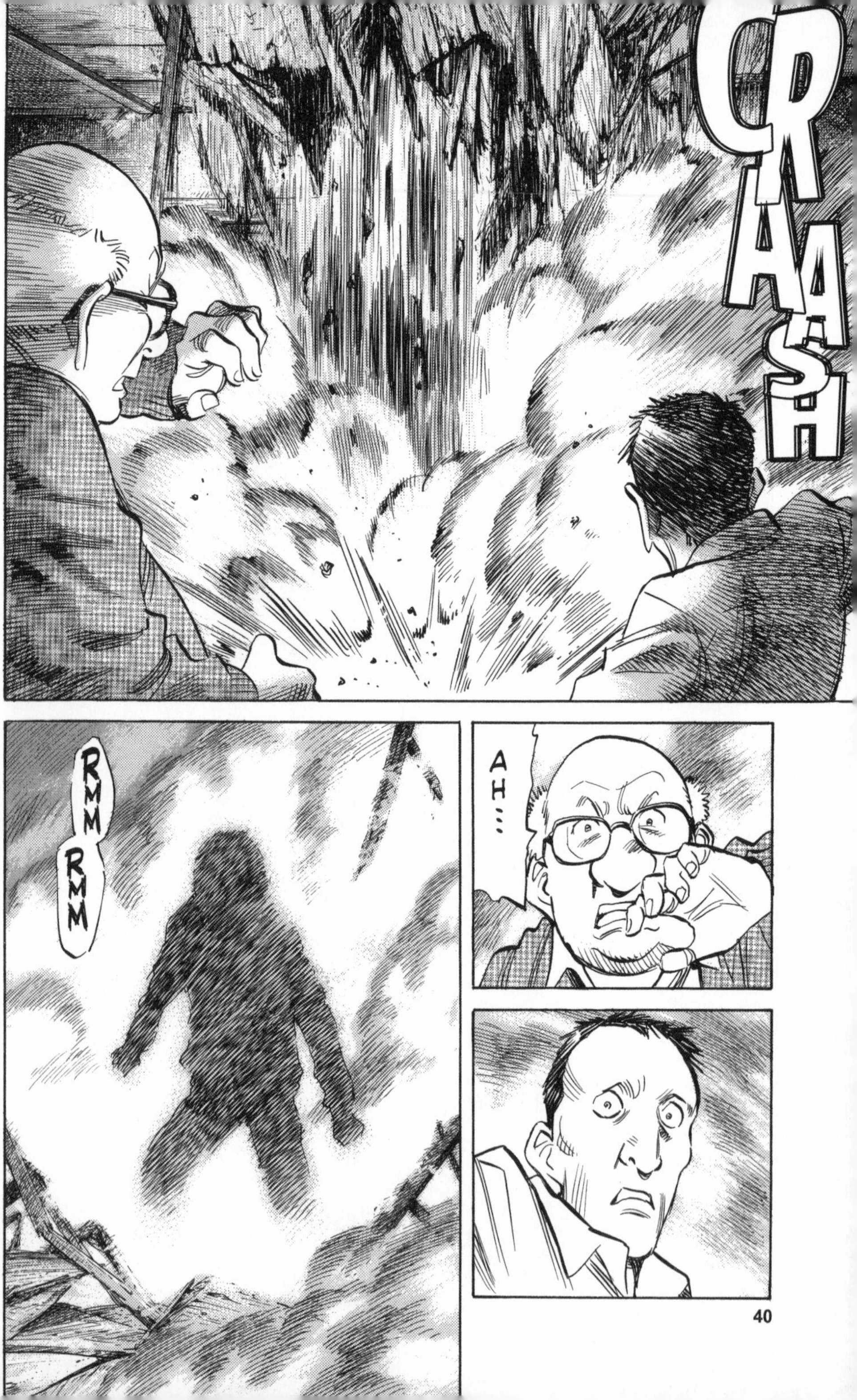
CRAASH
AH...
RMM RMM

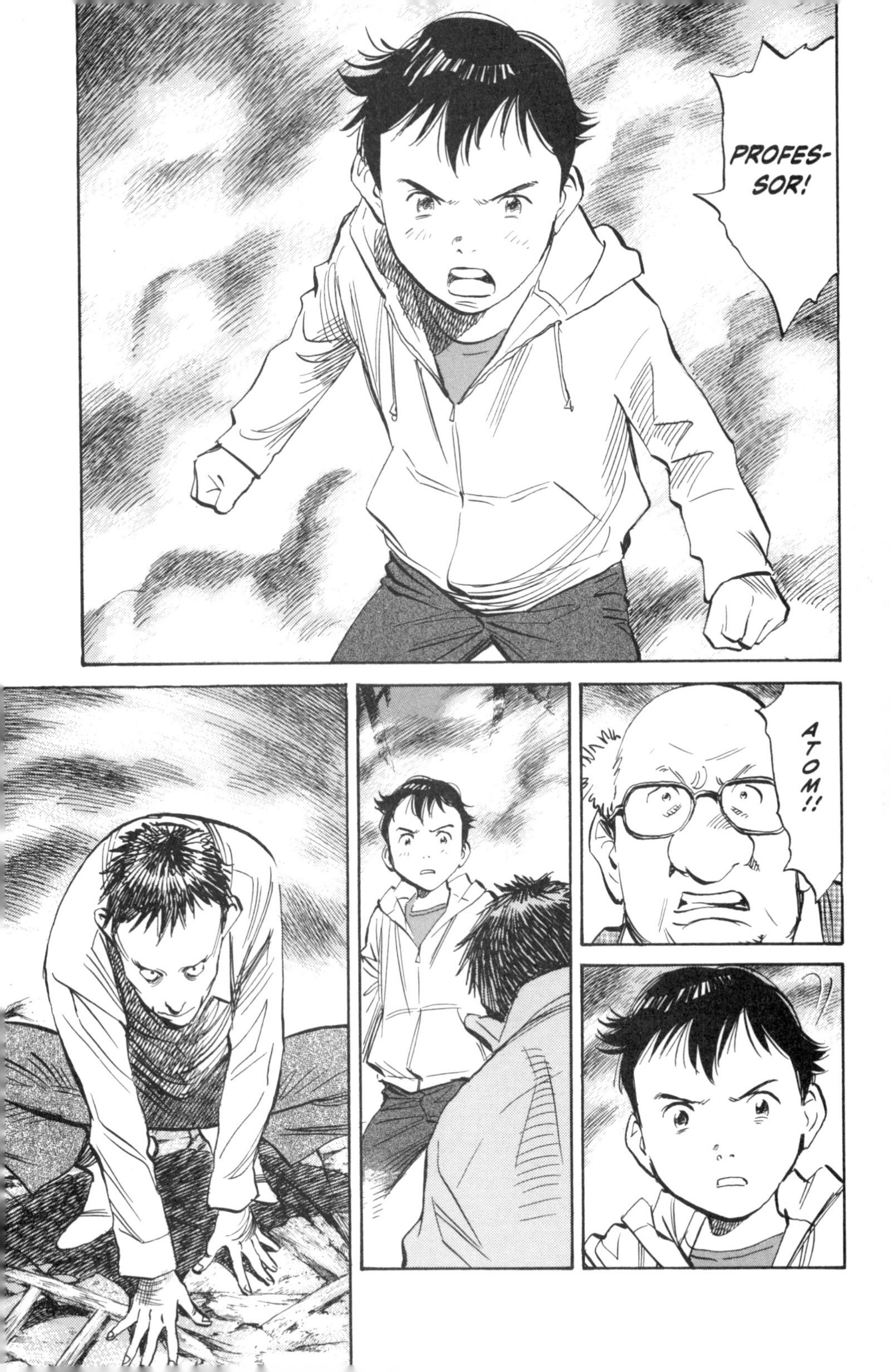
PROFES-
SOR!
ATOM!!

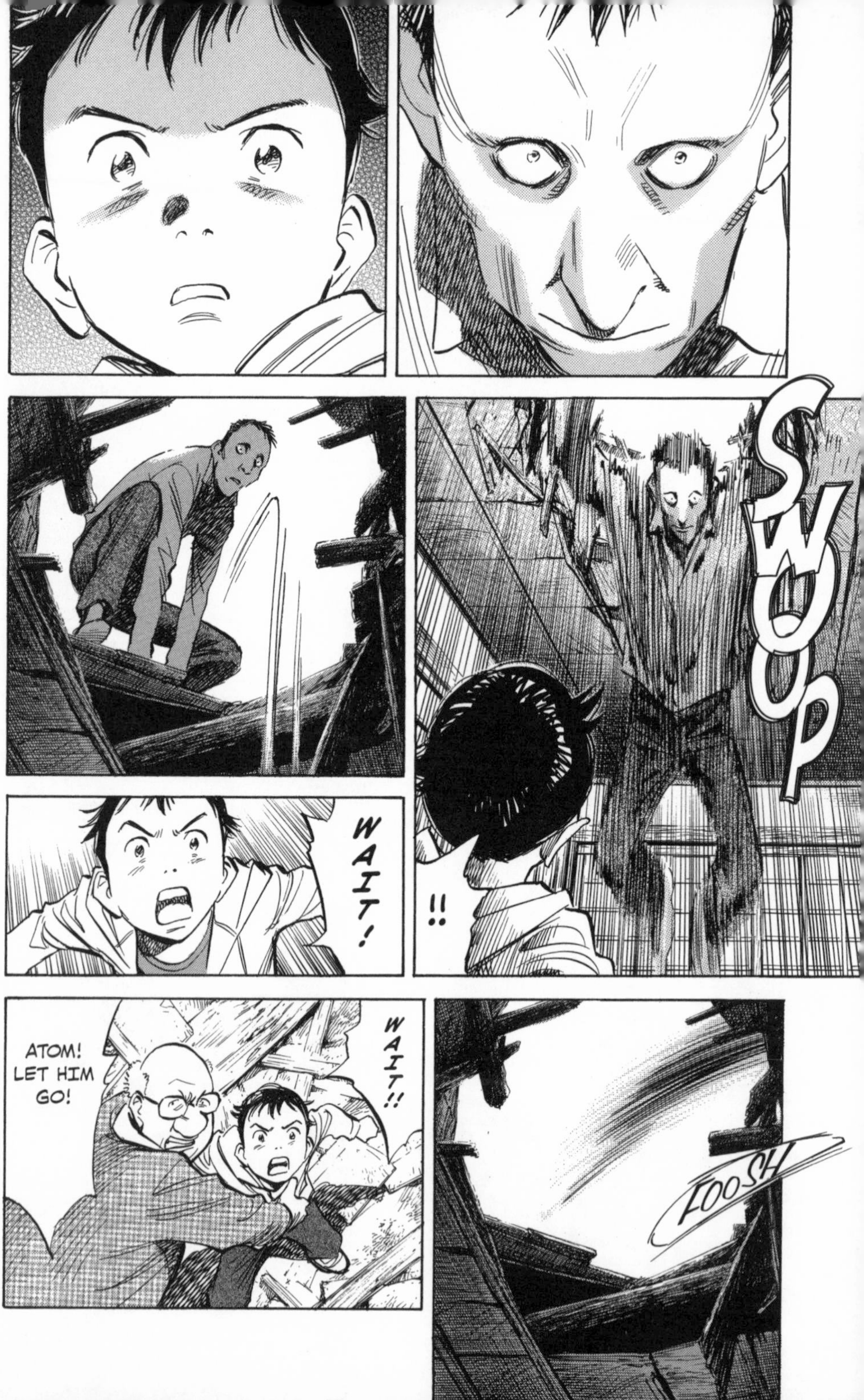
SWOOP
!!
WAIT!
FOOSH
WAIT!!
ATOM! LET HIM GO!

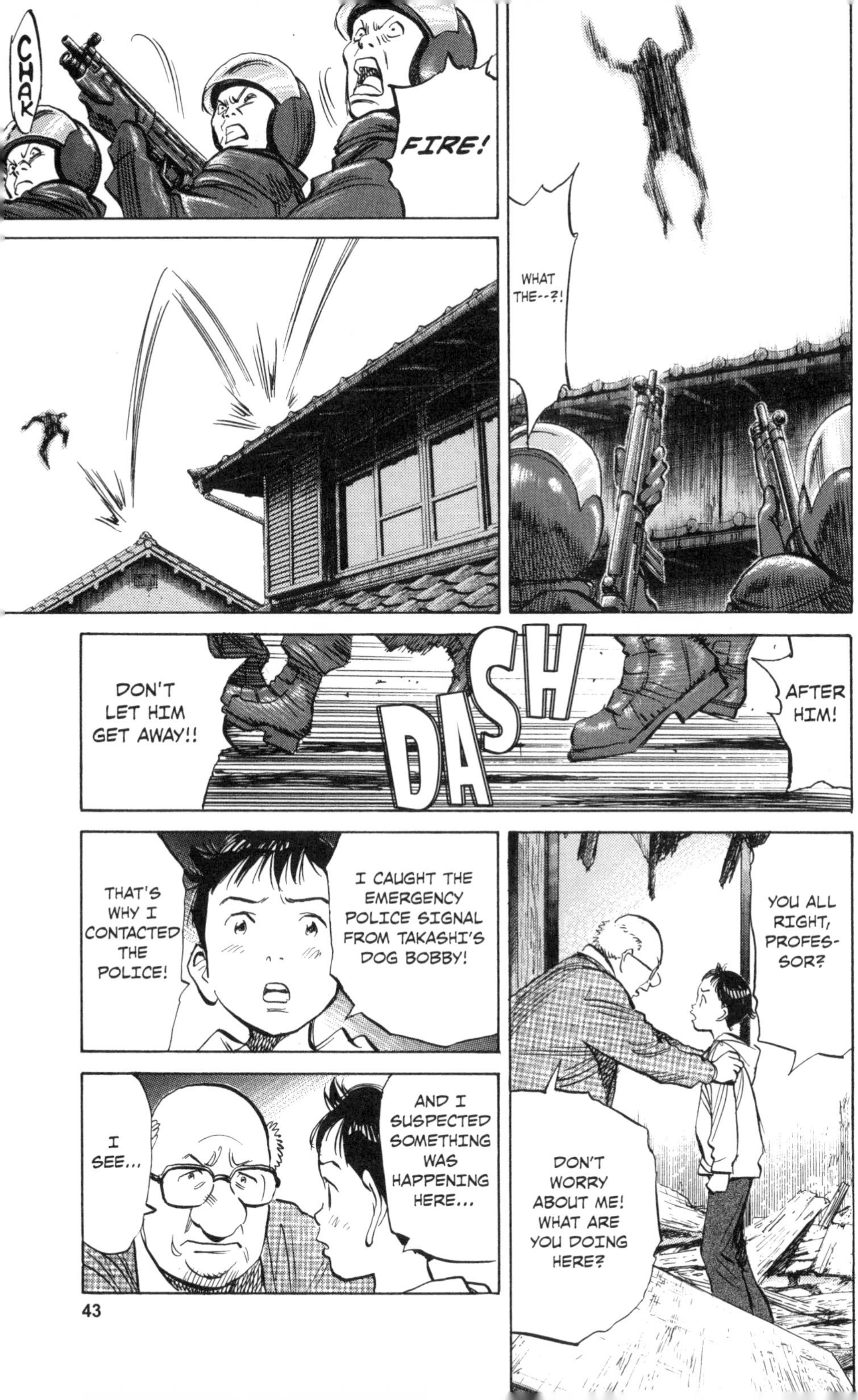
WHAT THE--?!
FIRE!
CHAK
AFTER HIM!
DASH
DON'T LET HIM GET AWAY!!
YOU ALL RIGHT, PROFES-SOR?
DON'T WORRY ABOUT ME! WHAT ARE YOU DOING HERE?
I CAUGHT THE EMERGENCY POLICE SIGNAL FROM TAKASHI'S DOG BOBBY!
THAT'S WHY I CONTACTED THE POLICE!
AND I SUSPECTED SOMETHING WAS HAPPENING HERE...
I SEE...

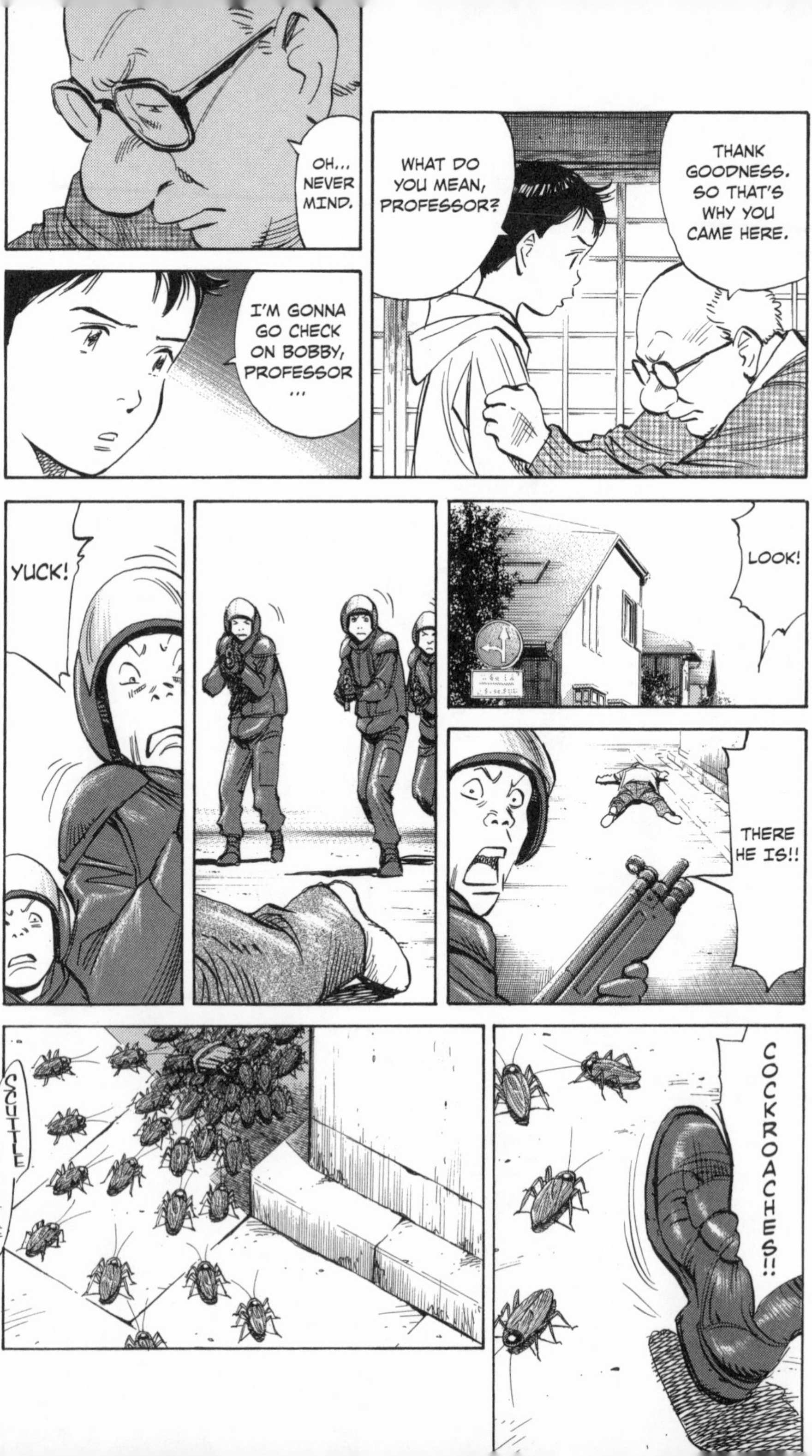
THANK GOODNESS. SO THAT'S WHY YOU CAME HERE.
WHAT DO YOU MEAN, PROFESSOR?
OH... NEVER MIND.
I'M GONNA GO CHECK ON BOBBY, PROFESSOR...
LOOK!
THERE HE IS!!
YUCK!
COCKROACHES!!
SCUTTLE
SCUTTLE

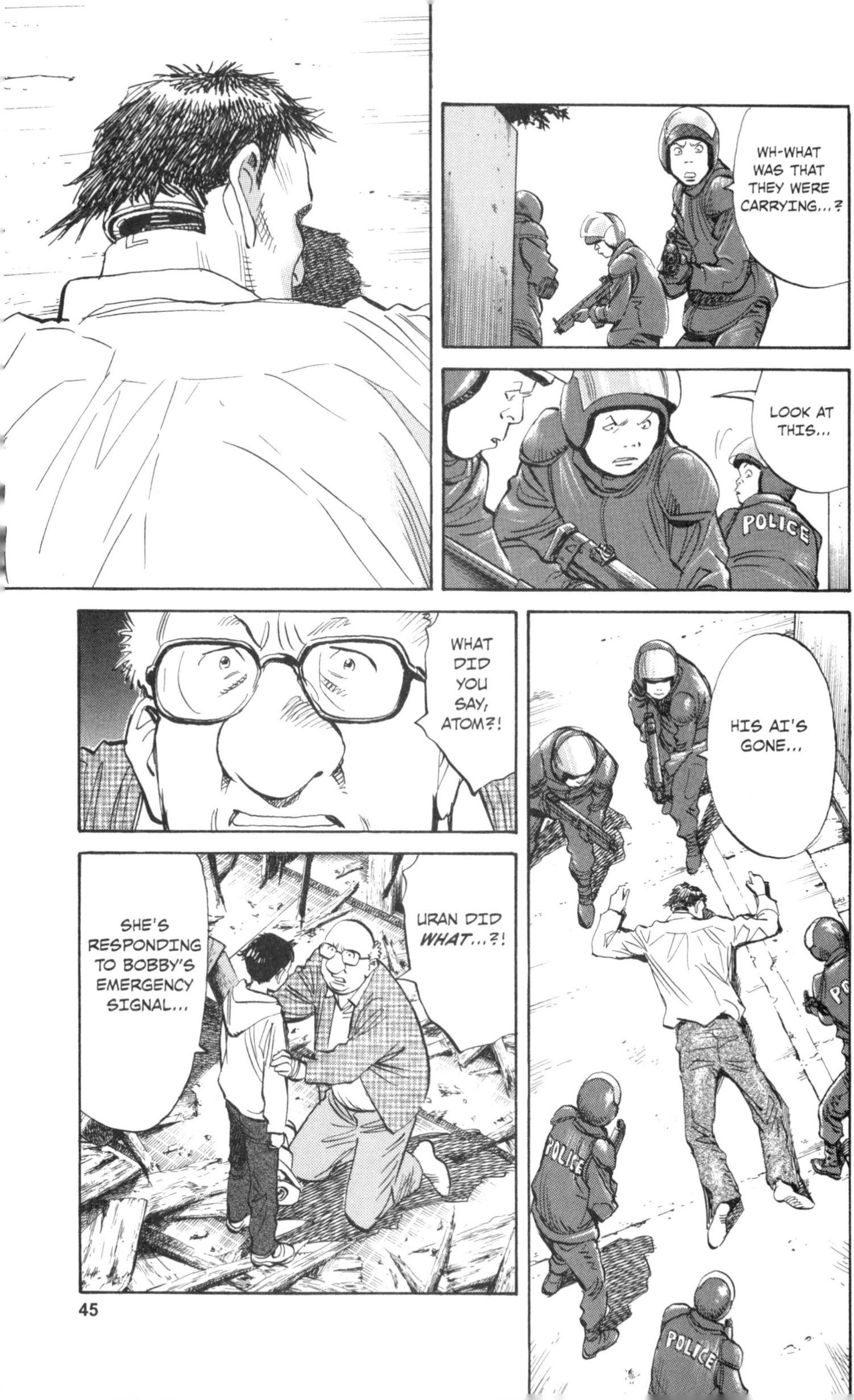
WH-WHAT WAS THAT THEY WERE CARRYING...?
LOOK AT THIS...
HIS AI'S GONE...
WHAT DID YOU SAY, ATOM?!
URAN DID *WHAT*...?!
SHE'S RESPONDING TO BOBBY'S EMERGENCY SIGNAL...

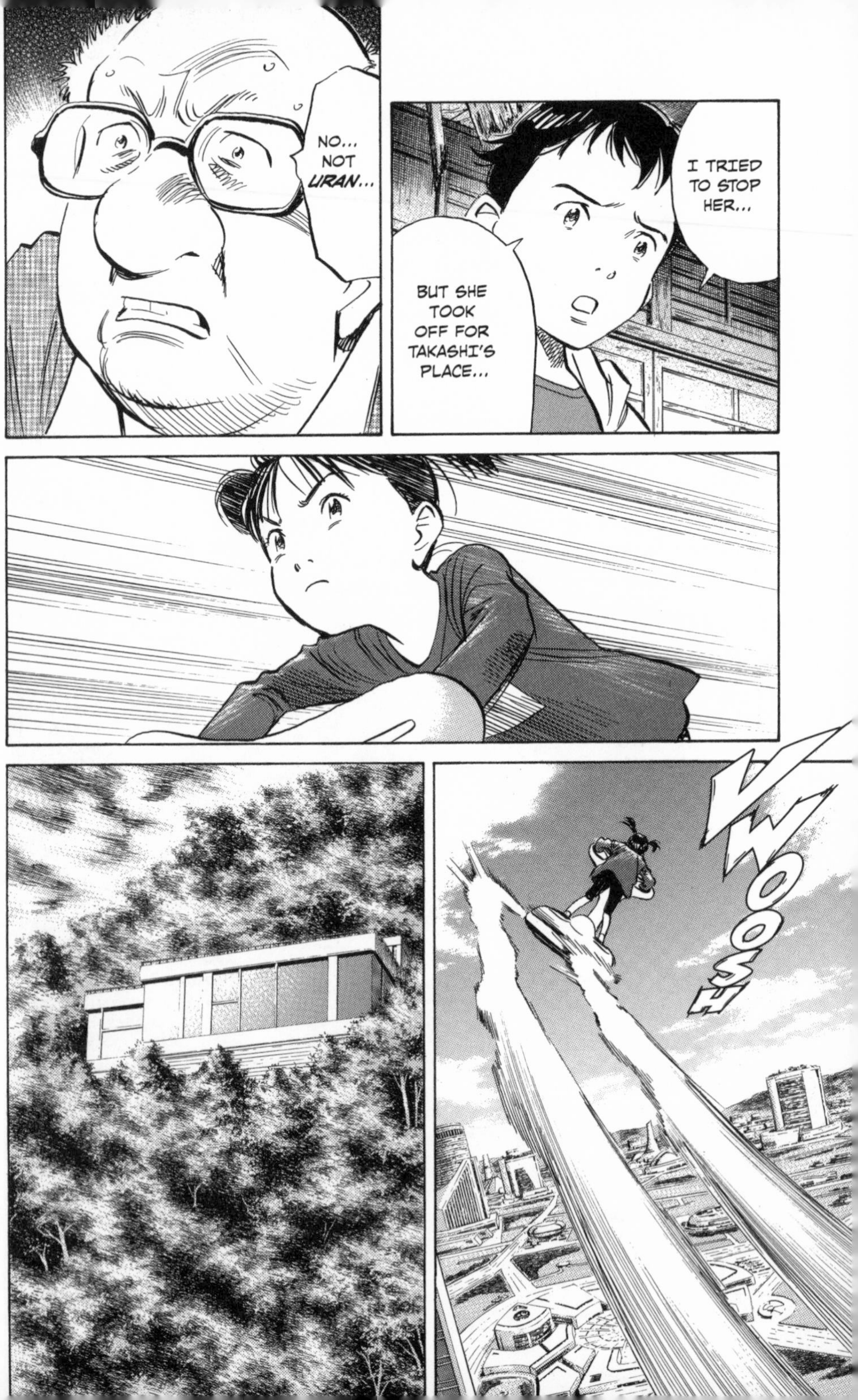
I TRIED TO STOP HER...
BUT SHE TOOK OFF FOR TAKASHI'S PLACE...
NO... NOT *URAN*...
VWOOSH

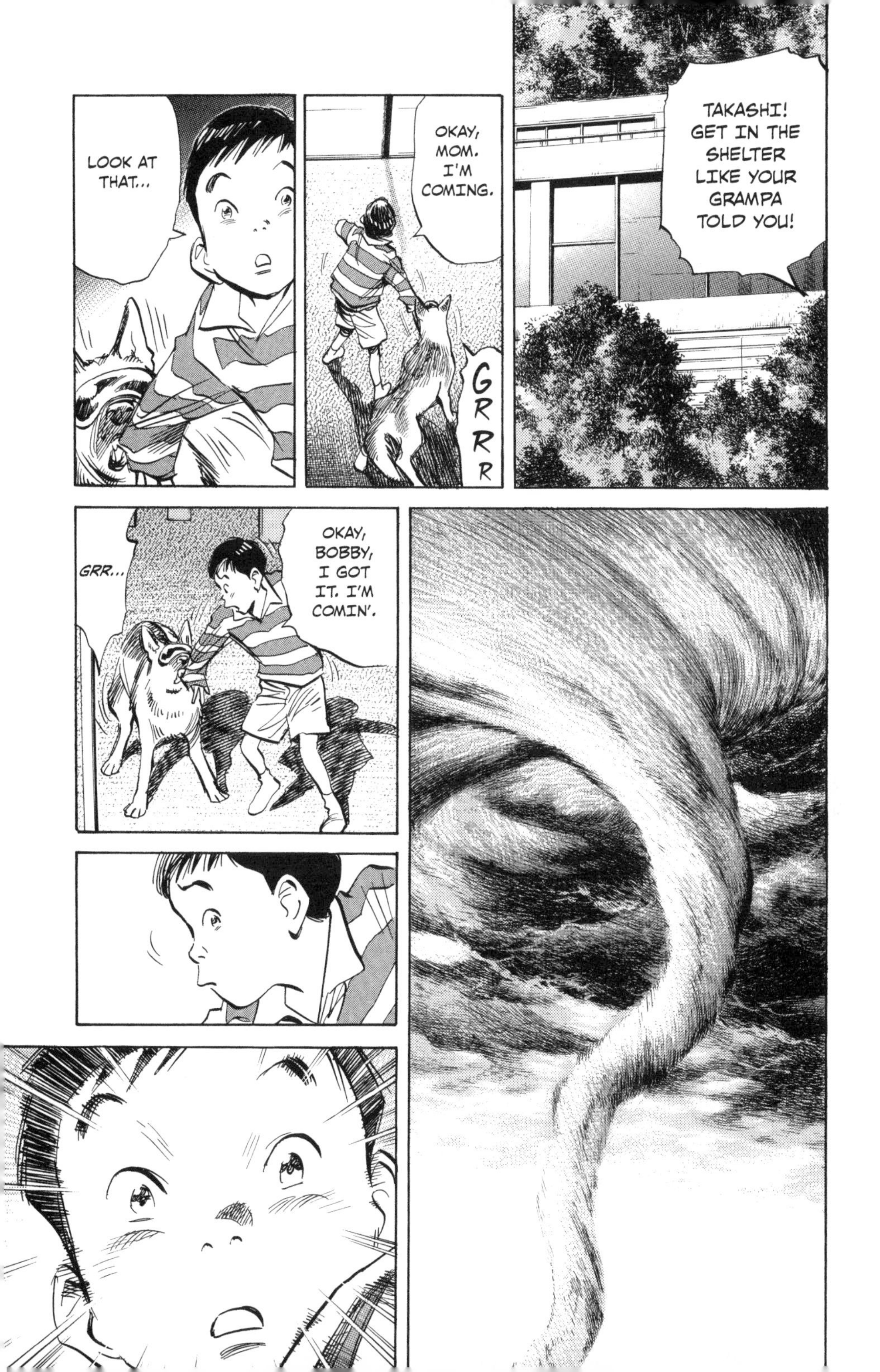
TAKASHI! GET IN THE SHELTER LIKE YOUR GRAMPA TOLD YOU!
OKAY, MOM. I'M COMING.
GRRR
LOOK AT THAT...
OKAY, BOBBY, I GOT IT. I'M COMIN'.
GRR...

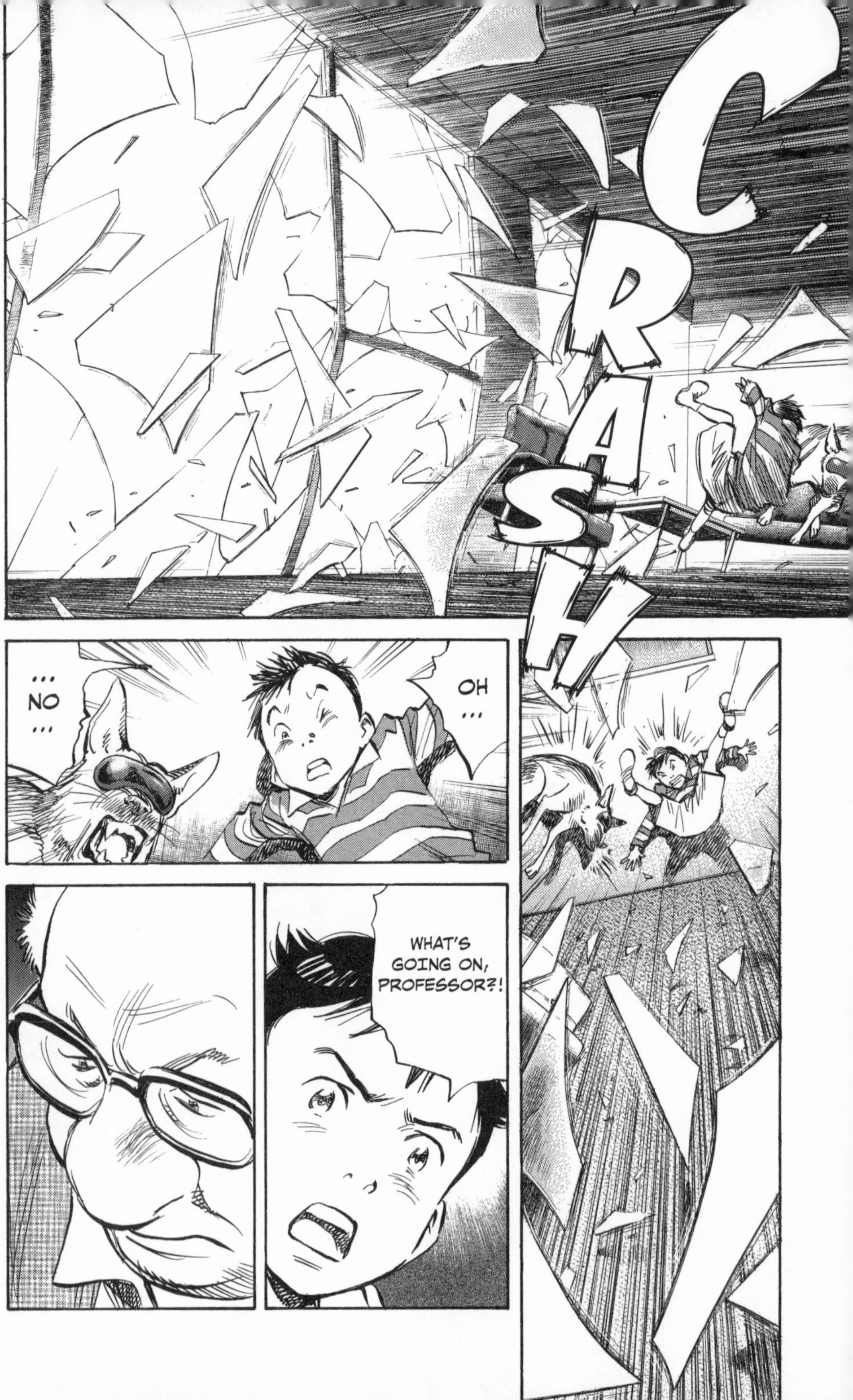
CRASH
OH ...
... NO ...
WHAT'S GOING ON, PROFESSOR?!

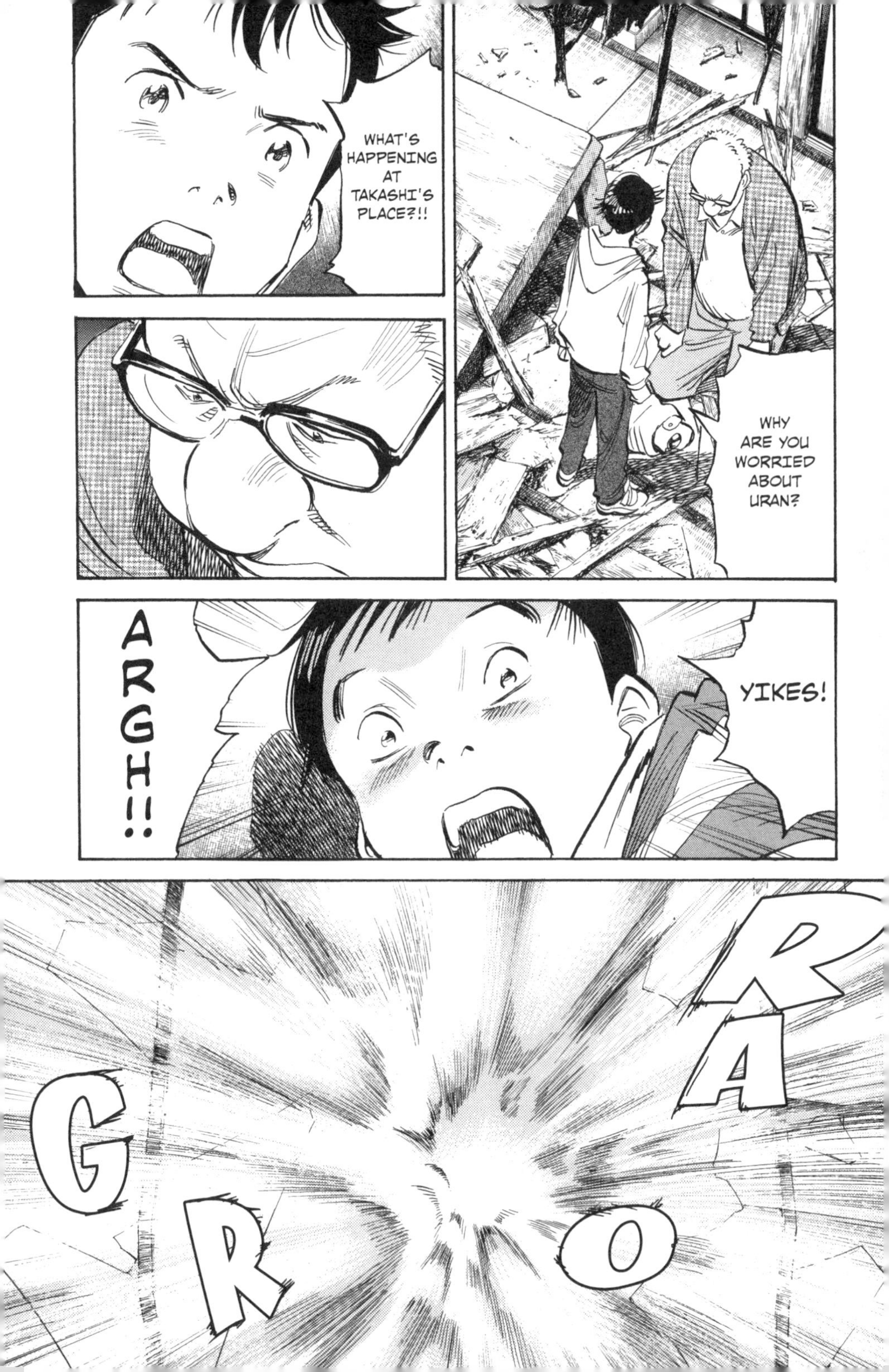
WHY ARE YOU WORRIED ABOUT URAN?
WHAT'S HAPPENING AT TAKASHI'S PLACE?!!
YIKES!
ARGH!!
GROAR

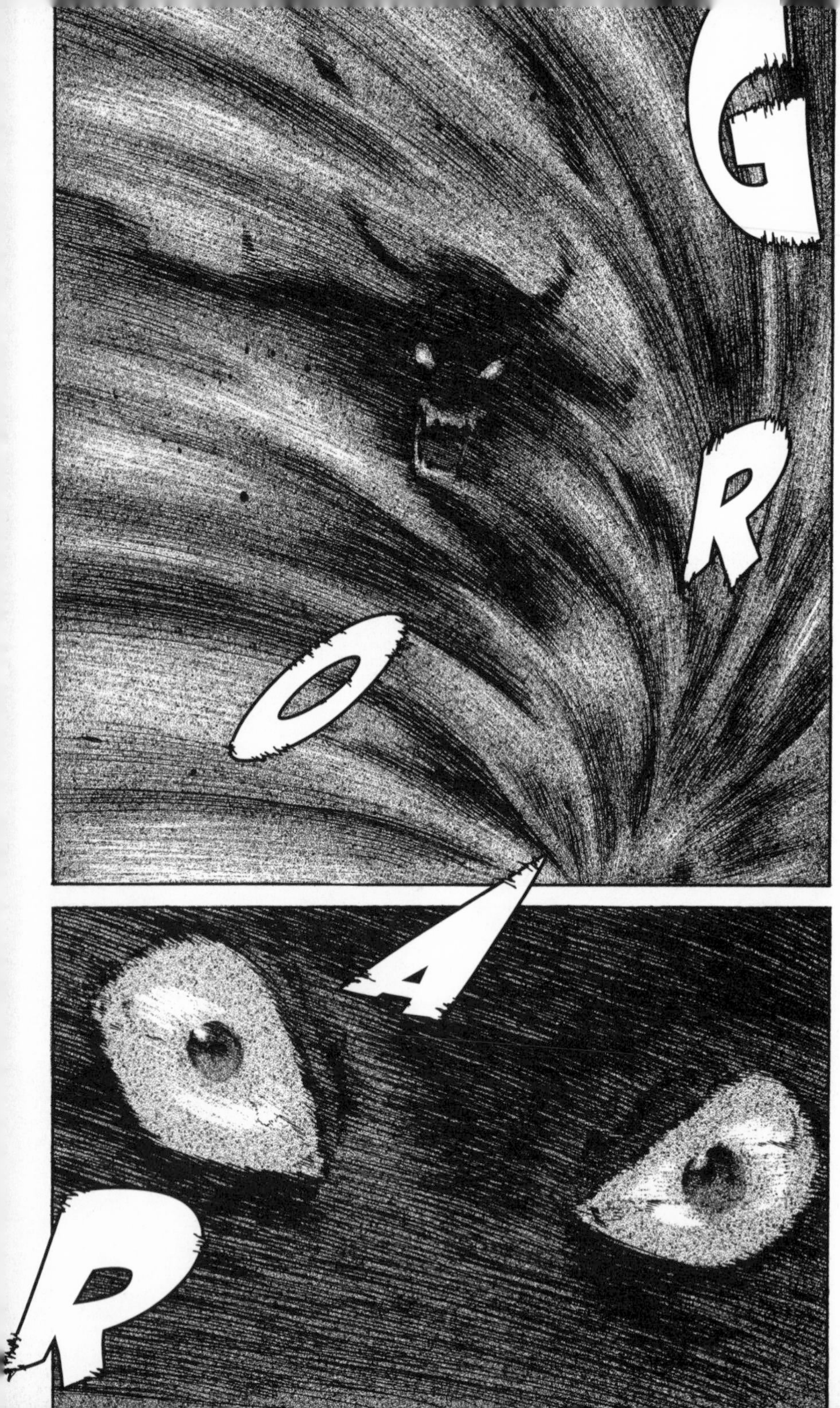
GROAR

Act 26 THE CONFRONTATION

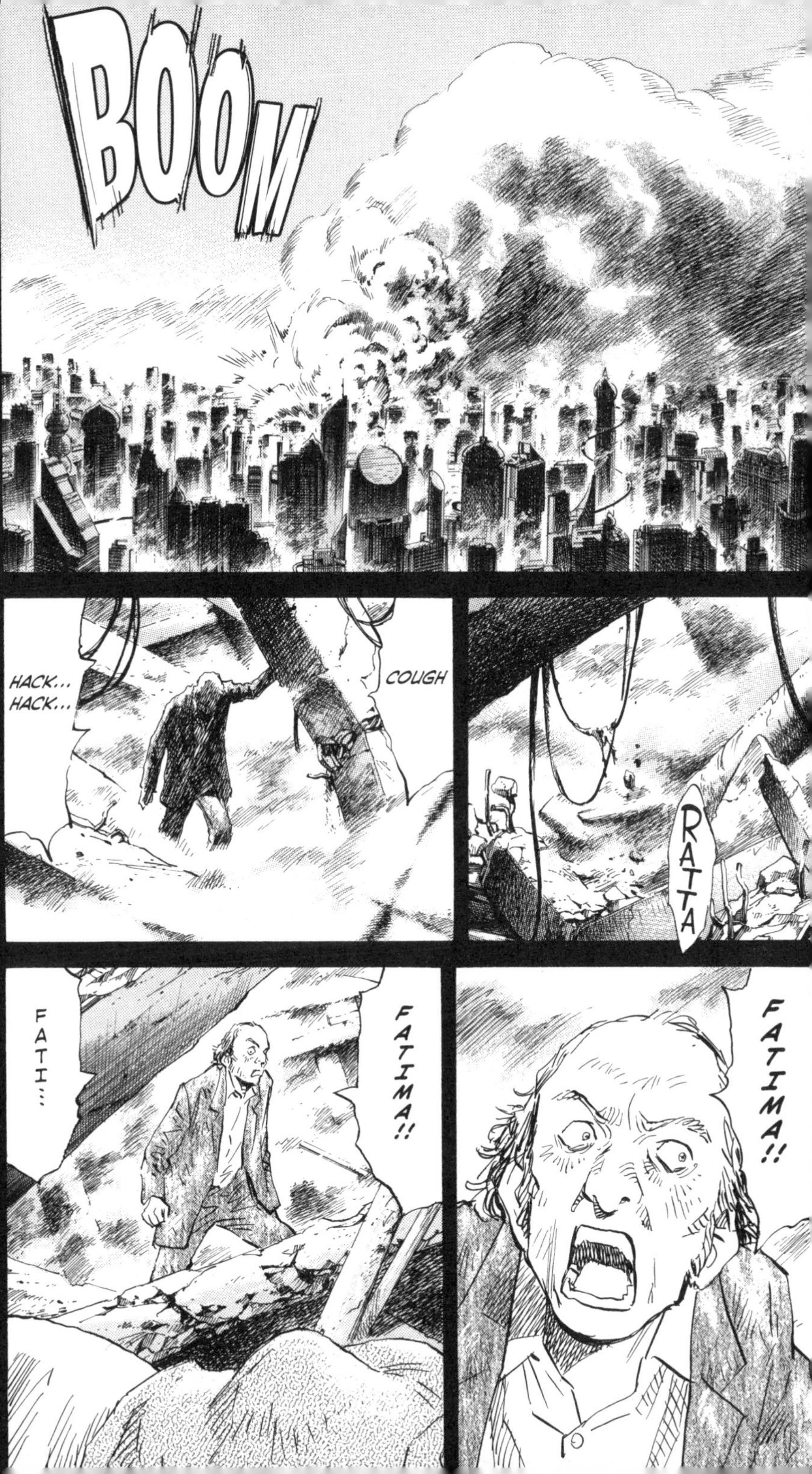
BOOM
RATTA
COUGH
HACK... HACK...
FATIMA!!
FATIMA!!
FATI...

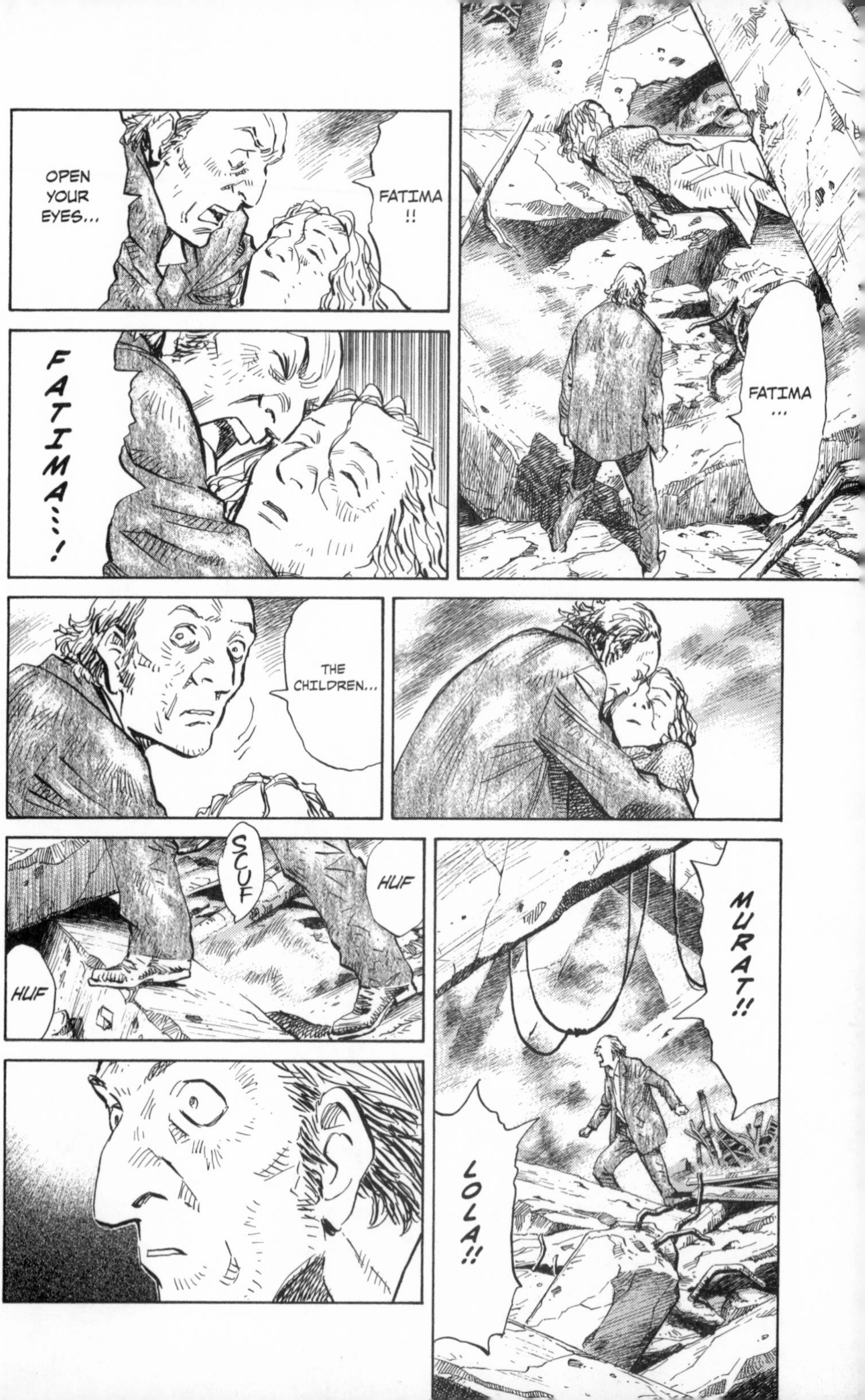
FATIMA ...
FATIMA !!
OPEN YOUR EYES...
FATIMA...!
THE CHILDREN...
MURAT!!
LOLA!!
HUF
SCUF
HUF

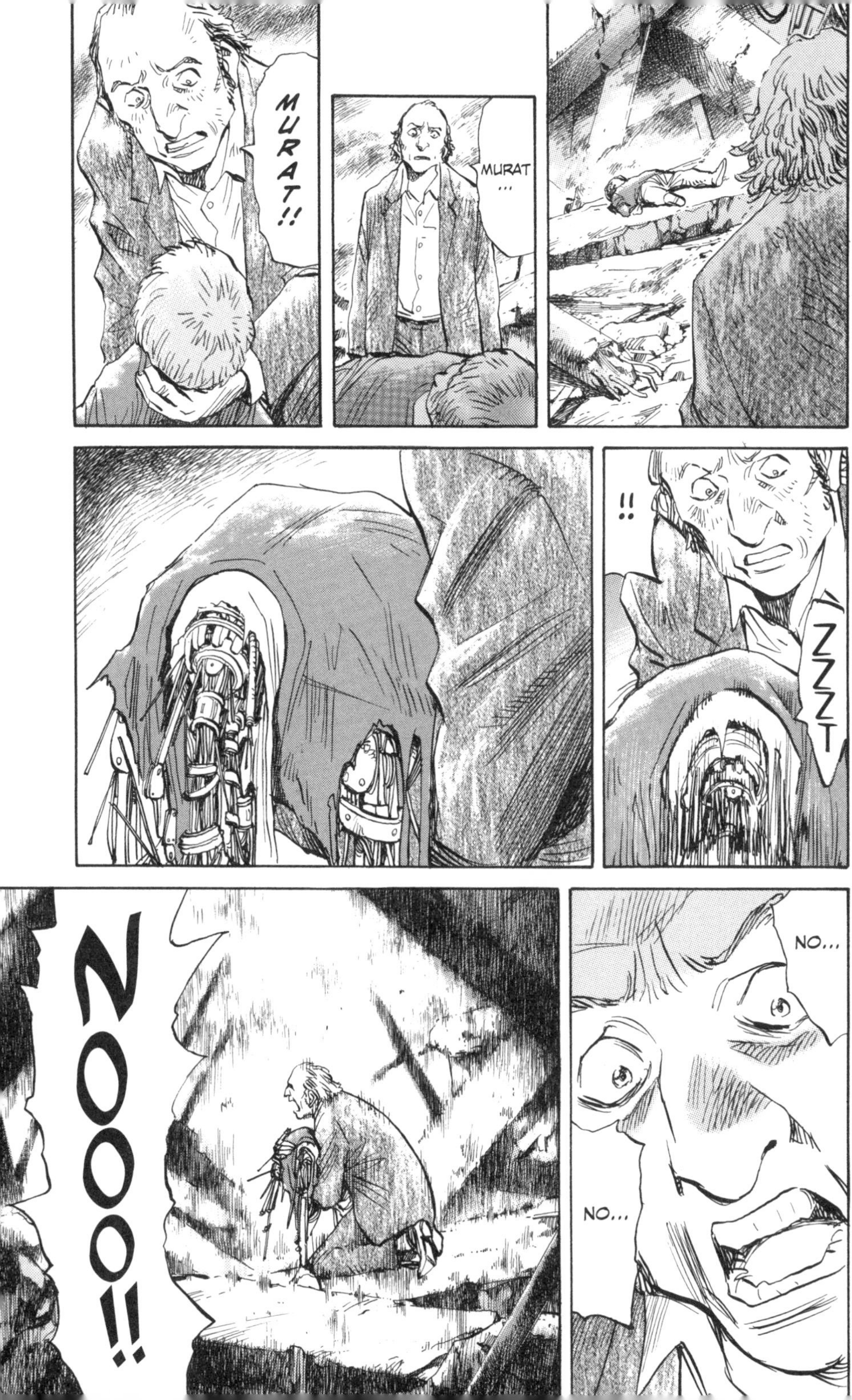
MURAT ...
MURAT!!
!!
ZZZT
NO...
NO...
NOOO!!

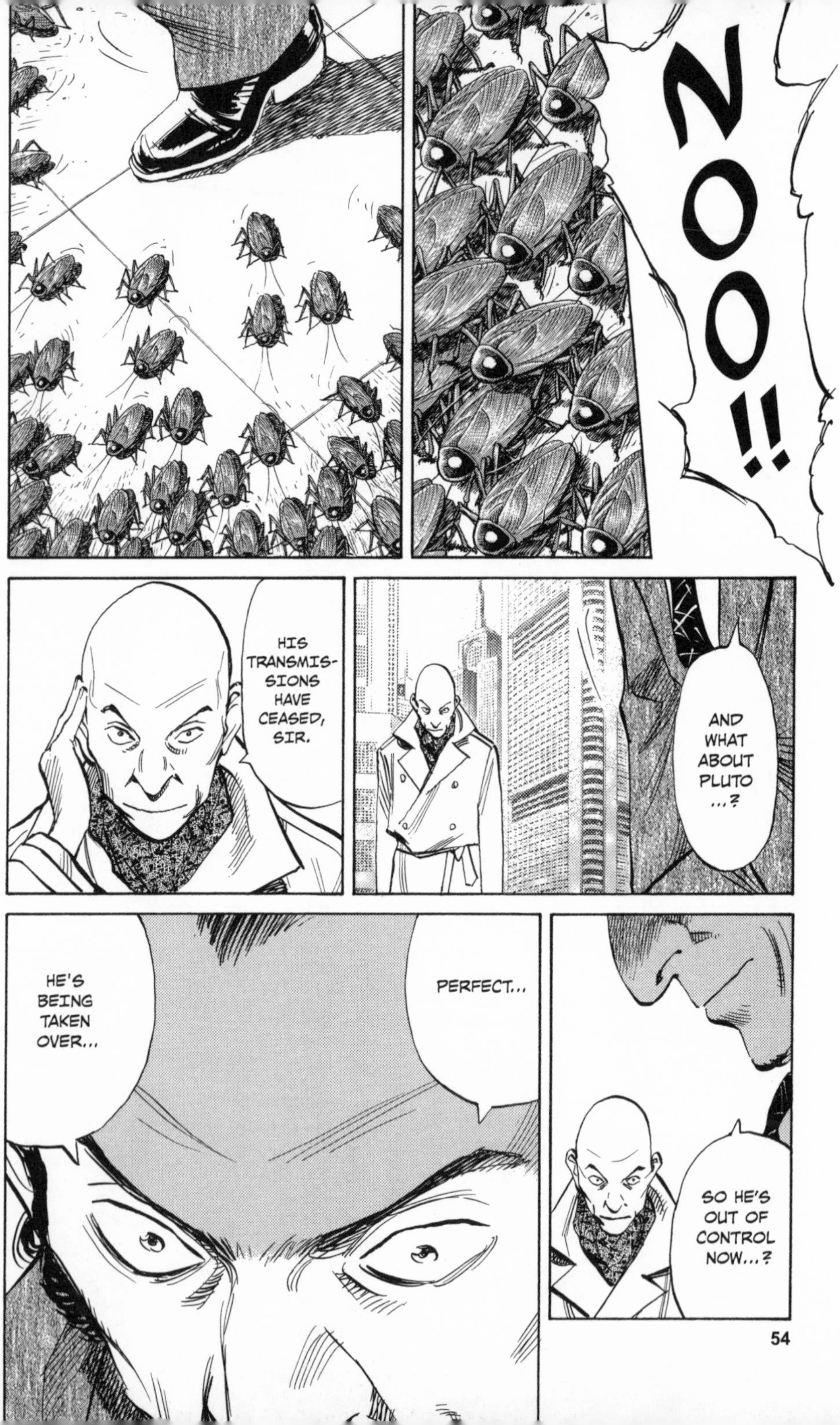
ZOOO!!
AND WHAT ABOUT PLUTO...?
HIS TRANSMIS-SIONS HAVE CEASED, SIR.
SO HE'S OUT OF CONTROL NOW...?
PERFECT...
HE'S BEING TAKEN OVER...

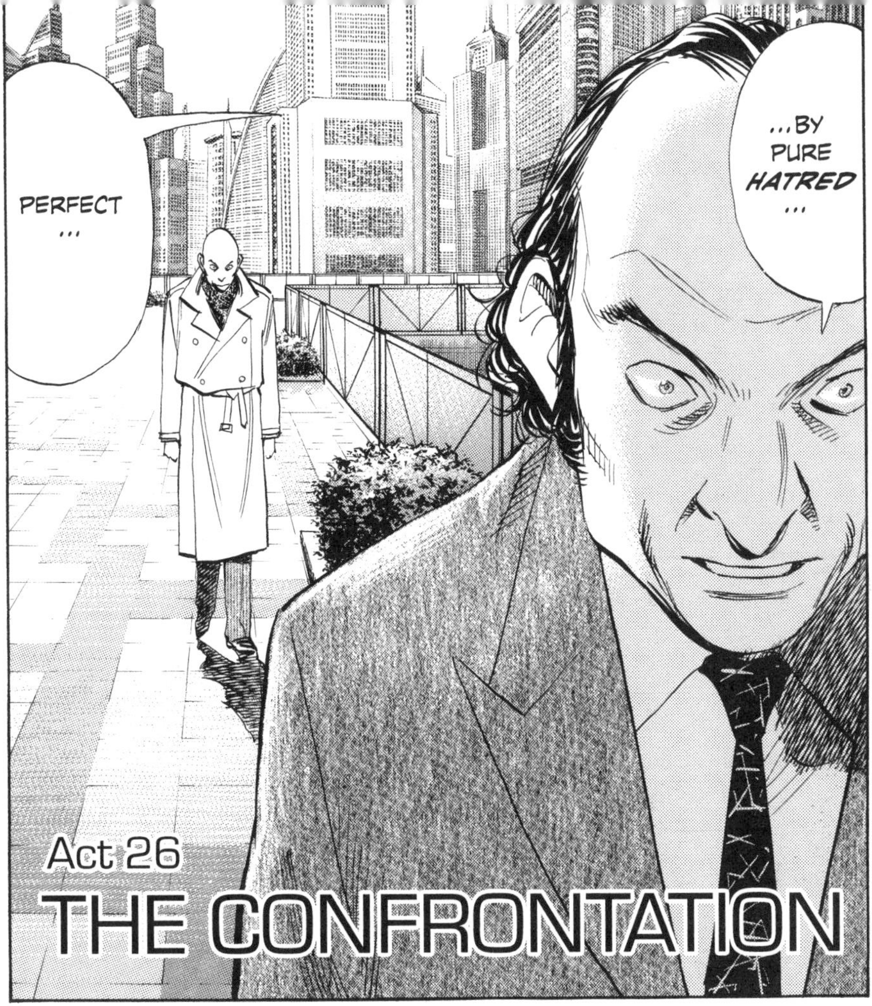
...BY PURE *HATRED* ...
PERFECT ...
Act 26
THE CONFRONTATION
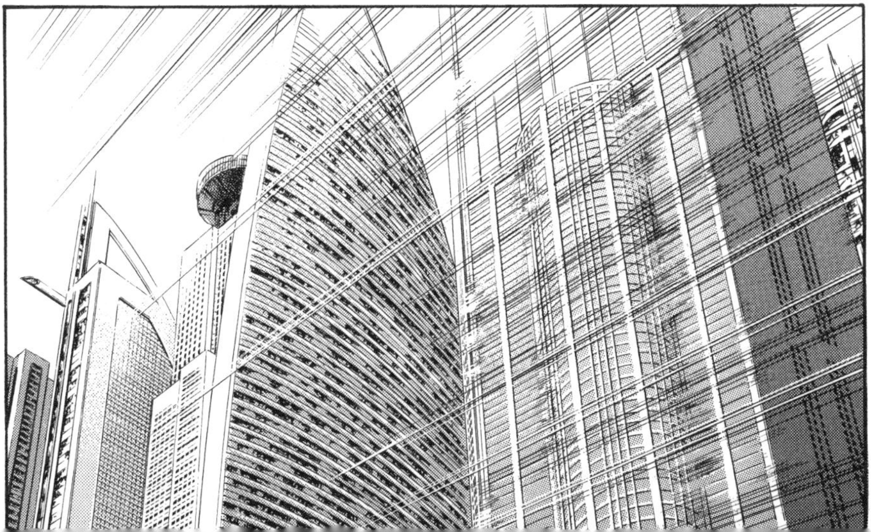

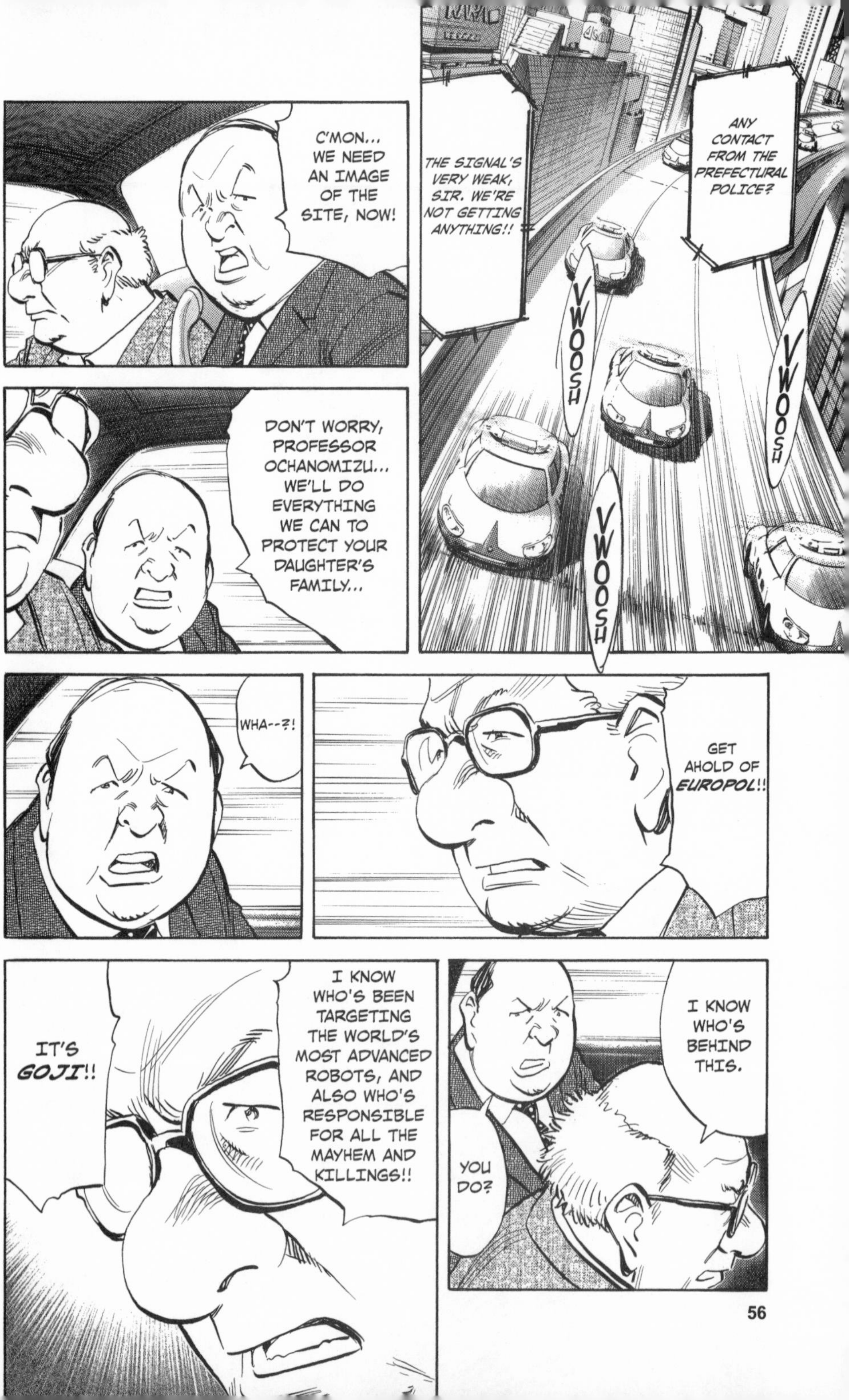
ANY CONTACT FROM THE PREFECTURAL POLICE?
THE SIGNAL'S VERY WEAK, SIR. WE'RE NOT GETTING ANYTHING!!
VWOOSH
VWOOSH
VWOOSH
C'MON... WE NEED AN IMAGE OF THE SITE, NOW!
DON'T WORRY, PROFESSOR OCHANOMIZU... WE'LL DO EVERYTHING WE CAN TO PROTECT YOUR DAUGHTER'S FAMILY...
GET AHOLD OF *EUROPOL*!!
WHA--?!
I KNOW WHO'S BEHIND THIS.
YOU DO?
I KNOW WHO'S BEEN TARGETING THE WORLD'S MOST ADVANCED ROBOTS, AND ALSO WHO'S RESPONSIBLE FOR ALL THE MAYHEM AND KILLINGS!!
IT'S *GOJI*!!

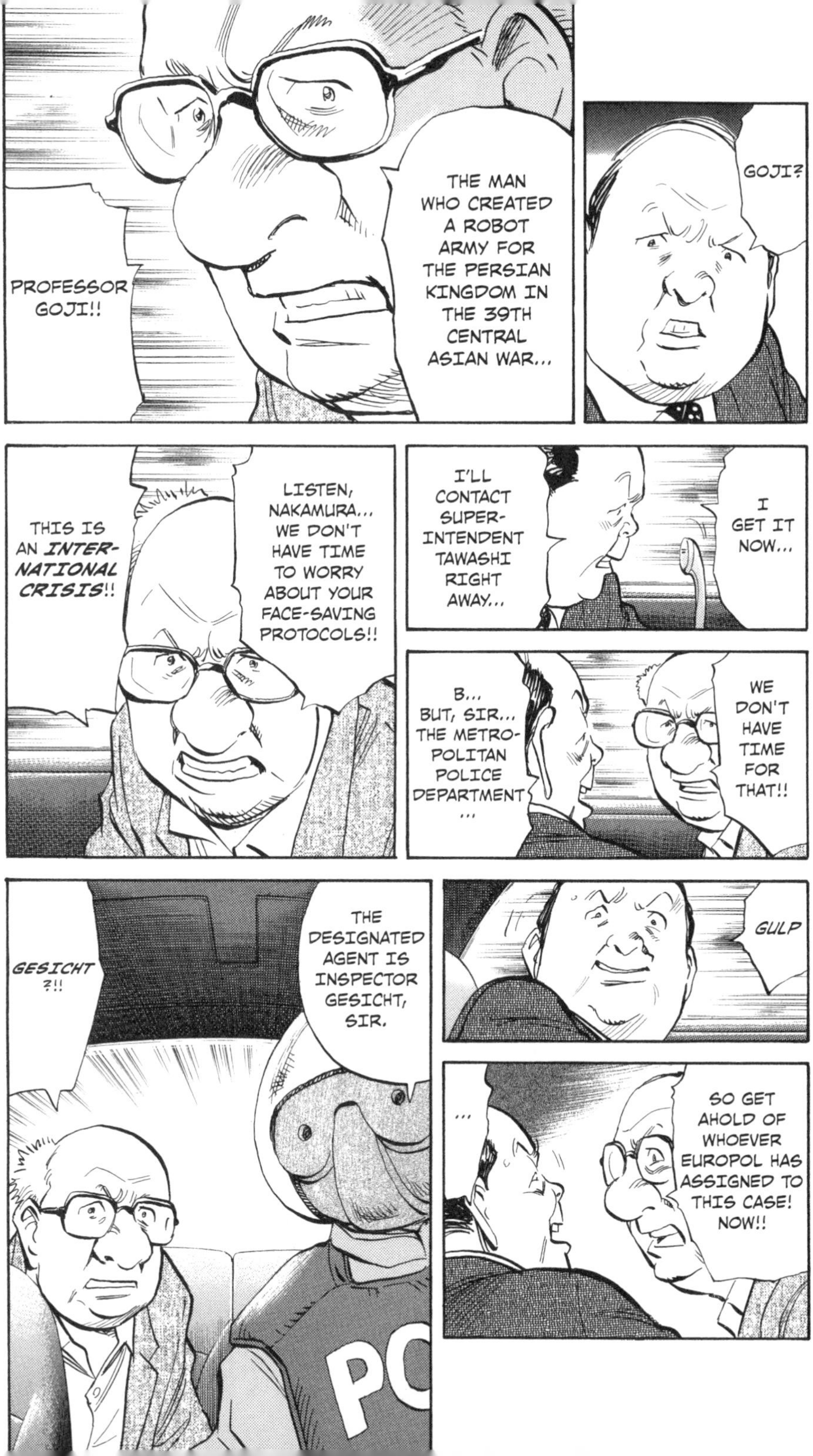
GOJI?
THE MAN WHO CREATED A ROBOT ARMY FOR THE PERSIAN KINGDOM IN THE 39TH CENTRAL ASIAN WAR...
PROFESSOR GOJI!!
I GET IT NOW...
I'LL CONTACT SUPER-INTENDENT TAWASHI RIGHT AWAY...
WE DON'T HAVE TIME FOR THAT!!
B... BUT, SIR... THE METRO-POLITAN POLICE DEPARTMENT...
LISTEN, NAKAMURA... WE DON'T HAVE TIME TO WORRY ABOUT YOUR FACE-SAVING PROTOCOLS!!
THIS IS AN *INTER-NATIONAL CRISIS*!!
GULP
SO GET AHOLD OF WHOEVER EUROPOL HAS ASSIGNED TO THIS CASE! NOW!!
...
THE DESIGNATED AGENT IS INSPECTOR GESICHT, SIR.
GESICHT ?!!
PO

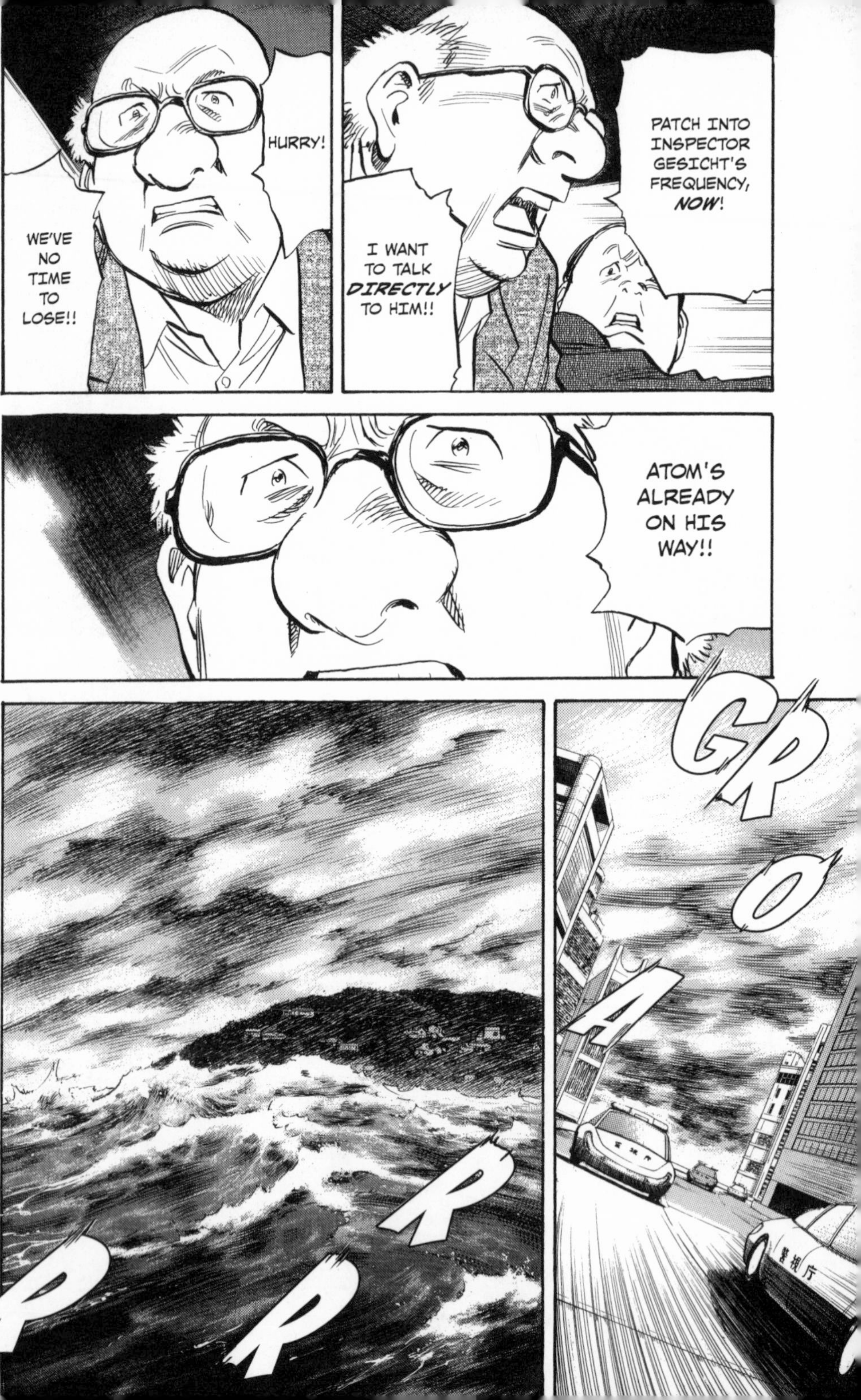
PATCH INTO INSPECTOR GESICHT'S FREQUENCY, **NOW**!
I WANT TO TALK **DIRECTLY** TO HIM!!
HURRY!
WE'VE NO TIME TO LOSE!!
ATOM'S ALREADY ON HIS WAY!!
GROARRR

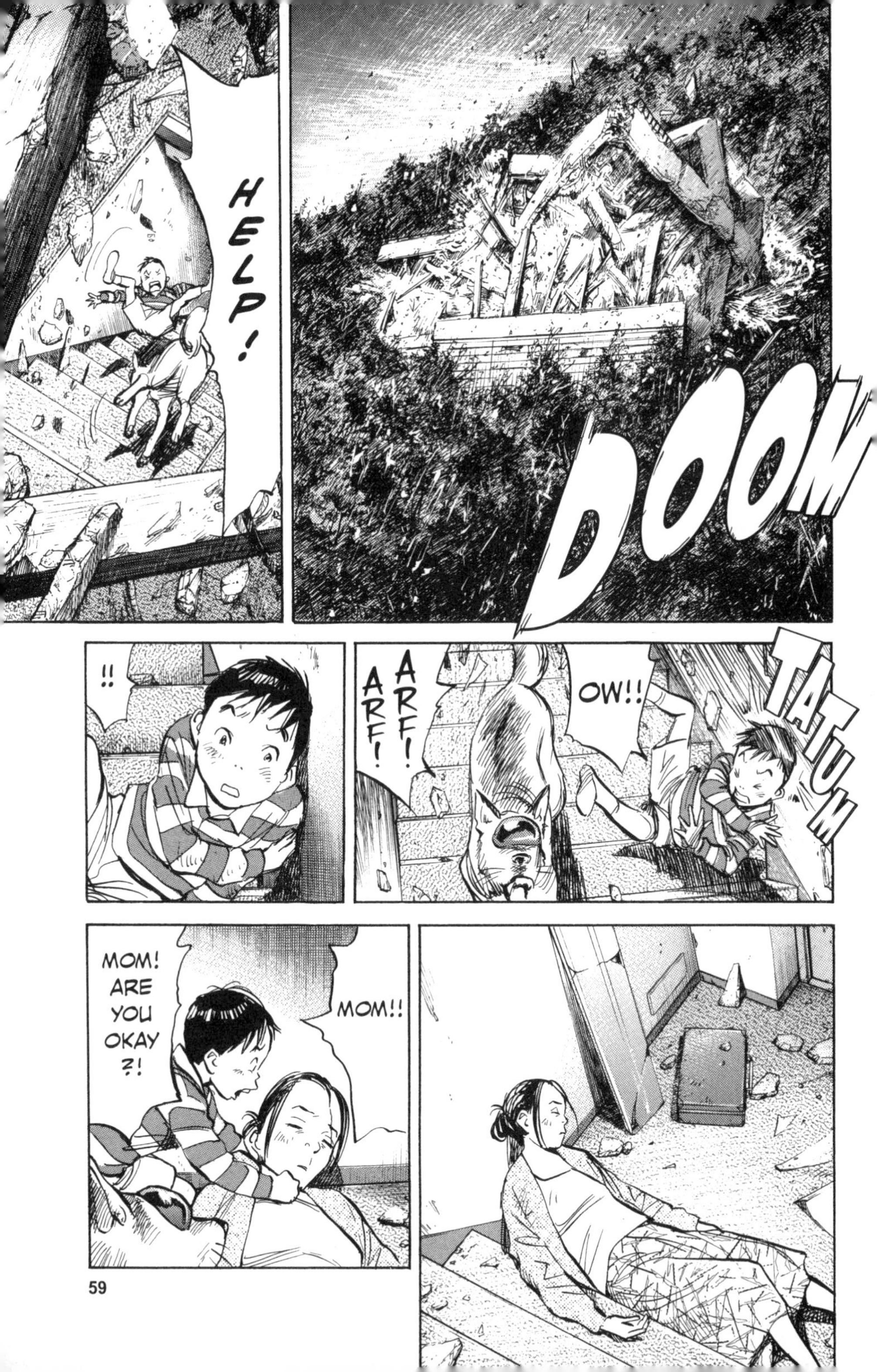
DOOM
HELP!
TATUM
OW!!
ARF! ARF!
!!
MOM!!
MOM! ARE YOU OKAY?!

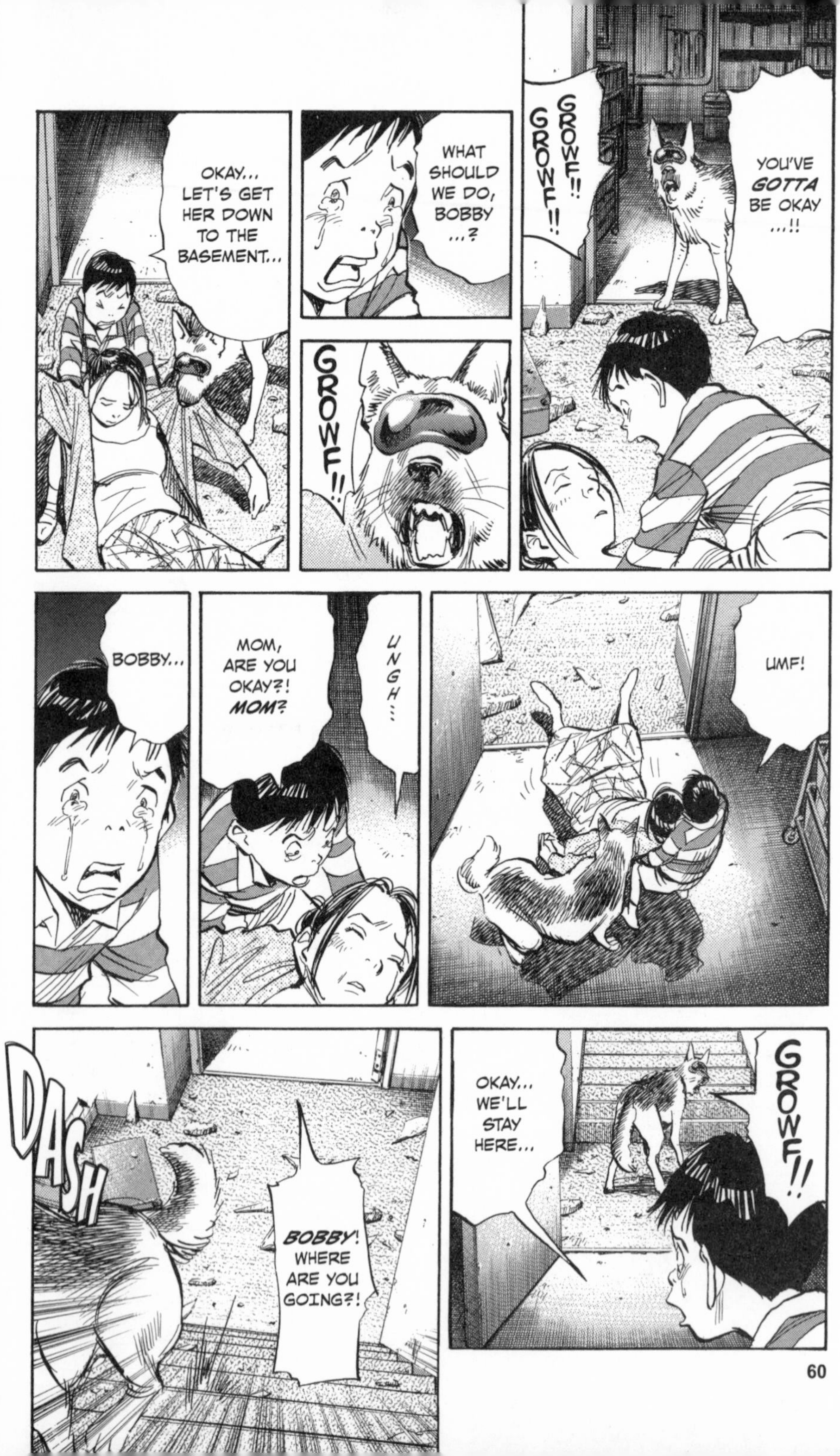
YOU'VE *GOTTA* BE OKAY ...!!
GROWF!! GROWF!!
WHAT SHOULD WE DO, BOBBY ...?
GROWF!!
OKAY... LET'S GET HER DOWN TO THE BASEMENT...
UMF!
UNGH...
MOM, ARE YOU OKAY?! *MOM?*
BOBBY...
GROWF!!
OKAY... WE'LL STAY HERE...
DASH
BOBBY! WHERE ARE YOU GOING?!

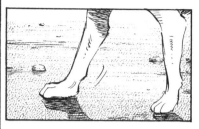

ANYONE HOME?

Z!

BOBBY! YOU OKAY?

BOBBY?

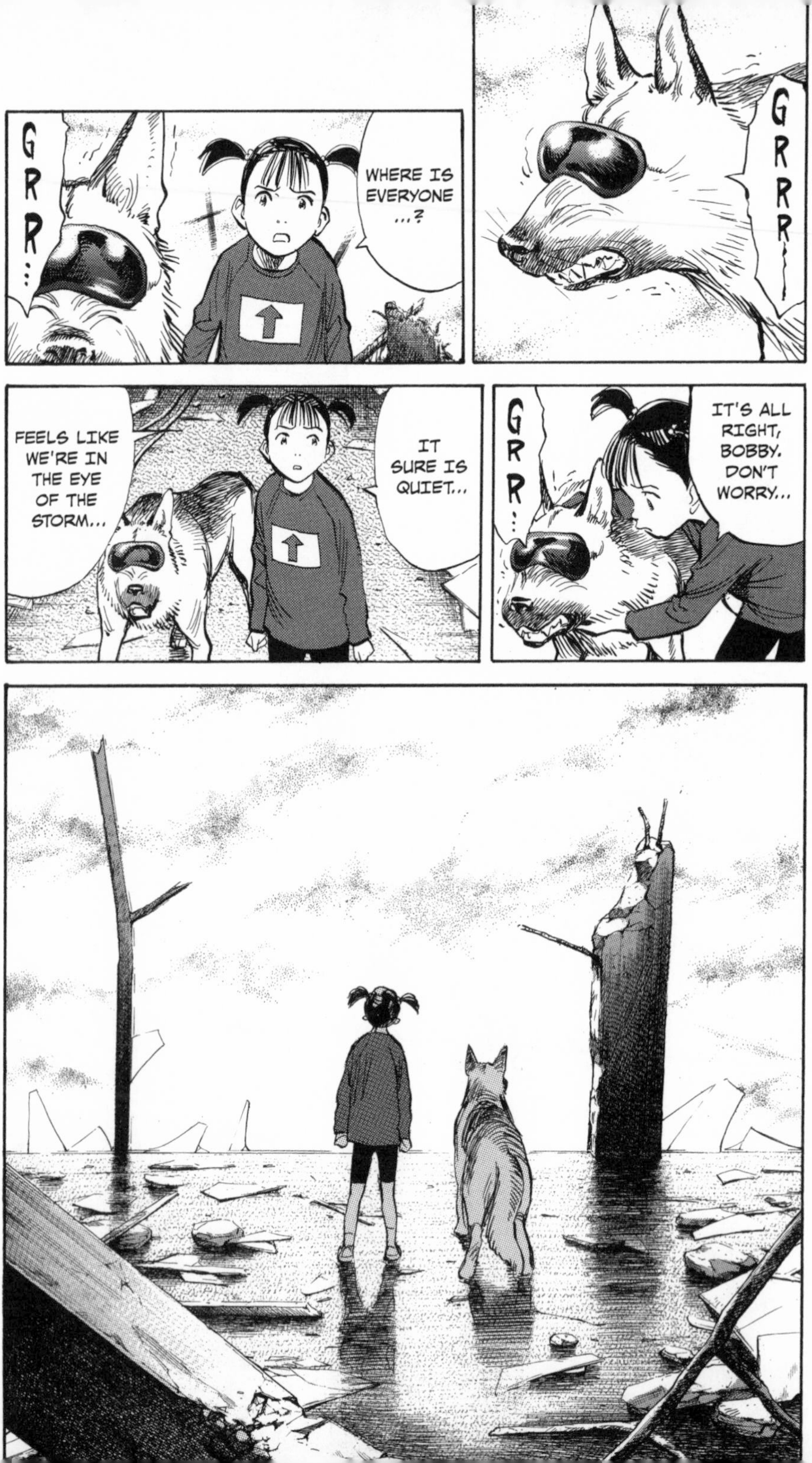
GRRR...
GRR...
WHERE IS EVERYONE ...?
IT'S ALL RIGHT, BOBBY. DON'T WORRY...
GRR...
IT SURE IS QUIET...
FEELS LIKE WE'RE IN THE EYE OF THE STORM...

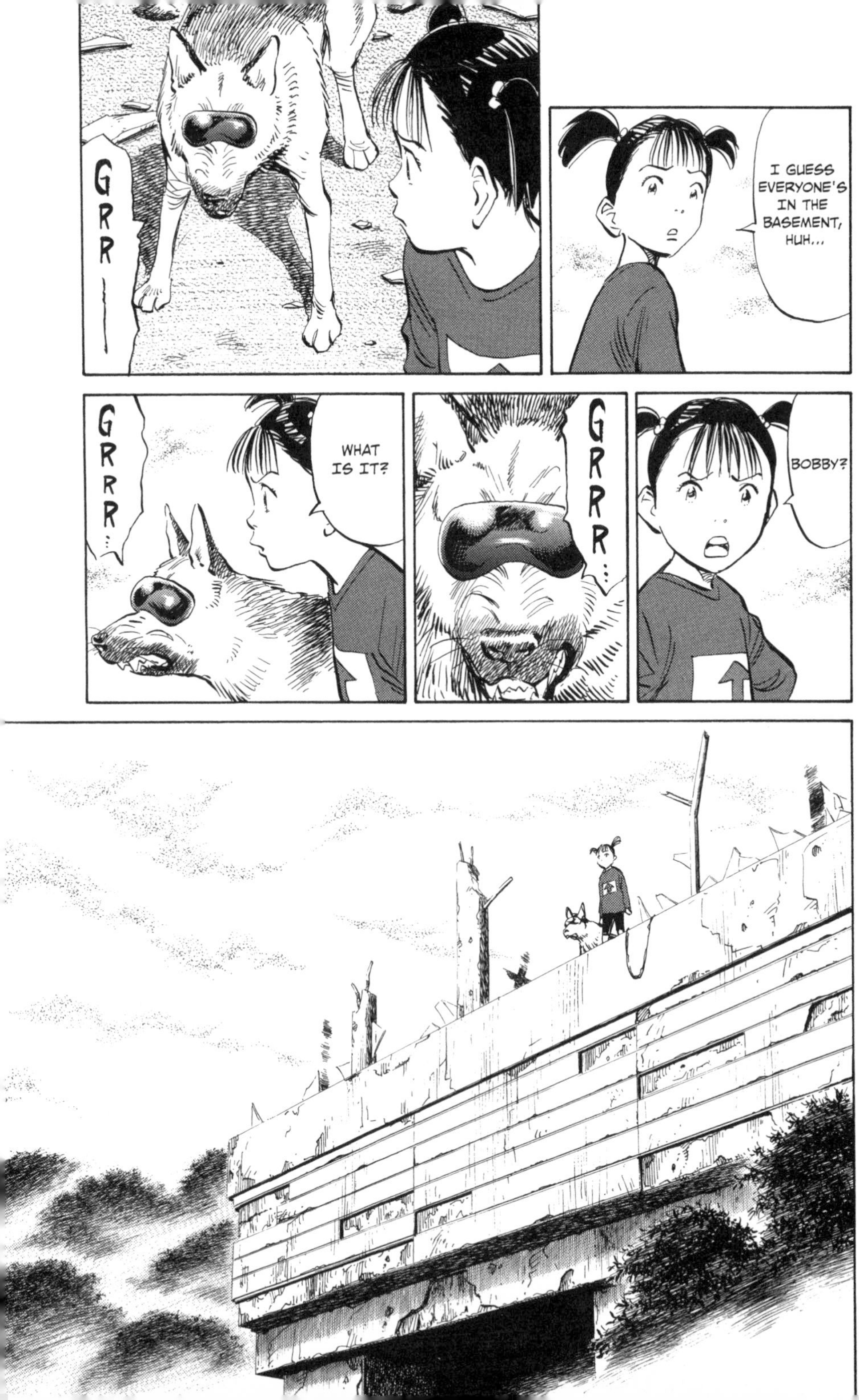
I GUESS EVERYONE'S IN THE BASEMENT, HUH...
GRR
BOBBY?
GRRR...
WHAT IS IT?
GRRR...

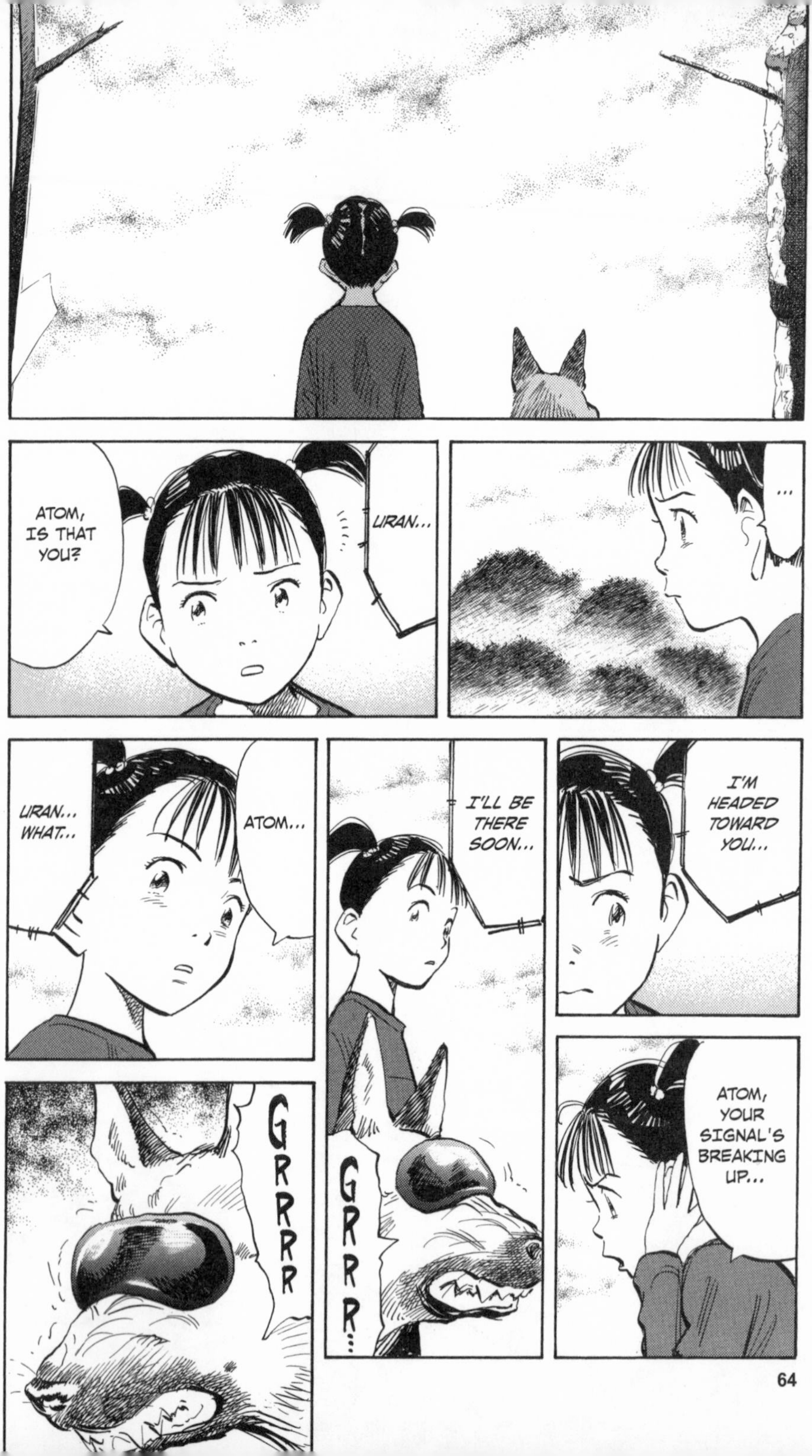
...
URAN...
ATOM, IS THAT YOU?
I'M HEADED TOWARD YOU...
ATOM, YOUR SIGNAL'S BREAKING UP...
I'LL BE THERE SOON...
GRRRR...
ATOM...
URAN... WHAT...
GRRRR

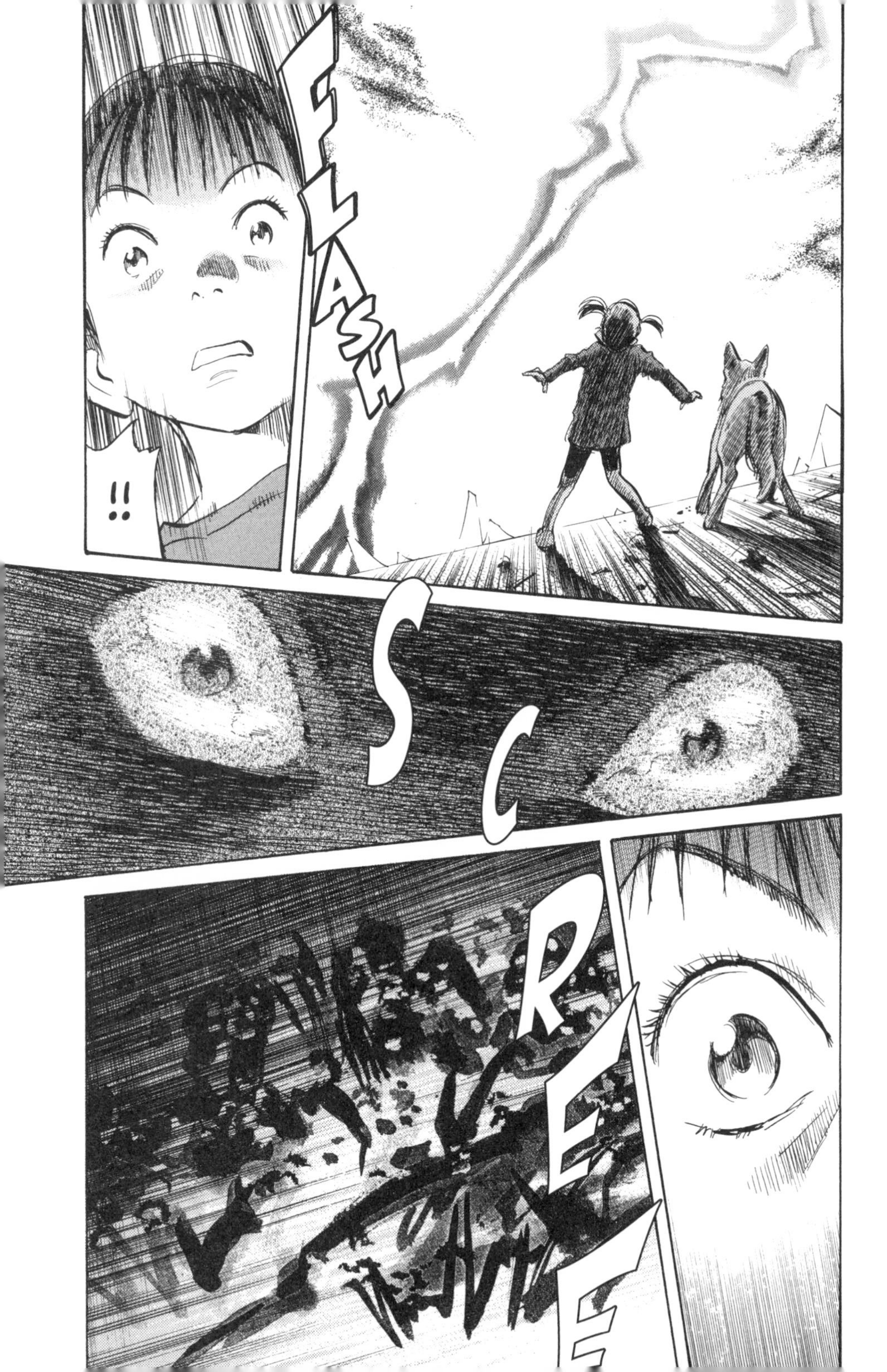
FLASH
!!
SCREE

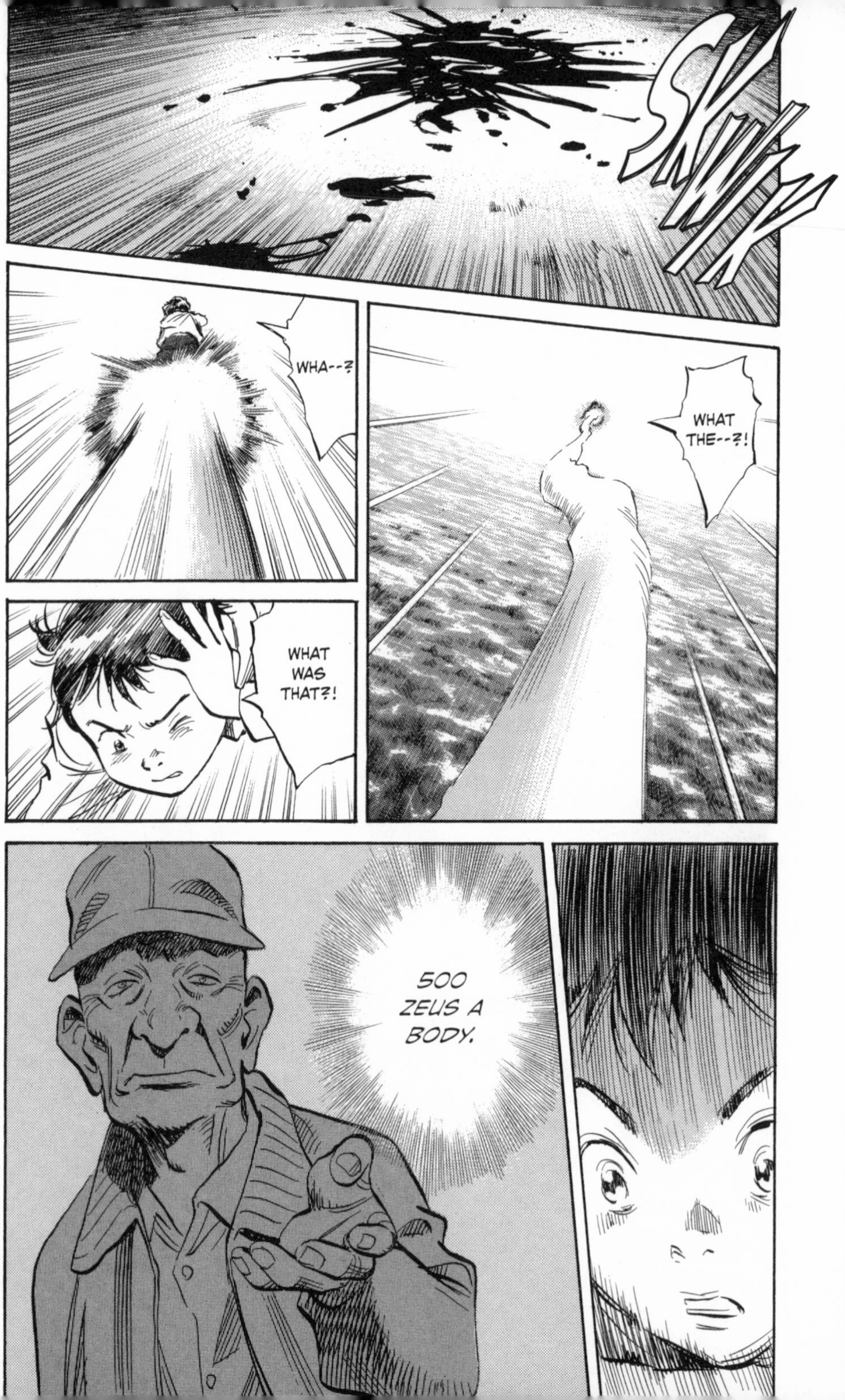
WHAT THE--?!
WHA--?
WHAT WAS THAT?!
500 ZEUS A BODY.

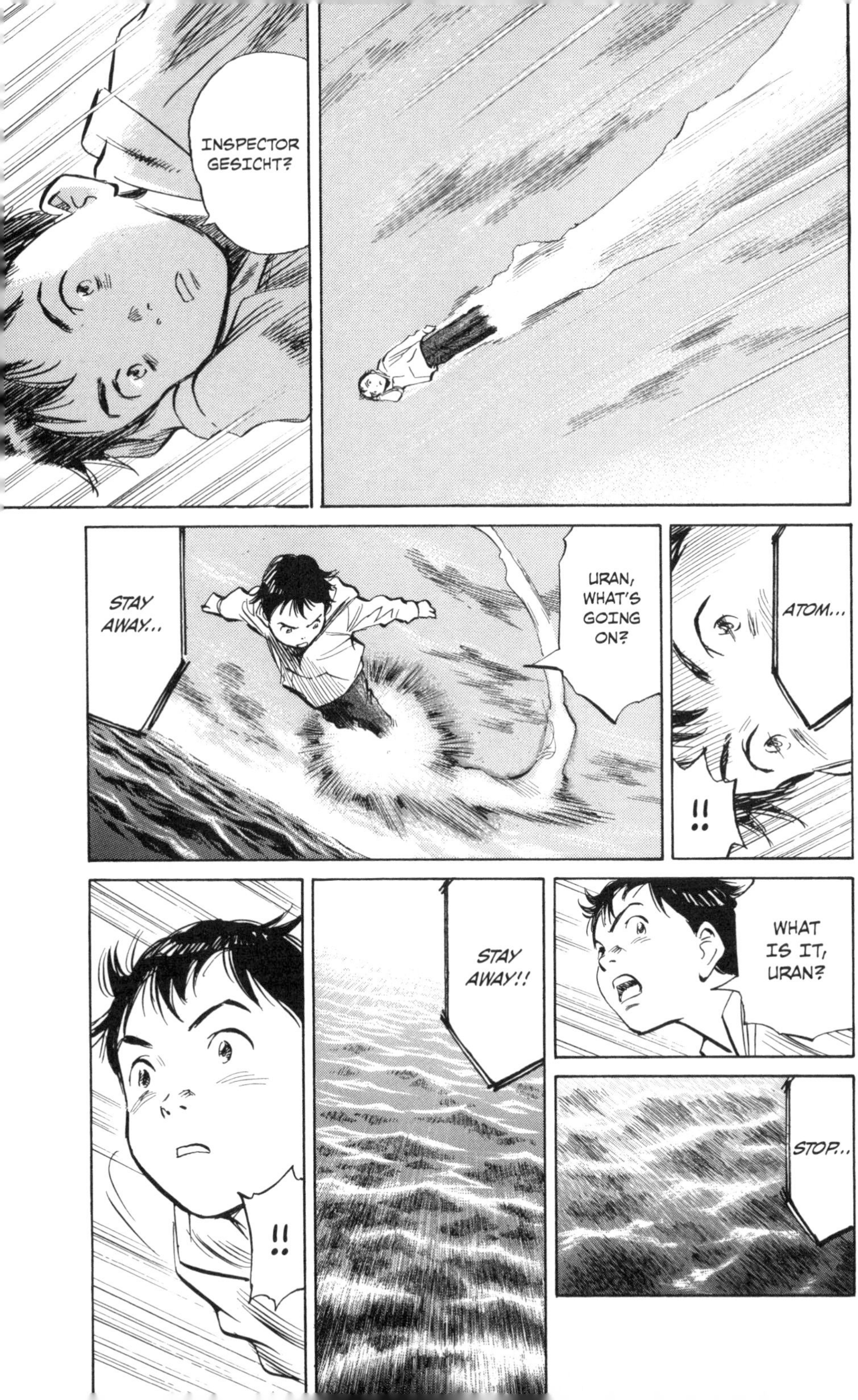
INSPECTOR GESICHT?
ATOM...
!!
URAN, WHAT'S GOING ON?
STAY AWAY...
WHAT IS IT, URAN?
STOP...
STAY AWAY!!
!!

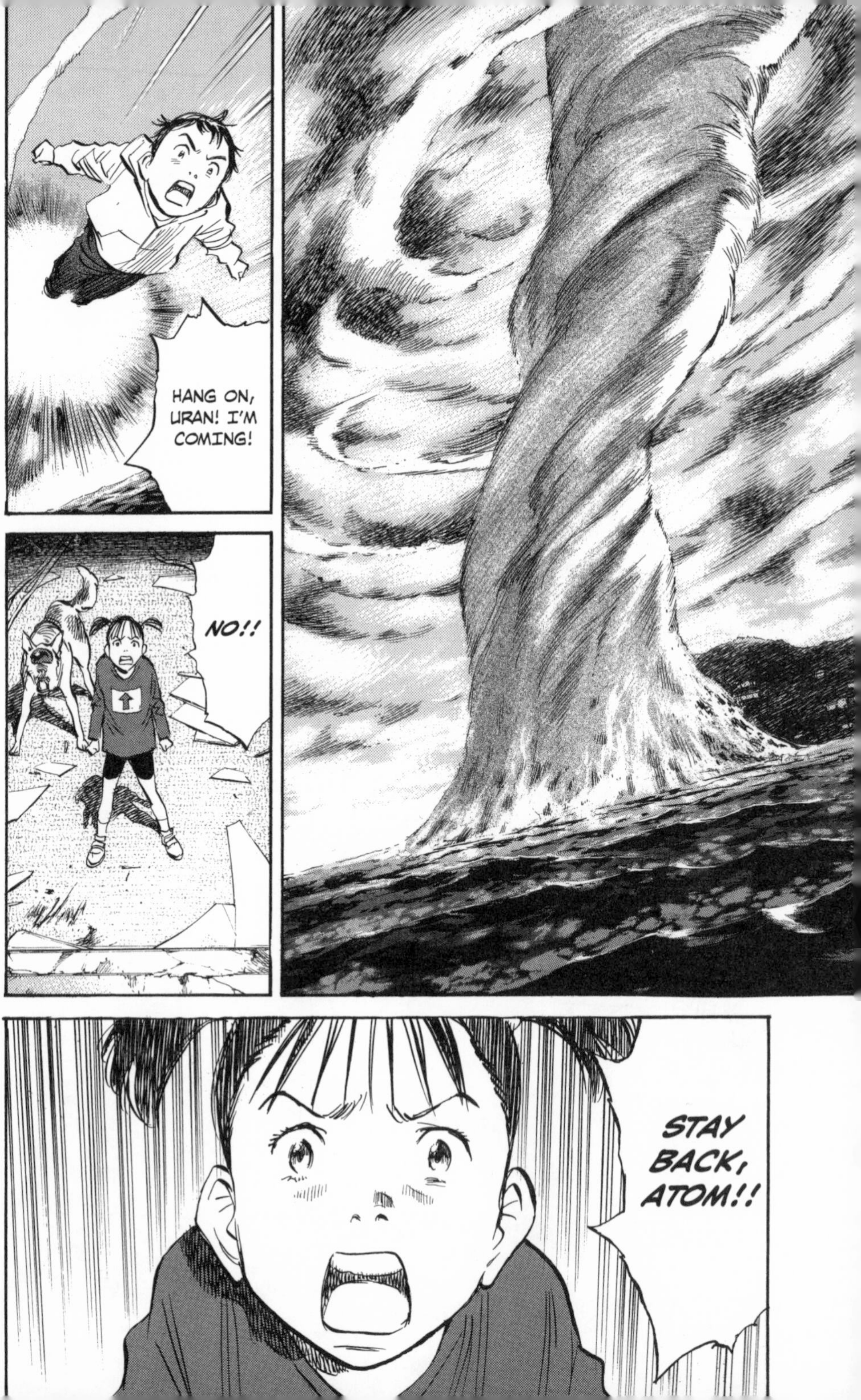
HANG ON, URAN! I'M COMING!
NO!!
STAY BACK, ATOM!!

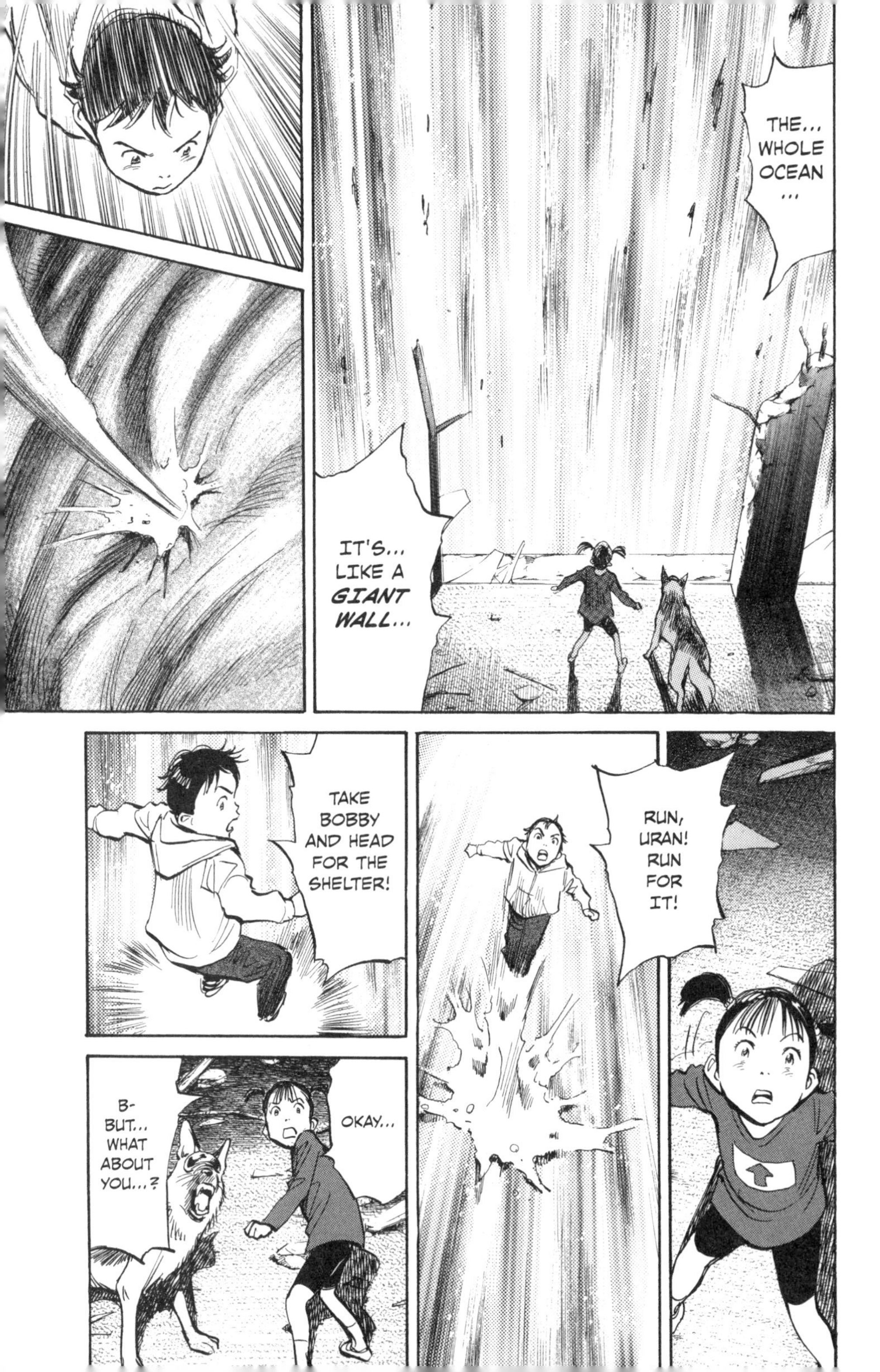
THE... WHOLE OCEAN...
IT'S... LIKE A *GIANT WALL*...
RUN, URAN! RUN FOR IT!
TAKE BOBBY AND HEAD FOR THE SHELTER!
OKAY...
B-BUT... WHAT ABOUT YOU...?

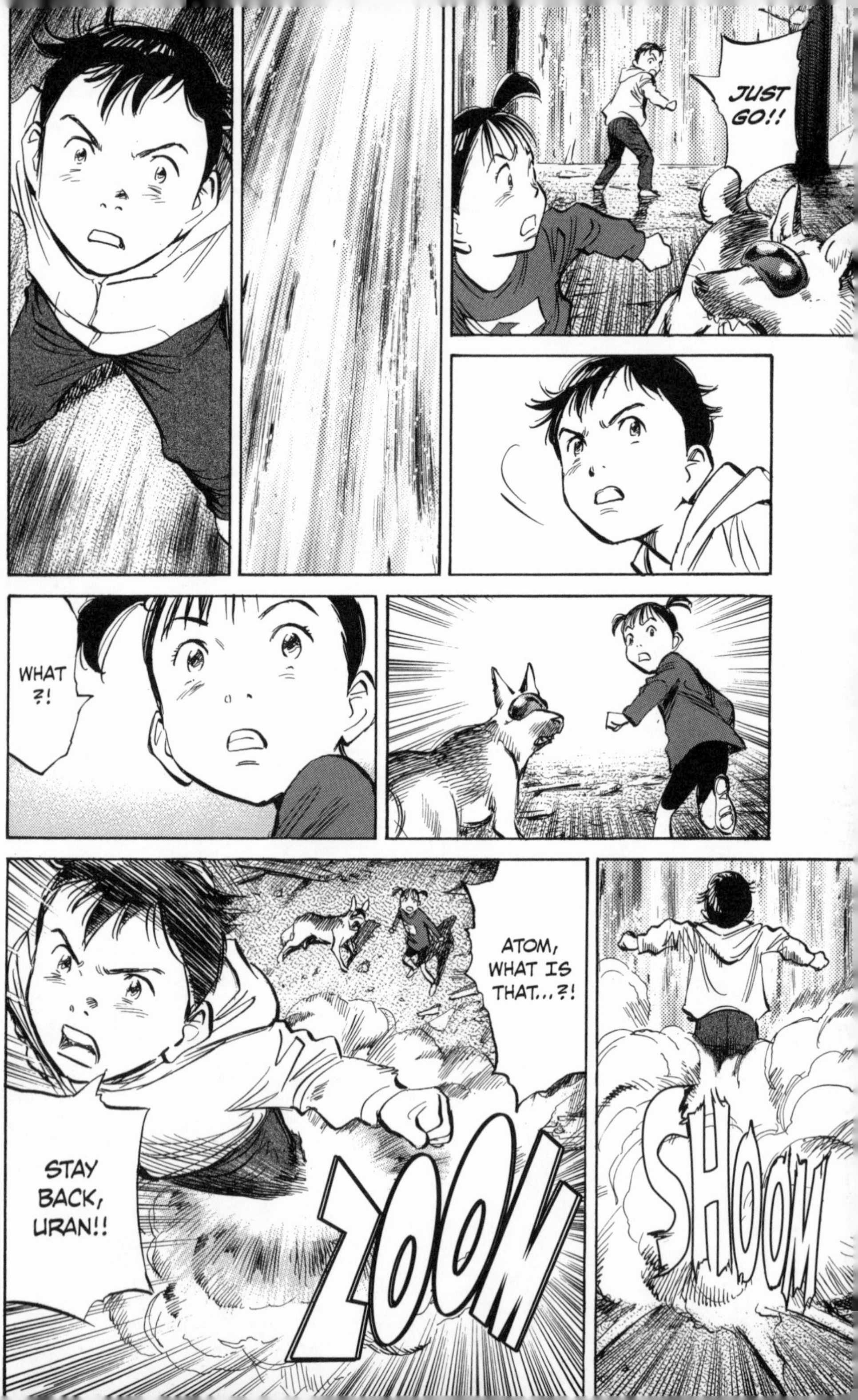
JUST GO!!
WHAT ?!
SHOOM
ATOM, WHAT IS THAT...?!
STAY BACK, URAN!!
ZOOM

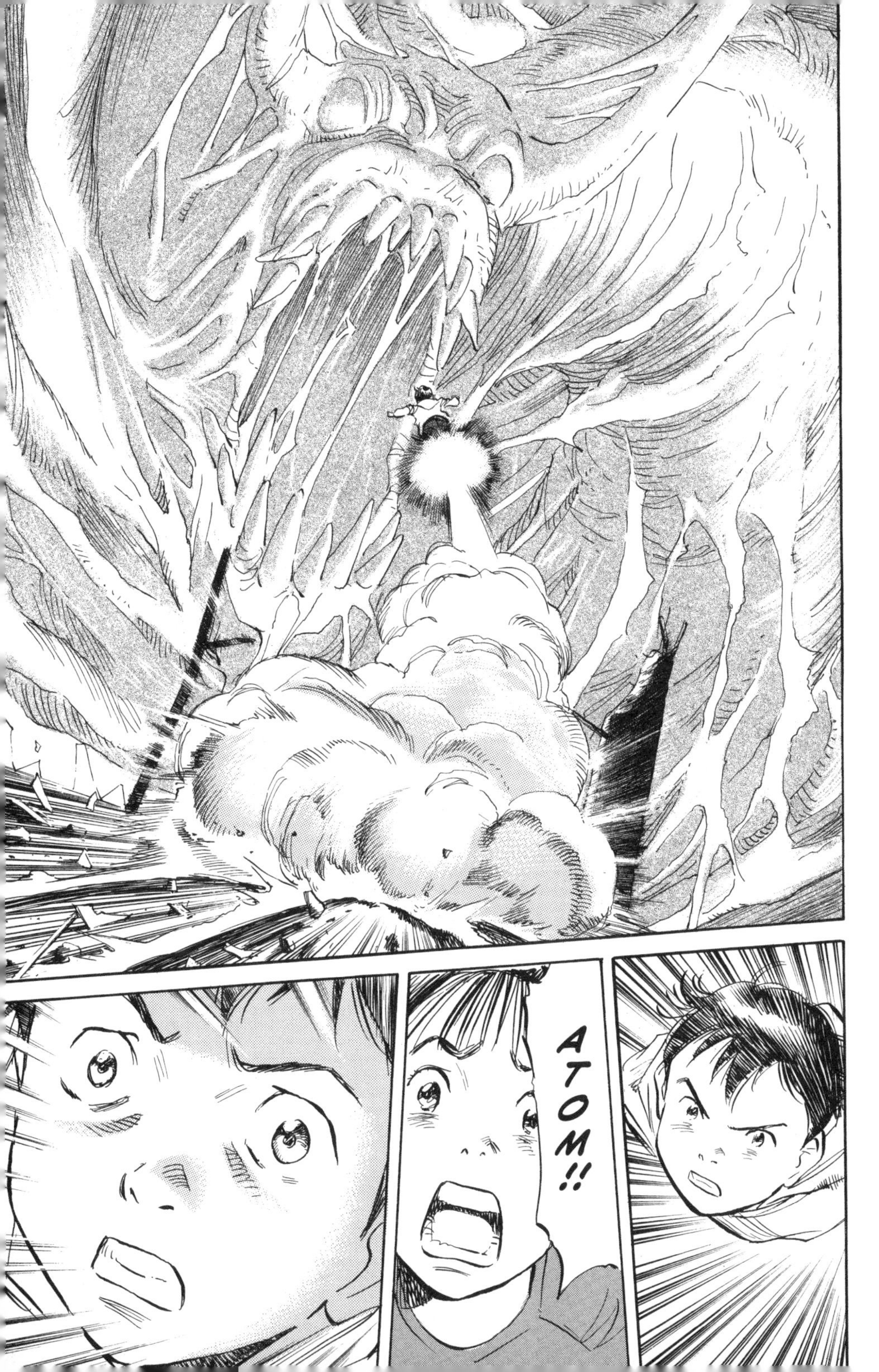
ATOM!!

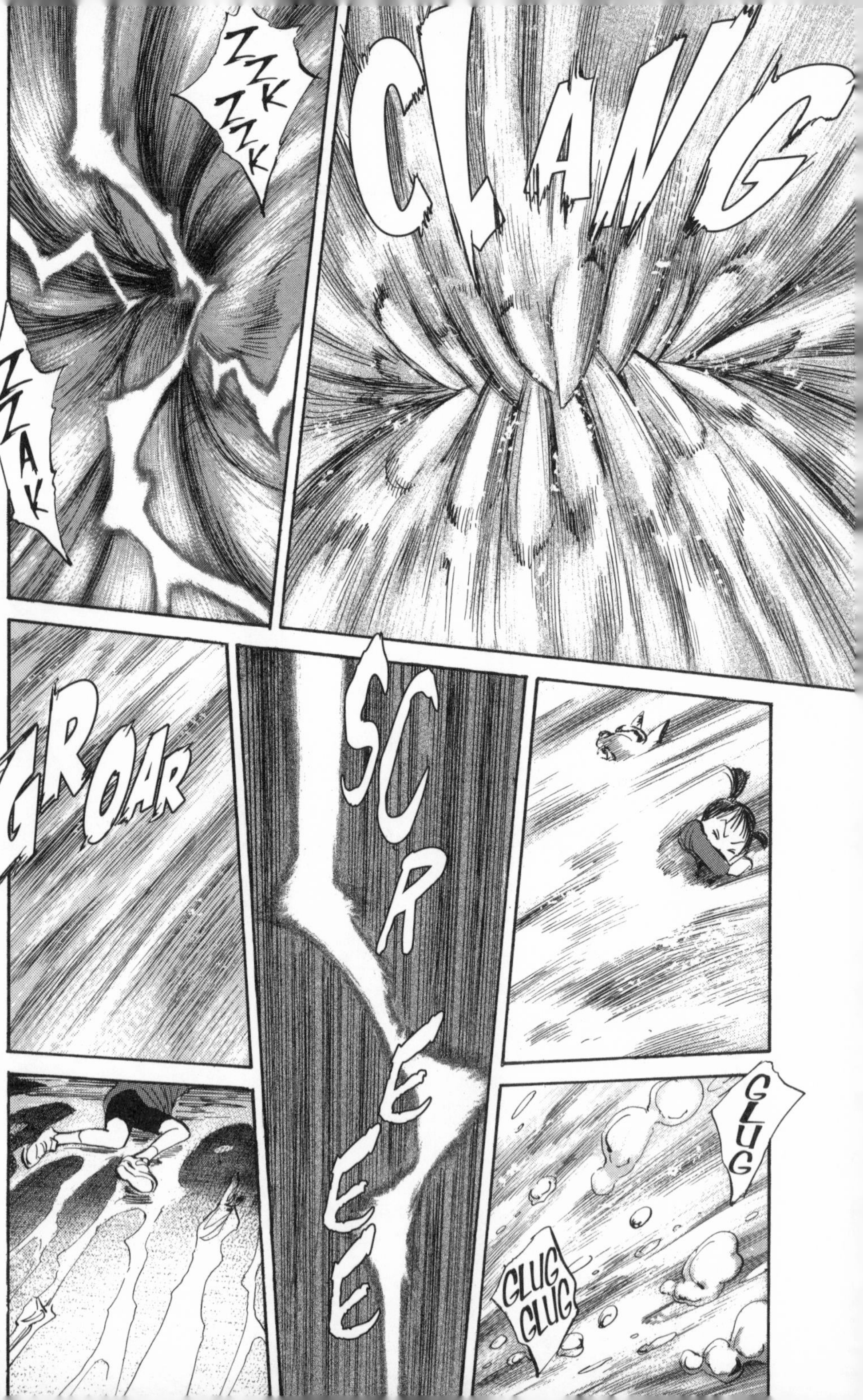
CLANG
ZZZK ZZZK
ZZZAK
GLUG
GLUG GLUG
SCREEEE
GROAR

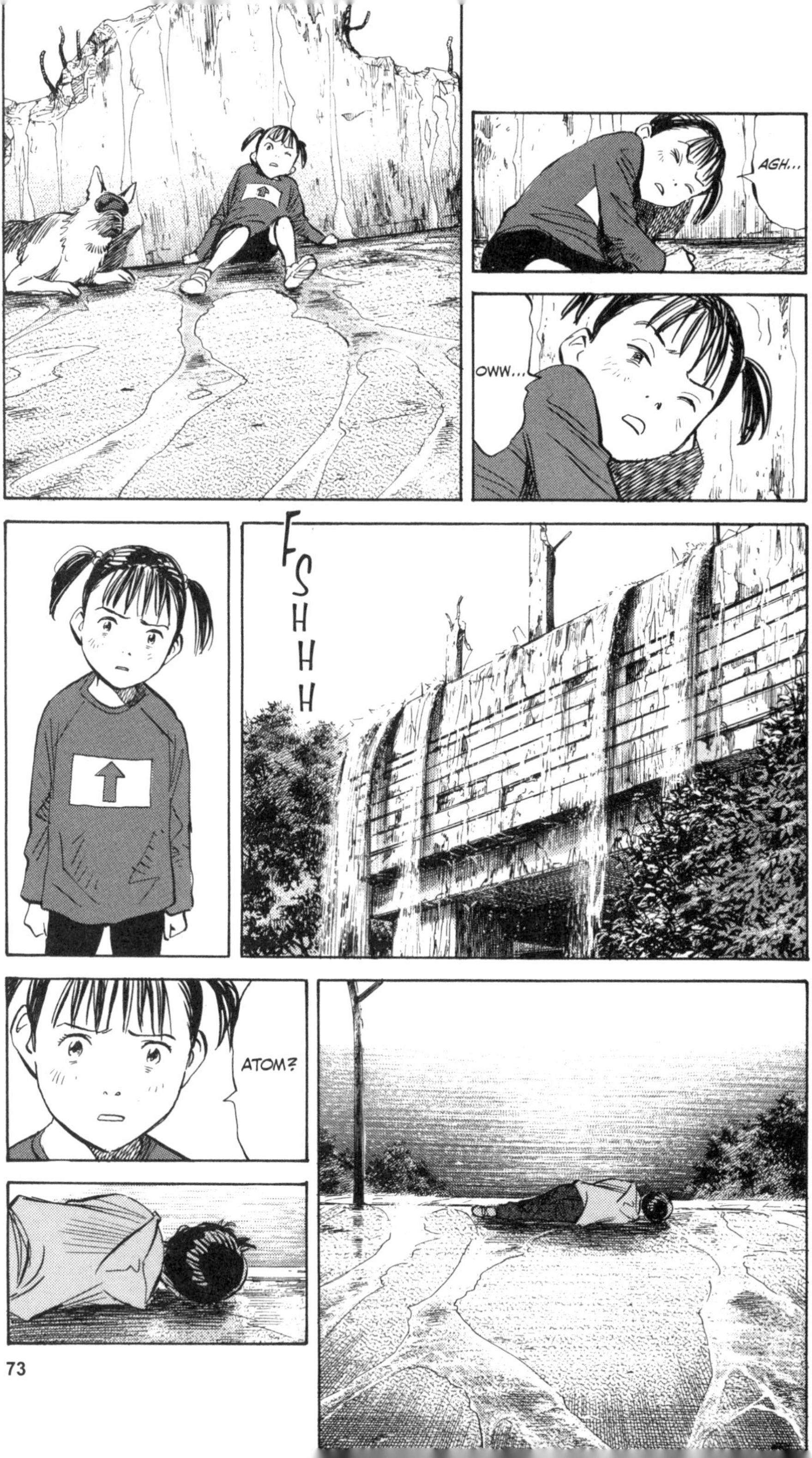
AGH...
OWW...
FSHHH
ATOM?

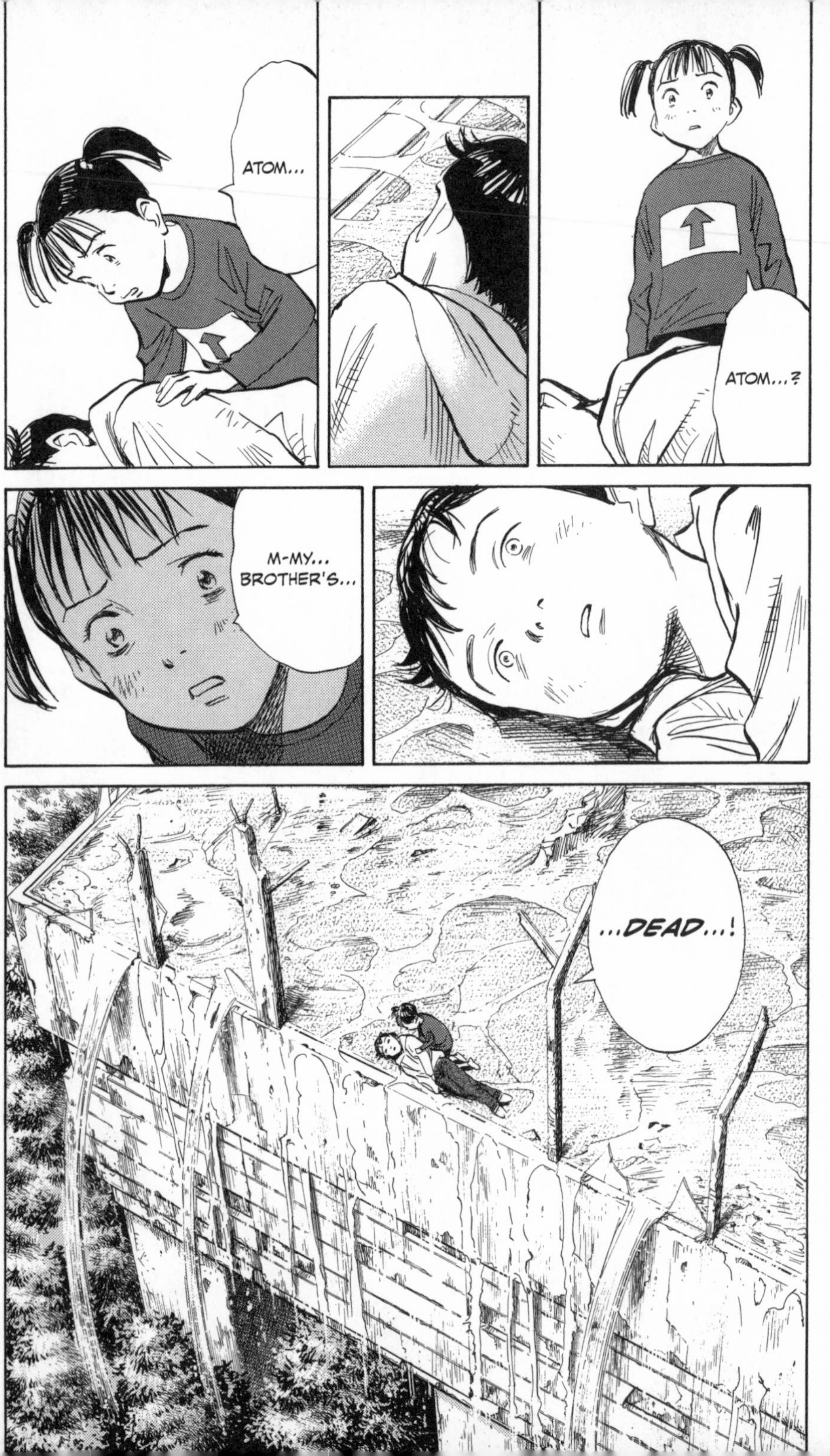
ATOM...?
ATOM...
M-MY... BROTHER'S...
...DEAD...!

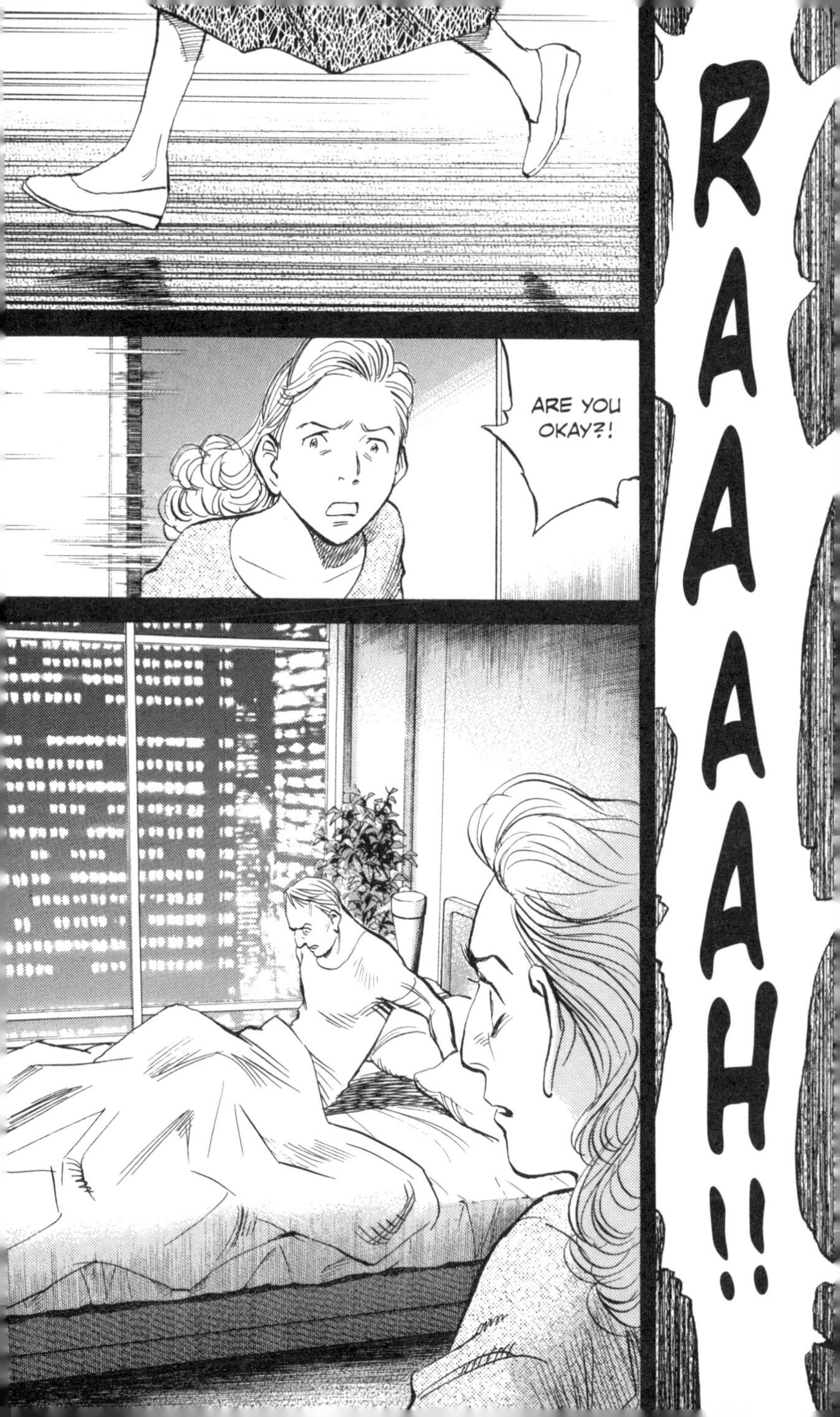
RAAAAH!!
ARE YOU OKAY?!

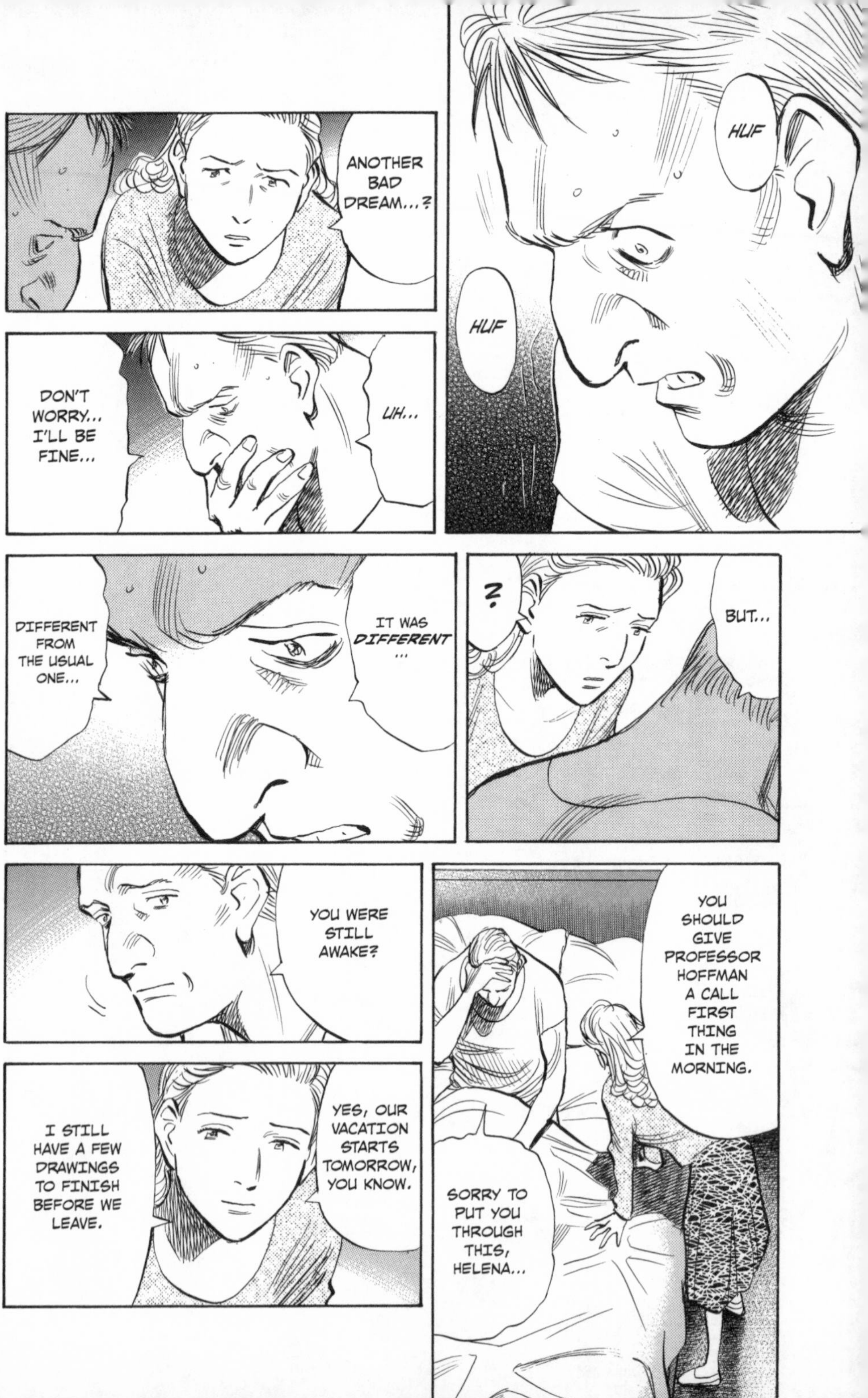
HUF
HUF
ANOTHER BAD DREAM...?
UH...
DON'T WORRY... I'LL BE FINE...
BUT...
?
IT WAS *DIFFERENT*...
DIFFERENT FROM THE USUAL ONE...
YOU SHOULD GIVE PROFESSOR HOFFMAN A CALL FIRST THING IN THE MORNING.
SORRY TO PUT YOU THROUGH THIS, HELENA...
YOU WERE STILL AWAKE?
YES, OUR VACATION STARTS TOMORROW, YOU KNOW.
I STILL HAVE A FEW DRAWINGS TO FINISH BEFORE WE LEAVE.

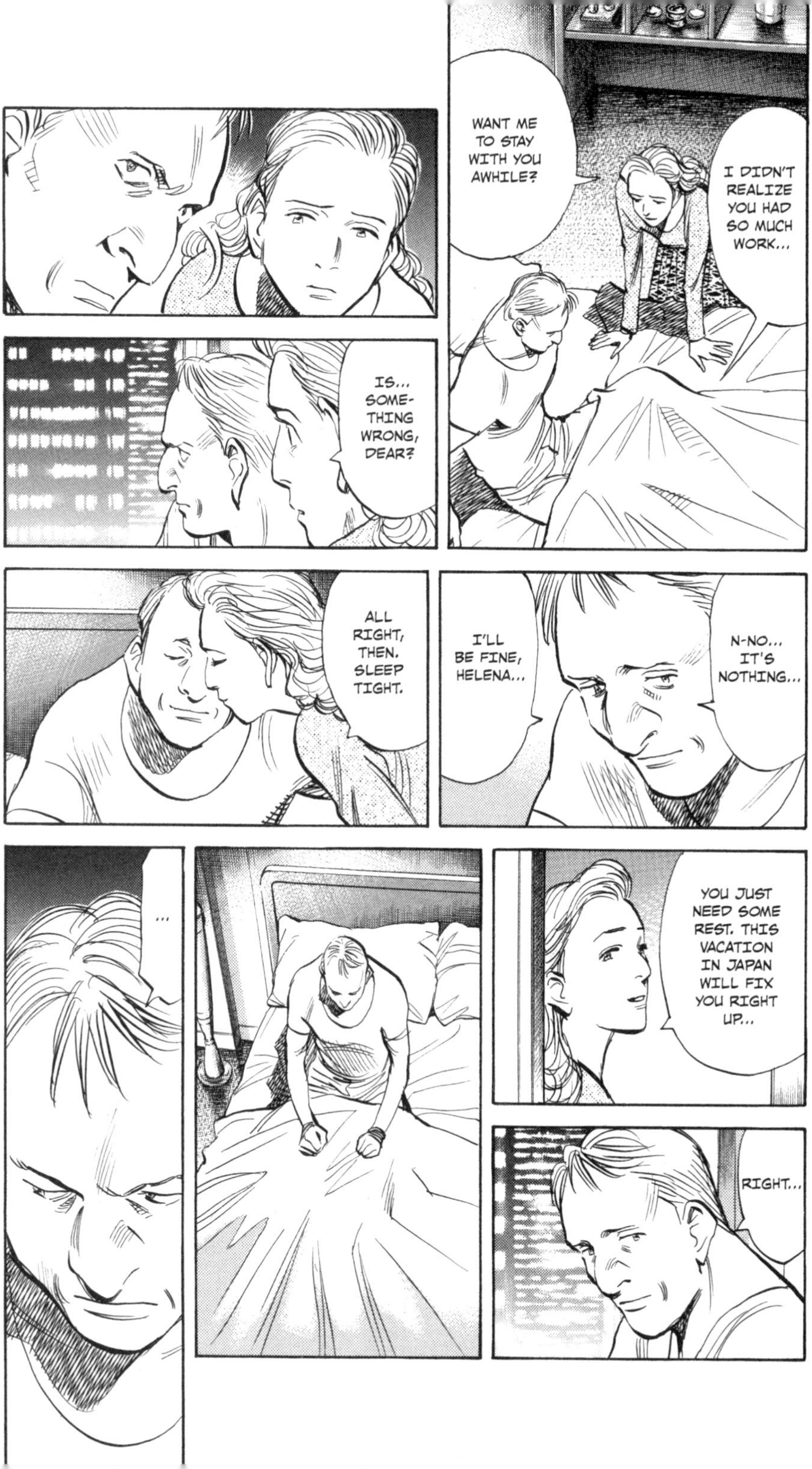
I DIDN'T REALIZE YOU HAD SO MUCH WORK...
WANT ME TO STAY WITH YOU AWHILE?
IS... SOME-THING WRONG, DEAR?
N-NO... IT'S NOTHING...
I'LL BE FINE, HELENA...
ALL RIGHT, THEN. SLEEP TIGHT.
YOU JUST NEED SOME REST. THIS VACATION IN JAPAN WILL FIX YOU RIGHT UP...
RIGHT...
...

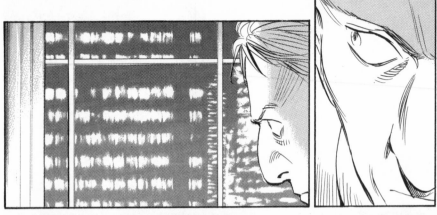

DAMN...
CAN'T
STOP
SHAKING...

TRBL
TRBL

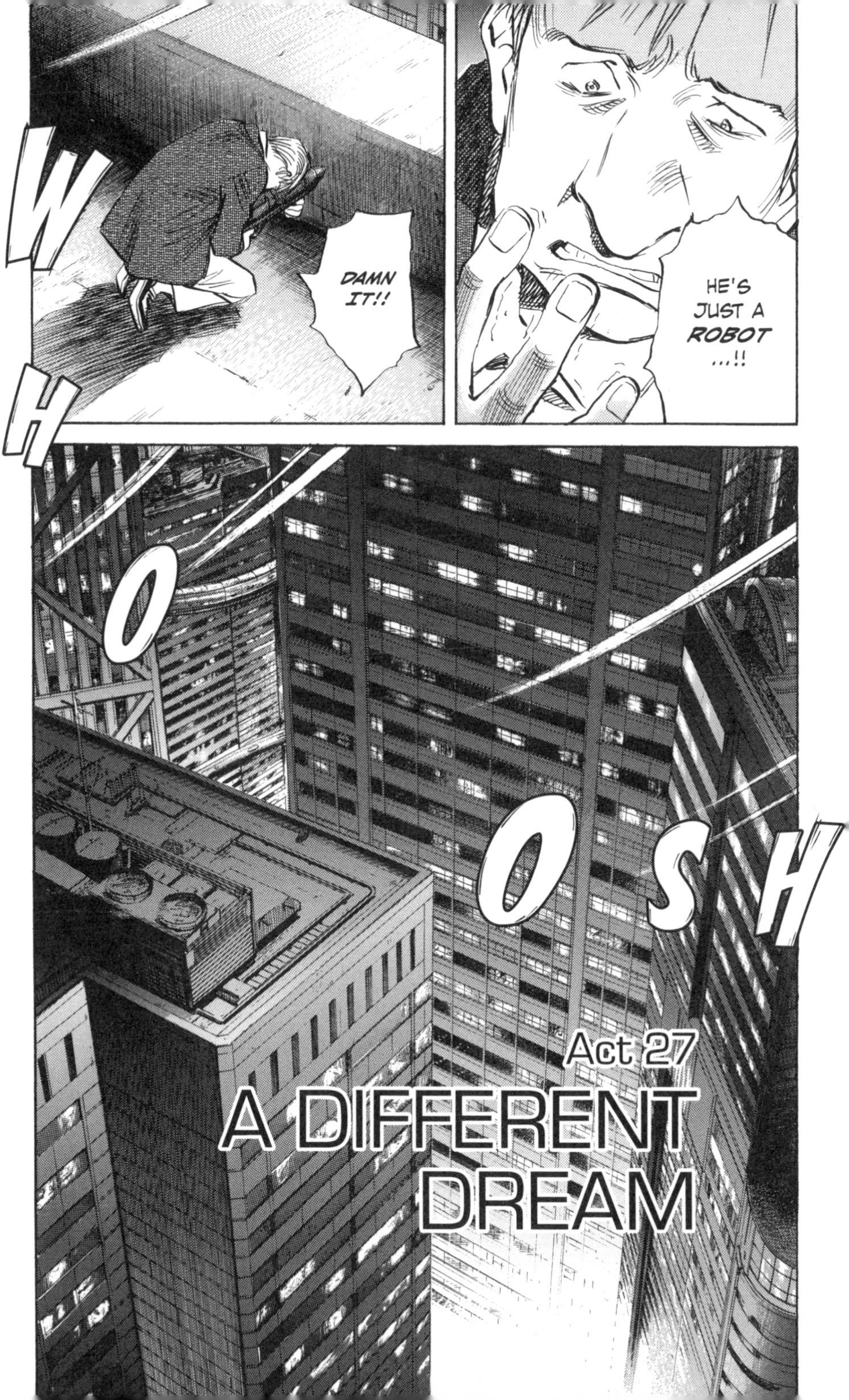
HE'S JUST A ROBOT ...!!
DAMN IT!!
WHOOSH

Act 27
A DIFFERENT DREAM

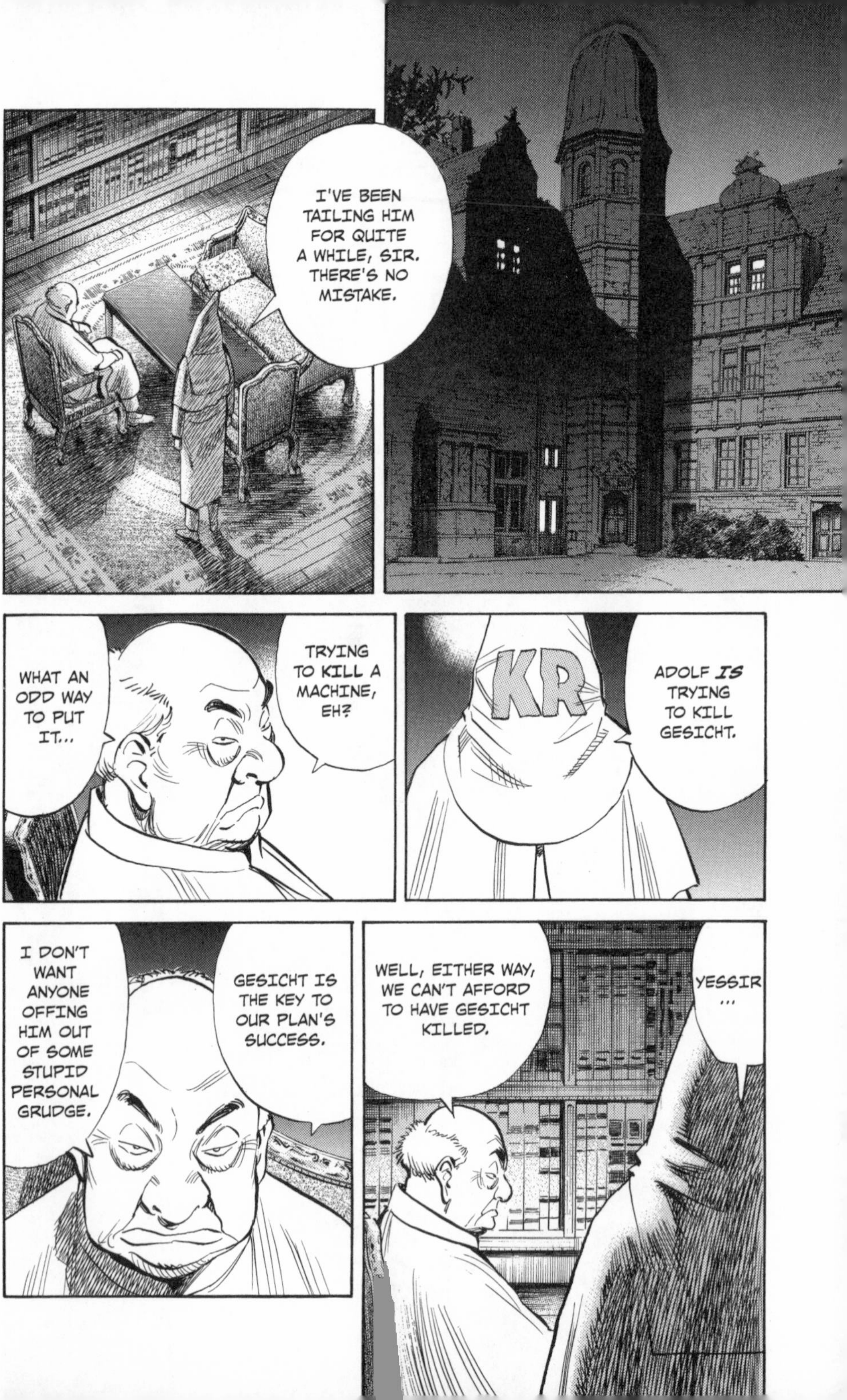
I'VE BEEN TAILING HIM FOR QUITE A WHILE, SIR. THERE'S NO MISTAKE.
ADOLF *IS* TRYING TO KILL GESICHT.
TRYING TO KILL A MACHINE, EH?
WHAT AN ODD WAY TO PUT IT...
WELL, EITHER WAY, WE CAN'T AFFORD TO HAVE GESICHT KILLED.
YESSIR ...
GESICHT IS THE KEY TO OUR PLAN'S SUCCESS.
I DON'T WANT ANYONE OFFING HIM OUT OF SOME STUPID PERSONAL GRUDGE.

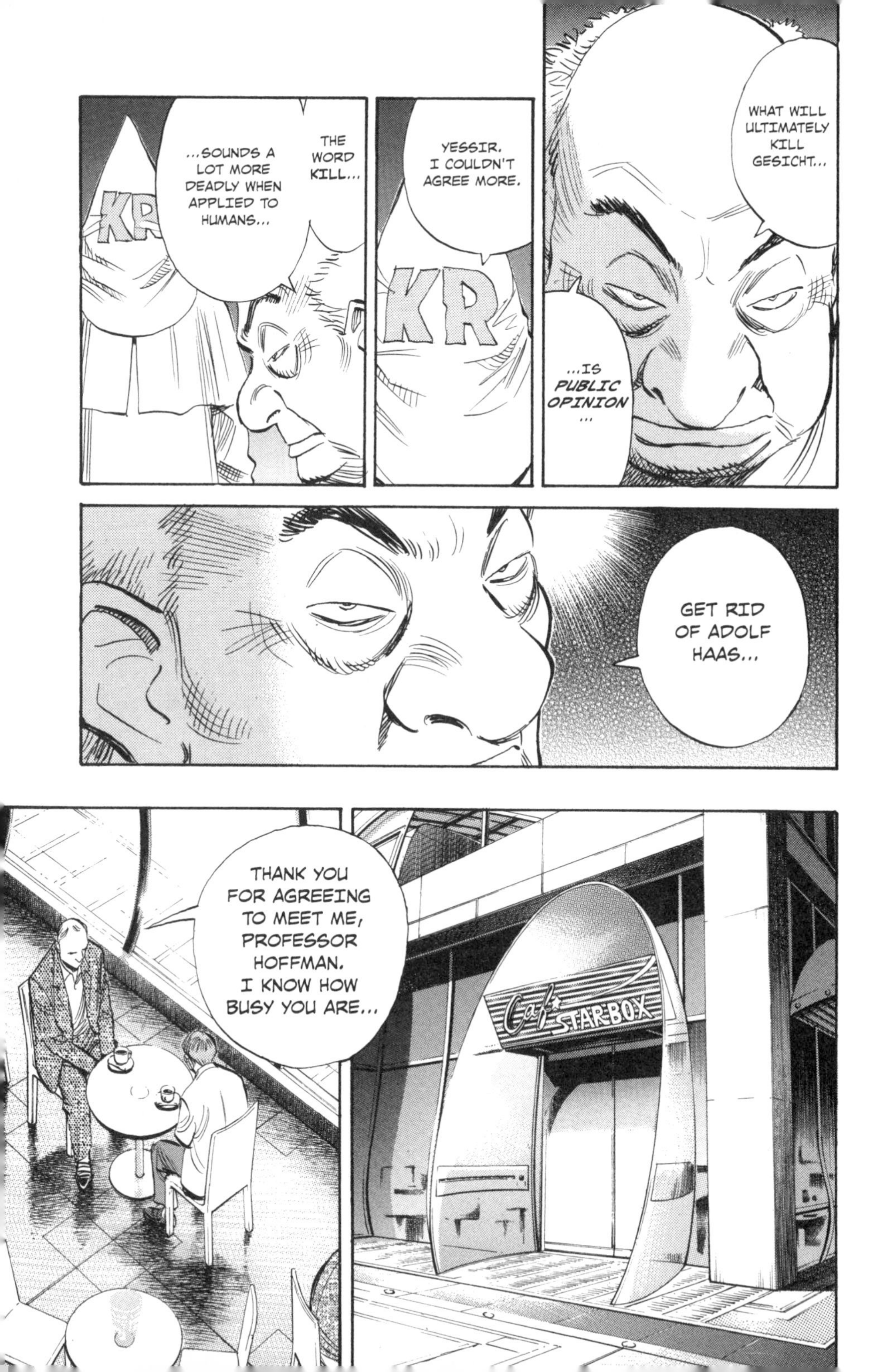
WHAT WILL ULTIMATELY KILL GESICHT...
...IS PUBLIC OPINION...
YESSIR. I COULDN'T AGREE MORE.
KR
THE WORD KILL...
...SOUNDS A LOT MORE DEADLY WHEN APPLIED TO HUMANS...
KR
GET RID OF ADOLF HAAS...
STAR BOX
THANK YOU FOR AGREEING TO MEET ME, PROFESSOR HOFFMAN. I KNOW HOW BUSY YOU ARE...

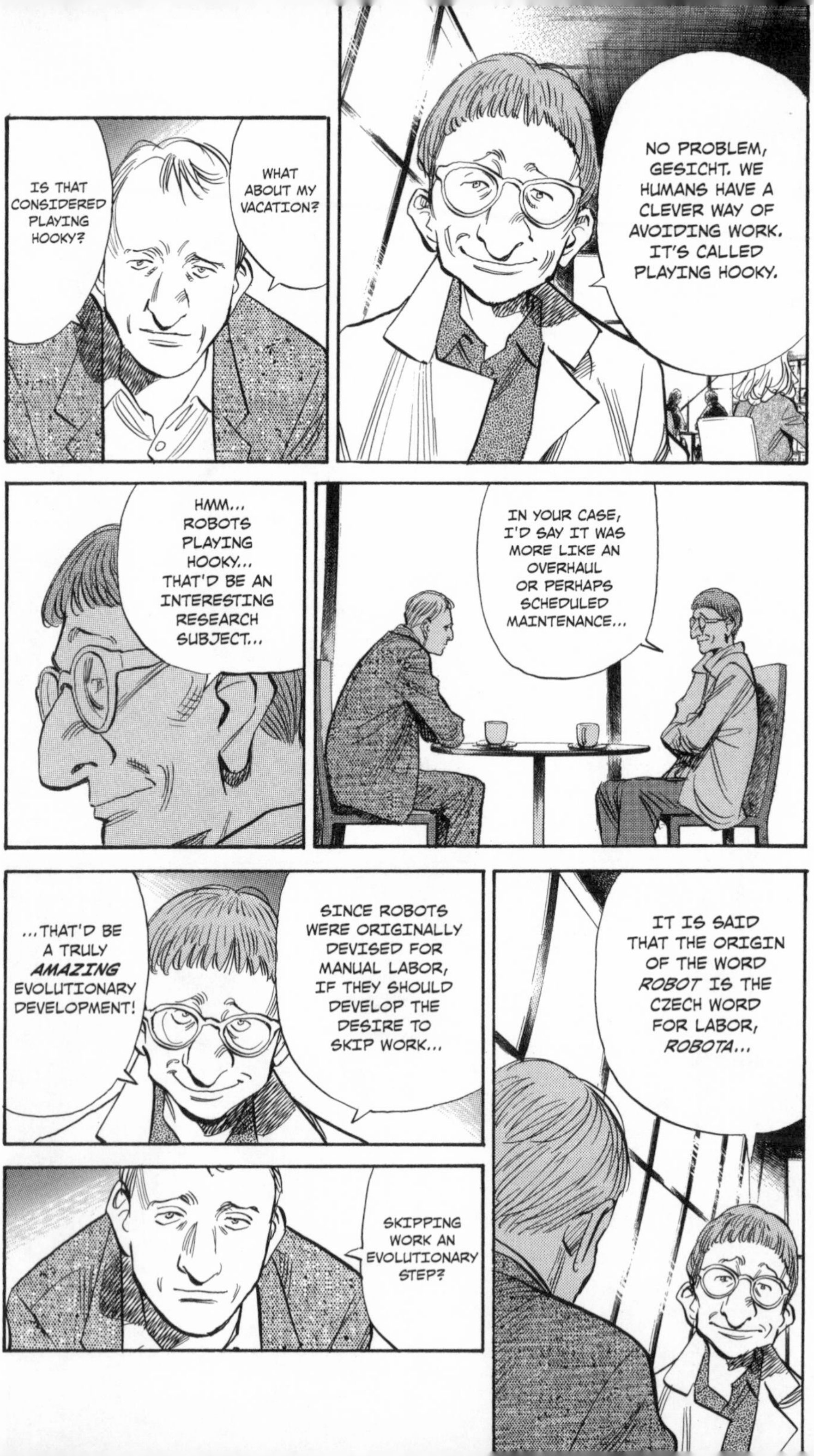
NO PROBLEM, GESICHT. WE HUMANS HAVE A CLEVER WAY OF AVOIDING WORK. IT'S CALLED PLAYING HOOKY.
WHAT ABOUT MY VACATION?
IS THAT CONSIDERED PLAYING HOOKY?
IN YOUR CASE, I'D SAY IT WAS MORE LIKE AN OVERHAUL OR PERHAPS SCHEDULED MAINTENANCE...
HMM... ROBOTS PLAYING HOOKY... THAT'D BE AN INTERESTING RESEARCH SUBJECT...
IT IS SAID THAT THE ORIGIN OF THE WORD *ROBOT* IS THE CZECH WORD FOR LABOR, *ROBOTA*...
SINCE ROBOTS WERE ORIGINALLY DEVISED FOR MANUAL LABOR, IF THEY SHOULD DEVELOP THE DESIRE TO SKIP WORK...
...THAT'D BE A TRULY ***AMAZING*** EVOLUTIONARY DEVELOPMENT!
SKIPPING WORK AN EVOLUTIONARY STEP?

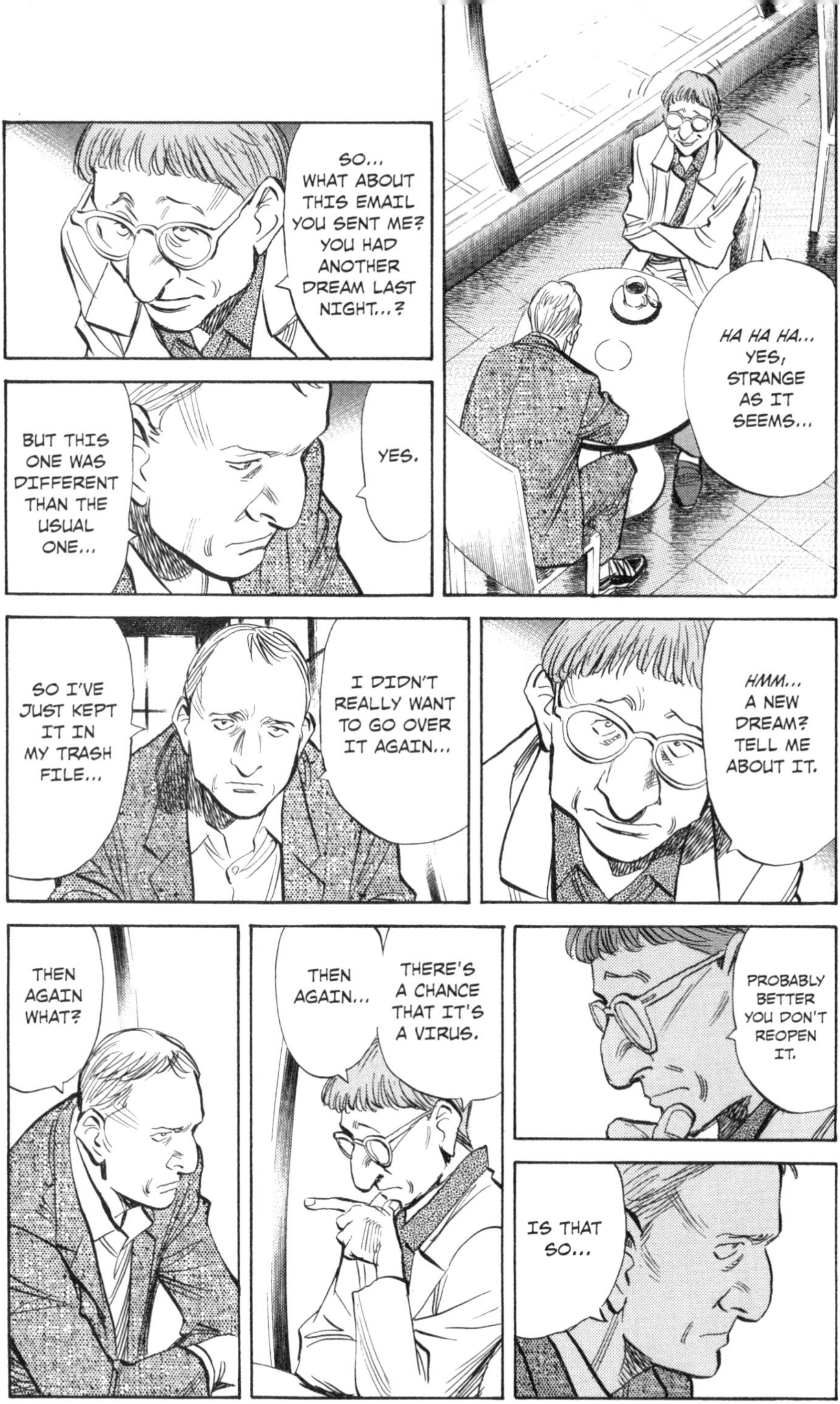
HA HA HA... YES, STRANGE AS IT SEEMS...
SO... WHAT ABOUT THIS EMAIL YOU SENT ME? YOU HAD ANOTHER DREAM LAST NIGHT...?
YES.
BUT THIS ONE WAS DIFFERENT THAN THE USUAL ONE...
HMM... A NEW DREAM? TELL ME ABOUT IT.
I DIDN'T REALLY WANT TO GO OVER IT AGAIN...
SO I'VE JUST KEPT IT IN MY TRASH FILE...
PROBABLY BETTER YOU DON'T REOPEN IT.
THERE'S A CHANCE THAT IT'S A VIRUS.
THEN AGAIN...
THEN AGAIN WHAT?
IS THAT SO...

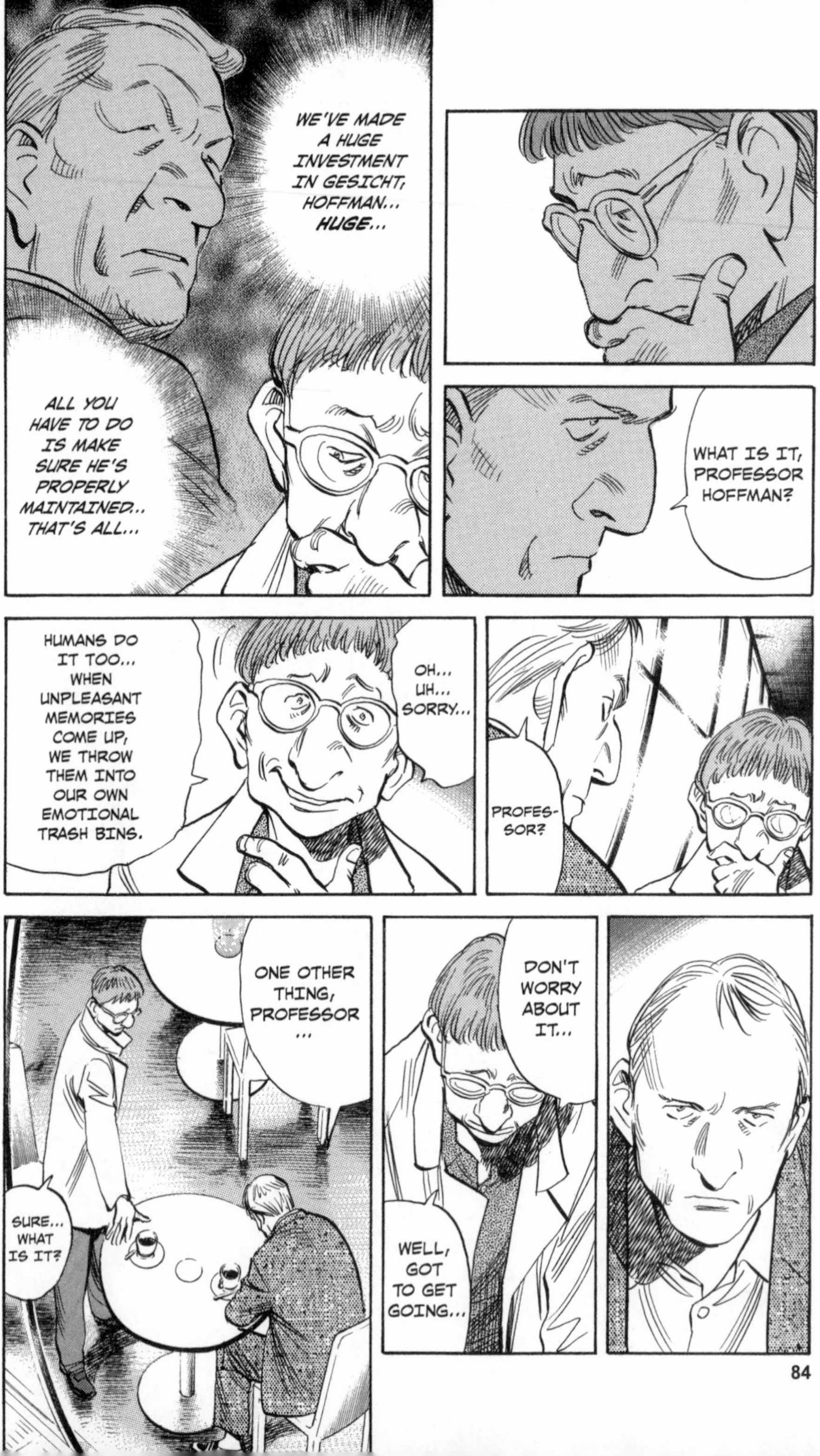
WHAT IS IT, PROFESSOR HOFFMAN?
WE'VE MADE A HUGE INVESTMENT IN GESICHT, HOFFMAN... **HUGE...**
ALL YOU HAVE TO DO IS MAKE SURE HE'S PROPERLY MAINTAINED... THAT'S ALL...
PROFES-SOR?
OH... UH... SORRY...
HUMANS DO IT TOO... WHEN UNPLEASANT MEMORIES COME UP, WE THROW THEM INTO OUR OWN EMOTIONAL TRASH BINS.
DON'T WORRY ABOUT IT...
WELL, GOT TO GET GOING...
ONE OTHER THING, PROFESSOR ...
SURE... WHAT IS IT?

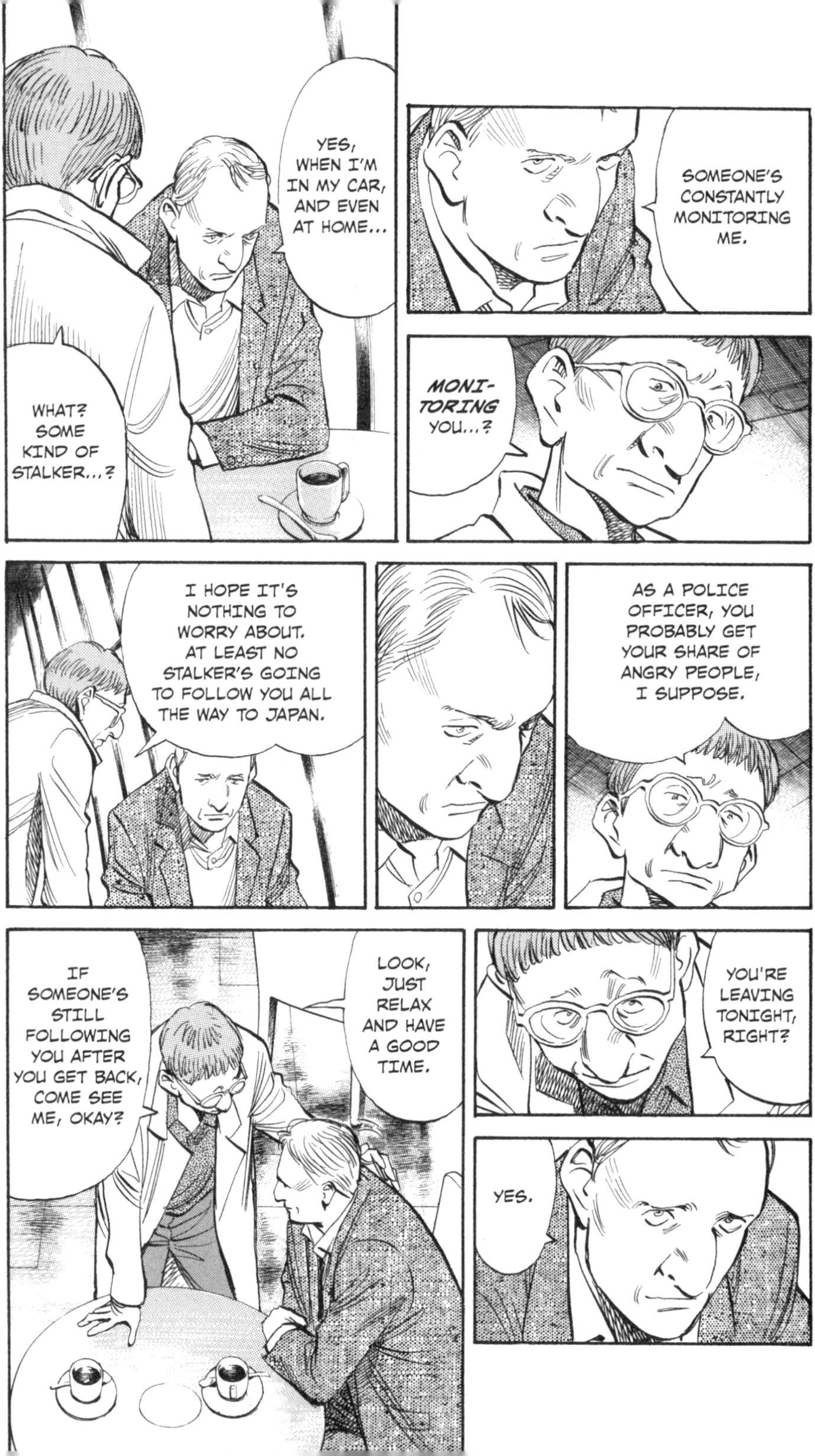
SOMEONE'S CONSTANTLY MONITORING ME.
MONI-TORING YOU...?
YES, WHEN I'M IN MY CAR, AND EVEN AT HOME...
WHAT? SOME KIND OF STALKER...?
AS A POLICE OFFICER, YOU PROBABLY GET YOUR SHARE OF ANGRY PEOPLE, I SUPPOSE.
I HOPE IT'S NOTHING TO WORRY ABOUT. AT LEAST NO STALKER'S GOING TO FOLLOW YOU ALL THE WAY TO JAPAN.
YOU'RE LEAVING TONIGHT, RIGHT?
YES.
LOOK, JUST RELAX AND HAVE A GOOD TIME.
IF SOMEONE'S STILL FOLLOWING YOU AFTER YOU GET BACK, COME SEE ME, OKAY?

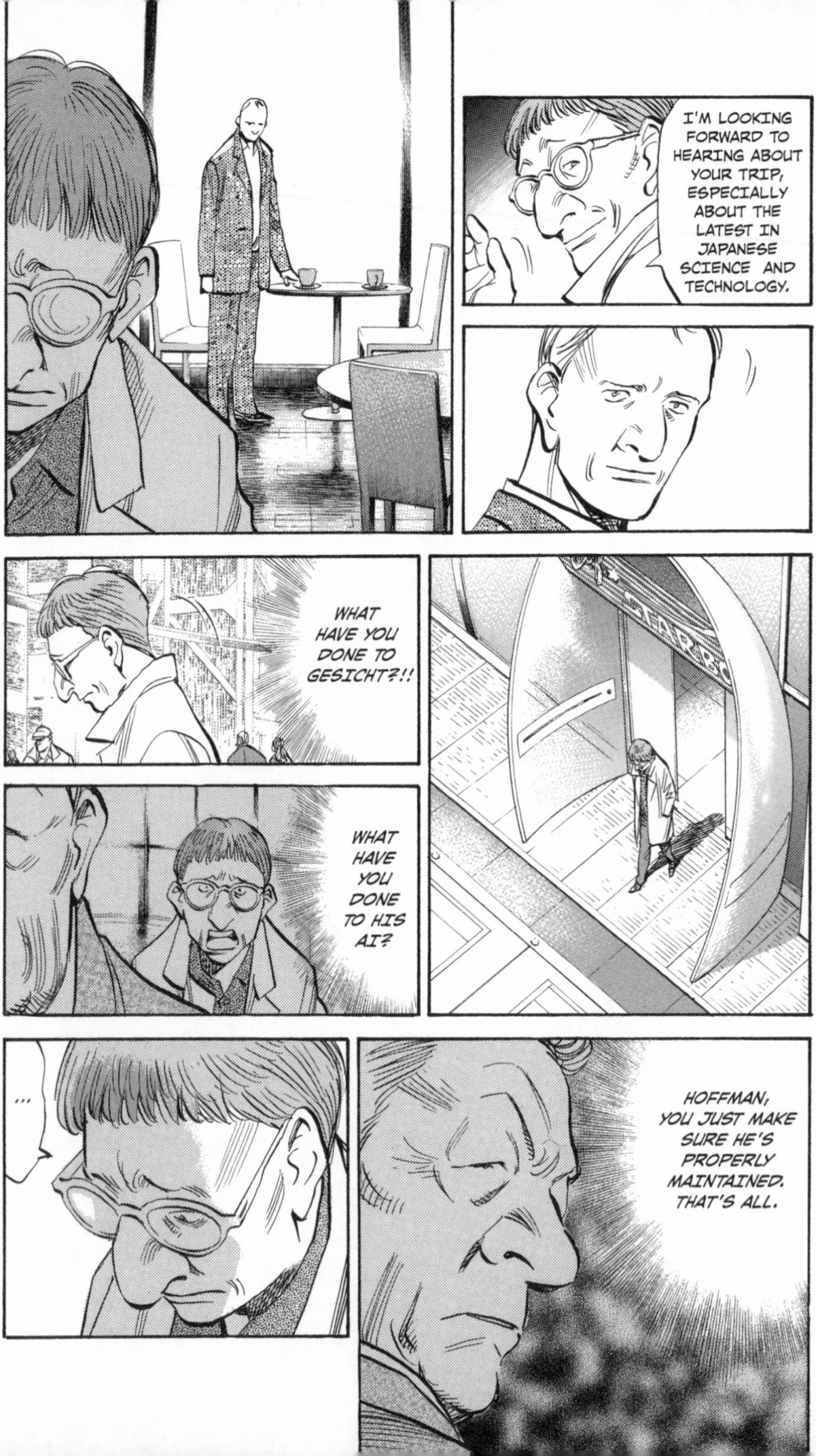
I'M LOOKING FORWARD TO HEARING ABOUT YOUR TRIP, ESPECIALLY ABOUT THE LATEST IN JAPANESE SCIENCE AND TECHNOLOGY.
WHAT HAVE YOU DONE TO GESICHT?!!
WHAT HAVE YOU DONE TO HIS AI?
HOFFMAN, YOU JUST MAKE SURE HE'S PROPERLY MAINTAINED. THAT'S ALL.
...

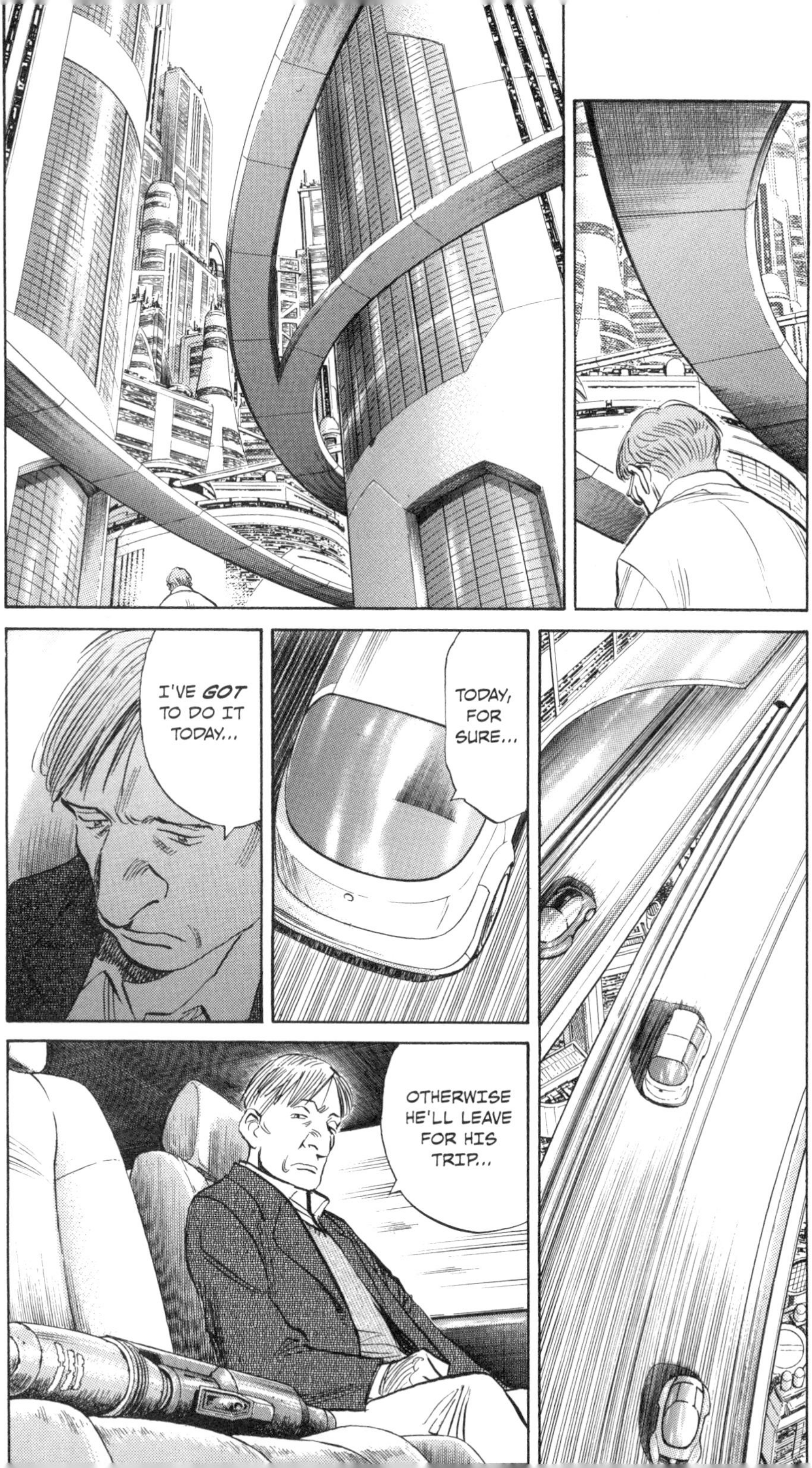
TODAY, FOR SURE...
I'VE *GOT* TO DO IT TODAY...
OTHERWISE HE'LL LEAVE FOR HIS TRIP...

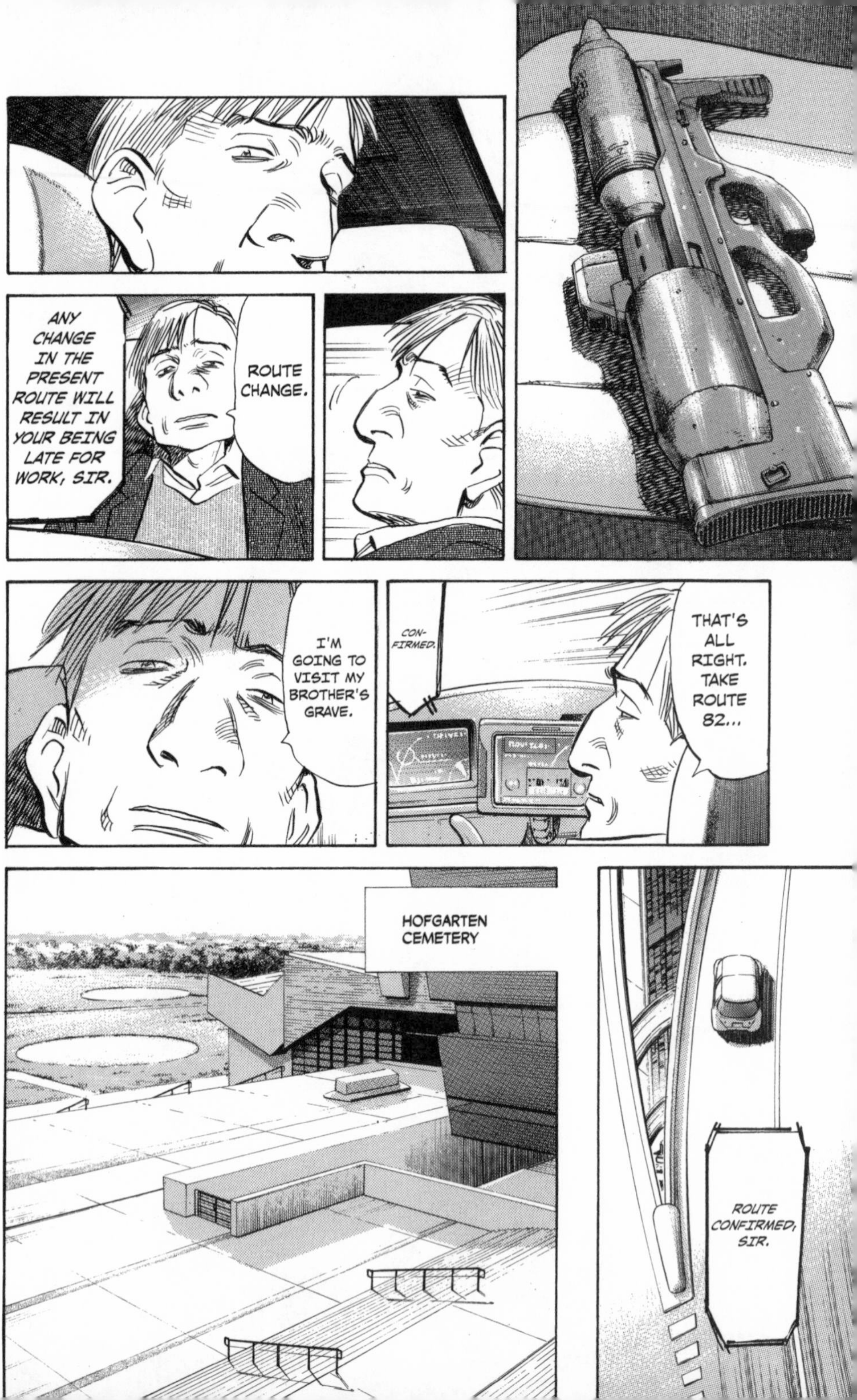
ROUTE CHANGE.
ANY CHANGE IN THE PRESENT ROUTE WILL RESULT IN YOUR BEING LATE FOR WORK, SIR.
THAT'S ALL RIGHT. TAKE ROUTE 82...
CON-FIRMED.
I'M GOING TO VISIT MY BROTHER'S GRAVE.
ROUTE CONFIRMED, SIR.
HOFGARTEN CEMETERY

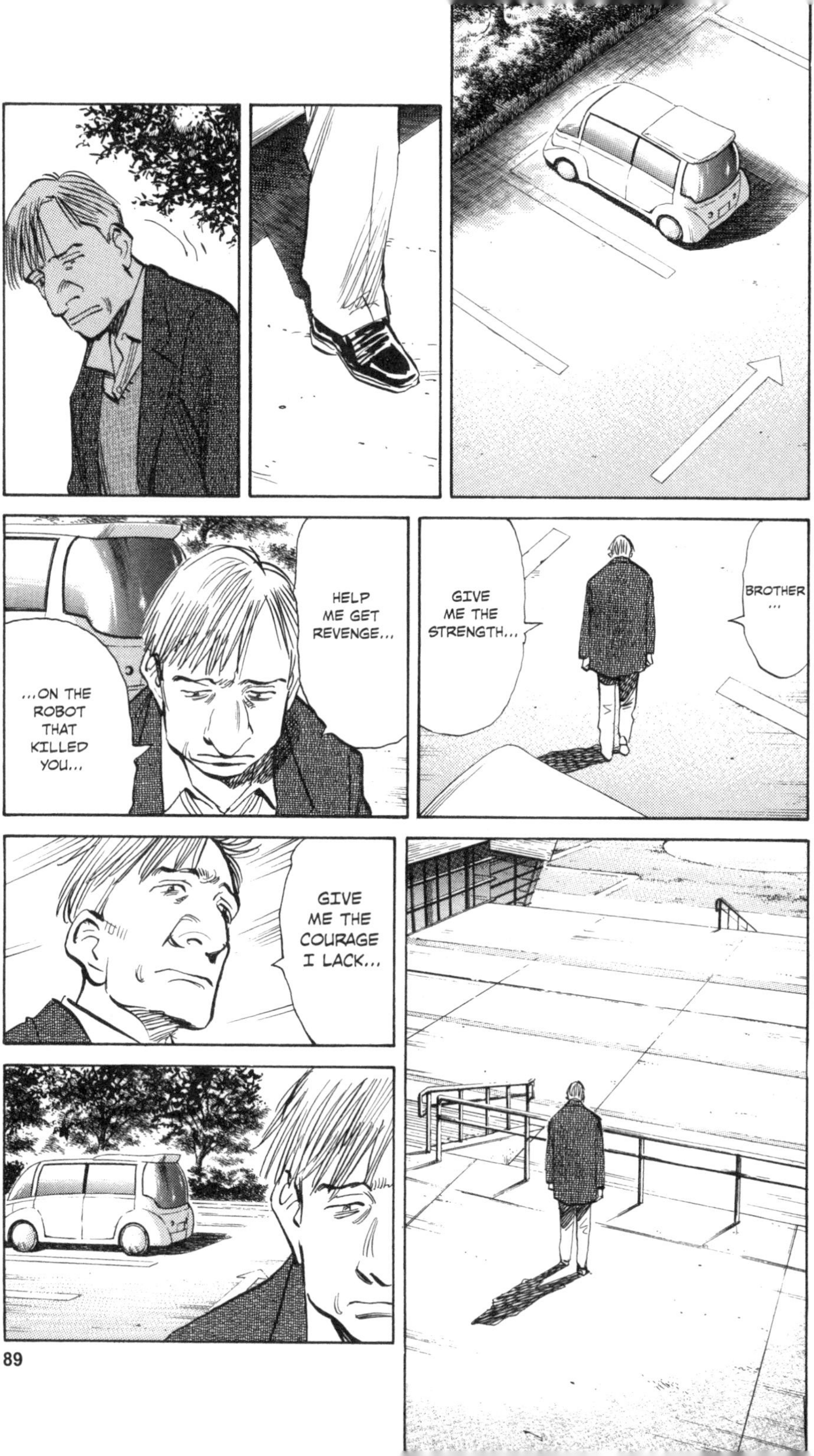
BROTHER...
GIVE ME THE STRENGTH...
HELP ME GET REVENGE...
...ON THE ROBOT THAT KILLED YOU...
GIVE ME THE COURAGE I LACK...

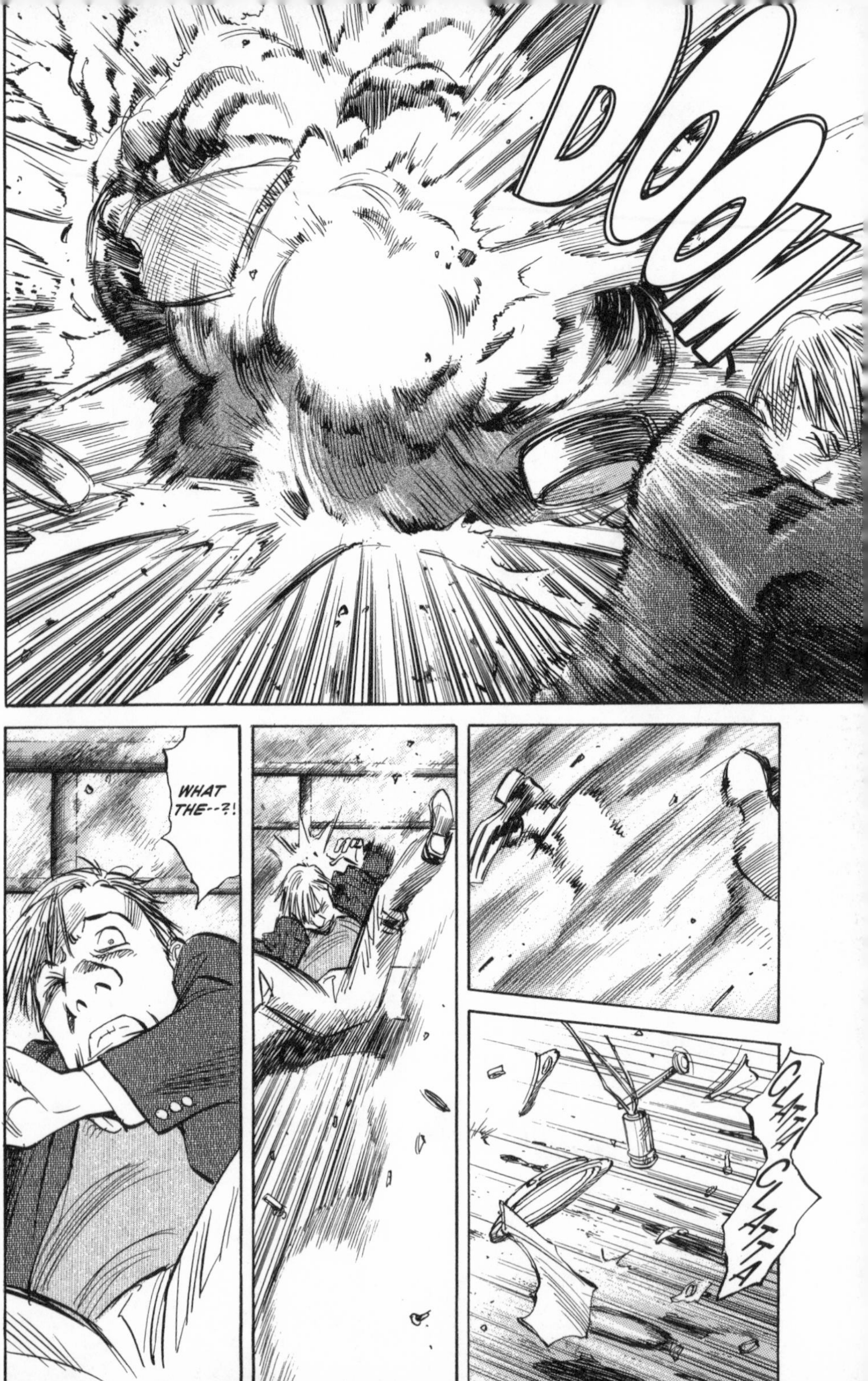
DOOOM
WHAT THE--?!
CLATTA CLATTA

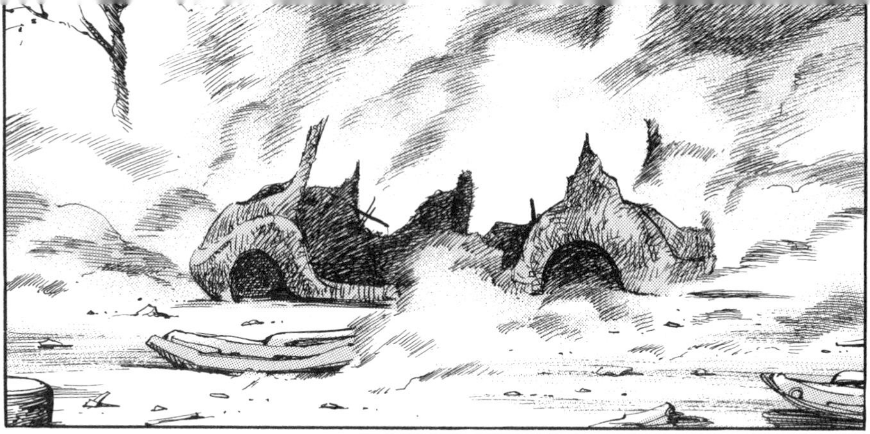

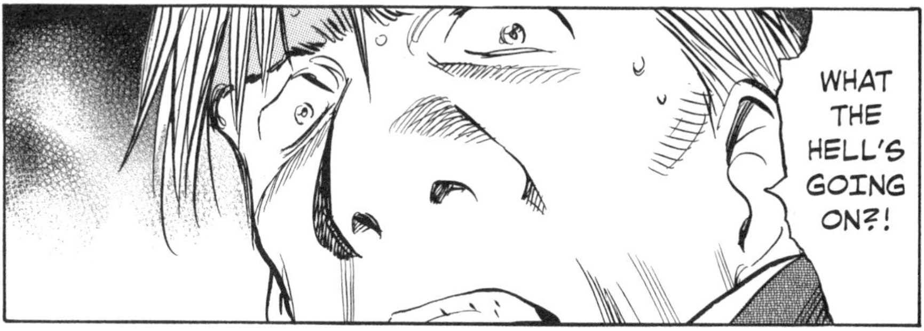
WHAT THE HELL'S GOING ON?!

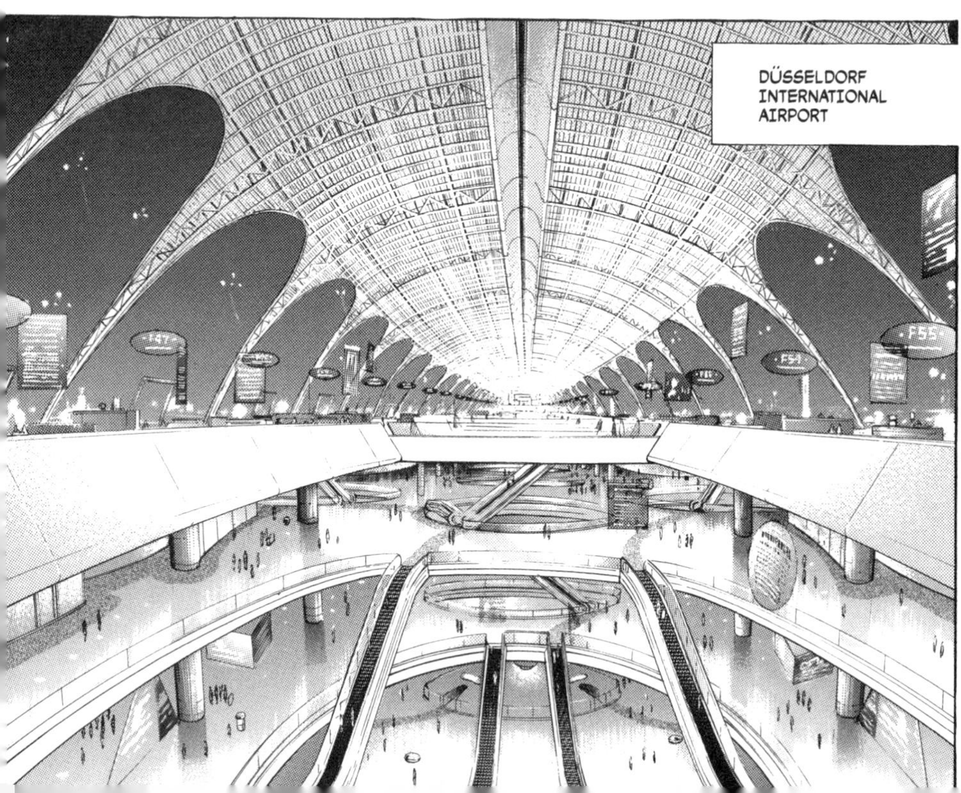
DÜSSELDORF INTERNATIONAL AIRPORT

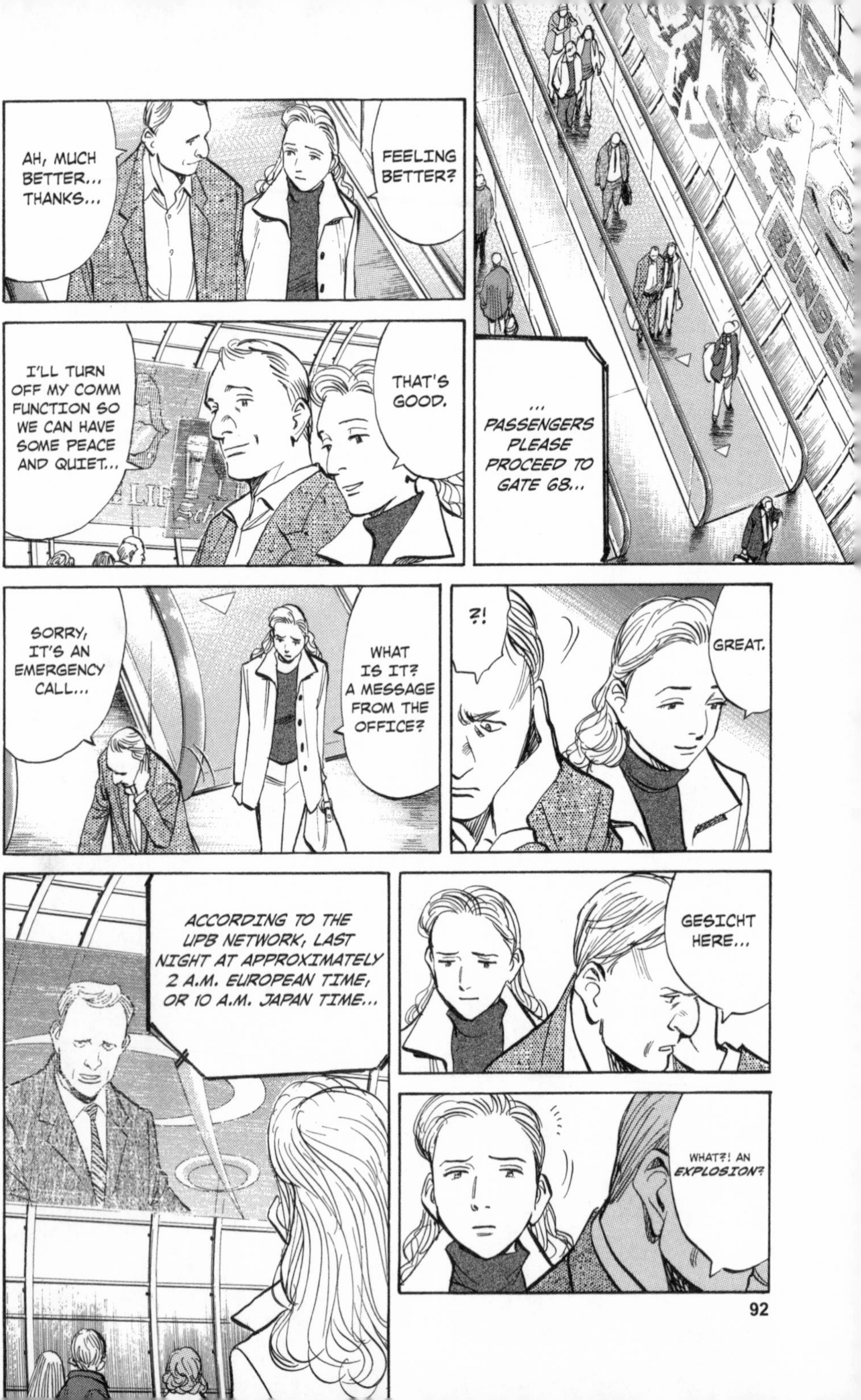
...PASSENGERS PLEASE PROCEED TO GATE 68...
FEELING BETTER?
AH, MUCH BETTER... THANKS...
THAT'S GOOD.
I'LL TURN OFF MY COMM FUNCTION SO WE CAN HAVE SOME PEACE AND QUIET...
GREAT.
?!
WHAT IS IT? A MESSAGE FROM THE OFFICE?
SORRY, IT'S AN EMERGENCY CALL...
GESICHT HERE...
WHAT?! AN EXPLOSION?
ACCORDING TO THE UPB NETWORK, LAST NIGHT AT APPROXIMATELY 2 A.M. EUROPEAN TIME, OR 10 A.M. JAPAN TIME...

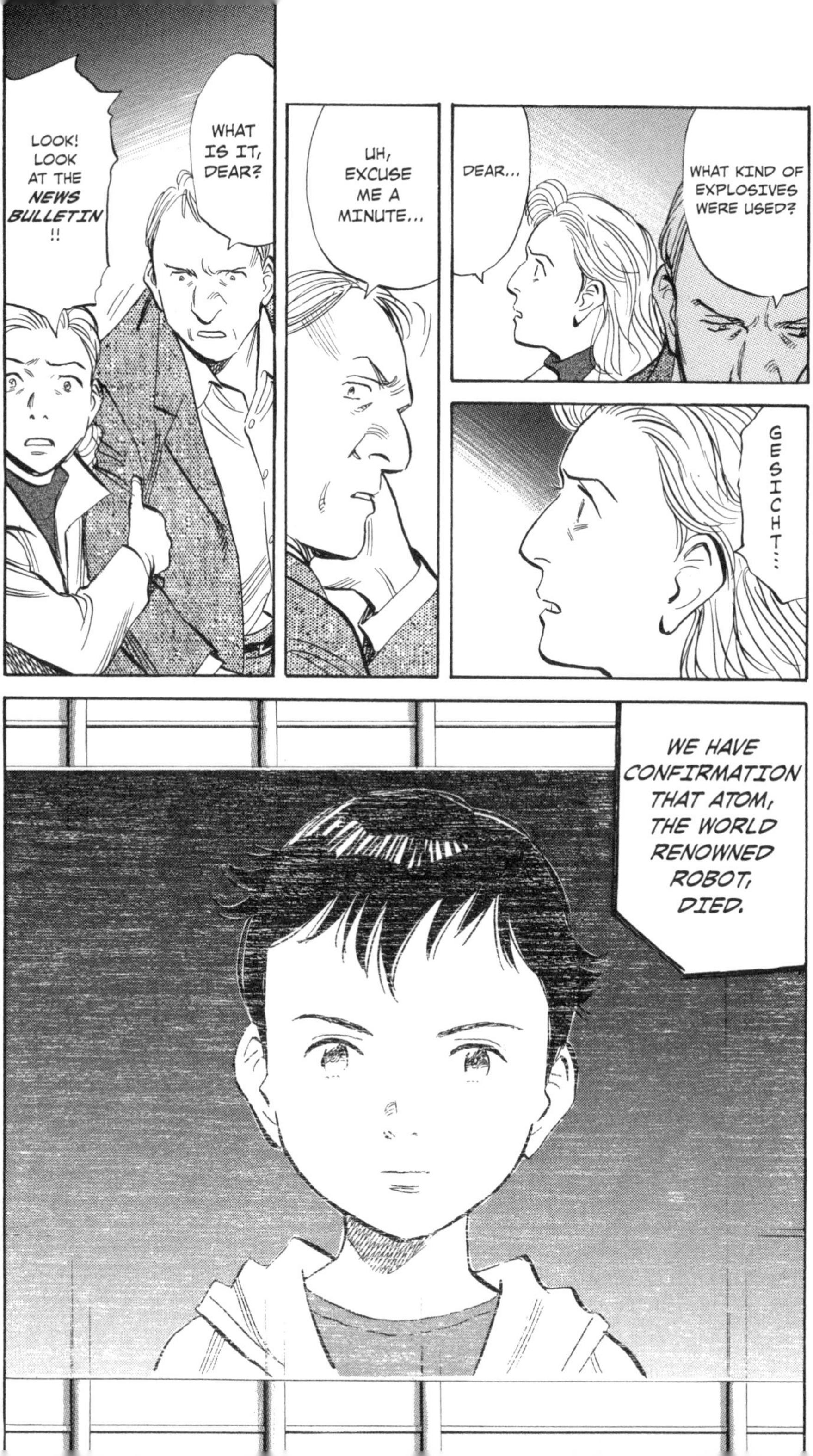
WHAT KIND OF EXPLOSIVES WERE USED?
DEAR...
GESICHT...
UH, EXCUSE ME A MINUTE...
WHAT IS IT, DEAR?
LOOK! LOOK AT THE NEWS BULLETIN!!
WE HAVE CONFIRMATION THAT ATOM, THE WORLD RENOWNED ROBOT, DIED.

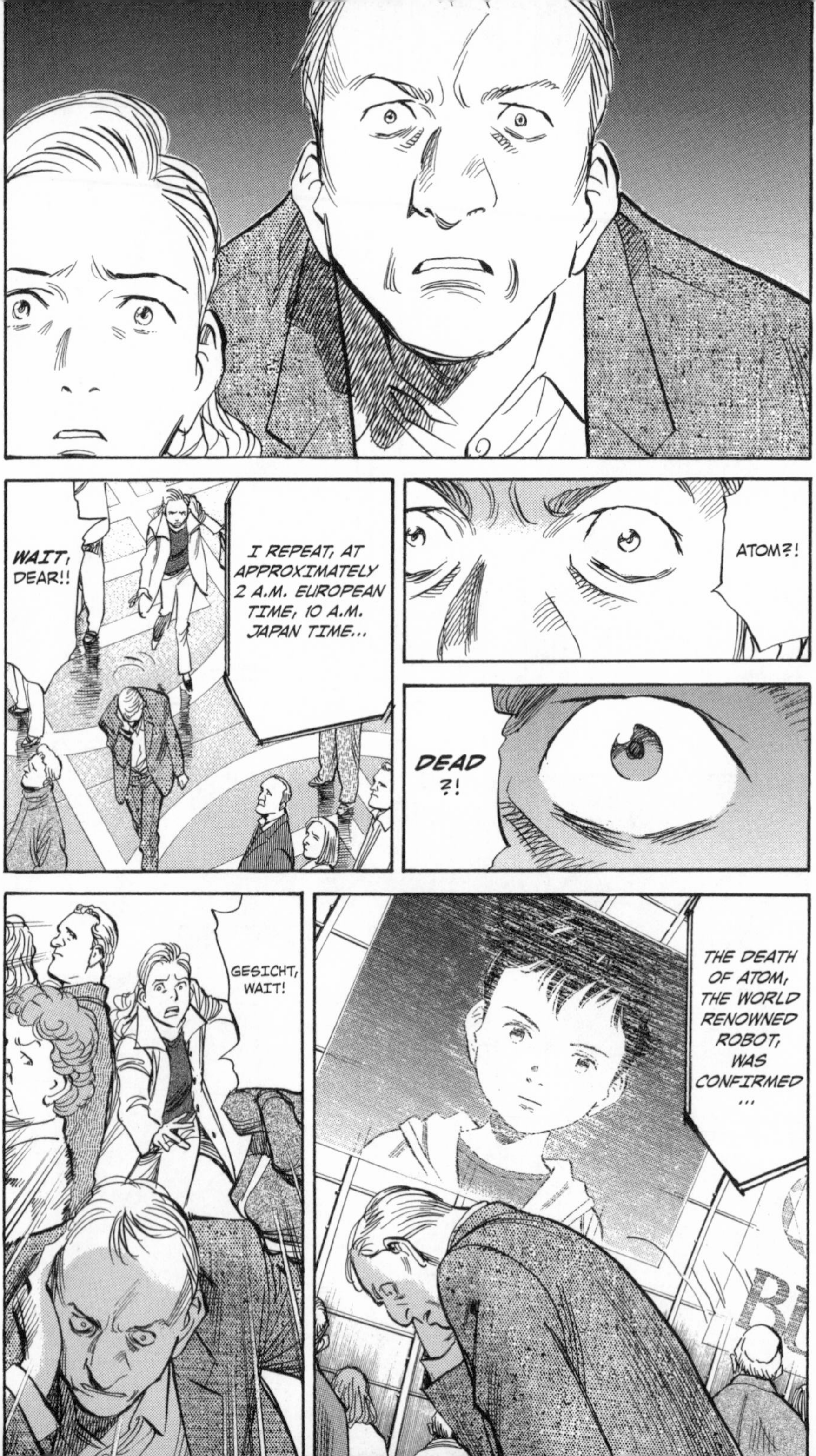
ATOM?!
DEAD ?!
I REPEAT, AT APPROXIMATELY 2 A.M. EUROPEAN TIME, 10 A.M. JAPAN TIME...
WAIT, DEAR!!
THE DEATH OF ATOM, THE WORLD RENOWNED ROBOT, WAS CONFIRMED ...
GESICHT, WAIT!

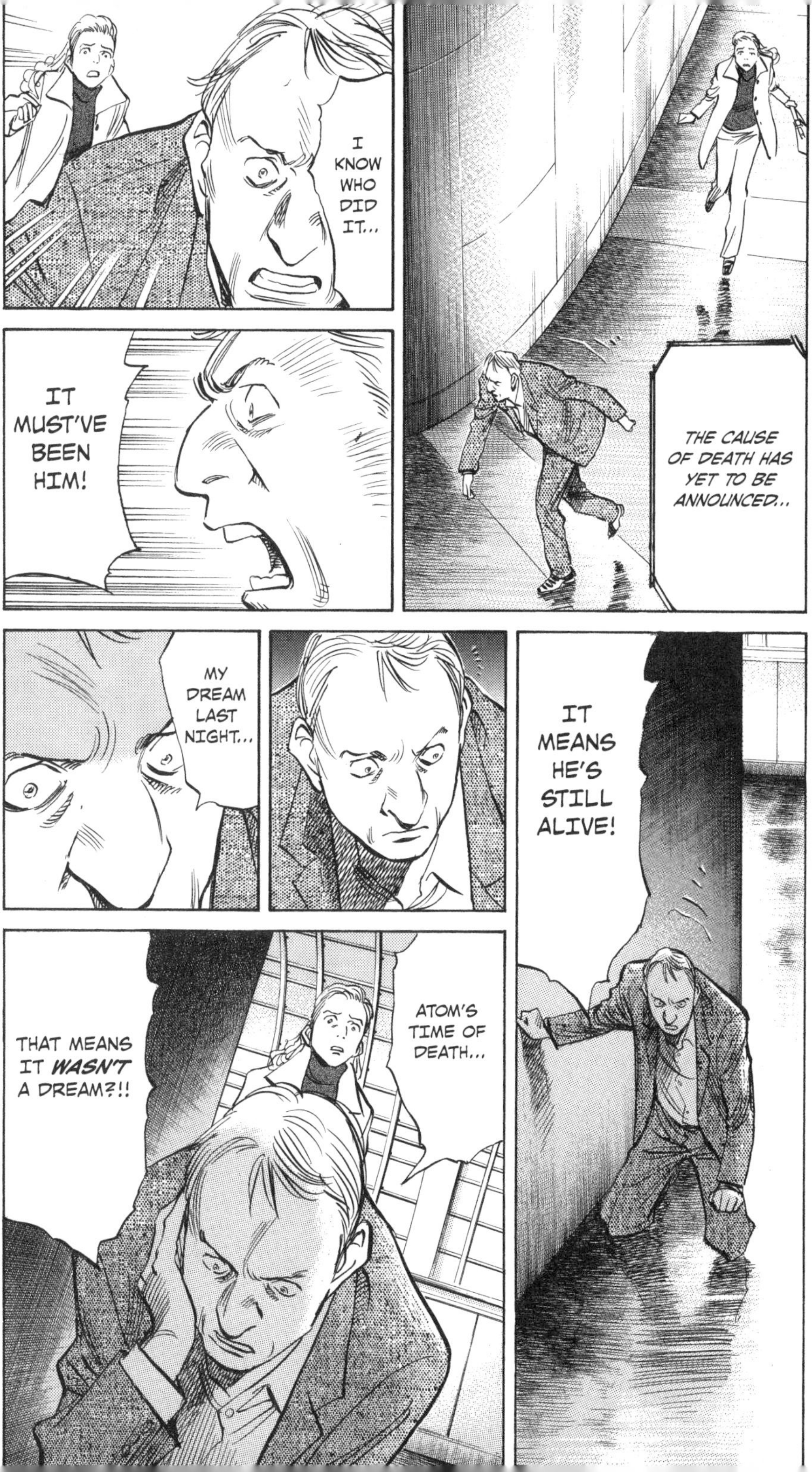
THE CAUSE OF DEATH HAS YET TO BE ANNOUNCED...
I KNOW WHO DID IT...
IT MUST'VE BEEN HIM!
IT MEANS HE'S STILL ALIVE!
MY DREAM LAST NIGHT...
ATOM'S TIME OF DEATH...
THAT MEANS IT *WASN'T* A DREAM?!!

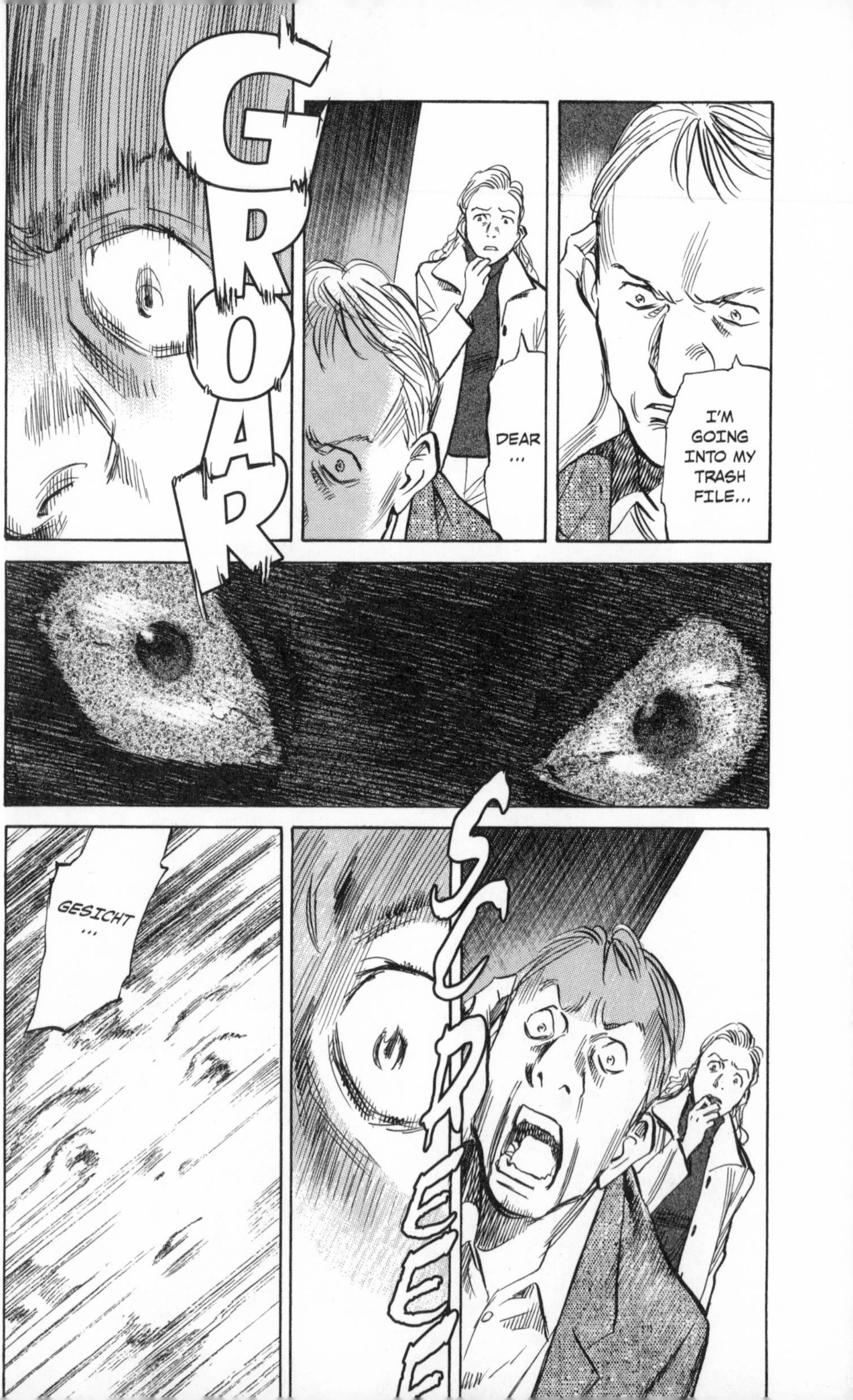
I'M GOING INTO MY TRASH FILE...
DEAR ...
GROAR
SCREEE
GESICHT ...

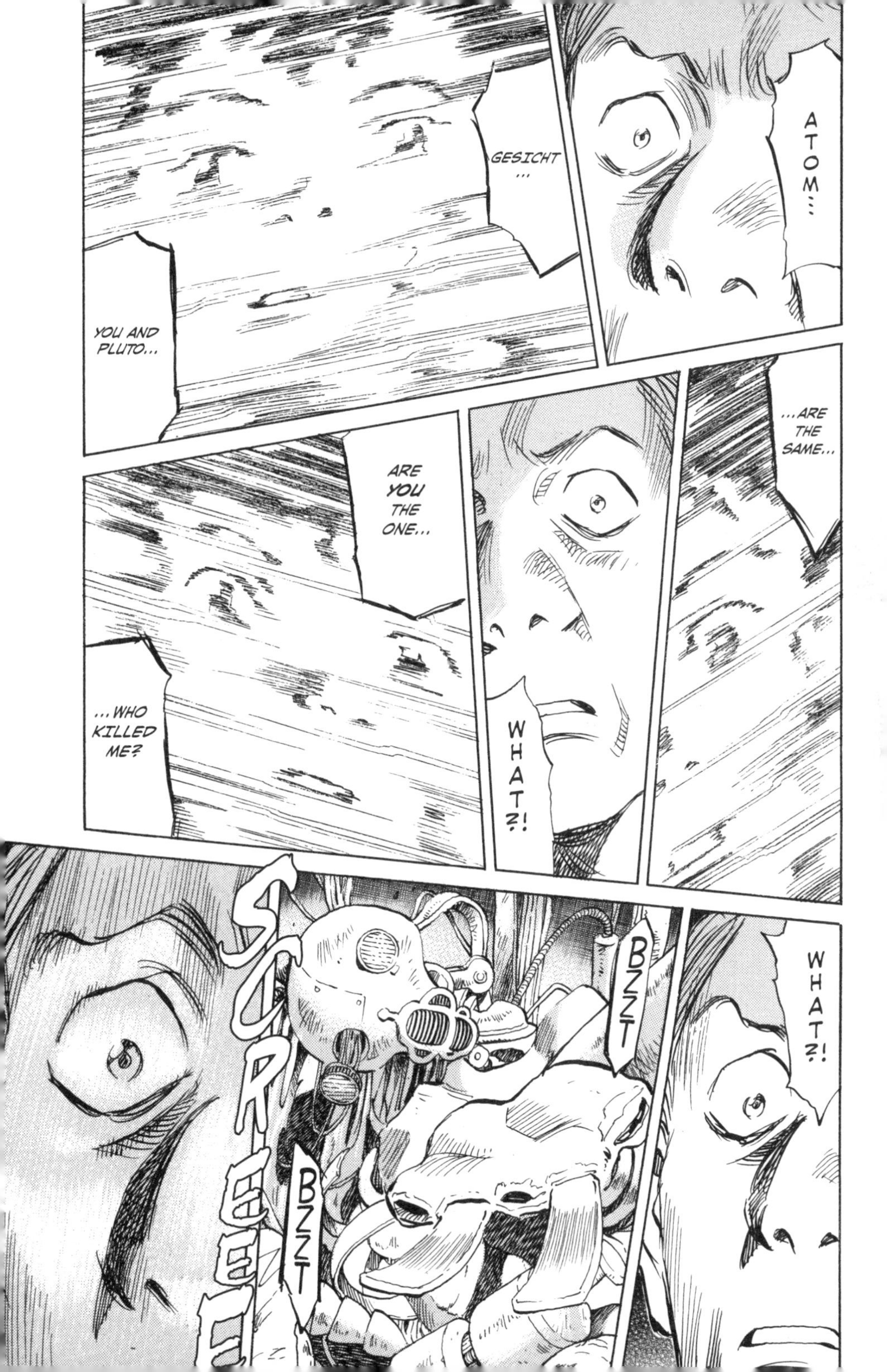
ATOM...
GESICHT...
YOU AND PLUTO...
...ARE THE SAME...
WHAT?!
ARE YOU THE ONE...
...WHO KILLED ME?
WHAT?!
BZZT
BZZT

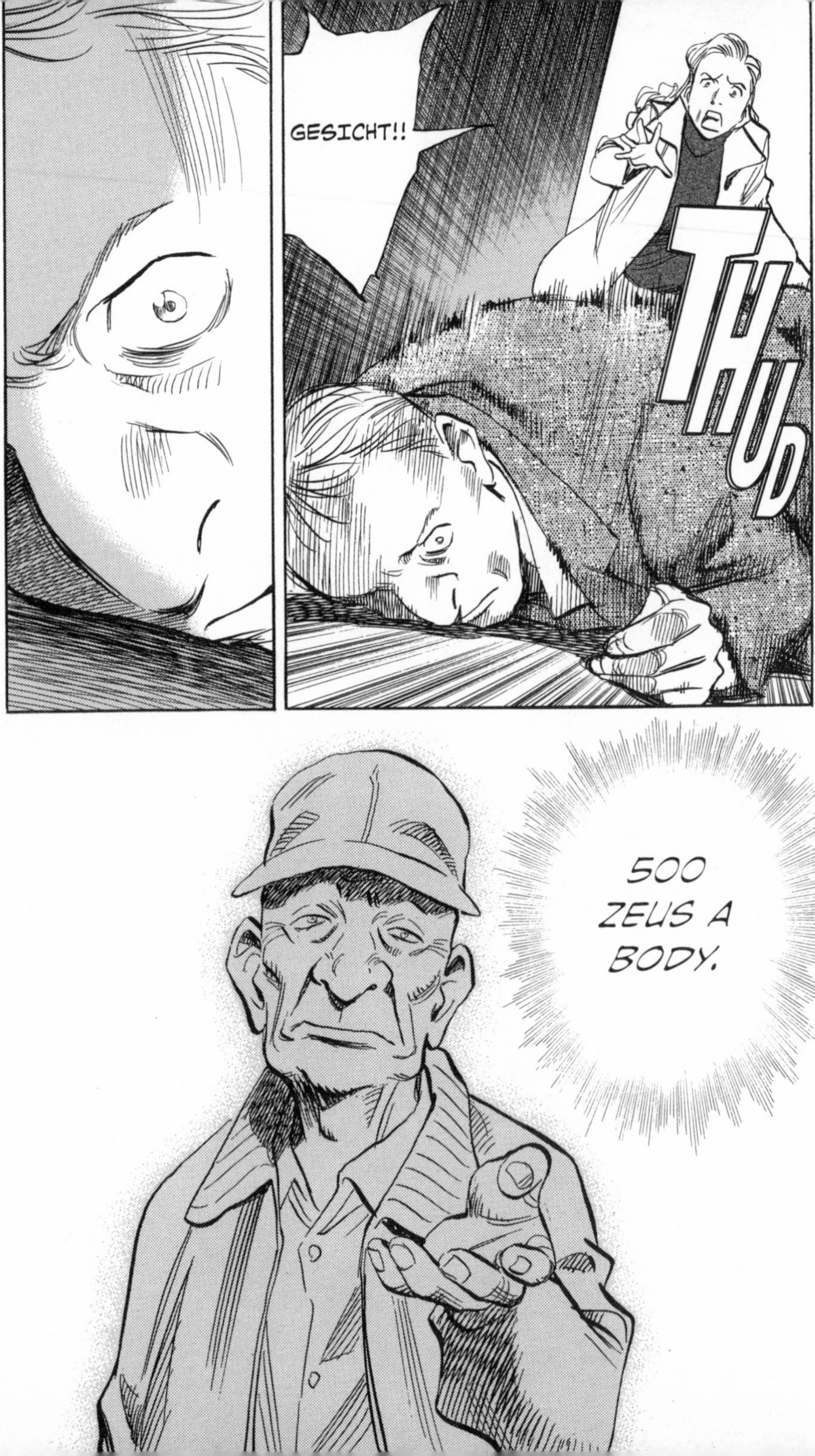
GESICHT!!
THUD
500 ZEUS A BODY.

Act 28 EMERGENCY CALL

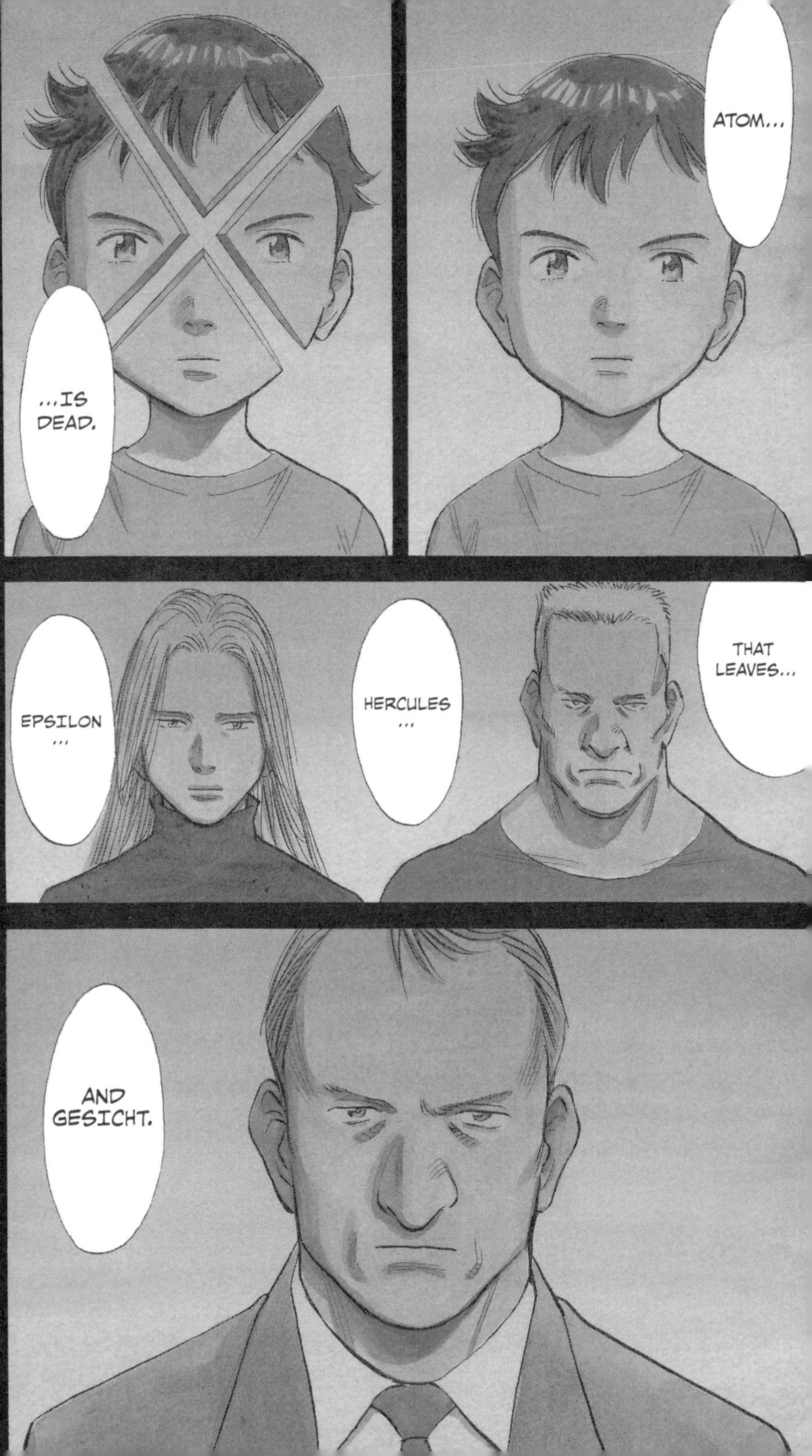
ATOM...
...IS DEAD.
THAT LEAVES...
HERCULES...
EPSILON...
AND GESICHT.

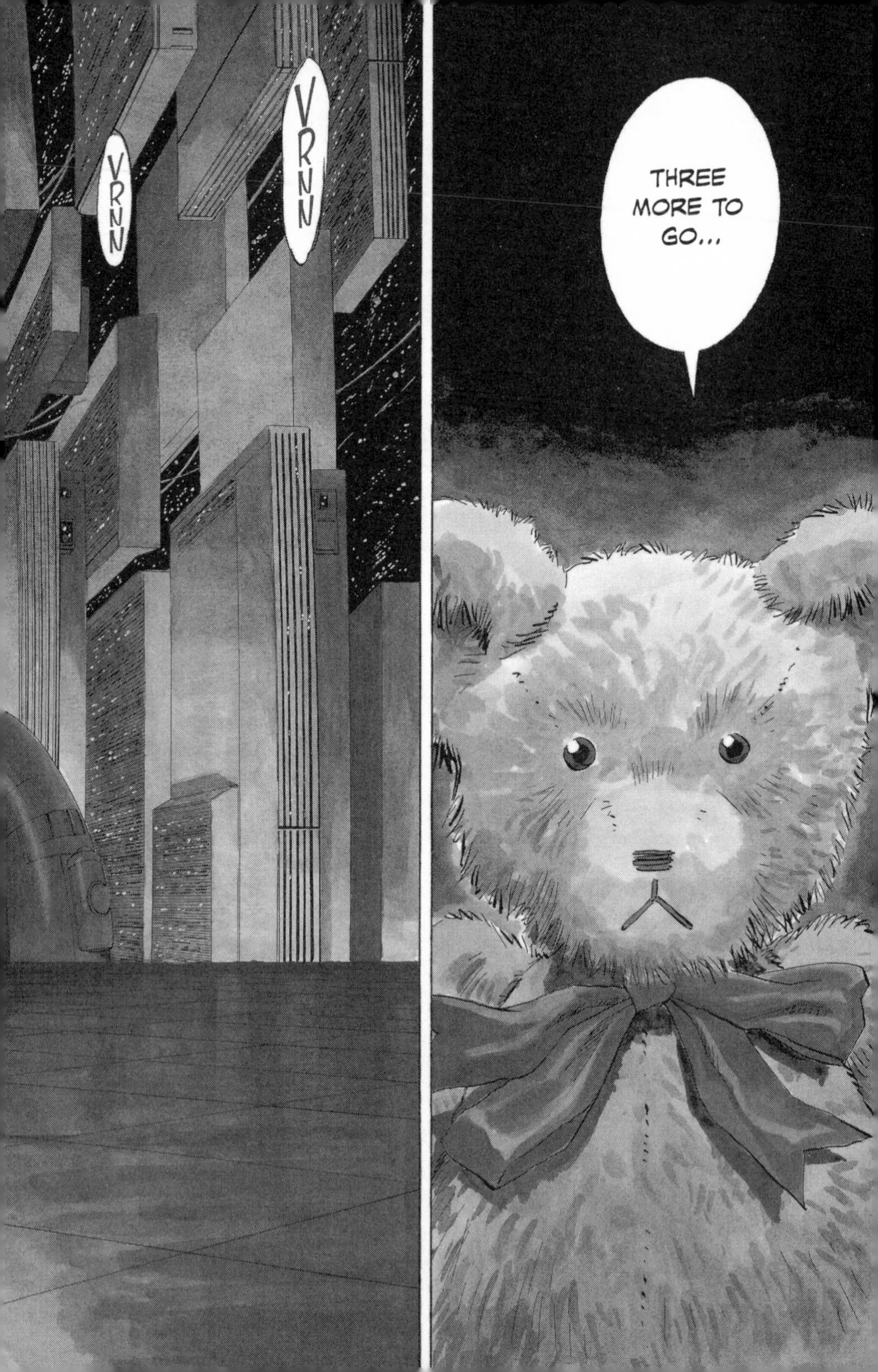
THREE MORE TO GO...
VRNN
VRNN

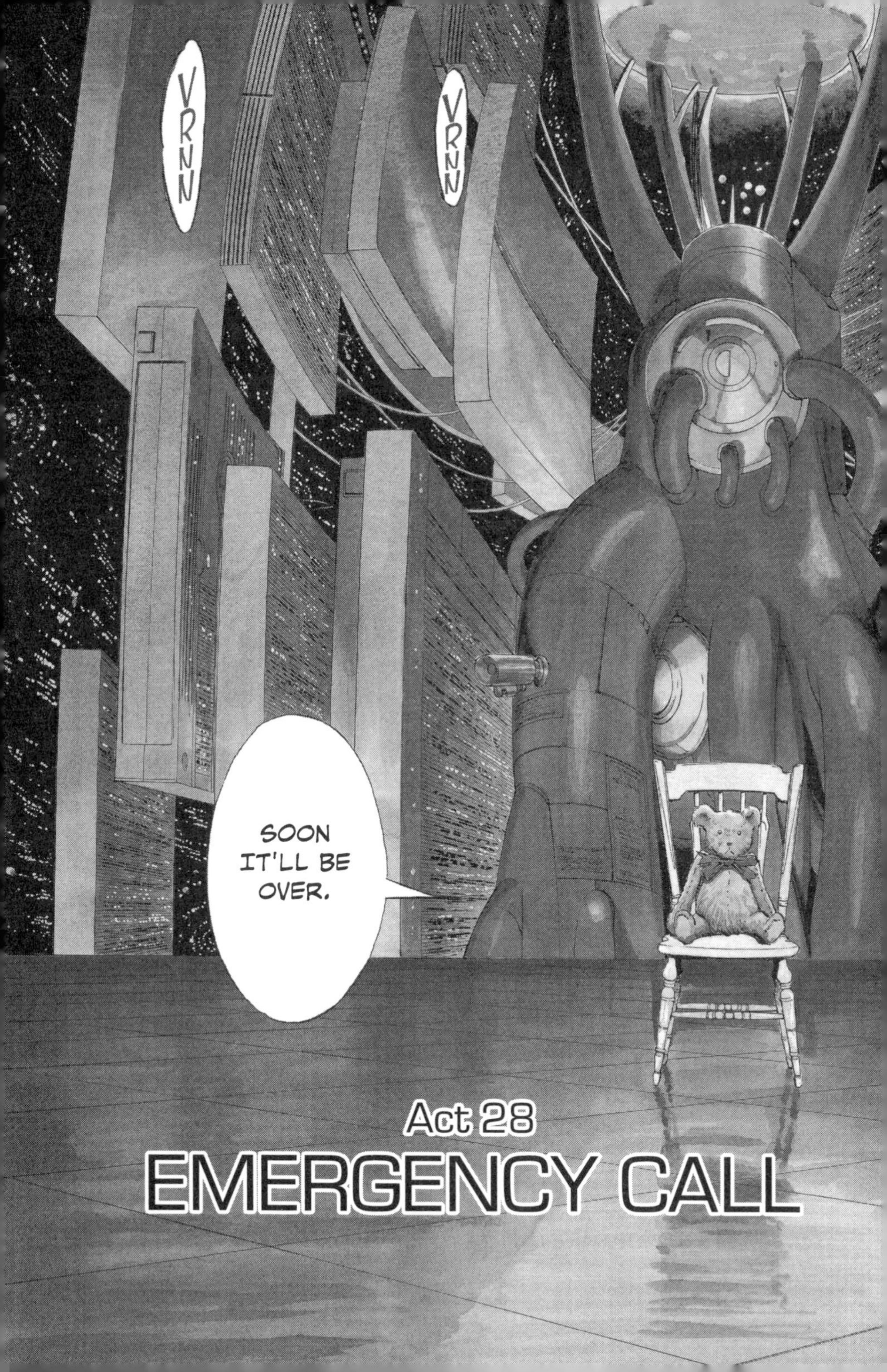
VRNN
VRNN
SOON IT'LL BE OVER.
Act 28
EMERGENCY CALL

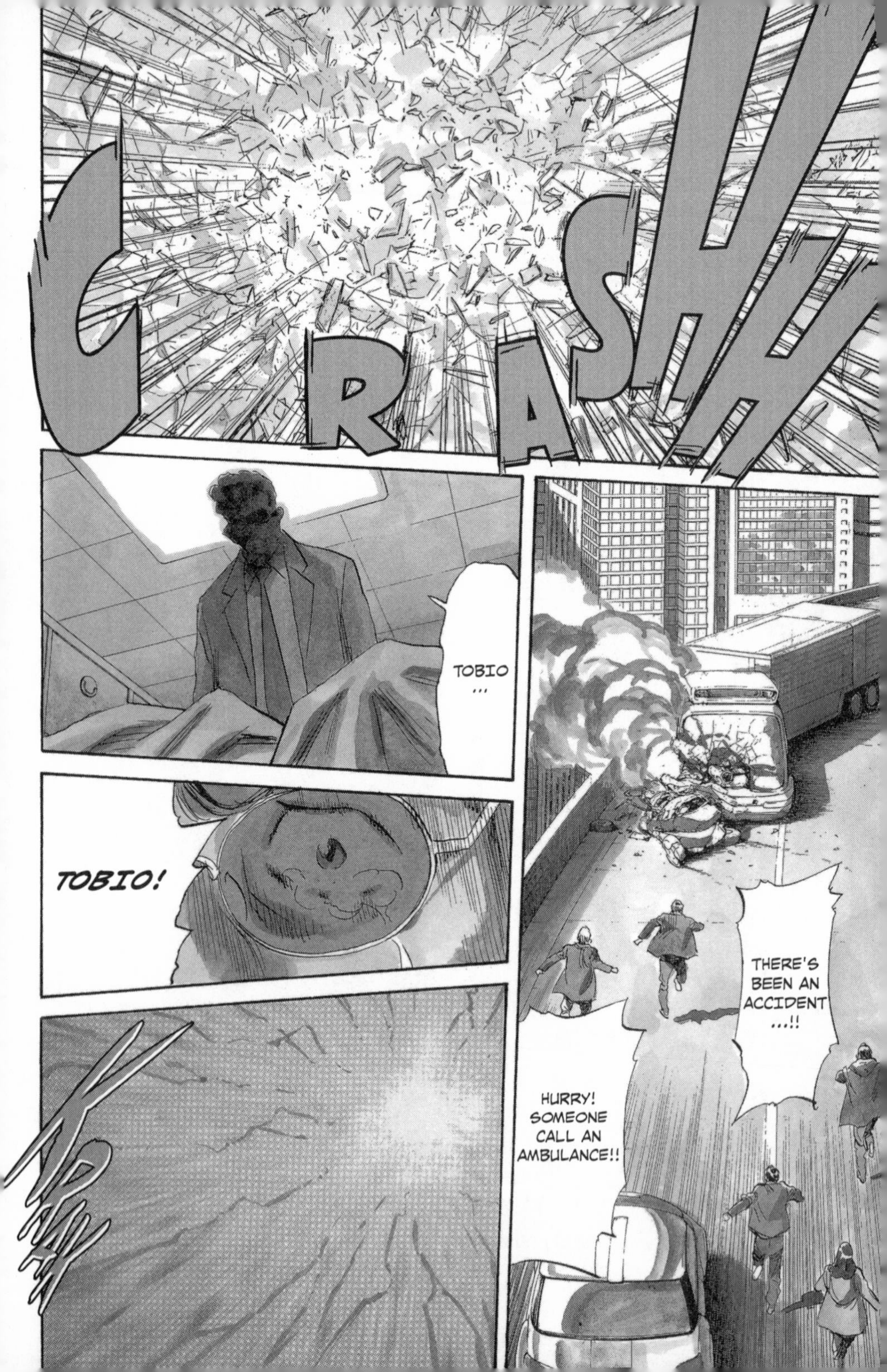
CRASH
THERE'S BEEN AN ACCIDENT ...!!
HURRY! SOMEONE CALL AN AMBULANCE!!
TOBIO ...
TOBIO!

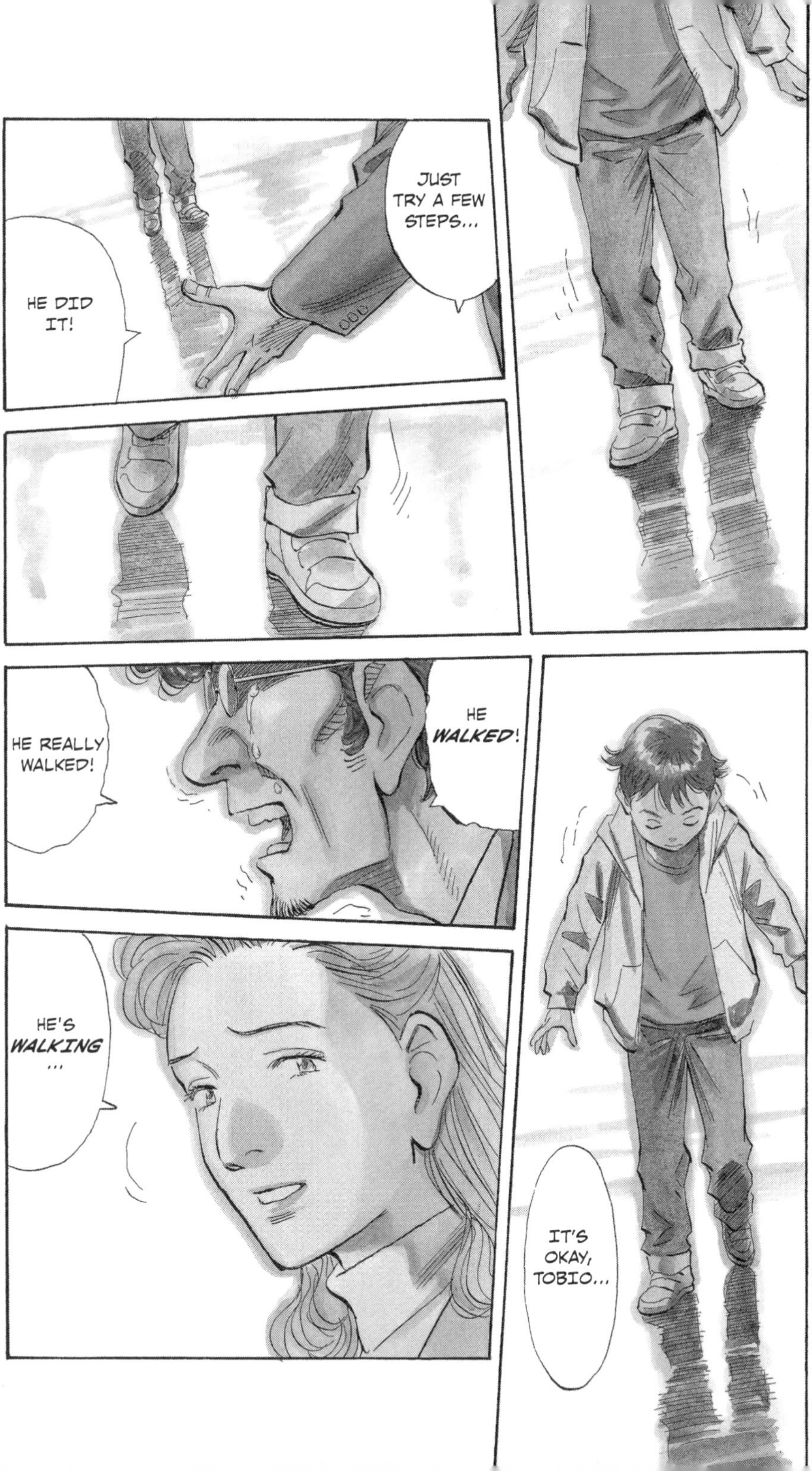
JUST TRY A FEW STEPS...
HE DID IT!
IT'S OKAY, TOBIO...
HE *WALKED*!
HE REALLY WALKED!
HE'S *WALKING* ...

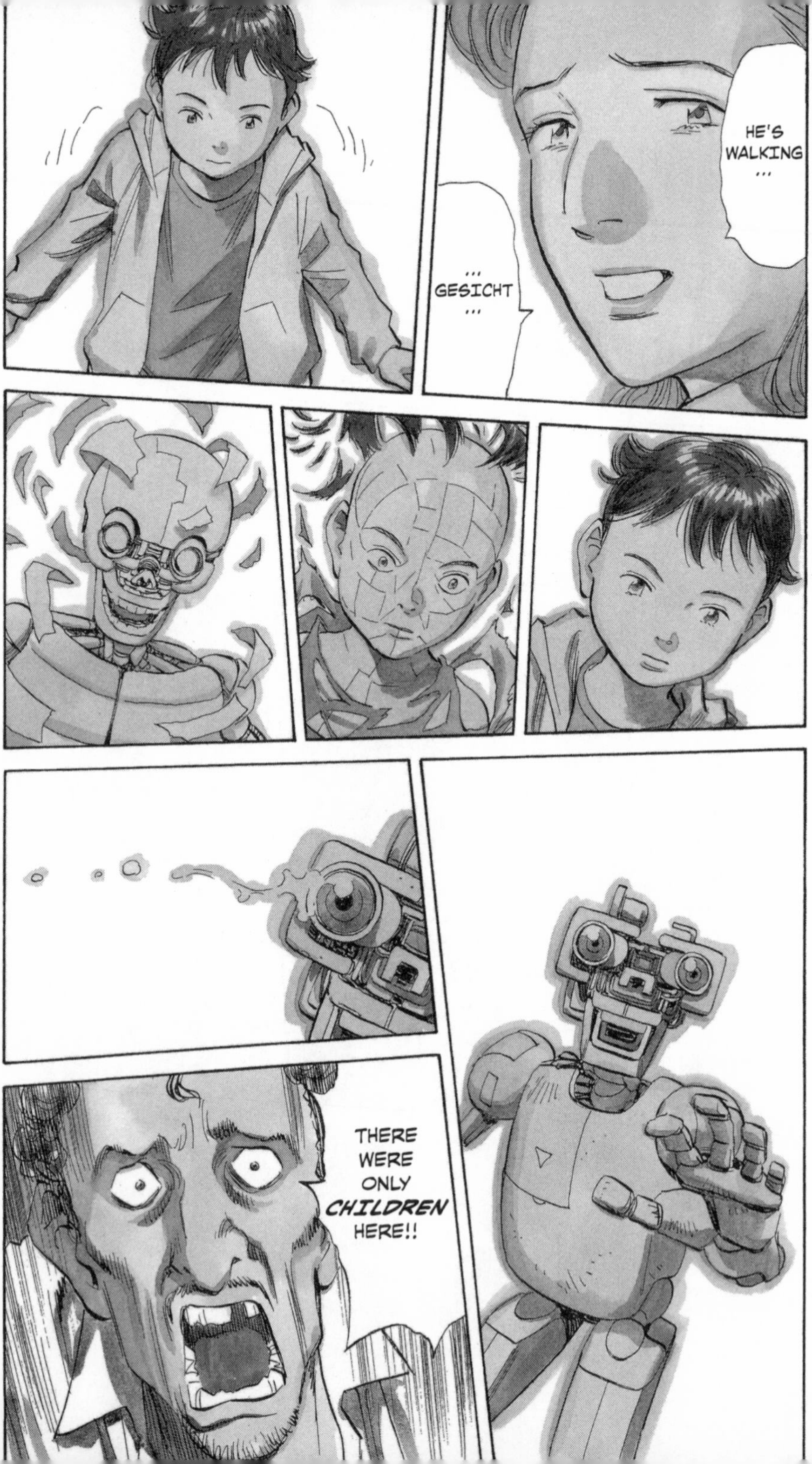
HE'S WALKING ...
... GESICHT ...
THERE WERE ONLY *CHILDREN* HERE!!

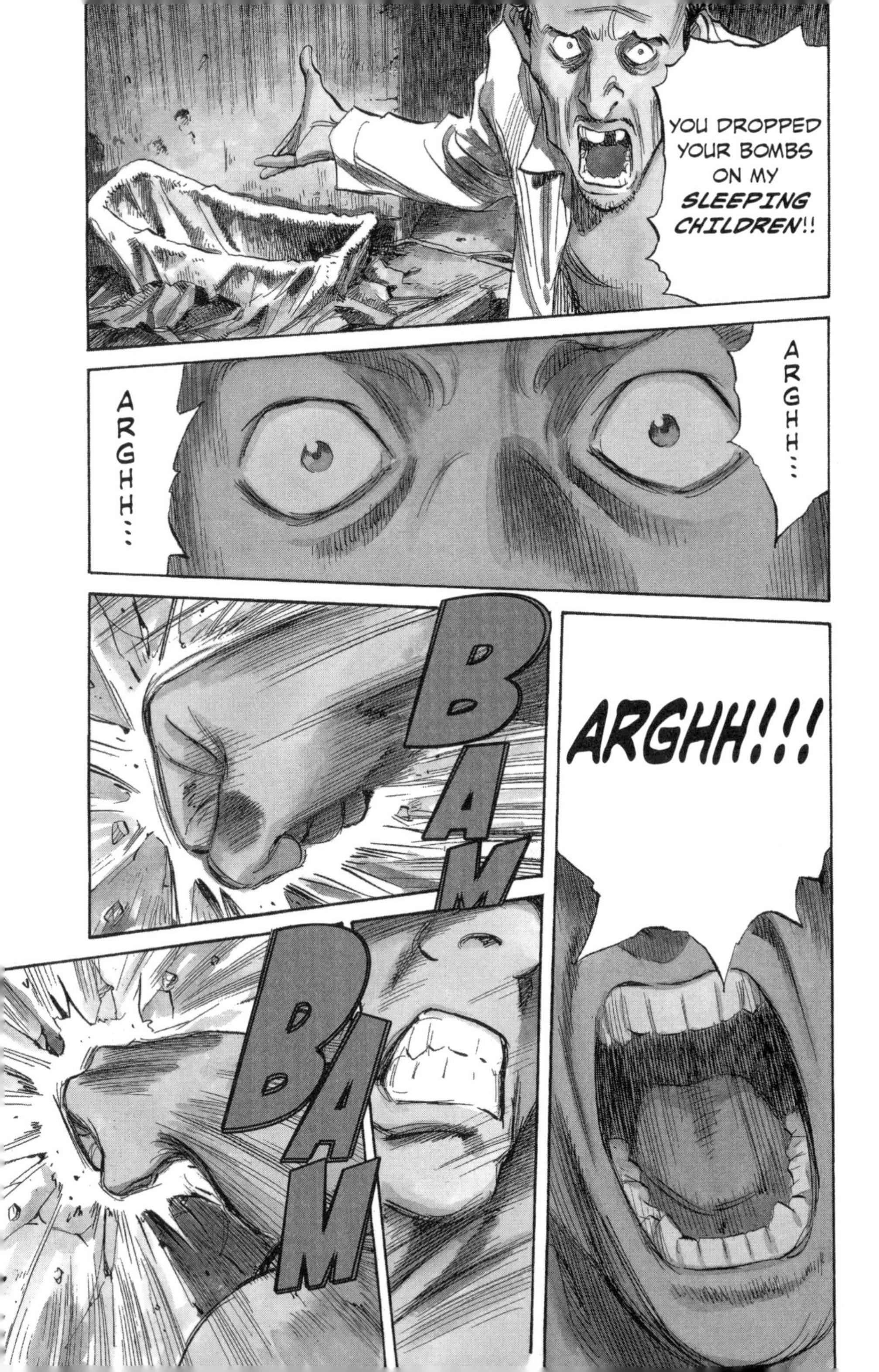
YOU DROPPED YOUR BOMBS ON MY *SLEEPING CHILDREN*!!
ARGHH...
ARGHH...
ARGHH!!!
BAM
BAM

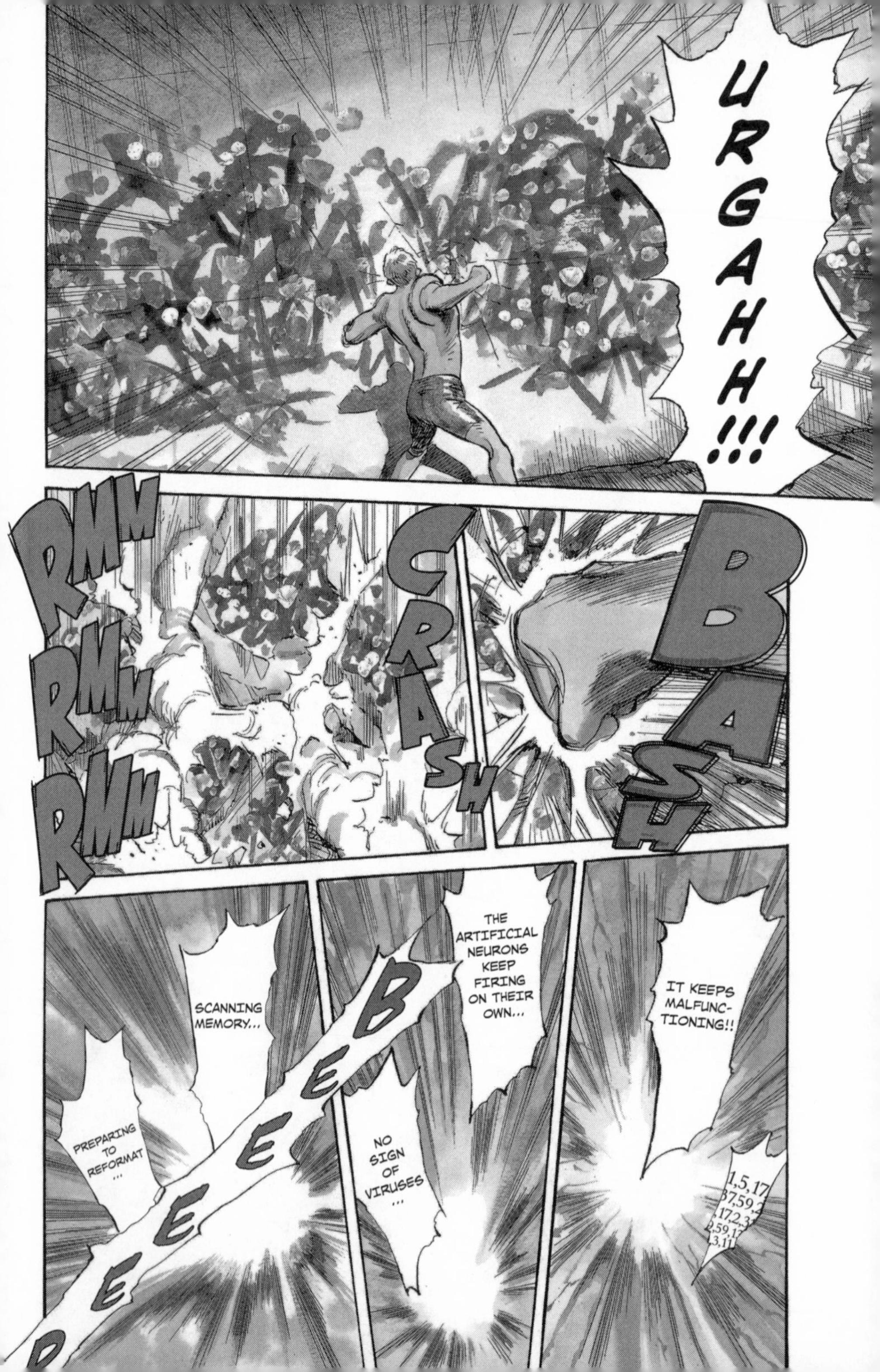
URGAHH!!!
BASH
CRASH
RMM RMM RMM
IT KEEPS MALFUNCTIONING!!
THE ARTIFICIAL NEURONS KEEP FIRING ON THEIR OWN...
NO SIGN OF VIRUSES...
BEEEEE
SCANNING MEMORY...
PREPARING TO REFORMAT...

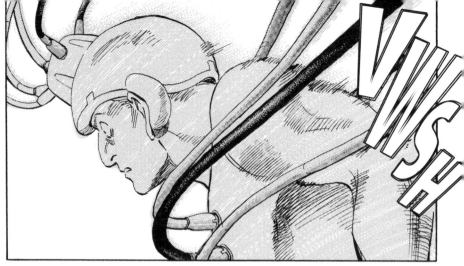

VWSH

UH...
Y-YES...

ARE
YOU ALL
RIGHT,
GESICHT?

ALL
FUNCTIONS
ARE BACK TO
NORMAL.

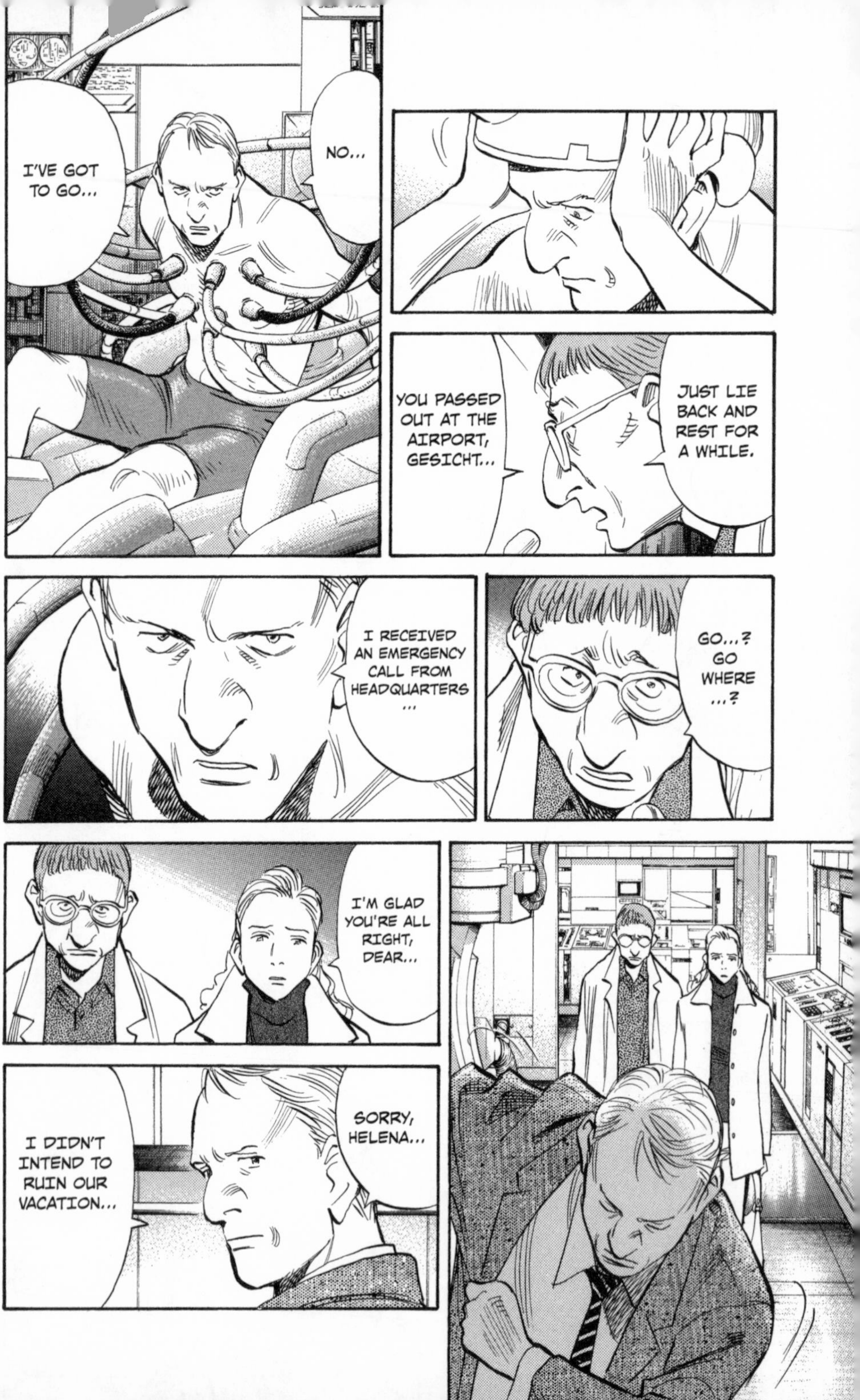
JUST LIE BACK AND REST FOR A WHILE.
YOU PASSED OUT AT THE AIRPORT, GESICHT...
NO...
I'VE GOT TO GO...
GO...? GO WHERE...?
I RECEIVED AN EMERGENCY CALL FROM HEADQUARTERS...
I'M GLAD YOU'RE ALL RIGHT, DEAR...
SORRY, HELENA...
I DIDN'T INTEND TO RUIN OUR VACATION...

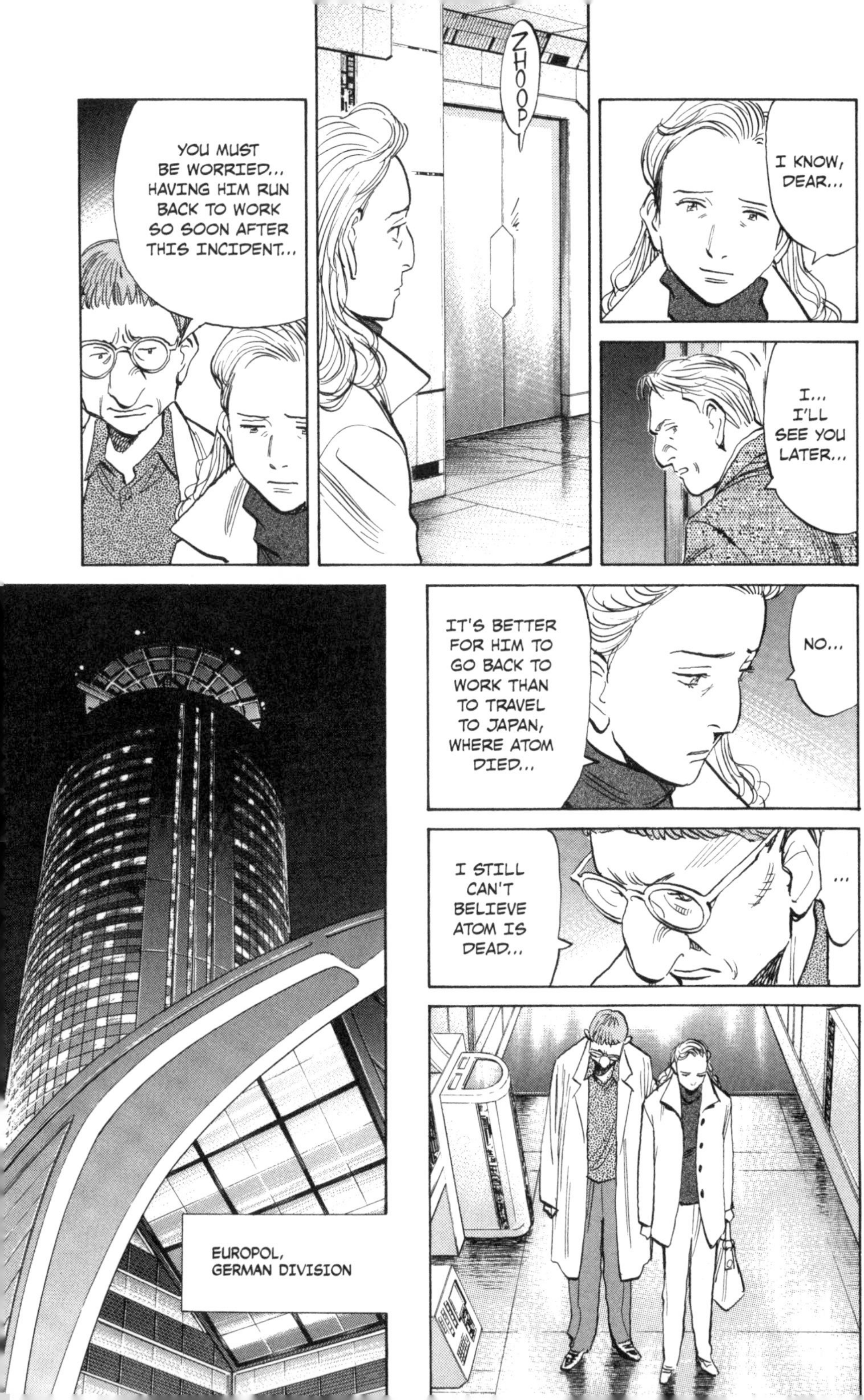
I KNOW, DEAR...
I... I'LL SEE YOU LATER...
ZHOOP
YOU MUST BE WORRIED... HAVING HIM RUN BACK TO WORK SO SOON AFTER THIS INCIDENT...
NO...
IT'S BETTER FOR HIM TO GO BACK TO WORK THAN TO TRAVEL TO JAPAN, WHERE ATOM DIED...
...
I STILL CAN'T BELIEVE ATOM IS DEAD...
EUROPOL, GERMAN DIVISION

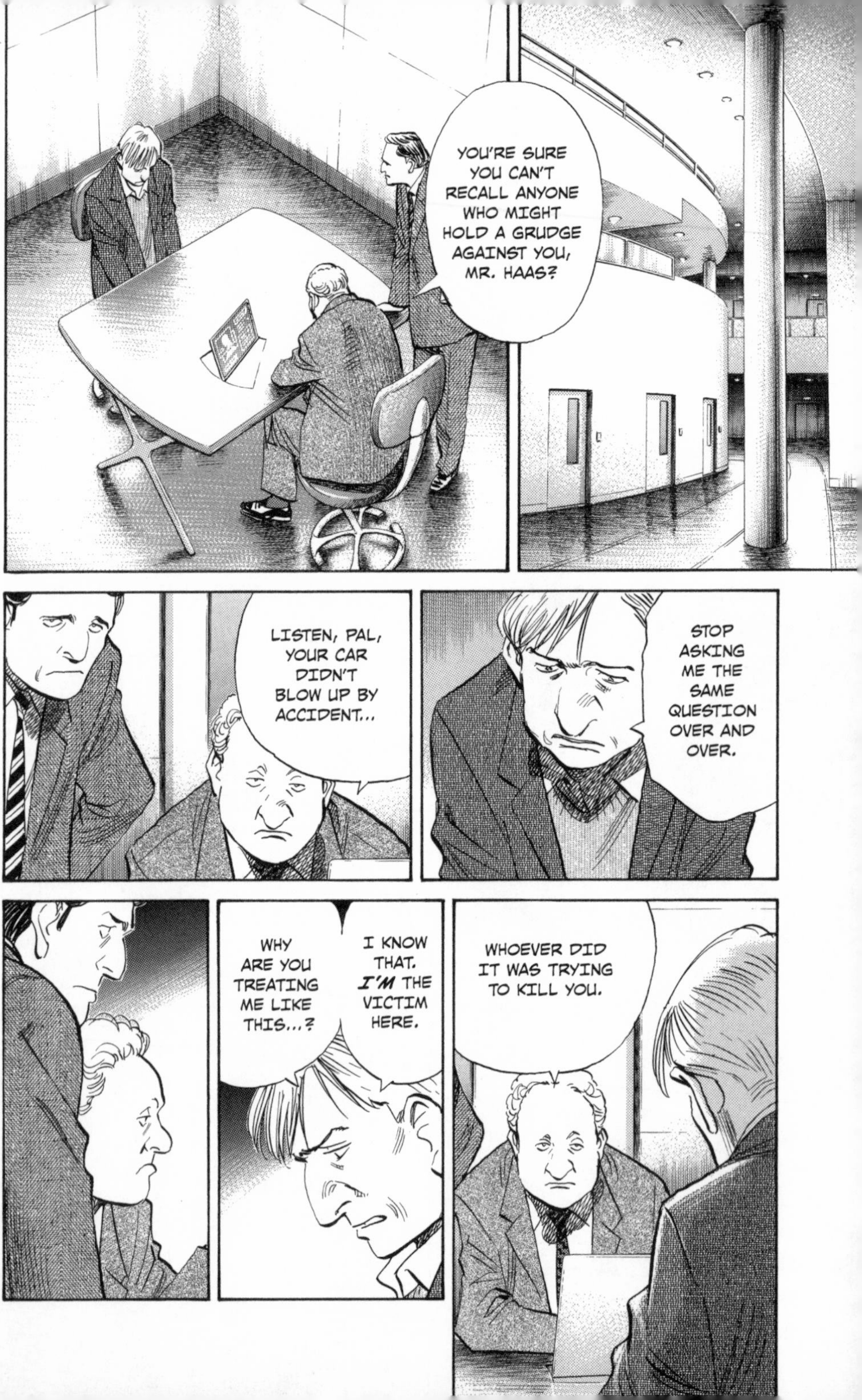
YOU'RE SURE YOU CAN'T RECALL ANYONE WHO MIGHT HOLD A GRUDGE AGAINST YOU, MR. HAAS?
STOP ASKING ME THE SAME QUESTION OVER AND OVER.
LISTEN, PAL, YOUR CAR DIDN'T BLOW UP BY ACCIDENT...
WHOEVER DID IT WAS TRYING TO KILL YOU.
I KNOW THAT. *I'M* THE VICTIM HERE.
WHY ARE YOU TREATING ME LIKE THIS...?

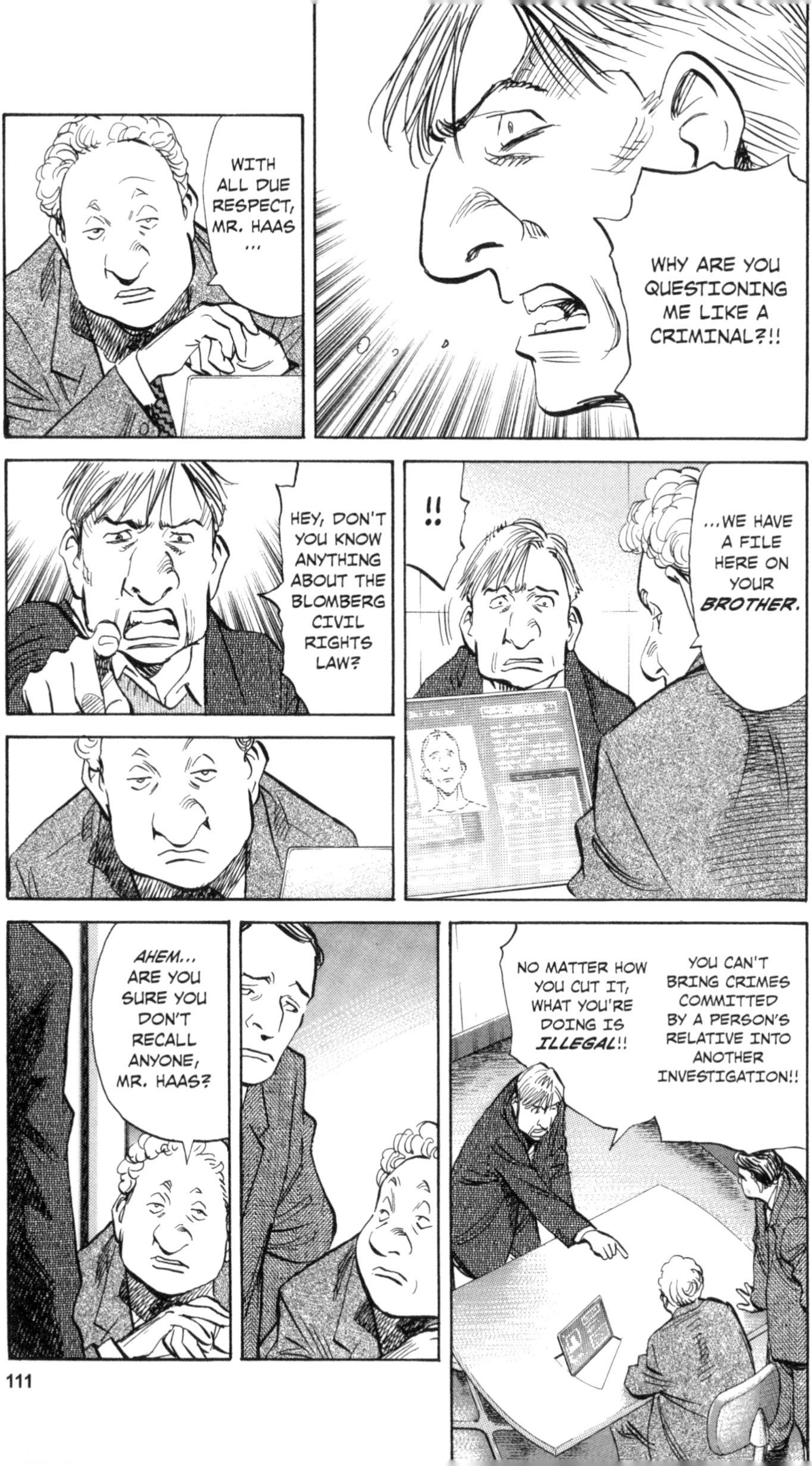
WHY ARE YOU QUESTIONING ME LIKE A CRIMINAL?!!
WITH ALL DUE RESPECT, MR. HAAS ...
...WE HAVE A FILE HERE ON YOUR *BROTHER.*
!!
HEY, DON'T YOU KNOW ANYTHING ABOUT THE BLOMBERG CIVIL RIGHTS LAW?
YOU CAN'T BRING CRIMES COMMITTED BY A PERSON'S RELATIVE INTO ANOTHER INVESTIGATION!!
NO MATTER HOW YOU CUT IT, WHAT YOU'RE DOING IS *ILLEGAL*!!
AHEM... ARE YOU SURE YOU DON'T RECALL ANYONE, MR. HAAS?

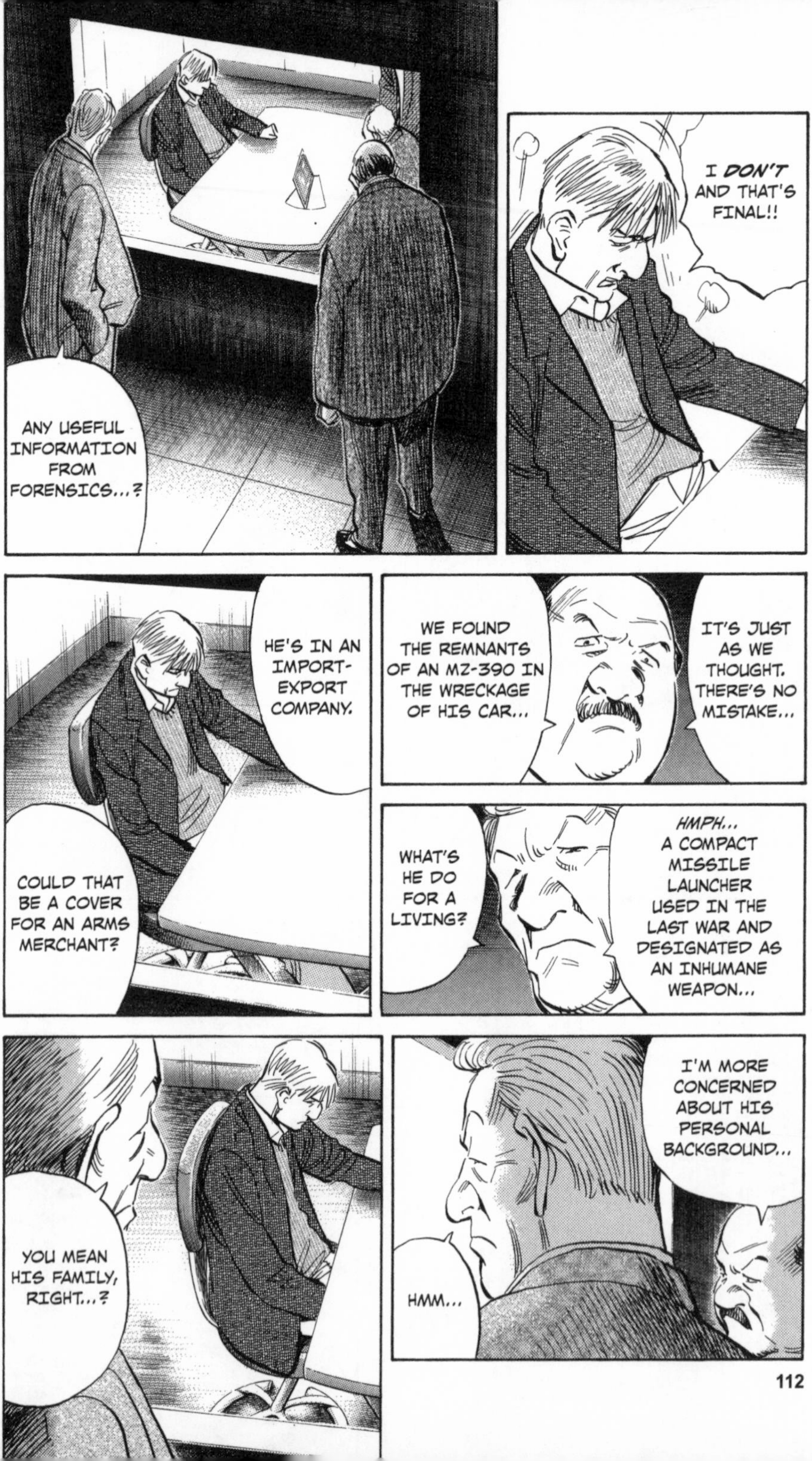
I *DON'T* AND THAT'S FINAL!!
ANY USEFUL INFORMATION FROM FORENSICS...?
IT'S JUST AS WE THOUGHT. THERE'S NO MISTAKE...
WE FOUND THE REMNANTS OF AN MZ-390 IN THE WRECKAGE OF HIS CAR...
HMPH... A COMPACT MISSILE LAUNCHER USED IN THE LAST WAR AND DESIGNATED AS AN INHUMANE WEAPON...
WHAT'S HE DO FOR A LIVING?
HE'S IN AN IMPORT-EXPORT COMPANY.
COULD THAT BE A COVER FOR AN ARMS MERCHANT?
I'M MORE CONCERNED ABOUT HIS PERSONAL BACKGROUND...
HMM...
YOU MEAN HIS FAMILY, RIGHT...?

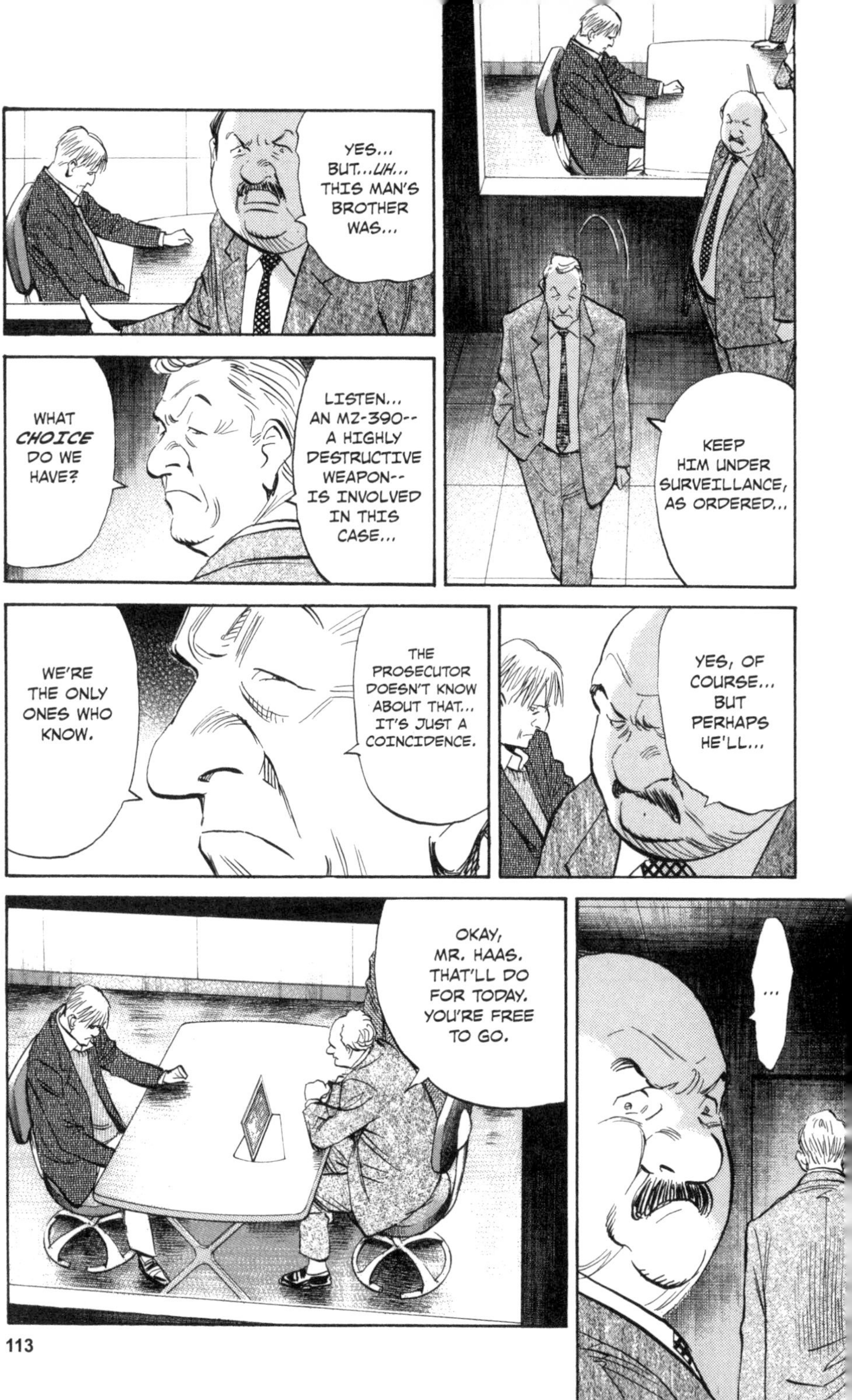
KEEP HIM UNDER SURVEILLANCE, AS ORDERED...
YES... BUT...UH... THIS MAN'S BROTHER WAS...
LISTEN... AN MZ-390-- A HIGHLY DESTRUCTIVE WEAPON-- IS INVOLVED IN THIS CASE...
WHAT CHOICE DO WE HAVE?
YES, OF COURSE... BUT PERHAPS HE'LL...
THE PROSECUTOR DOESN'T KNOW ABOUT THAT... IT'S JUST A COINCIDENCE.
WE'RE THE ONLY ONES WHO KNOW.
...
OKAY, MR. HAAS. THAT'LL DO FOR TODAY. YOU'RE FREE TO GO.

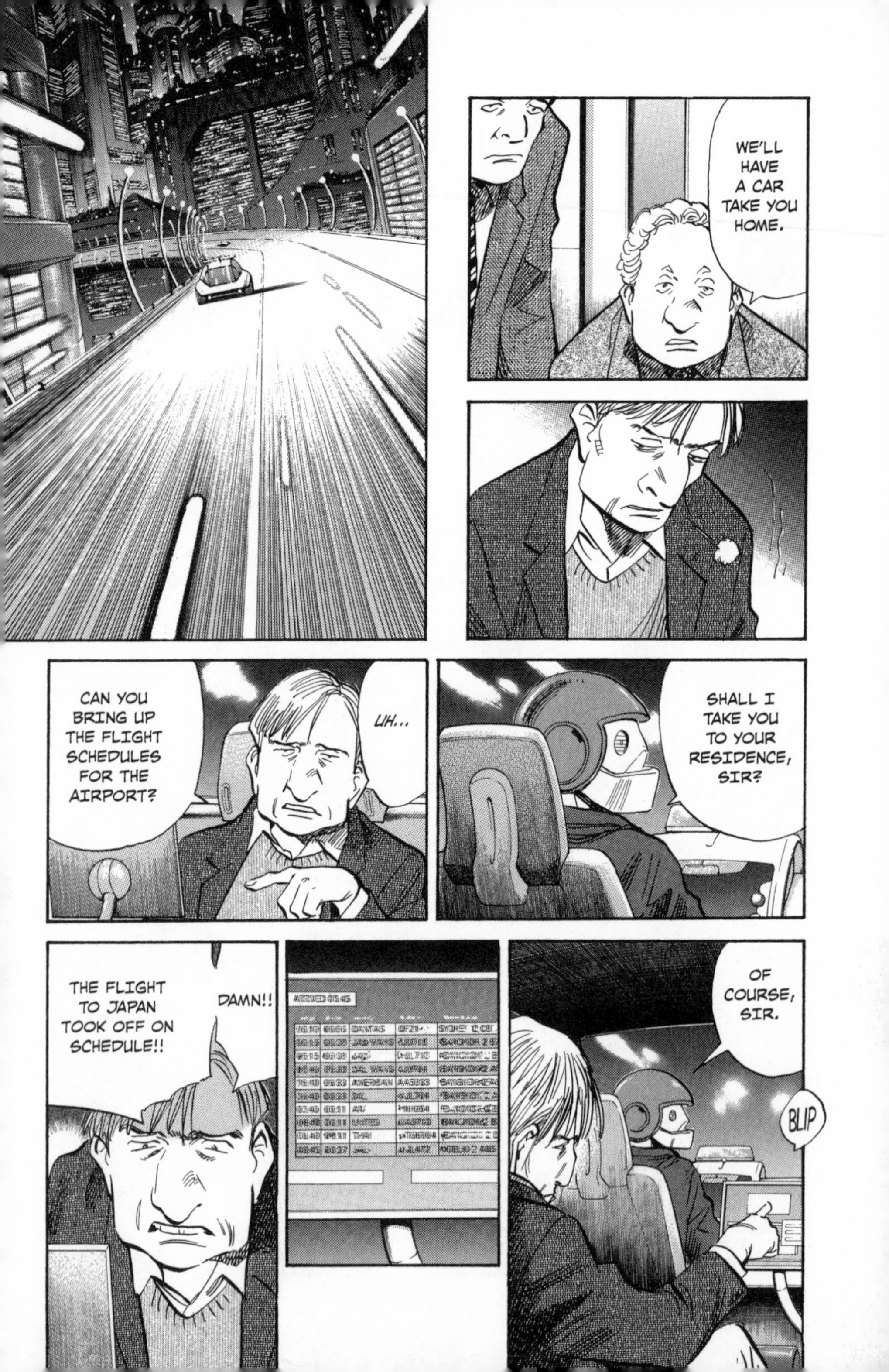
WE'LL HAVE A CAR TAKE YOU HOME.
SHALL I TAKE YOU TO YOUR RESIDENCE, SIR?
UH...
CAN YOU BRING UP THE FLIGHT SCHEDULES FOR THE AIRPORT?
OF COURSE, SIR.
BLIP
DAMN!!
THE FLIGHT TO JAPAN TOOK OFF ON SCHEDULE!!

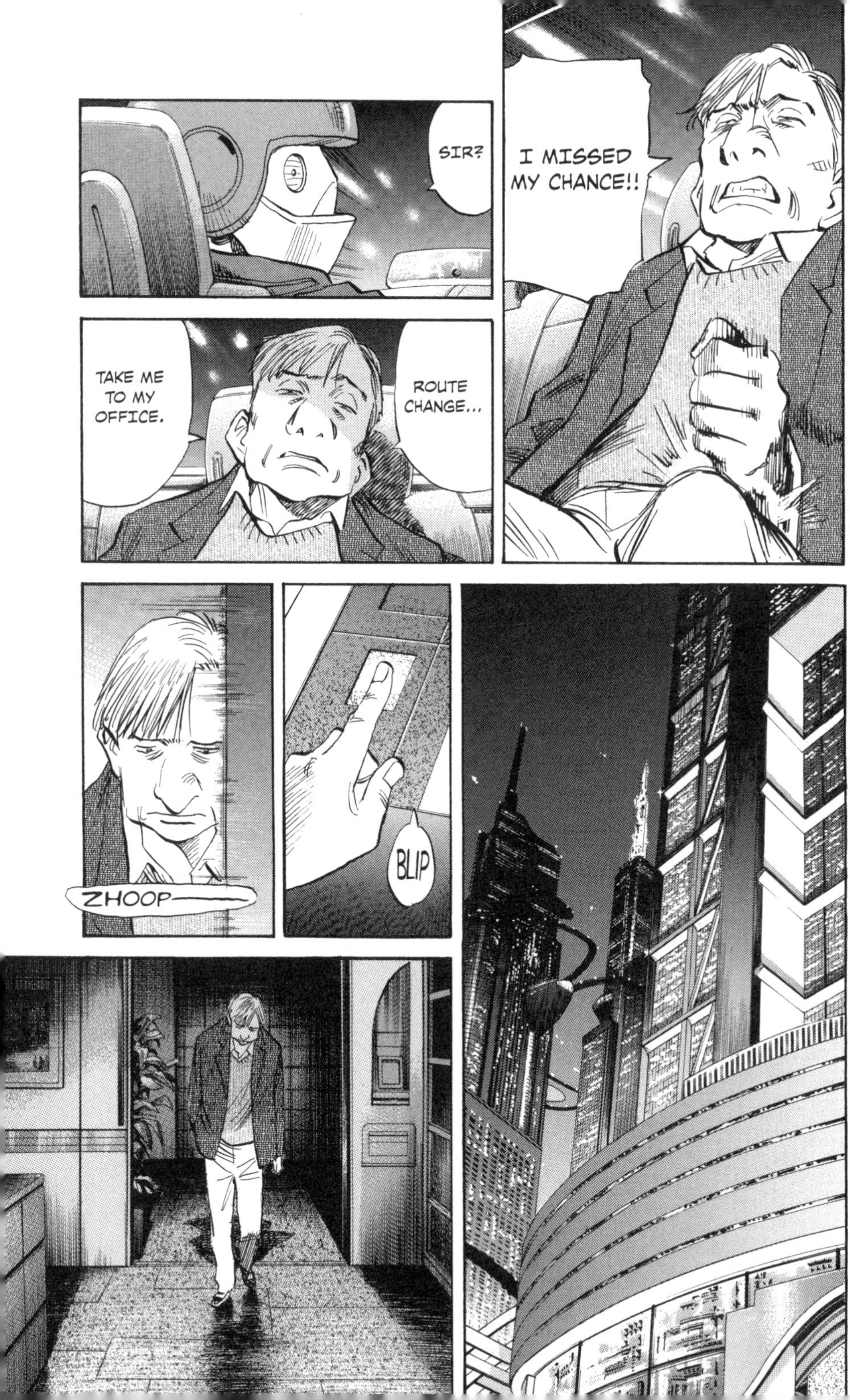
I MISSED MY CHANCE!!
SIR?
TAKE ME TO MY OFFICE.
ROUTE CHANGE...
BLIP
ZHOOP——

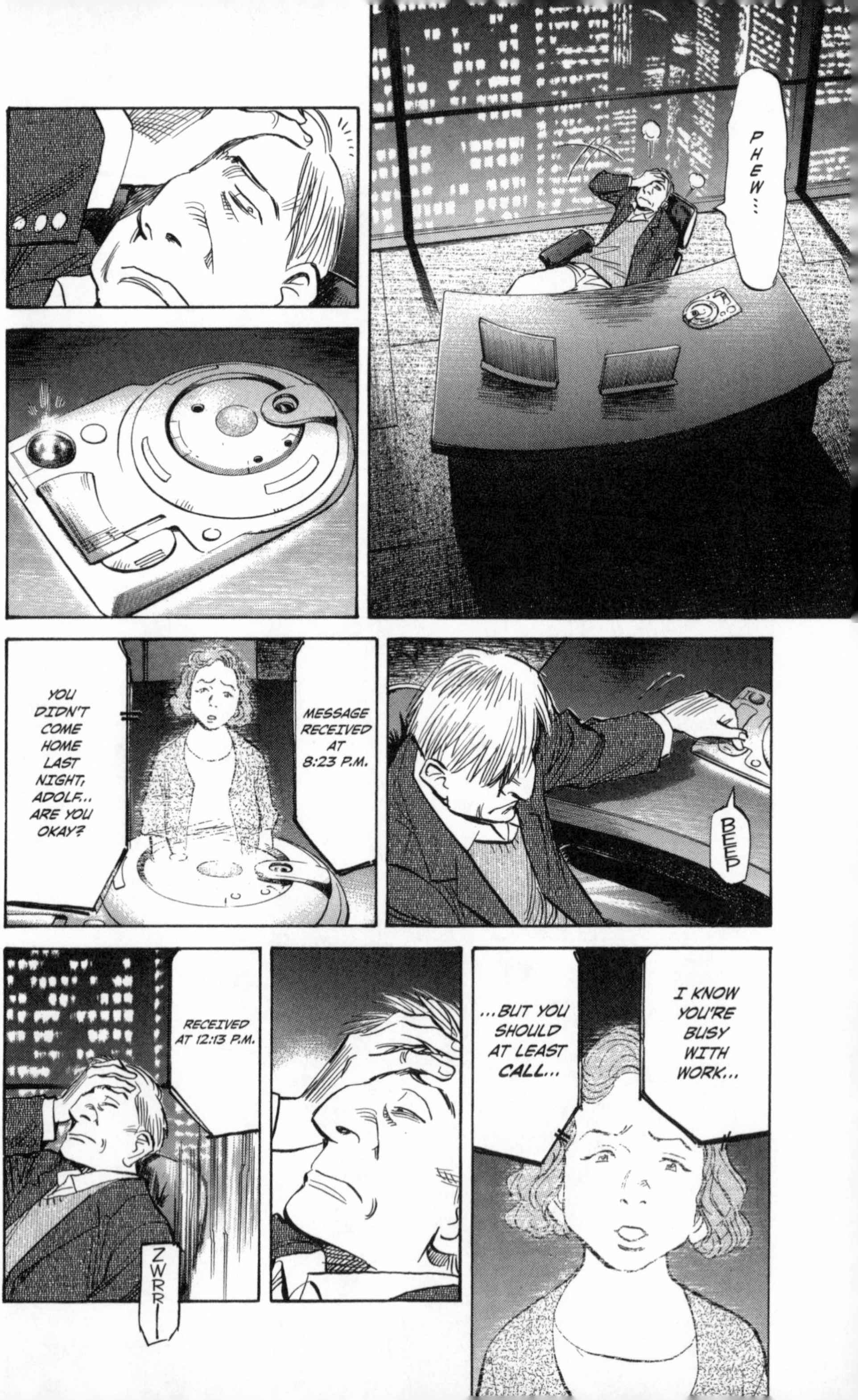
PHEW...
BEEP
MESSAGE RECEIVED AT 8:23 P.M.
YOU DIDN'T COME HOME LAST NIGHT, ADOLF... ARE YOU OKAY?
I KNOW YOU'RE BUSY WITH WORK...
...BUT YOU SHOULD AT LEAST CALL...
RECEIVED AT 12:13 P.M.
ZWRR

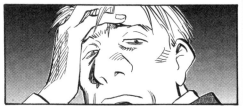

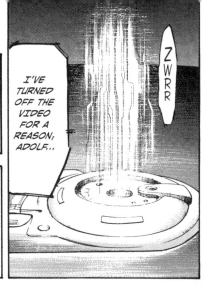

ZWRR
I'VE TURNED OFF THE VIDEO FOR A REASON, ADOLF...
I MUST WARN YOU...
ZWRRI
YOU'RE IN DANGER...
THAT "JOB" YOU WERE TRYING TO FINISH...
ZWRRI
...HAS BECOME A LIABILITY FOR THE COUNCIL...
THE CHAIRMAN WANTS TO GET RID OF YOU... **PERMANENTLY...**
ZWRRI
BLIP

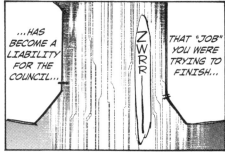

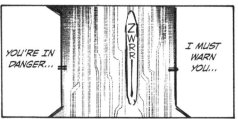

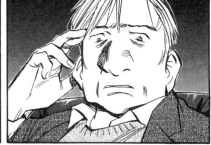

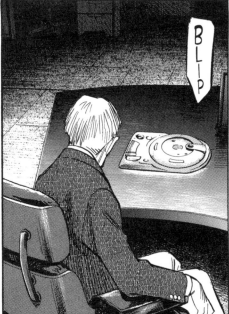

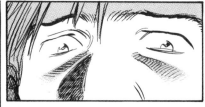

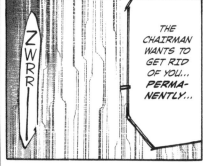

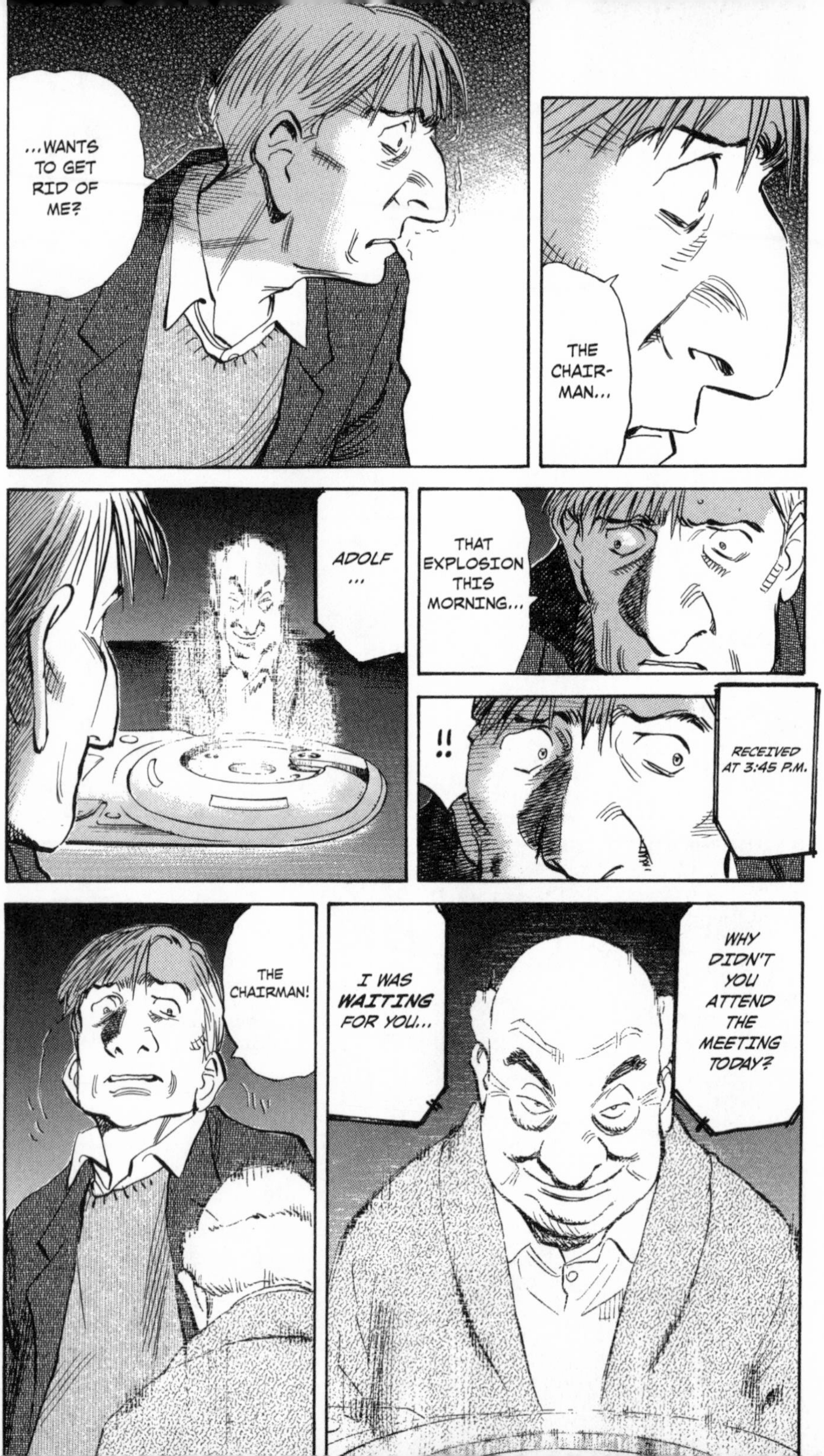
THE CHAIR-MAN...
...WANTS TO GET RID OF ME?
THAT EXPLOSION THIS MORNING...
RECEIVED AT 3:45 P.M.
!!
ADOLF ...
WHY DIDN'T YOU ATTEND THE MEETING TODAY?
I WAS **WAITING** FOR YOU...
THE CHAIRMAN!

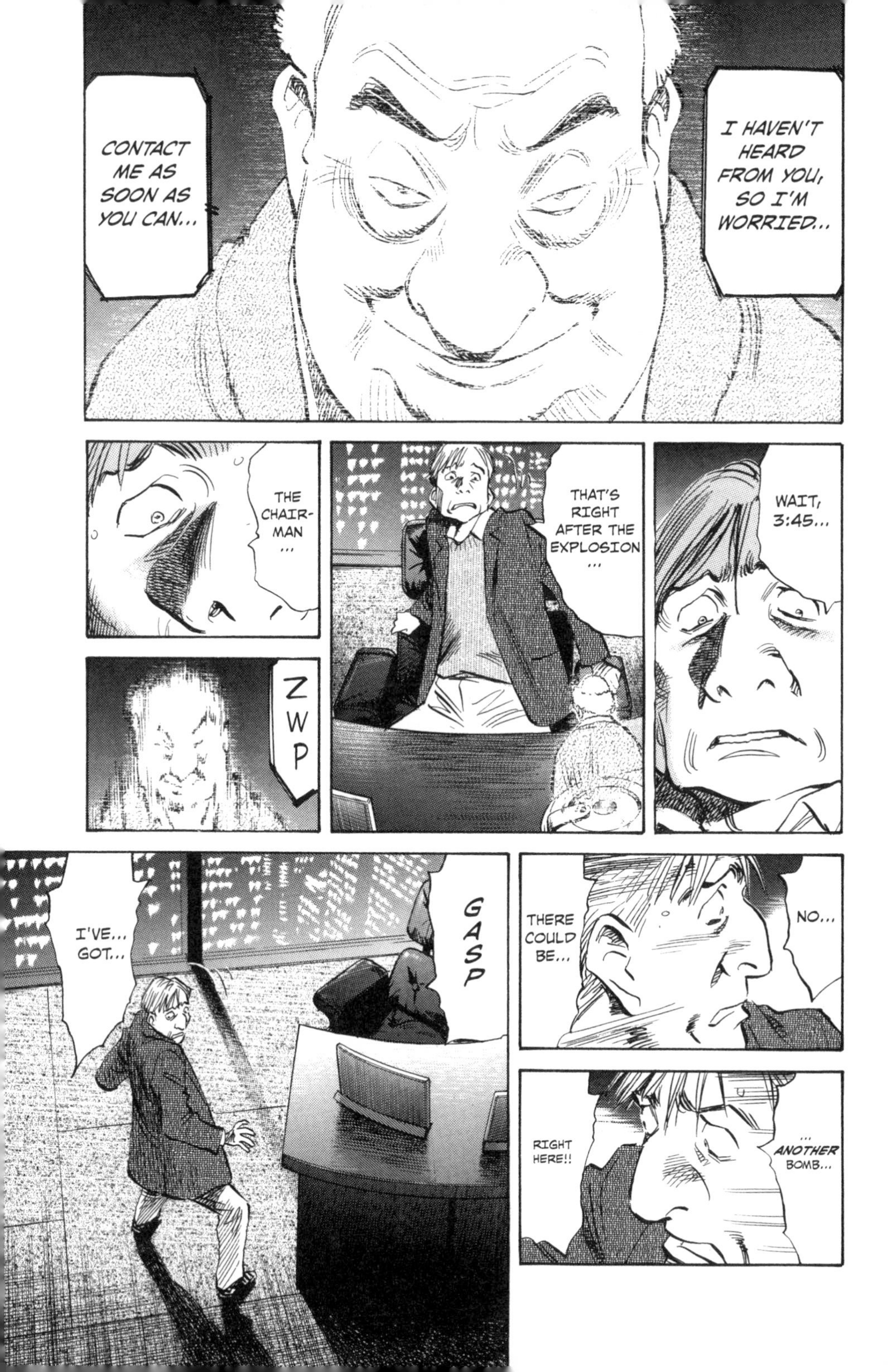
I HAVEN'T HEARD FROM YOU, SO I'M WORRIED...
CONTACT ME AS SOON AS YOU CAN...
WAIT, 3:45...
THAT'S RIGHT AFTER THE EXPLOSION ...
THE CHAIR-MAN ...
ZWP
NO...
THERE COULD BE...
... ANOTHER BOMB...
RIGHT HERE!!
GASP
I'VE... GOT...

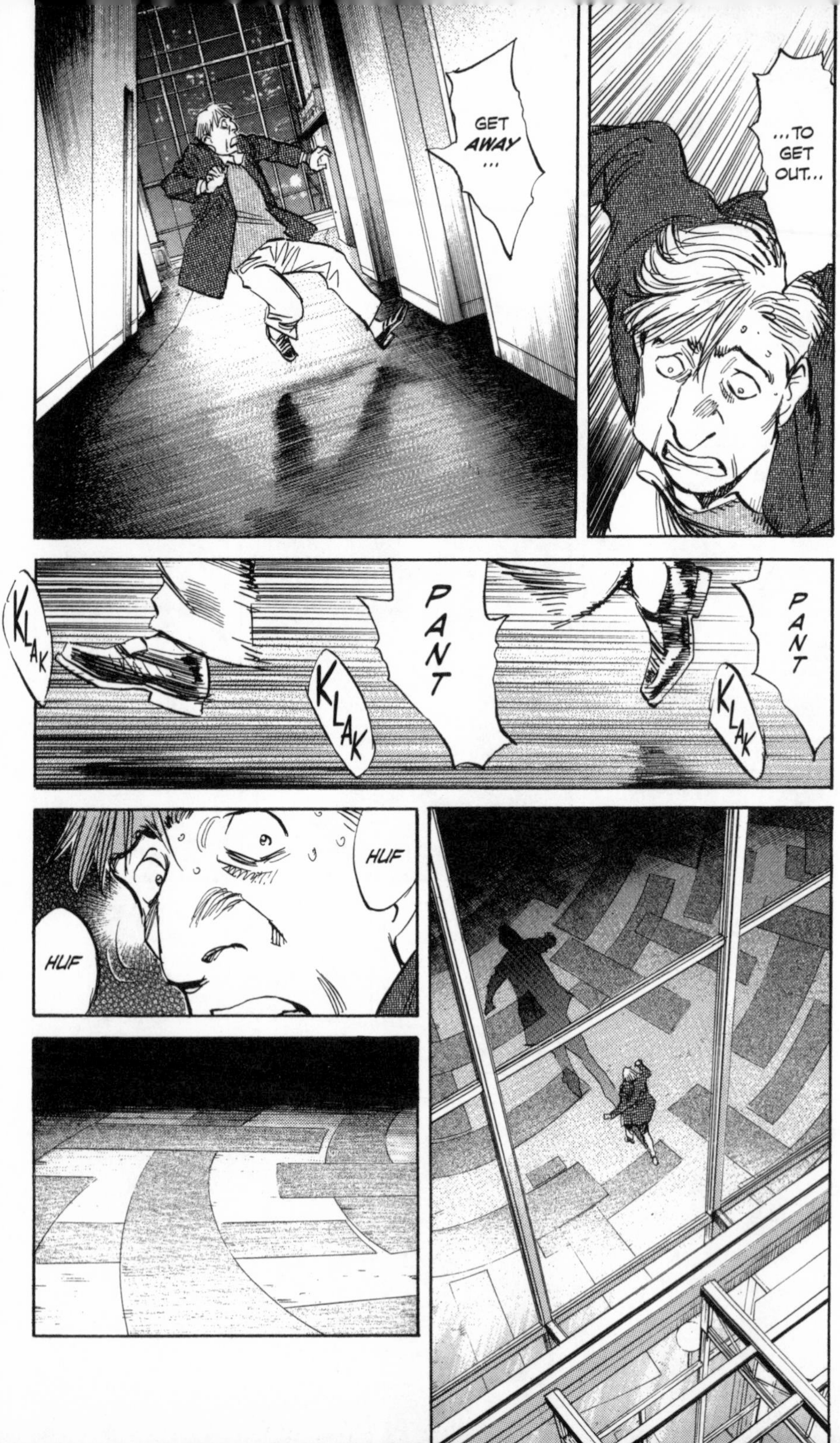
...TO GET OUT...
GET AWAY ...
PANT
KLAK
PANT
KLAK
KLAK
HUF
HUF

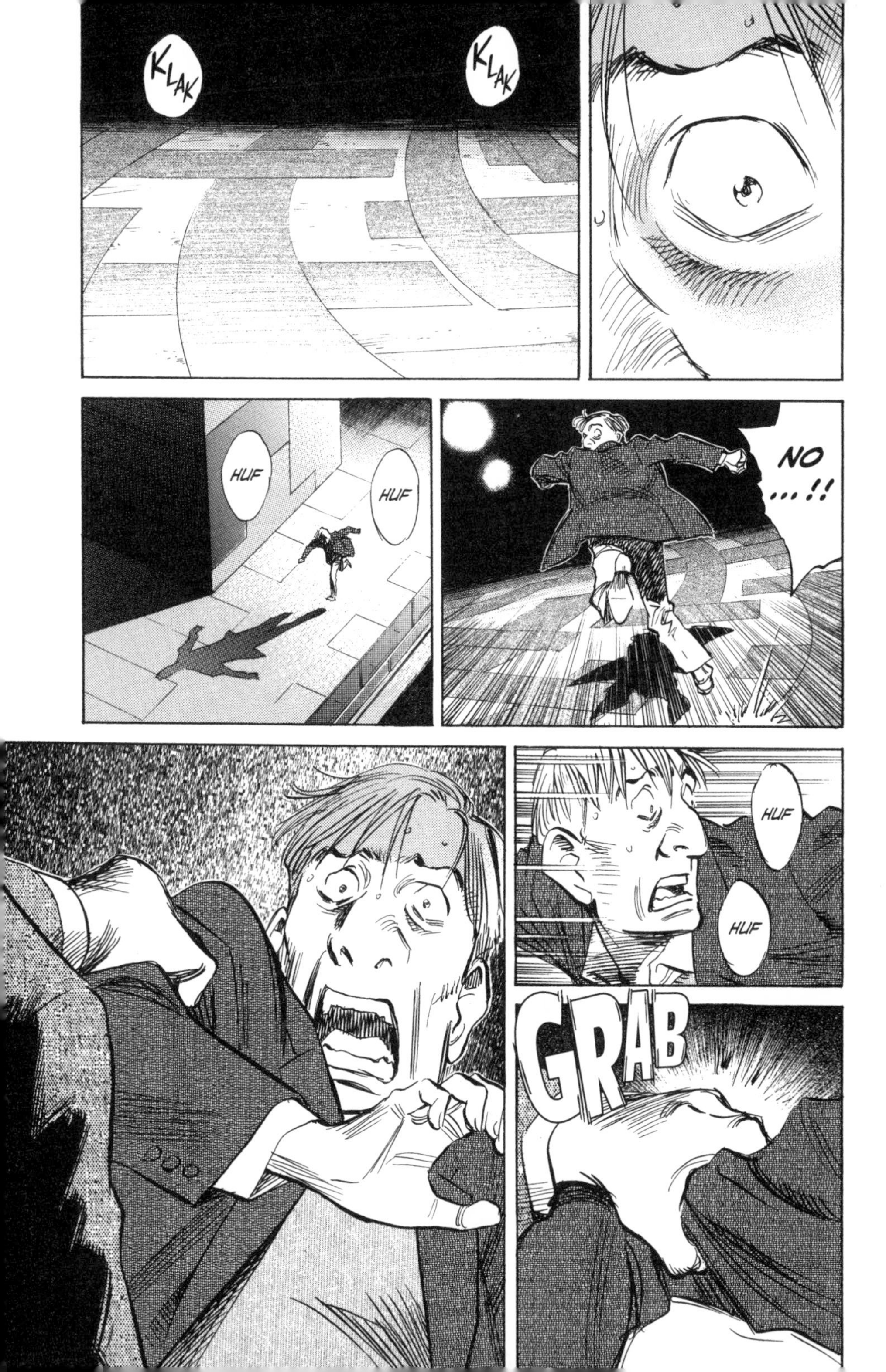
KLAK
KLAK
NO ...!!
HUF
HUF
HUF
HUF
GRAB

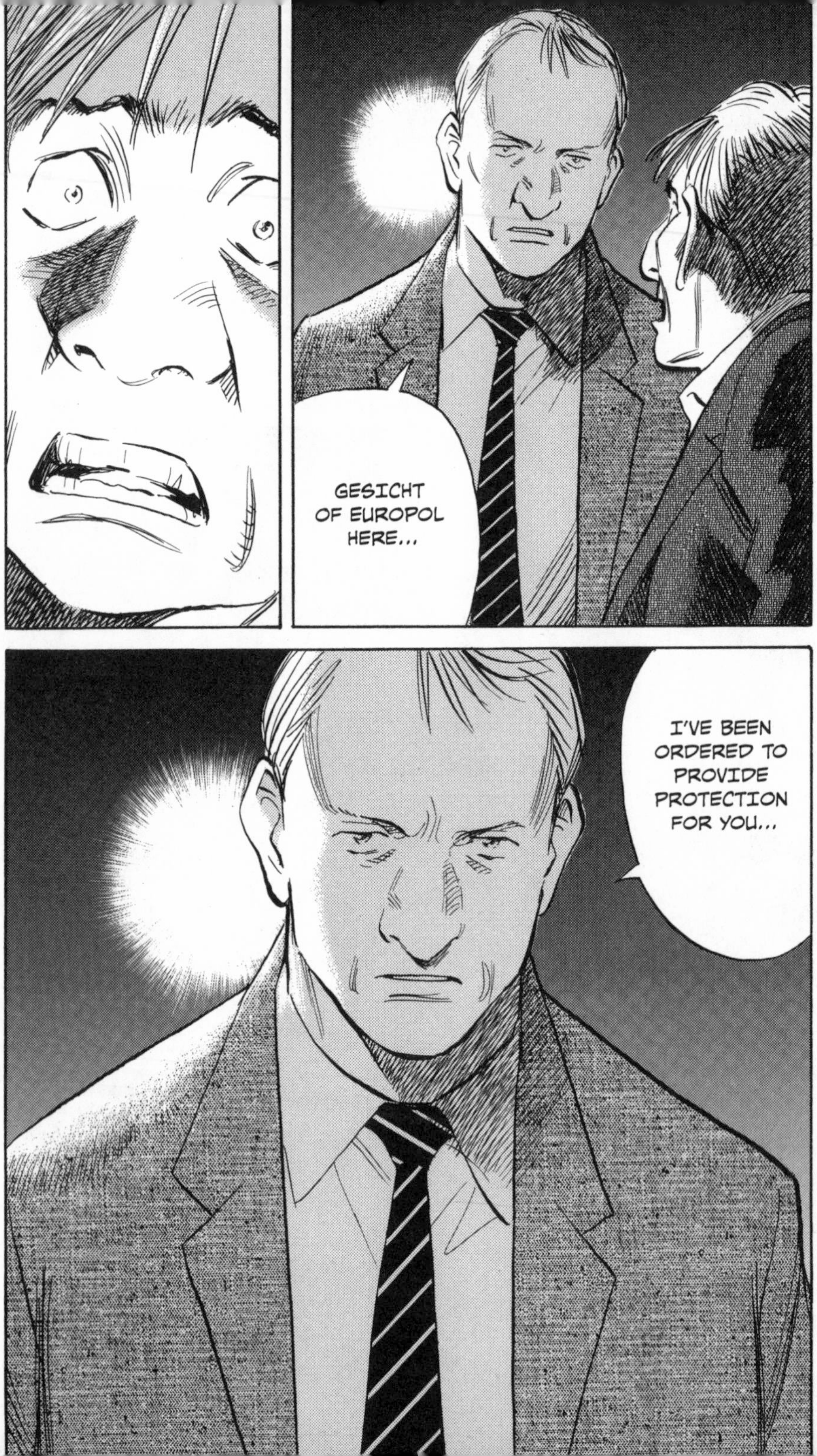
GESICHT OF EUROPOL HERE...
I'VE BEEN ORDERED TO PROVIDE PROTECTION FOR YOU...

Act 29 Whispering Shadows

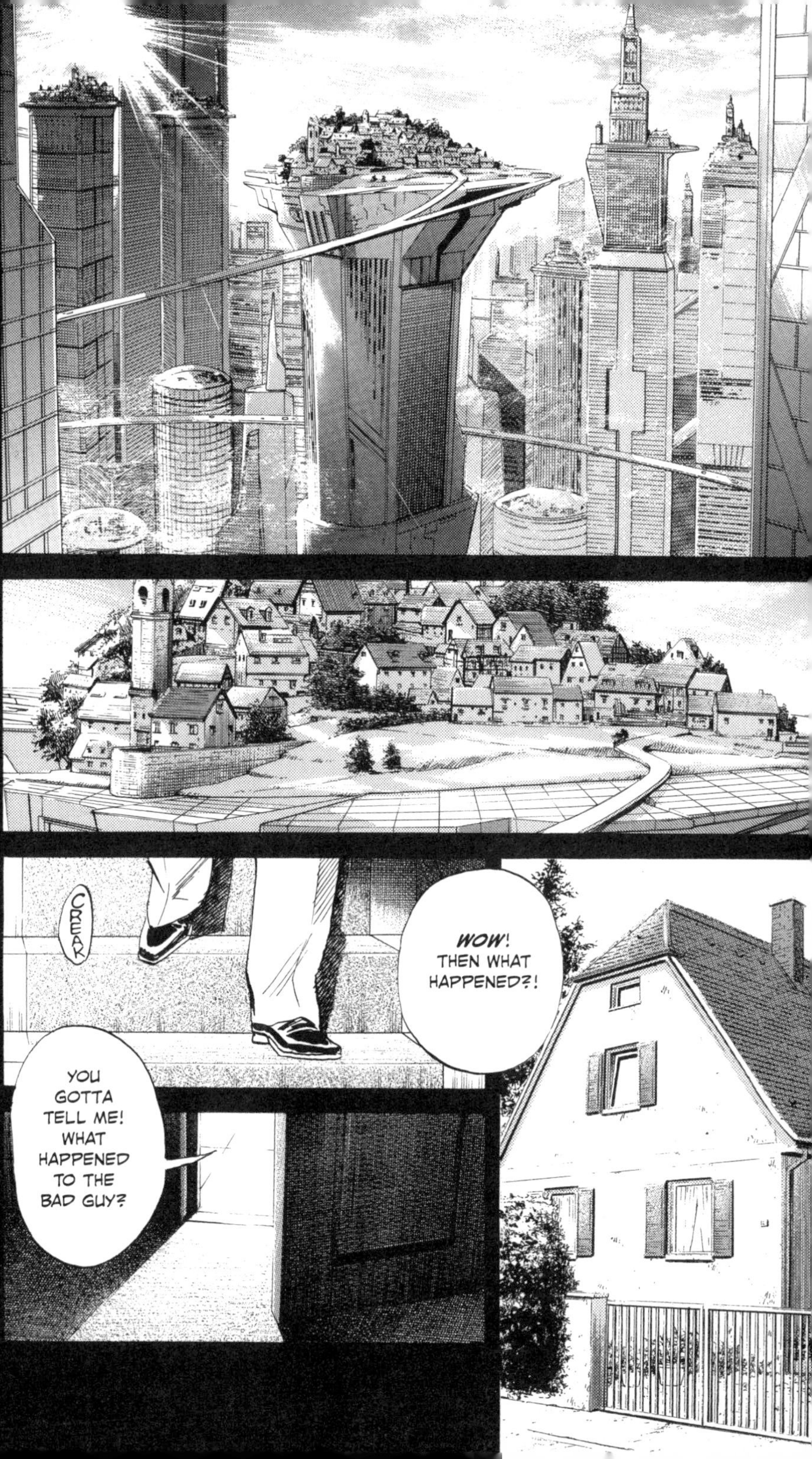
WOW! THEN WHAT HAPPENED?!
CREAK
YOU GOTTA TELL ME! WHAT HAPPENED TO THE BAD GUY?

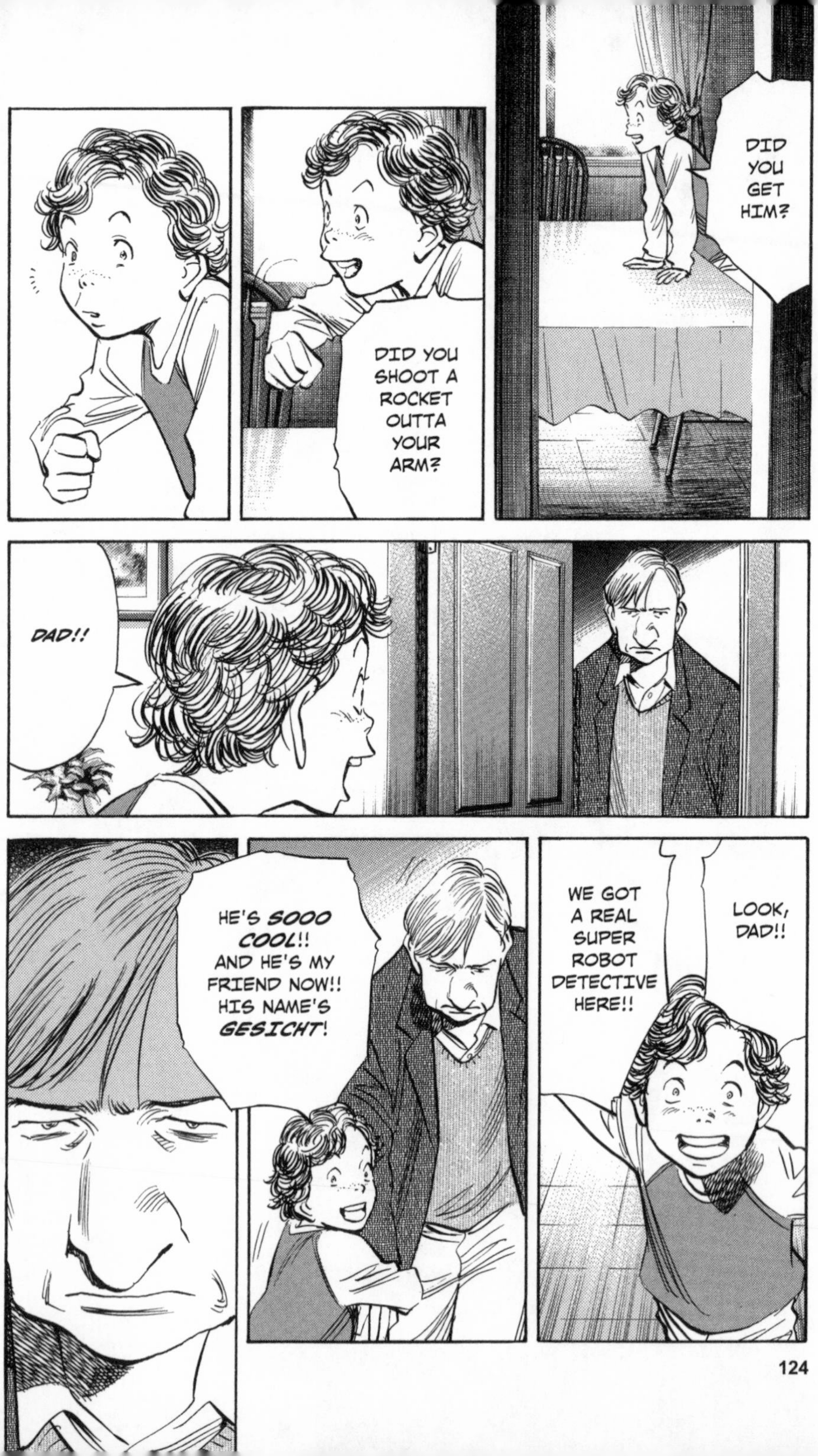
DID YOU GET HIM?
DID YOU SHOOT A ROCKET OUTTA YOUR ARM?
DAD!!
LOOK, DAD!!
WE GOT A REAL SUPER ROBOT DETECTIVE HERE!!
HE'S ***SOOO COOL***!! AND HE'S MY FRIEND NOW!! HIS NAME'S ***GESICHT***!

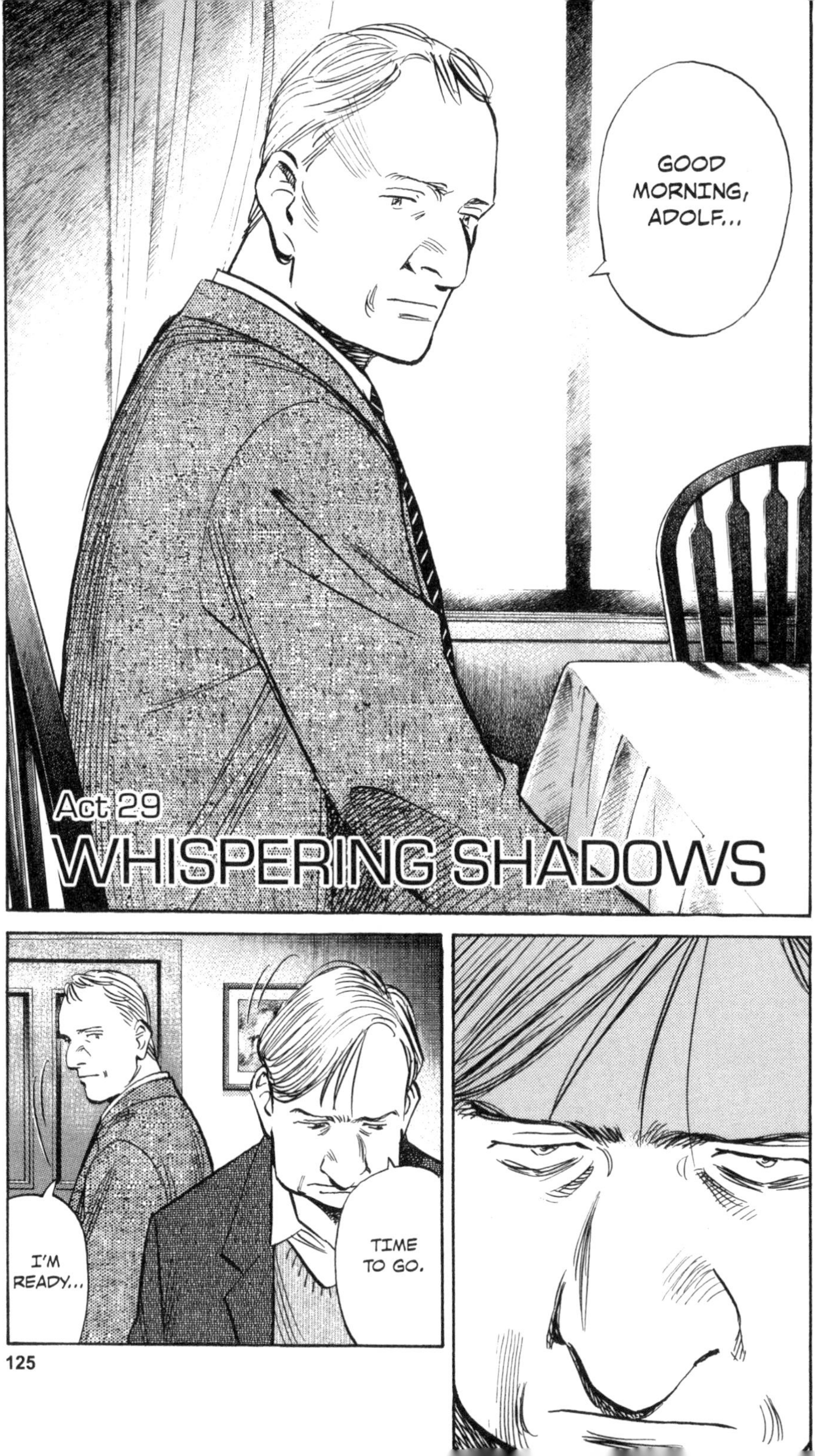
GOOD MORNING, ADOLF...
Act 29
WHISPERING SHADOWS
TIME TO GO.
I'M READY...

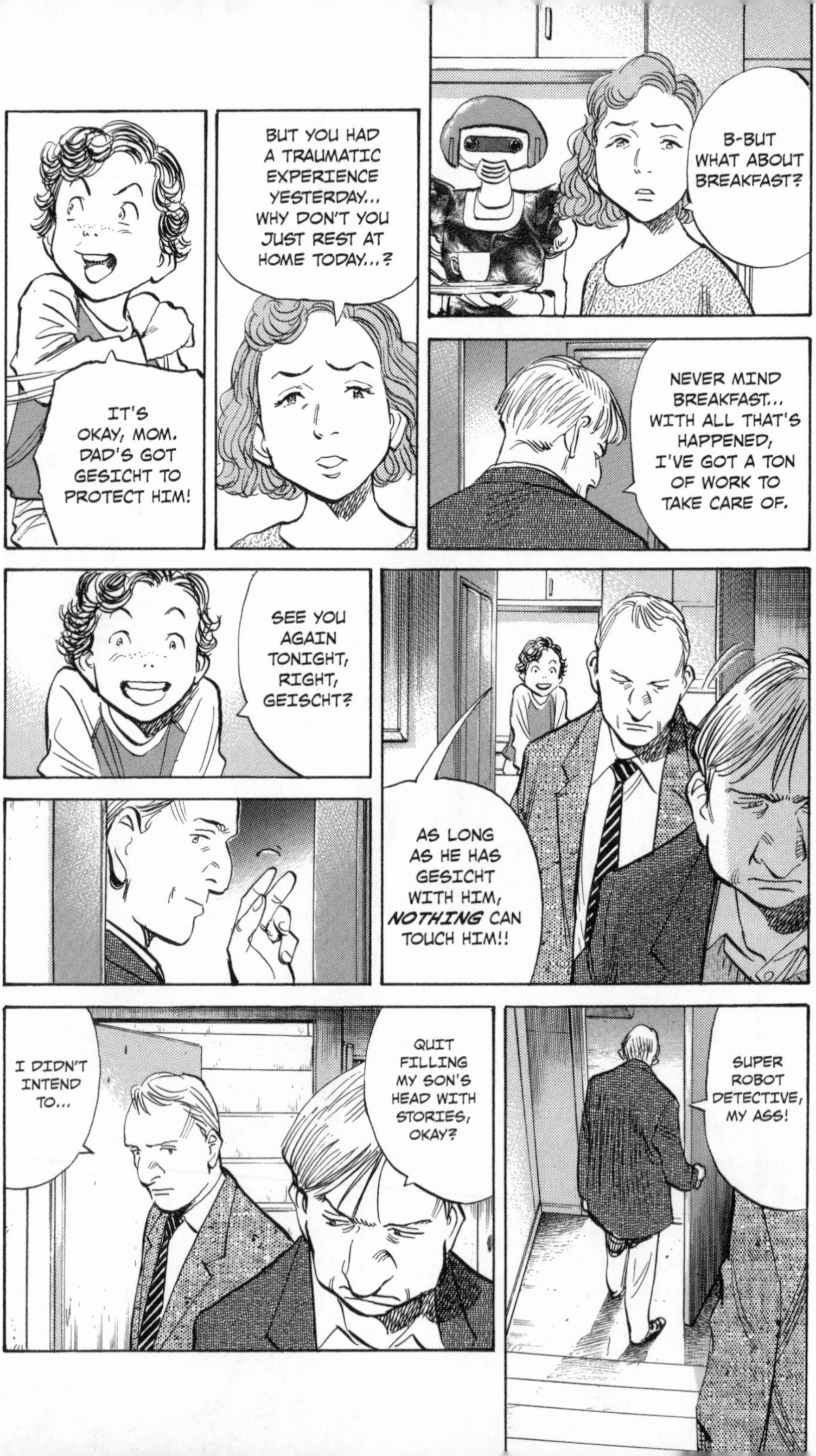
B-BUT WHAT ABOUT BREAKFAST?
NEVER MIND BREAKFAST... WITH ALL THAT'S HAPPENED, I'VE GOT A TON OF WORK TO TAKE CARE OF.
BUT YOU HAD A TRAUMATIC EXPERIENCE YESTERDAY... WHY DON'T YOU JUST REST AT HOME TODAY...?
IT'S OKAY, MOM. DAD'S GOT GESICHT TO PROTECT HIM!
AS LONG AS HE HAS GESICHT WITH HIM, ***NOTHING*** CAN TOUCH HIM!!
SEE YOU AGAIN TONIGHT, RIGHT, GEISCHT?
SUPER ROBOT DETECTIVE, MY ASS!
QUIT FILLING MY SON'S HEAD WITH STORIES, OKAY?
I DIDN'T INTEND TO...

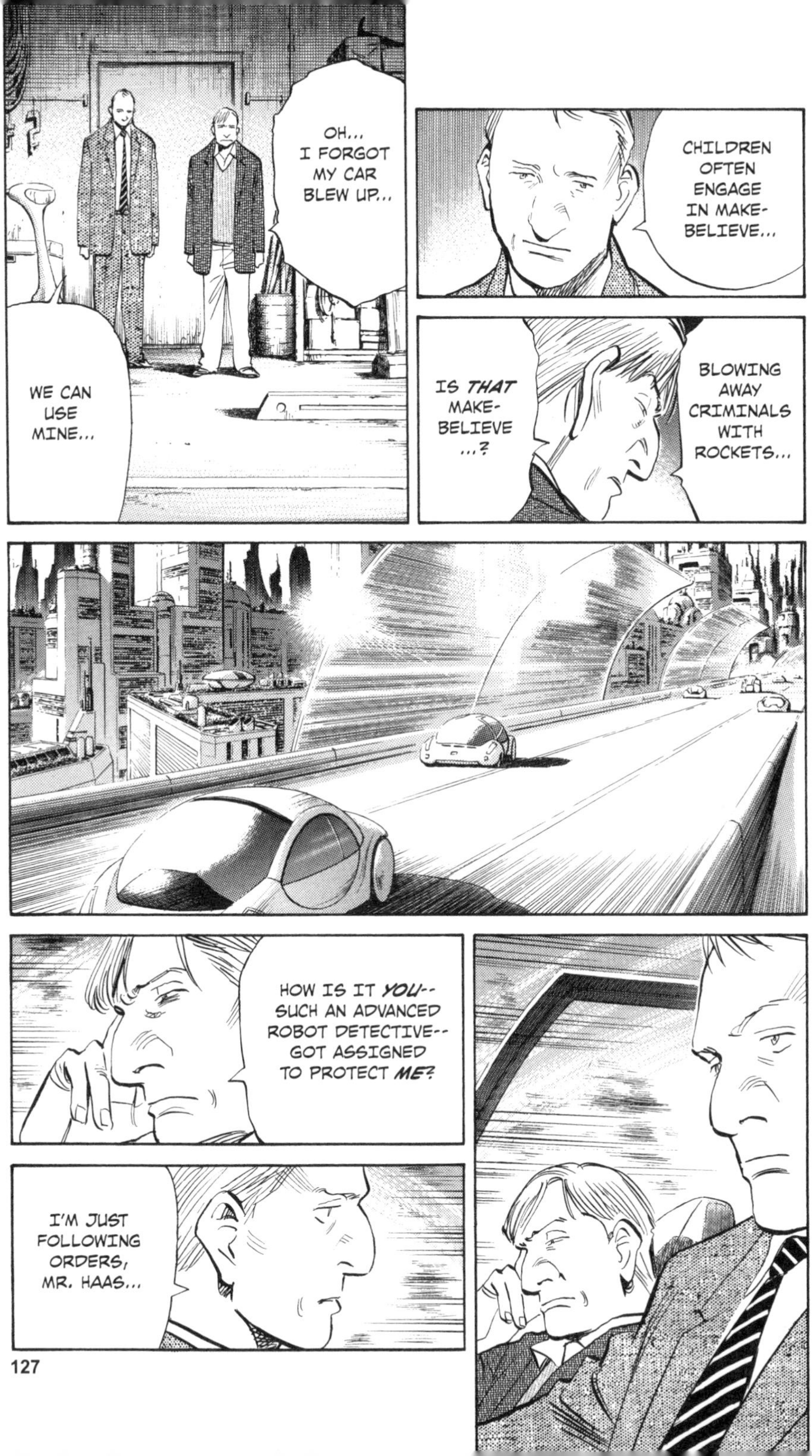
CHILDREN OFTEN ENGAGE IN MAKE-BELIEVE...
BLOWING AWAY CRIMINALS WITH ROCKETS...
IS *THAT* MAKE-BELIEVE...?
OH... I FORGOT MY CAR BLEW UP...
WE CAN USE MINE...
HOW IS IT *YOU*--SUCH AN ADVANCED ROBOT DETECTIVE--GOT ASSIGNED TO PROTECT *ME*?
I'M JUST FOLLOWING ORDERS, MR. HAAS...

!!

HOW DID YOU KNOW THAT?

SO IS *THIS* WHY YOU CANCELLED YOUR VACATION?

DO YOU HATE ROBOTS?

LET ME ASK YOU, MR. HAAS...

...FROM YOUR BOSS...

I... *UH...* HEARD ABOUT IT...

IF SO, I'M SORRY YOU WOUND UP WITH A ROBOT BODYGUARD...

BUT PLEASE DON'T FORGET, I'M ONLY CARRYING OUT ORDERS.

128

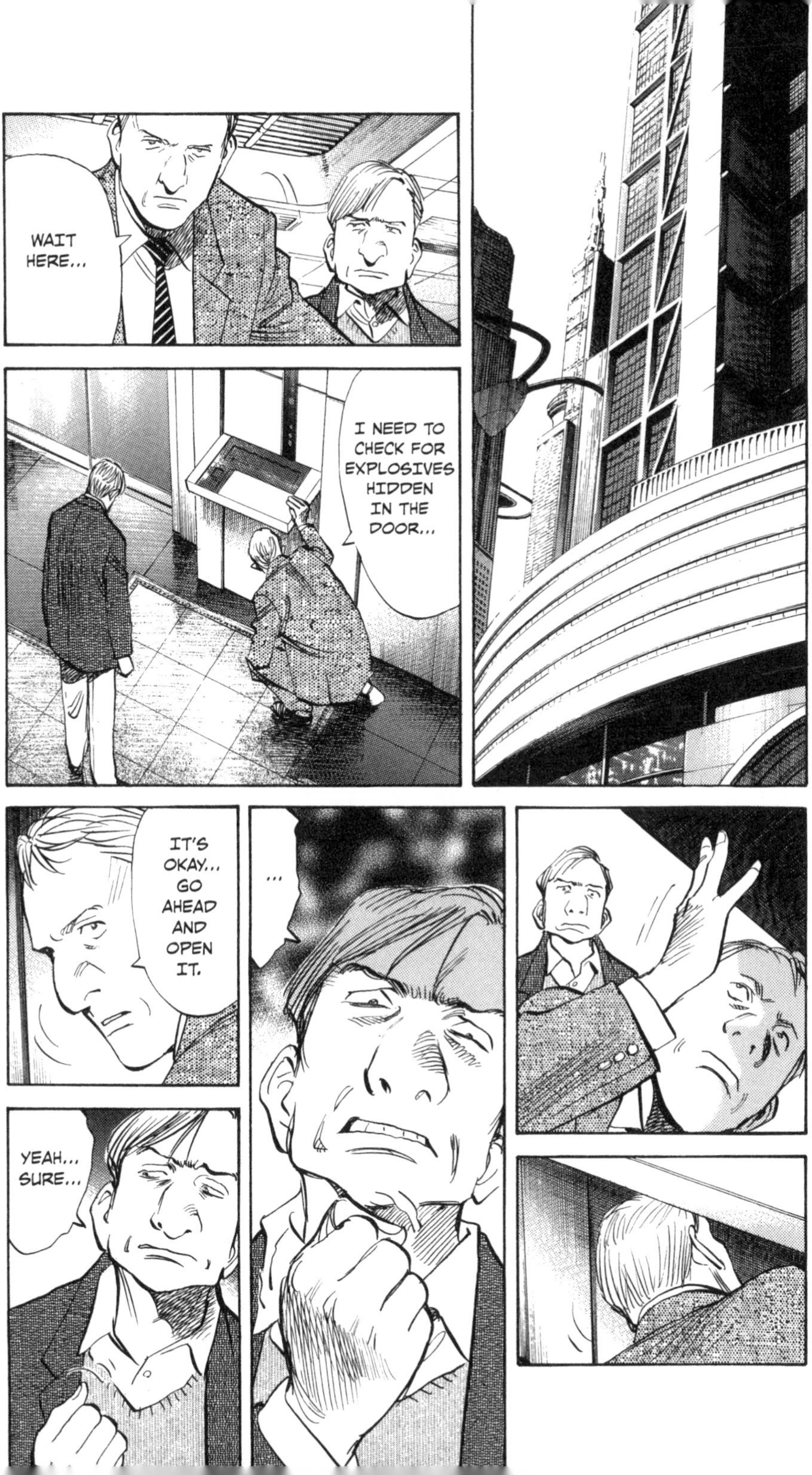
WAIT HERE...
I NEED TO CHECK FOR EXPLOSIVES HIDDEN IN THE DOOR...
...
IT'S OKAY... GO AHEAD AND OPEN IT.
YEAH... SURE...

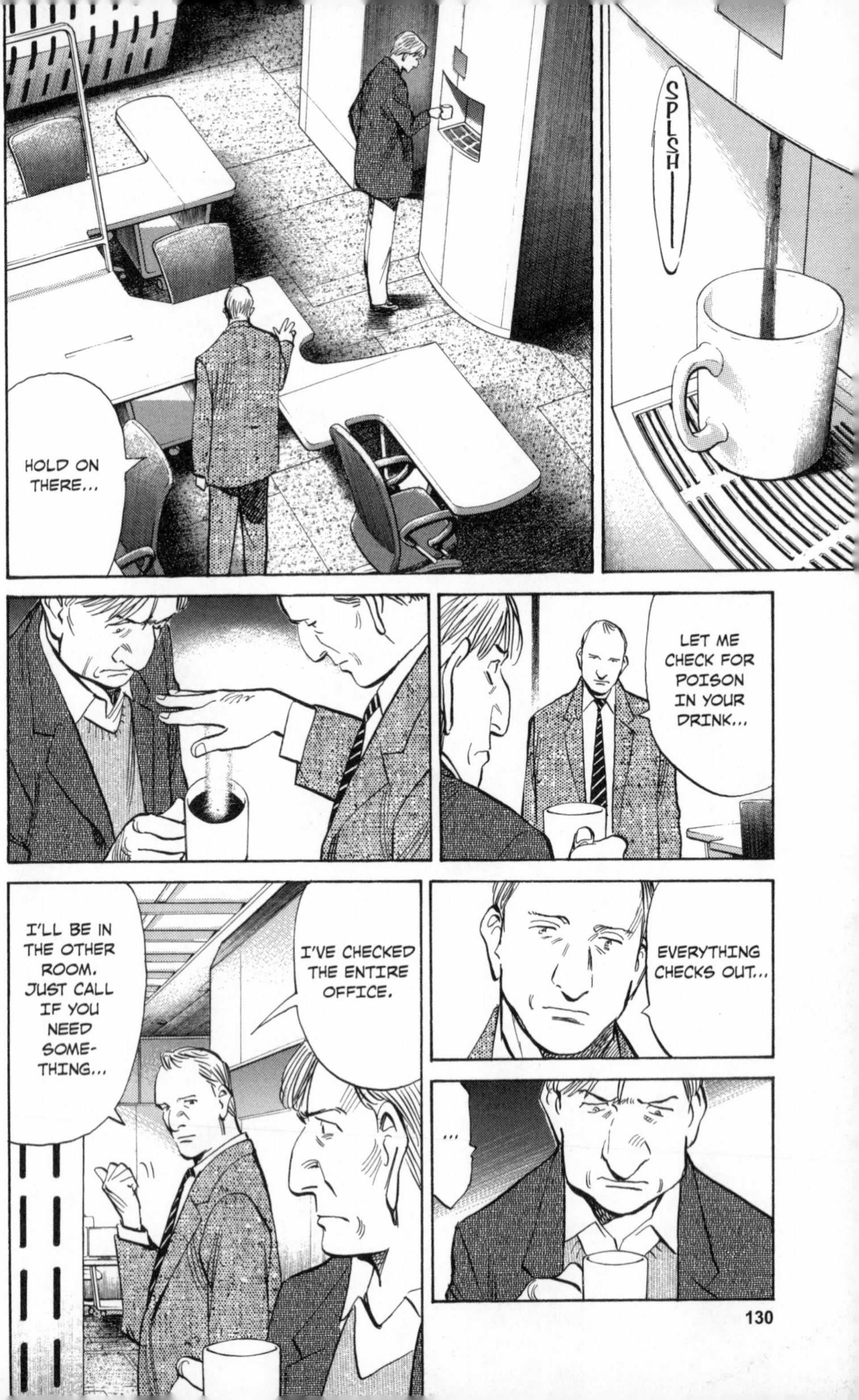
SPLSH
HOLD ON THERE...
LET ME CHECK FOR POISON IN YOUR DRINK...
EVERYTHING CHECKS OUT...
...
I'VE CHECKED THE ENTIRE OFFICE.
I'LL BE IN THE OTHER ROOM. JUST CALL IF YOU NEED SOME-THING...

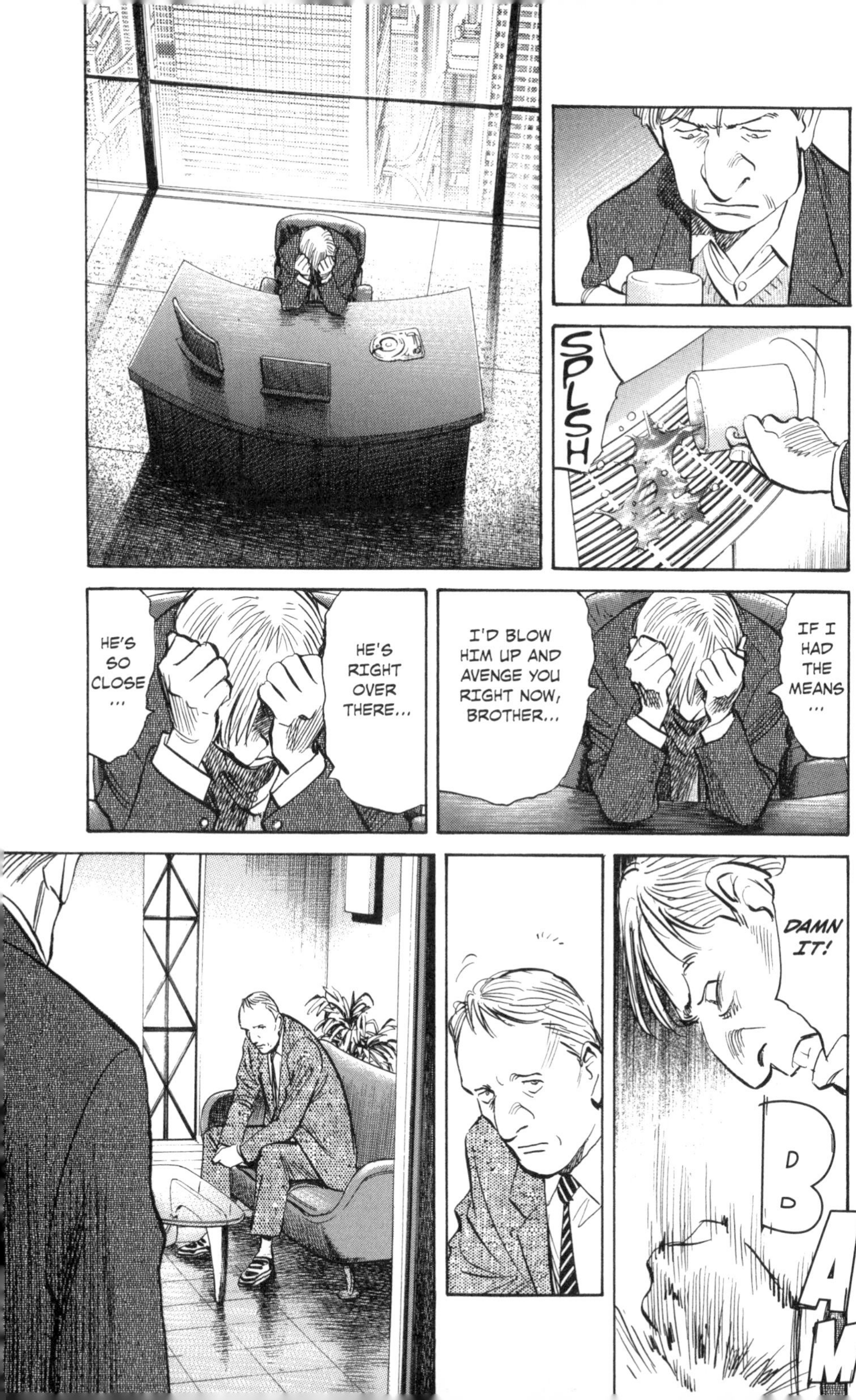
SPLSH
IF I HAD THE MEANS...
I'D BLOW HIM UP AND AVENGE YOU RIGHT NOW, BROTHER...
HE'S RIGHT OVER THERE...
HE'S SO CLOSE...
DAMN IT!
BAM

I CAN'T THINK STRAIGHT WITH YOU HERE.

CAN'T YOU JUST LEAVE?

SOME-THING WRONG?

WE'RE TRYING TO PROTECT...

JUST WHAT ARE YOU AFTER?

I'VE BEEN ORDERED TO GUARD YOU...

I'M SORRY, MR. HAAS...

PLEASE, MR. HAAS...

YOU SAY YOU'RE PROTECTING ME, BUT WHAT YOU'RE REALLY TRYING TO DO IS GET INFORMATION ABOUT ME, RIGHT?

LIAR!!

LOOK, I KNOW THAT ALL YOU COPS THINK I'M A *SUSPECT*!!

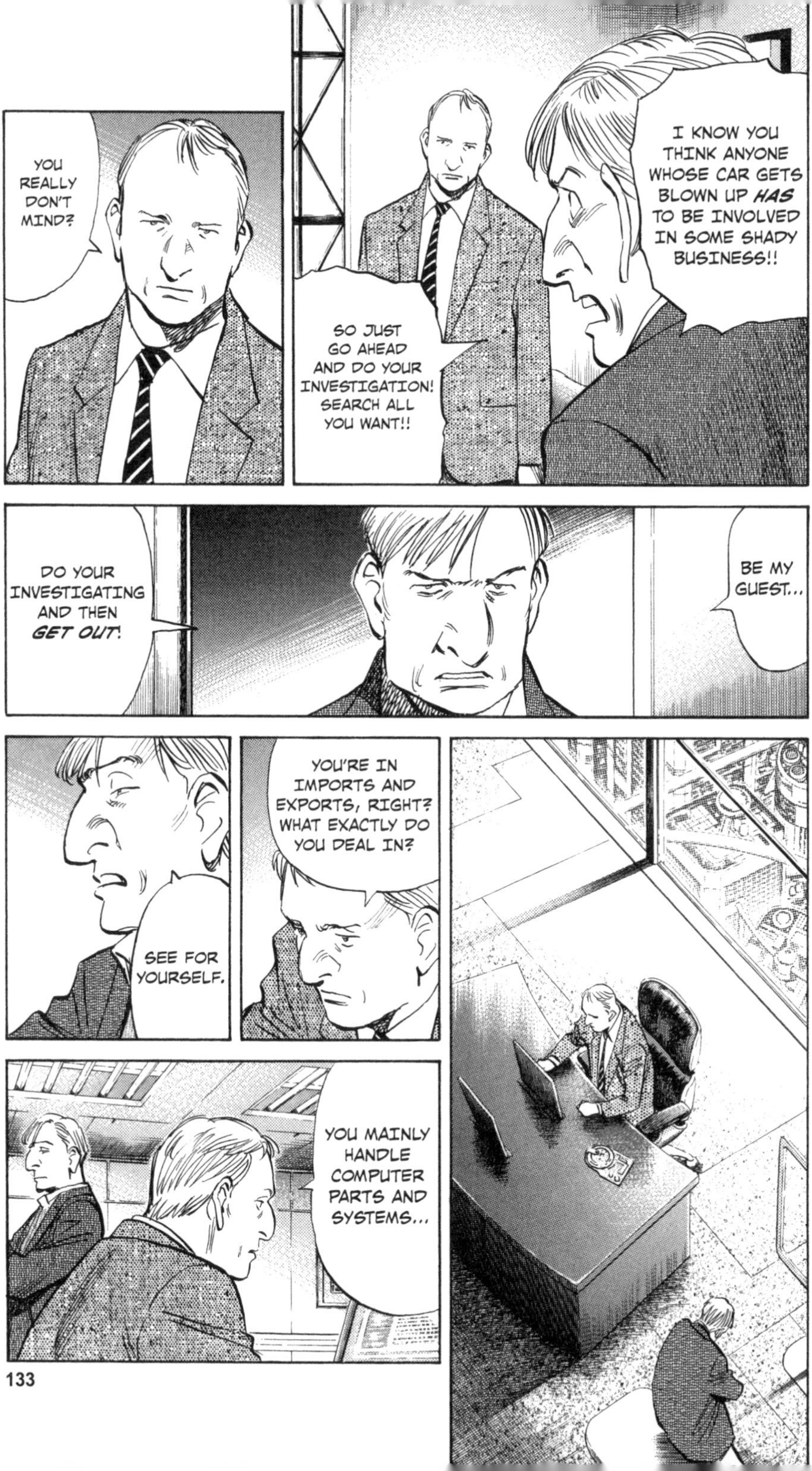
I KNOW YOU THINK ANYONE WHOSE CAR GETS BLOWN UP ***HAS*** TO BE INVOLVED IN SOME SHADY BUSINESS!!
SO JUST GO AHEAD AND DO YOUR INVESTIGATION! SEARCH ALL YOU WANT!!
YOU REALLY DON'T MIND?
BE MY GUEST...
DO YOUR INVESTIGATING AND THEN ***GET OUT***!
YOU'RE IN IMPORTS AND EXPORTS, RIGHT? WHAT EXACTLY DO YOU DEAL IN?
SEE FOR YOURSELF.
YOU MAINLY HANDLE COMPUTER PARTS AND SYSTEMS...

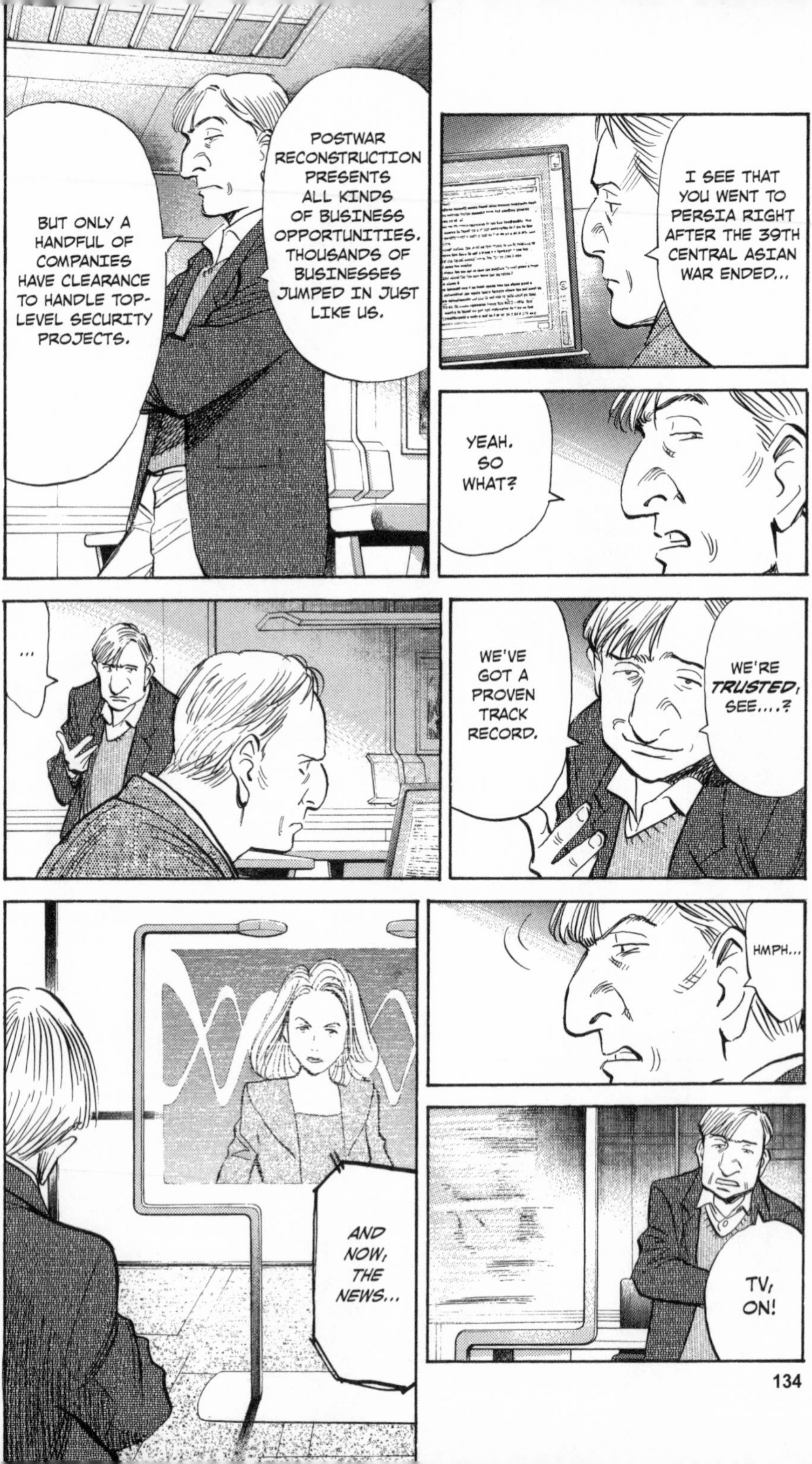
I SEE THAT YOU WENT TO PERSIA RIGHT AFTER THE 39TH CENTRAL ASIAN WAR ENDED...
YEAH. SO WHAT?
POSTWAR RECONSTRUCTION PRESENTS ALL KINDS OF BUSINESS OPPORTUNITIES. THOUSANDS OF BUSINESSES JUMPED IN JUST LIKE US.
BUT ONLY A HANDFUL OF COMPANIES HAVE CLEARANCE TO HANDLE TOP-LEVEL SECURITY PROJECTS.
WE'RE *TRUSTED*, SEE....?
WE'VE GOT A PROVEN TRACK RECORD.
...
HMPH...
TV, ON!
AND NOW, THE NEWS...

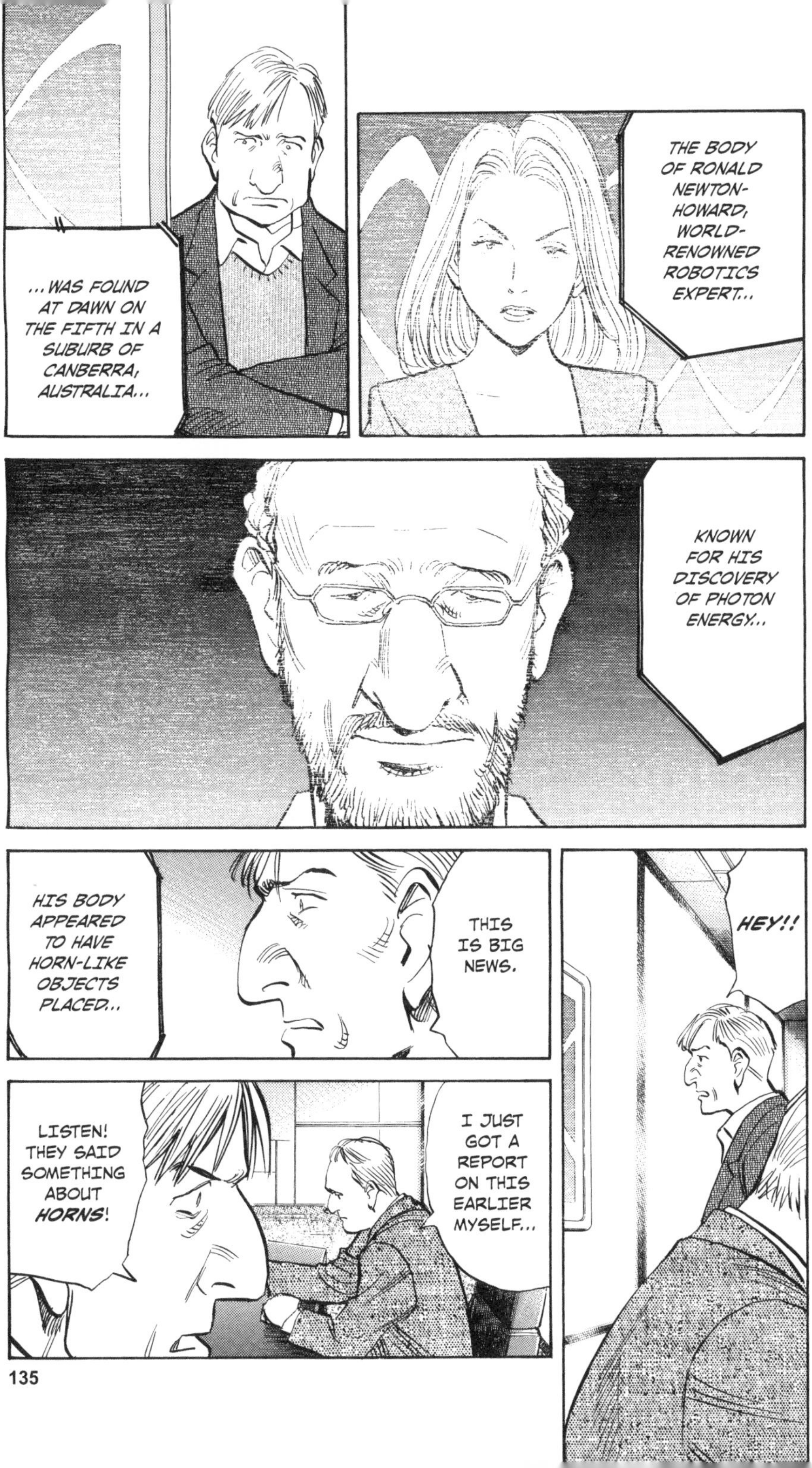
THE BODY OF RONALD NEWTON-HOWARD, WORLD-RENOWNED ROBOTICS EXPERT...
...WAS FOUND AT DAWN ON THE FIFTH IN A SUBURB OF CANBERRA, AUSTRALIA...
KNOWN FOR HIS DISCOVERY OF PHOTON ENERGY...
HEY!!
THIS IS BIG NEWS.
HIS BODY APPEARED TO HAVE HORN-LIKE OBJECTS PLACED...
I JUST GOT A REPORT ON THIS EARLIER MYSELF...
LISTEN! THEY SAID SOMETHING ABOUT HORNS!

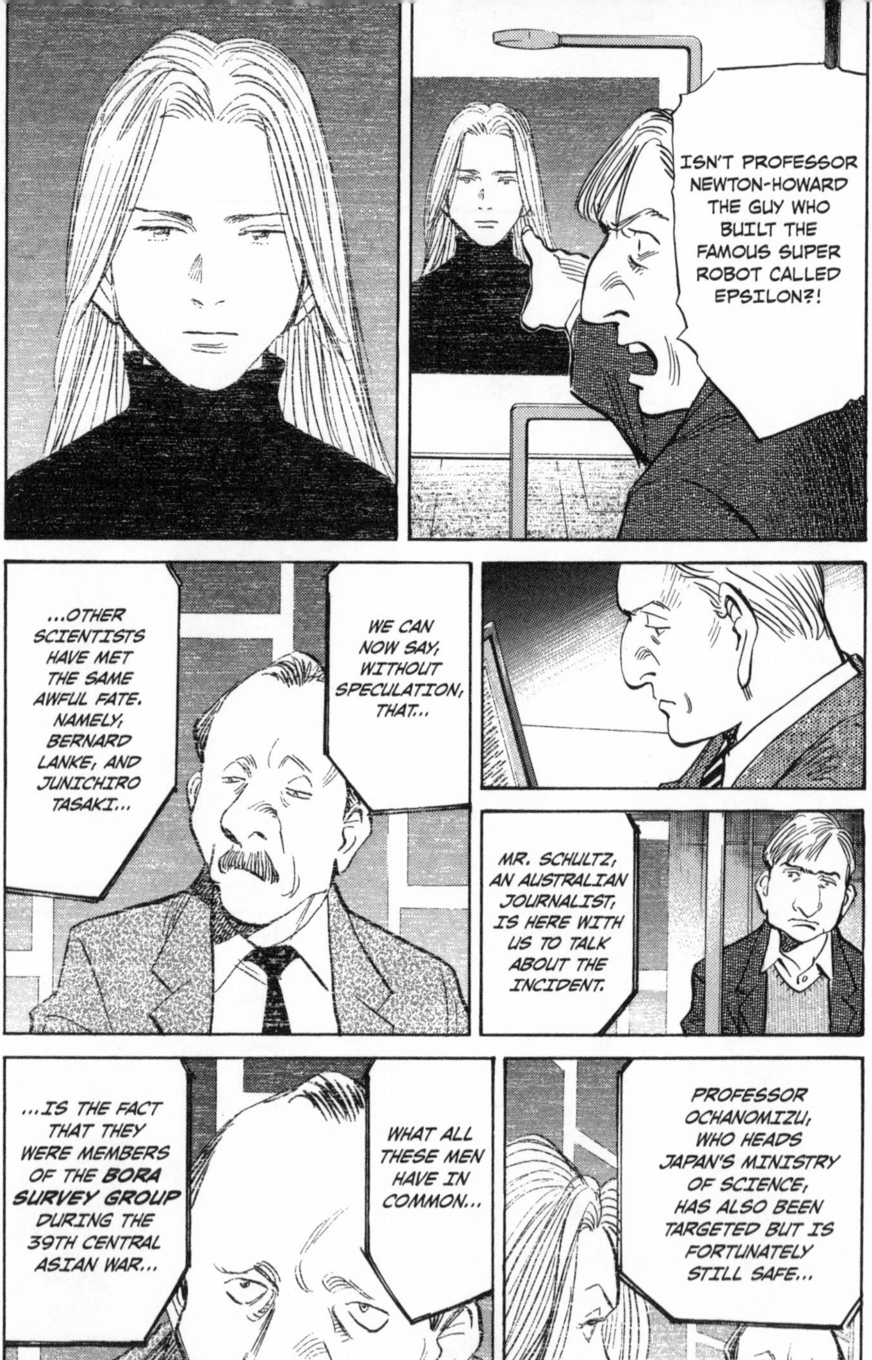
ISN'T PROFESSOR NEWTON-HOWARD THE GUY WHO BUILT THE FAMOUS SUPER ROBOT CALLED EPSILON?!
MR. SCHULTZ, AN AUSTRALIAN JOURNALIST, IS HERE WITH US TO TALK ABOUT THE INCIDENT.
WE CAN NOW SAY, WITHOUT SPECULATION, THAT...
...OTHER SCIENTISTS HAVE MET THE SAME AWFUL FATE. NAMELY, BERNARD LANKE, AND JUNICHIRO TASAKI...
PROFESSOR OCHANOMIZU, WHO HEADS JAPAN'S MINISTRY OF SCIENCE, HAS ALSO BEEN TARGETED BUT IS FORTUNATELY STILL SAFE...
WHAT ALL THESE MEN HAVE IN COMMON...
...IS THE FACT THAT THEY WERE MEMBERS OF THE BORA SURVEY GROUP DURING THE 39TH CENTRAL ASIAN WAR...

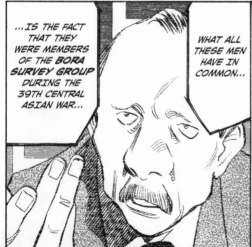

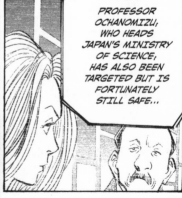

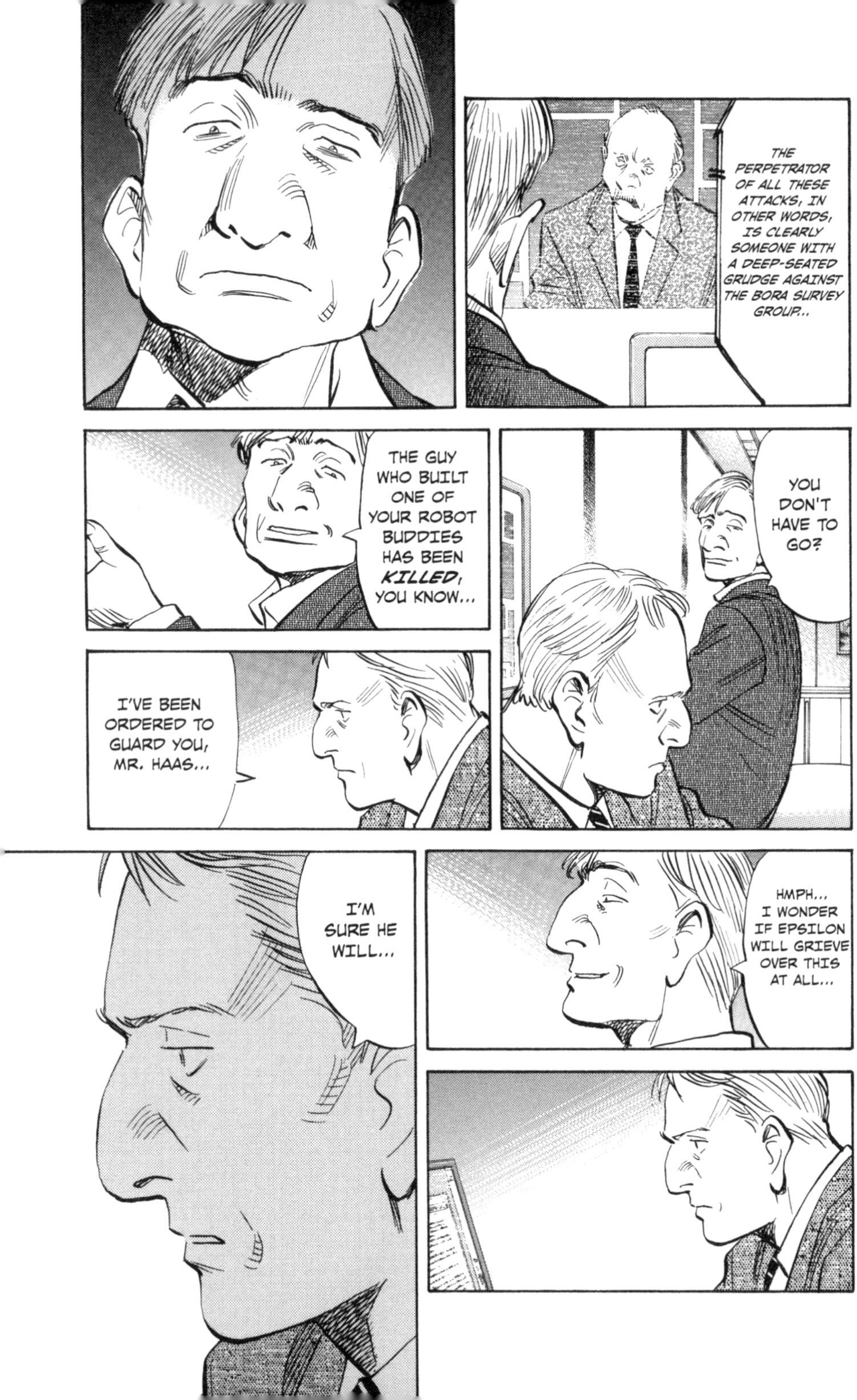
THE PERPETRATOR OF ALL THESE ATTACKS, IN OTHER WORDS, IS CLEARLY SOMEONE WITH A DEEP-SEATED GRUDGE AGAINST THE BORA SURVEY GROUP...
YOU DON'T HAVE TO GO?
THE GUY WHO BUILT ONE OF YOUR ROBOT BUDDIES HAS BEEN KILLED, YOU KNOW...
I'VE BEEN ORDERED TO GUARD YOU, MR. HAAS...
HMPH... I WONDER IF EPSILON WILL GRIEVE OVER THIS AT ALL...
I'M SURE HE WILL...

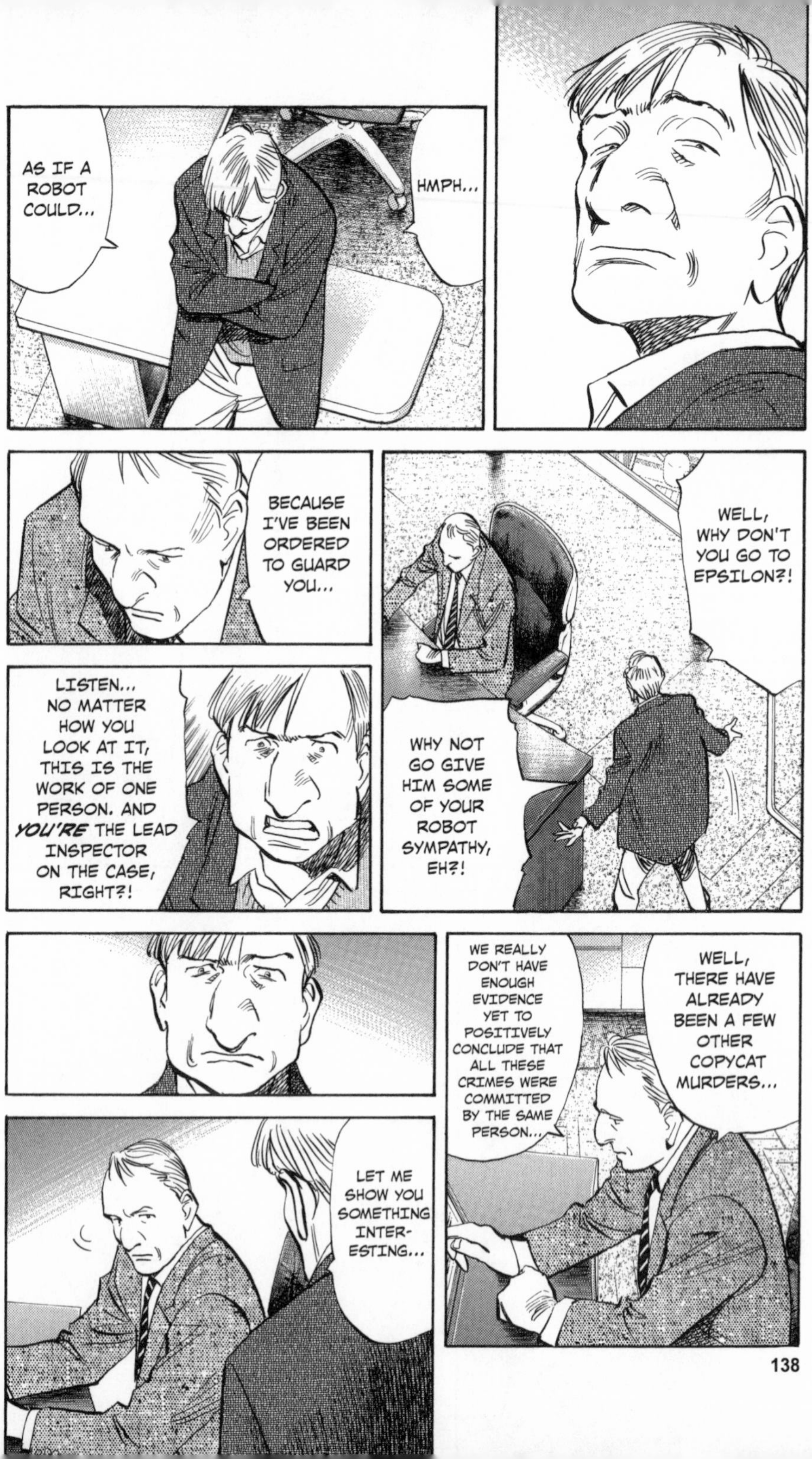
HMPH...
AS IF A ROBOT COULD...
WELL, WHY DON'T YOU GO TO EPSILON?!
WHY NOT GO GIVE HIM SOME OF YOUR ROBOT SYMPATHY, EH?!
BECAUSE I'VE BEEN ORDERED TO GUARD YOU...
LISTEN... NO MATTER HOW YOU LOOK AT IT, THIS IS THE WORK OF ONE PERSON. AND *YOU'RE* THE LEAD INSPECTOR ON THE CASE, RIGHT?!
WELL, THERE HAVE ALREADY BEEN A FEW OTHER COPYCAT MURDERS...
WE REALLY DON'T HAVE ENOUGH EVIDENCE YET TO POSITIVELY CONCLUDE THAT ALL THESE CRIMES WERE COMMITTED BY THE SAME PERSON...
LET ME SHOW YOU SOMETHING INTER-ESTING...

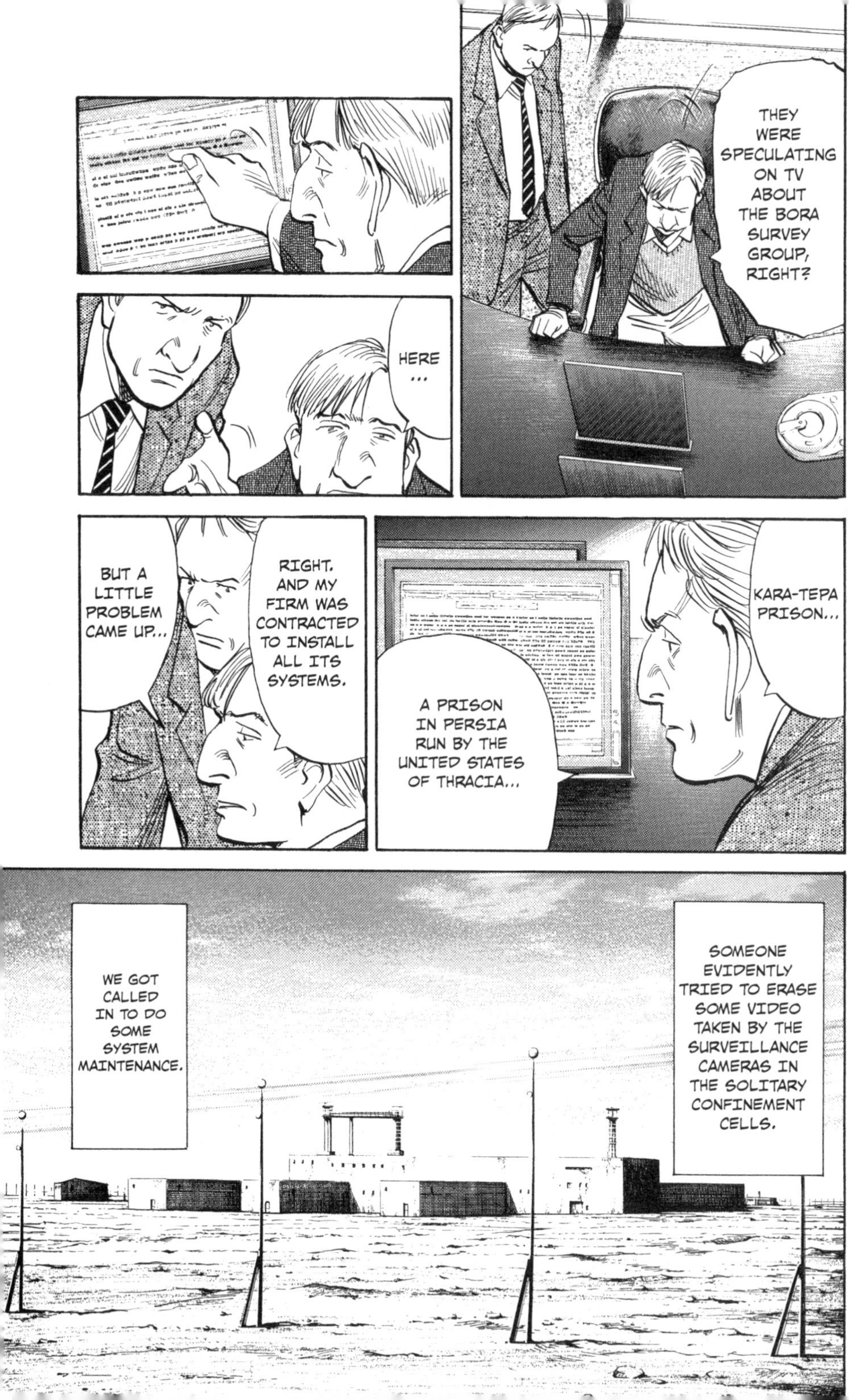
THEY WERE SPECULATING ON TV ABOUT THE BORA SURVEY GROUP, RIGHT?
HERE...
KARA-TEPA PRISON...
A PRISON IN PERSIA RUN BY THE UNITED STATES OF THRACIA...
RIGHT. AND MY FIRM WAS CONTRACTED TO INSTALL ALL ITS SYSTEMS.
BUT A LITTLE PROBLEM CAME UP...
SOMEONE EVIDENTLY TRIED TO ERASE SOME VIDEO TAKEN BY THE SURVEILLANCE CAMERAS IN THE SOLITARY CONFINEMENT CELLS.
WE GOT CALLED IN TO DO SOME SYSTEM MAINTENANCE.

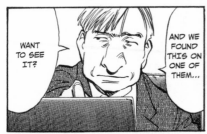

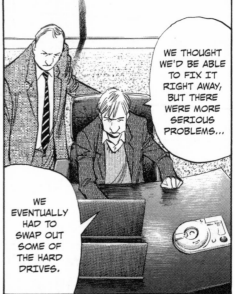

WE THOUGHT WE'D BE ABLE TO FIX IT RIGHT AWAY, BUT THERE WERE MORE SERIOUS PROBLEMS...
WE EVENTUALLY HAD TO SWAP OUT SOME OF THE HARD DRIVES.
AND WE FOUND THIS ON ONE OF THEM...
WANT TO SEE IT?
GO AHEAD...
BZZ... BZZ...
BZ... BZZ...
BZ...
B... BZ...
B... R...
LANKE...
TASAKI...
HOWARD...
IS THAT A HUMAN VOICE?
HERE... I CAN CLEAN IT UP A BIT...

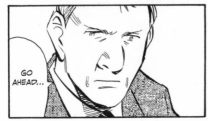

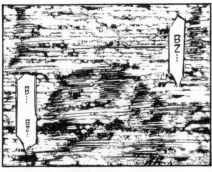

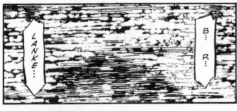

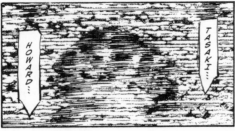

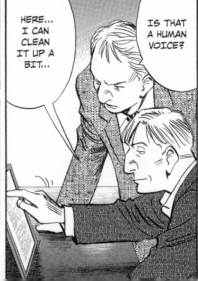

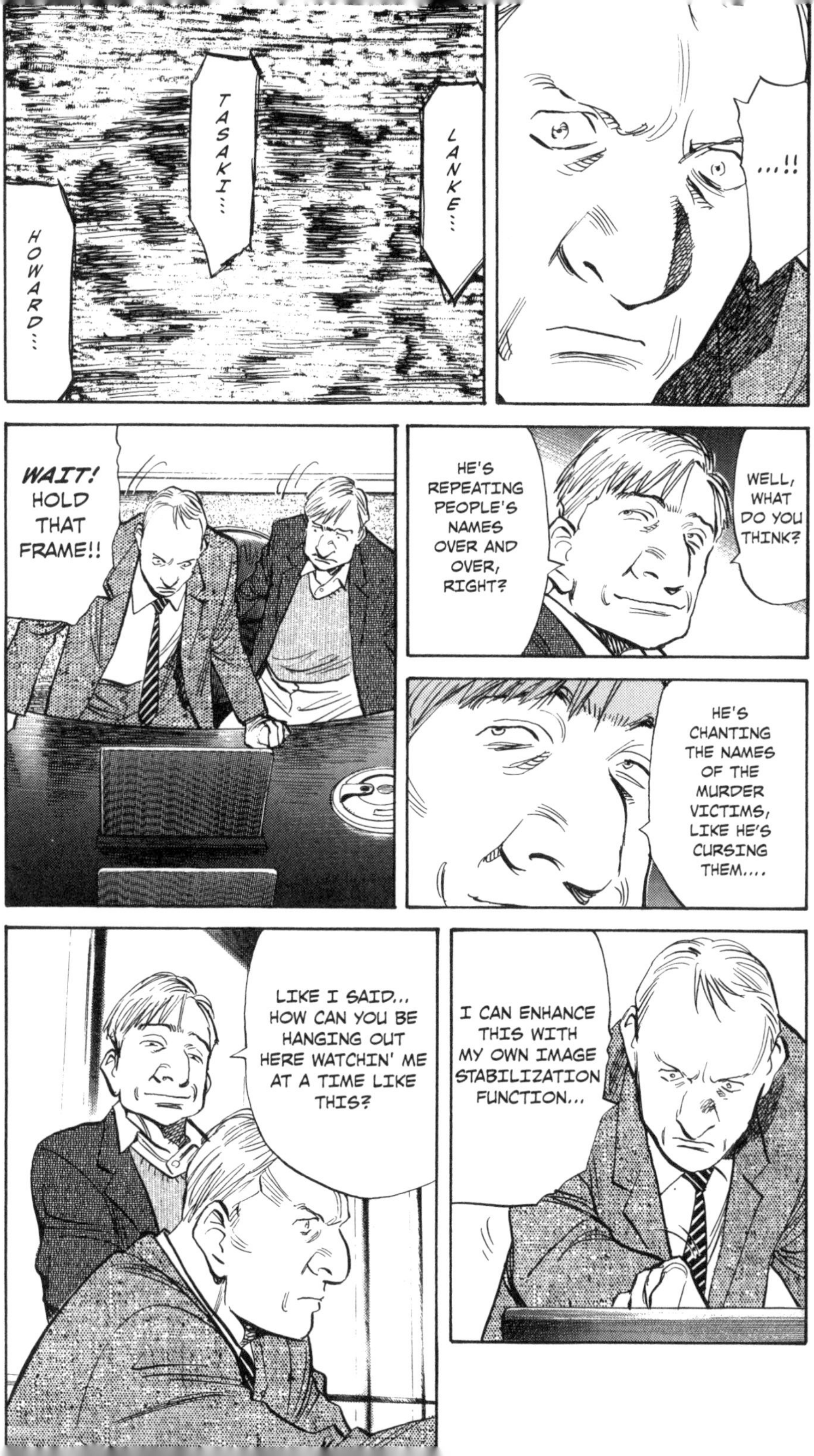
...!!
LANKE...
TASAKI...
HOWARD...
WELL, WHAT DO YOU THINK?
HE'S REPEATING PEOPLE'S NAMES OVER AND OVER, RIGHT?
HE'S CHANTING THE NAMES OF THE MURDER VICTIMS, LIKE HE'S CURSING THEM....
WAIT! HOLD THAT FRAME!!
I CAN ENHANCE THIS WITH MY OWN IMAGE STABILIZATION FUNCTION...
LIKE I SAID... HOW CAN YOU BE HANGING OUT HERE WATCHIN' ME AT A TIME LIKE THIS?

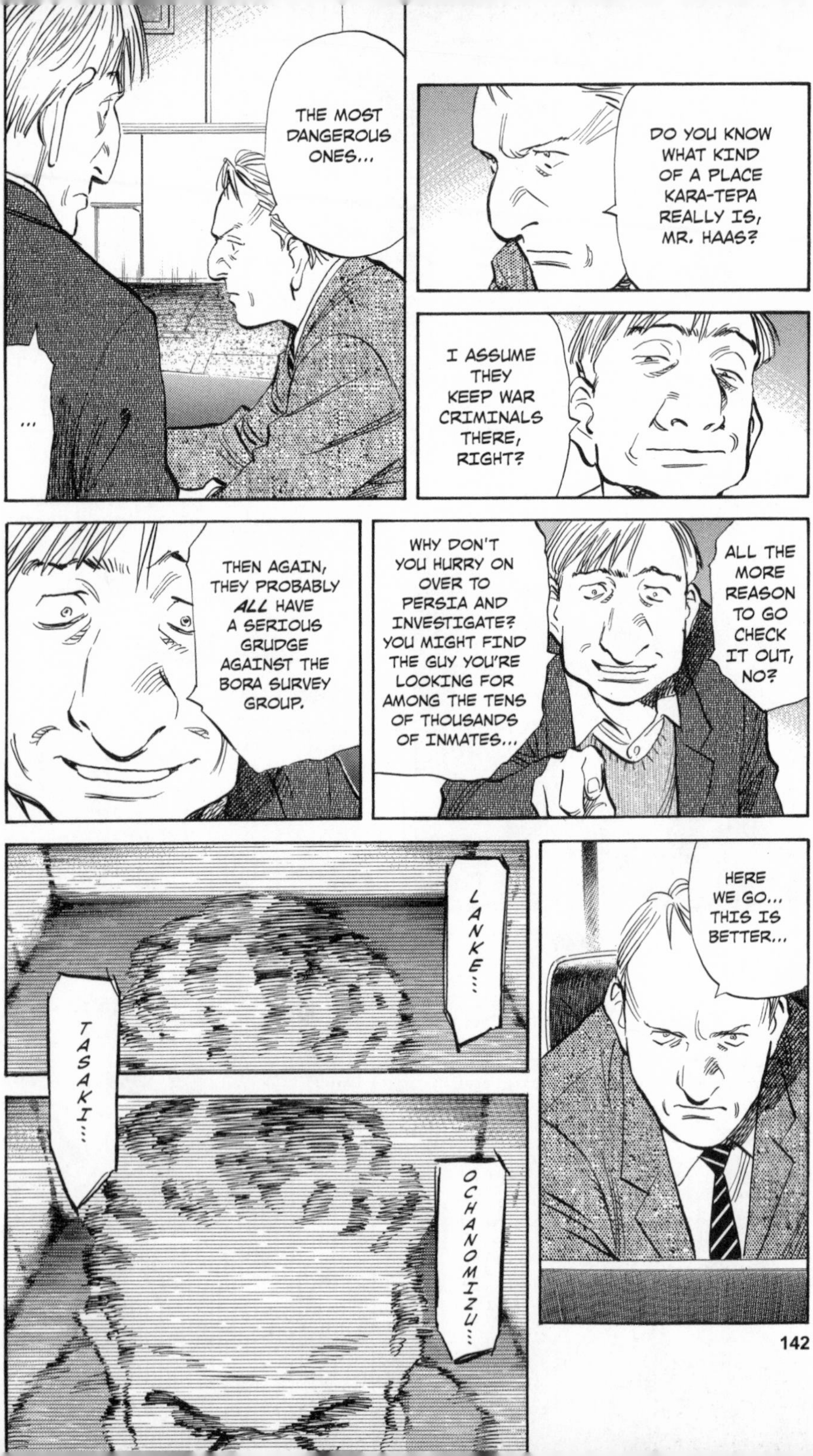
DO YOU KNOW WHAT KIND OF A PLACE KARA-TEPA REALLY IS, MR. HAAS?
I ASSUME THEY KEEP WAR CRIMINALS THERE, RIGHT?
THE MOST DANGEROUS ONES...
...
ALL THE MORE REASON TO GO CHECK IT OUT, NO?
WHY DON'T YOU HURRY ON OVER TO PERSIA AND INVESTIGATE? YOU MIGHT FIND THE GUY YOU'RE LOOKING FOR AMONG THE TENS OF THOUSANDS OF INMATES...
THEN AGAIN, THEY PROBABLY ALL HAVE A SERIOUS GRUDGE AGAINST THE BORA SURVEY GROUP.
HERE WE GO... THIS IS BETTER...
LANKE...
TASAKI...
OCHANOMIZU...

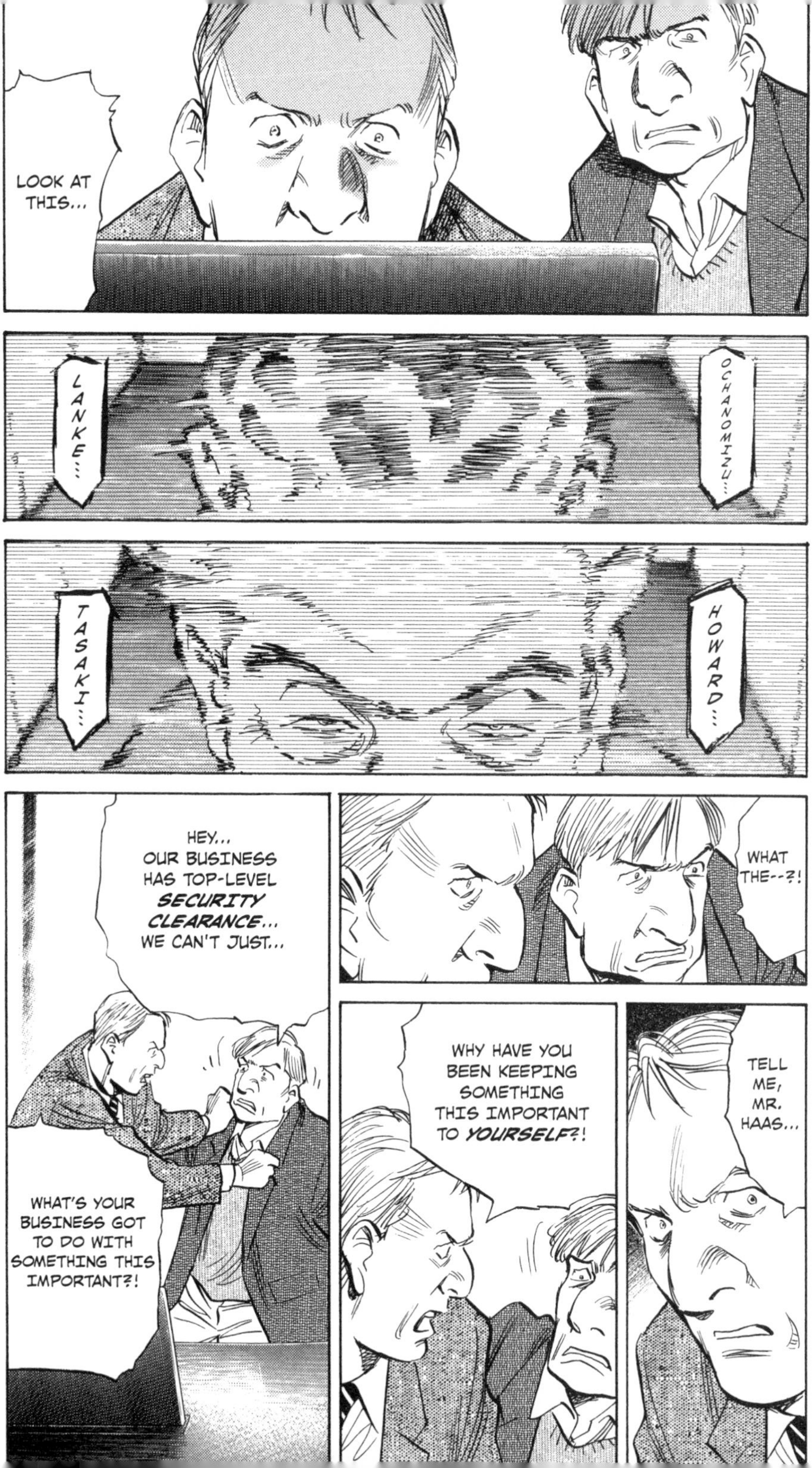
LOOK AT THIS...
OCHANOMIZU...
LANKE...
HOWARD...
TASAKI...
WHAT THE--?!
TELL ME, MR. HAAS...
WHY HAVE YOU BEEN KEEPING SOMETHING THIS IMPORTANT TO *YOURSELF*?!
HEY... OUR BUSINESS HAS TOP-LEVEL ***SECURITY CLEARANCE***... WE CAN'T JUST...
WHAT'S YOUR BUSINESS GOT TO DO WITH SOMETHING THIS IMPORTANT?!

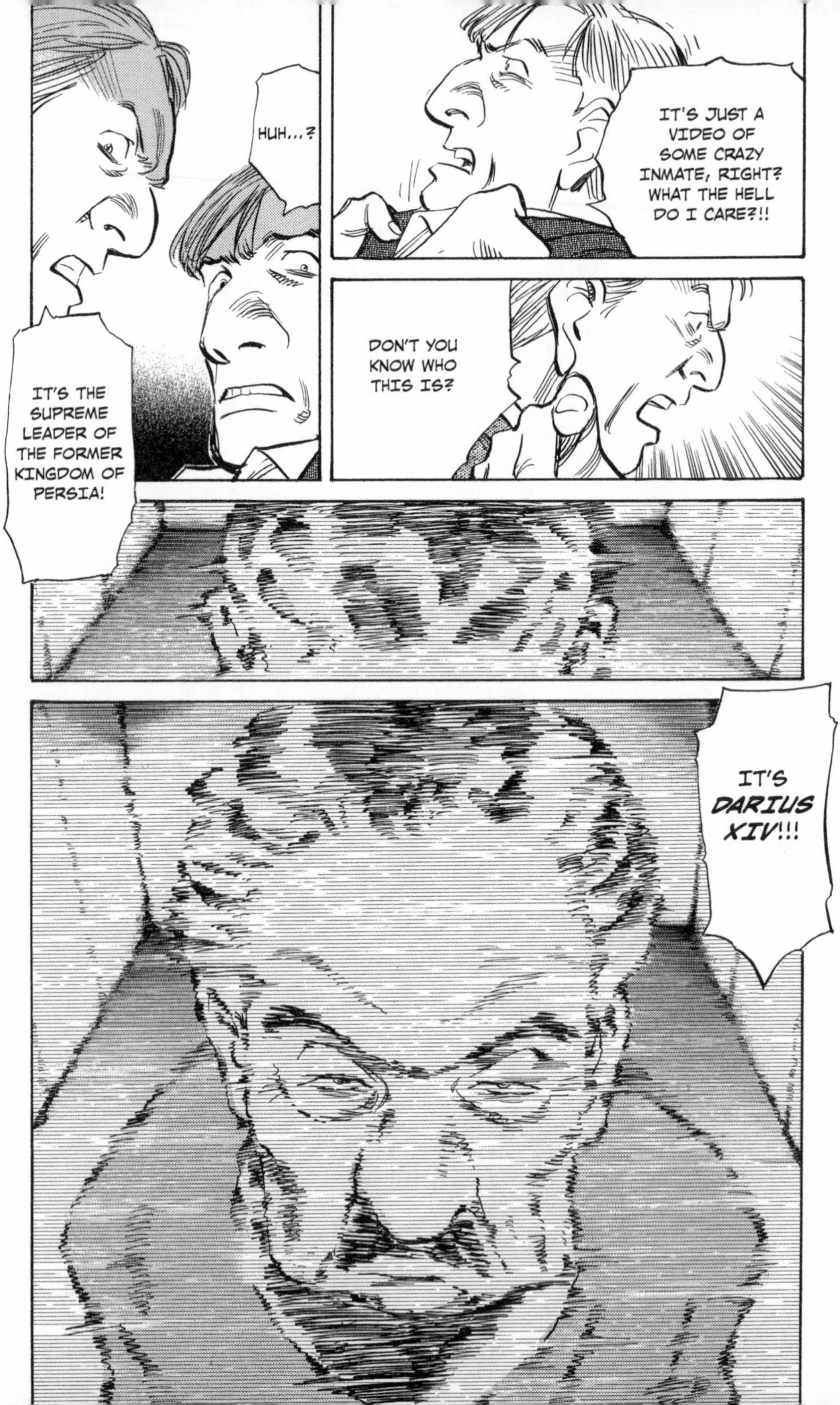
IT'S JUST A VIDEO OF SOME CRAZY INMATE, RIGHT? WHAT THE HELL DO I CARE?!!
DON'T YOU KNOW WHO THIS IS?
HUH...?
IT'S THE SUPREME LEADER OF THE FORMER KINGDOM OF PERSIA!
IT'S *DARIUS XIV*!!!

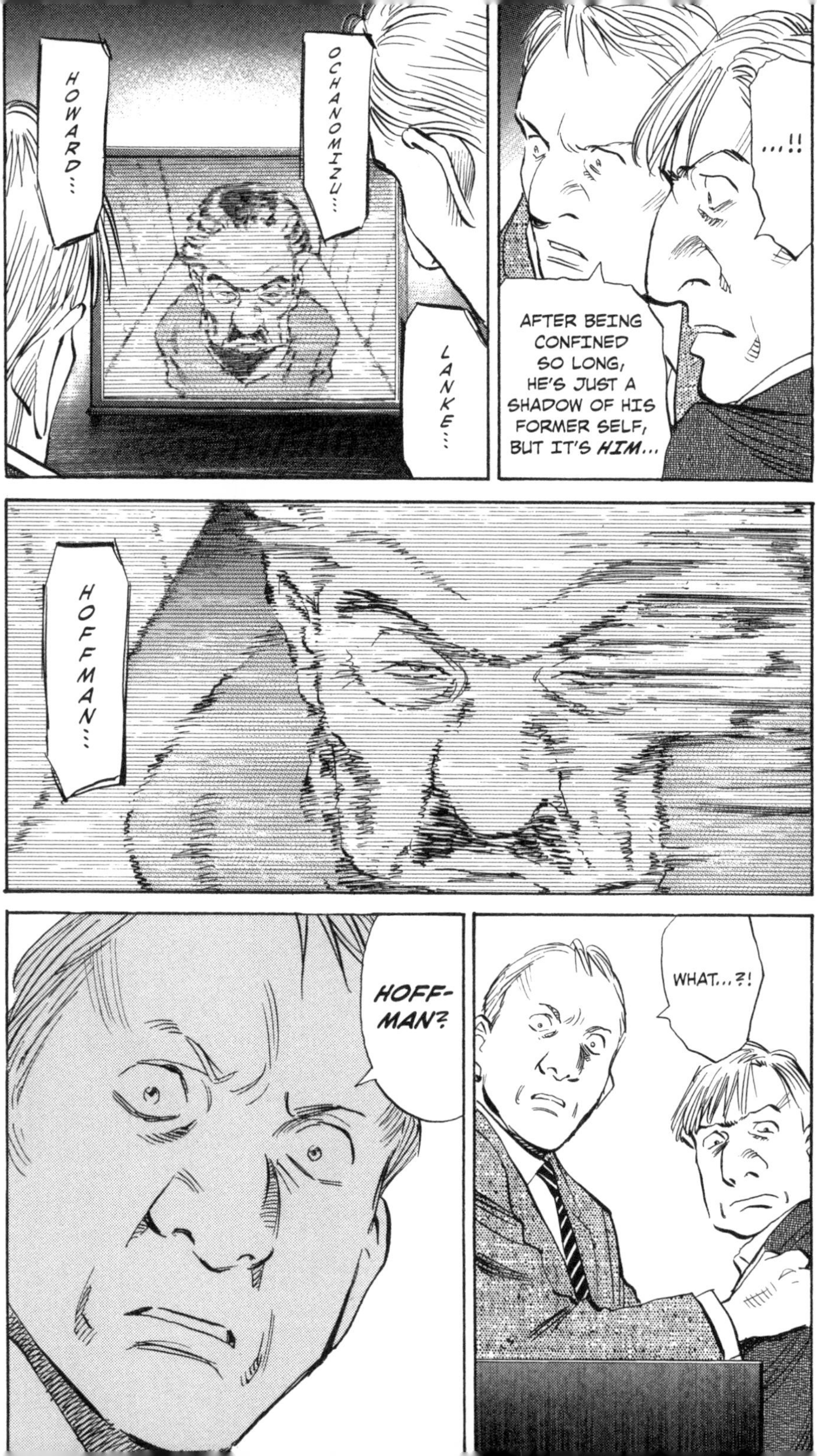

...!!
AFTER BEING CONFINED SO LONG, HE'S JUST A SHADOW OF HIS FORMER SELF, BUT IT'S *HIM*...
OCHANOMIZU...
HOWARD...
LANKE...
HOFFMAN...
WHAT...?!
HOFF-MAN?

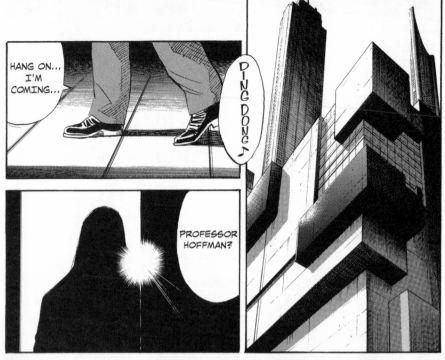

HANG ON...
I'M COMING...

DING DONG♪

PROFESSOR HOFFMAN?

THAT'S RIGHT.
AND YOU ARE...?

Act 30 Three Scientists at Kimberley

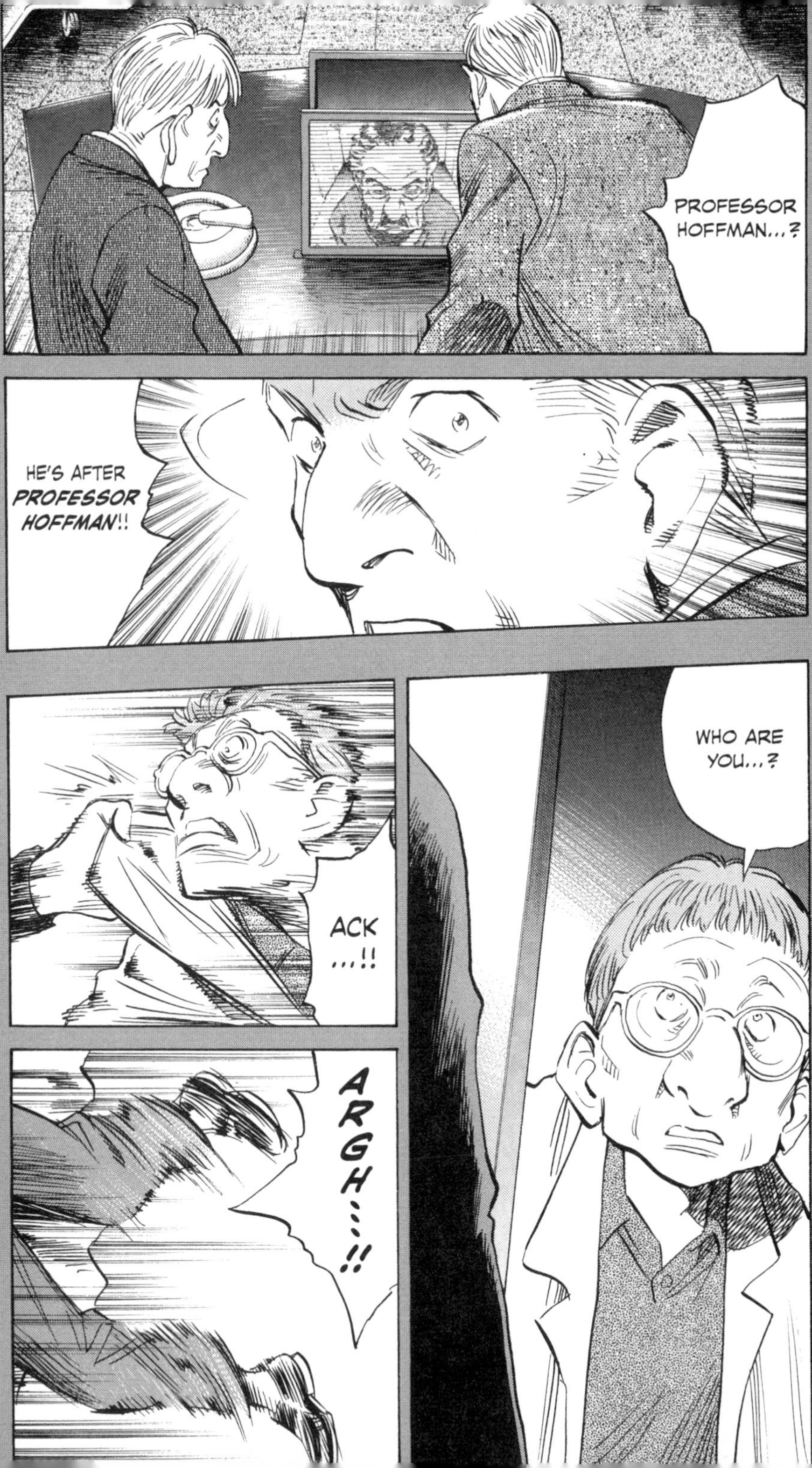
PROFESSOR HOFFMAN...?
HE'S AFTER *PROFESSOR HOFFMAN*!!
WHO ARE YOU...?
ACK ...!!
ARGH...!!

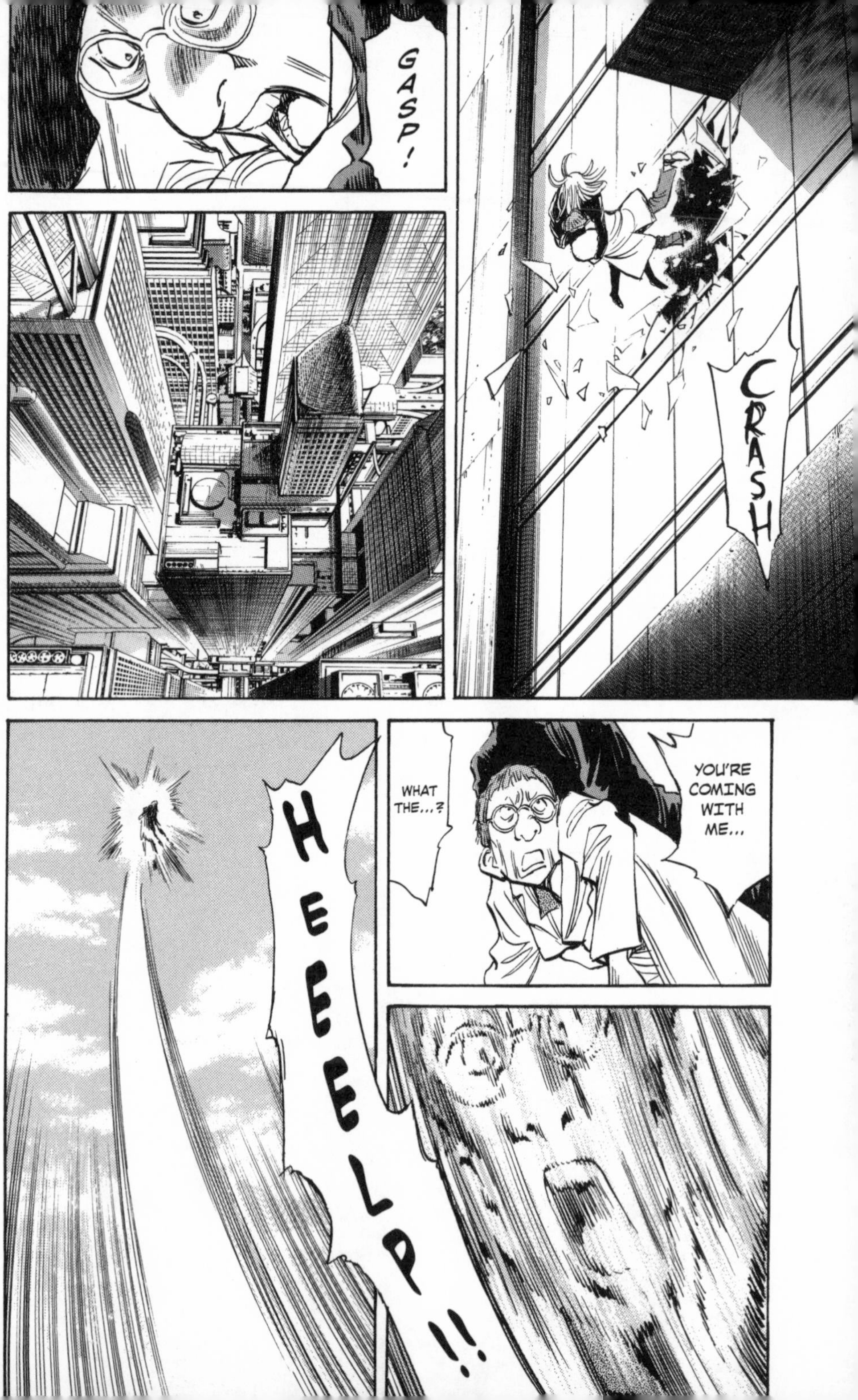
CRASH
GASP!
YOU'RE COMING WITH ME...
WHAT THE...?
HEEEELP!!

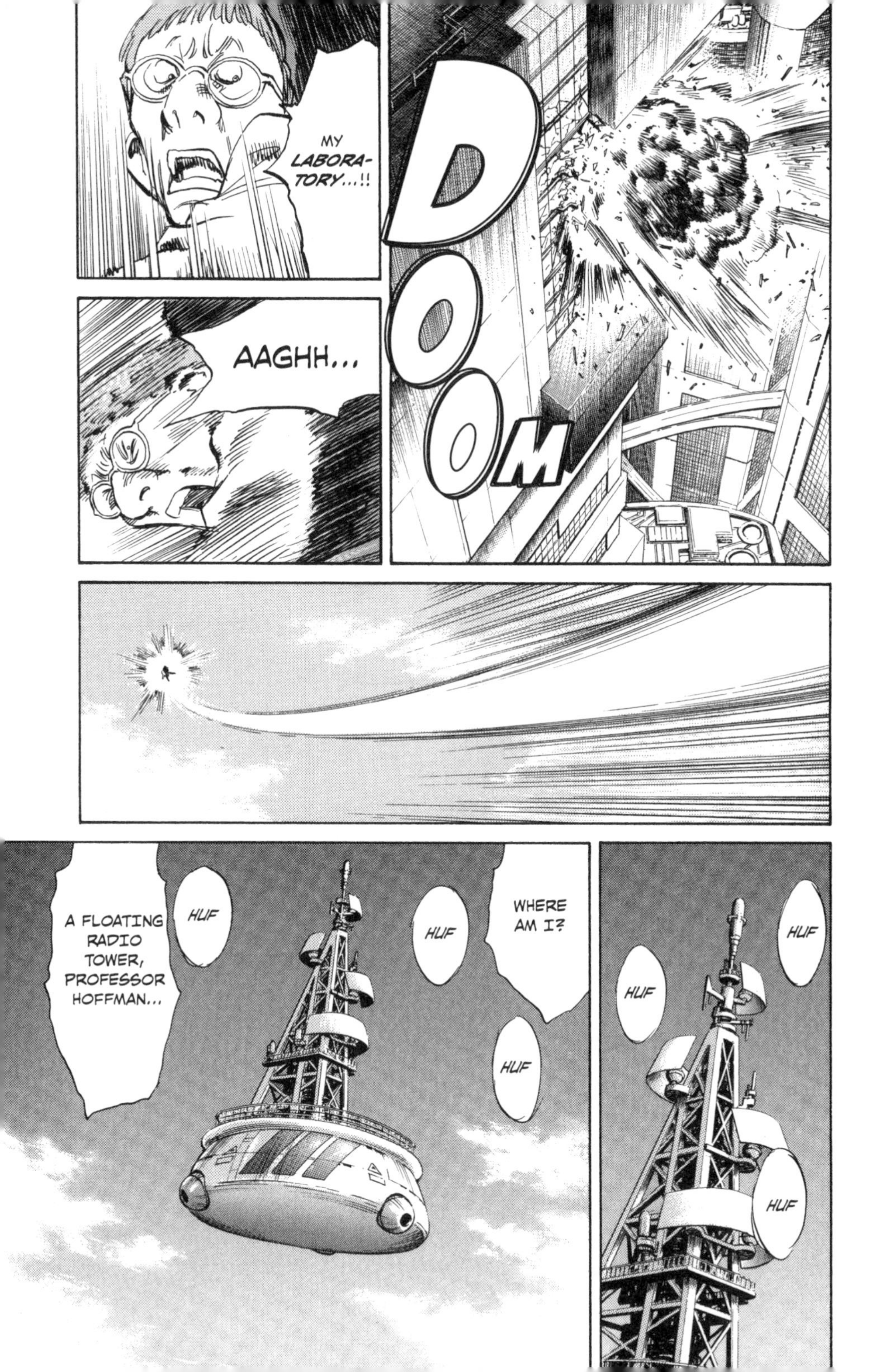
DOOOM
MY LABORATORY...!!
AAGHH...
HUF
HUF
HUF
WHERE AM I?
HUF
HUF
A FLOATING RADIO TOWER, PROFESSOR HOFFMAN...
HUF

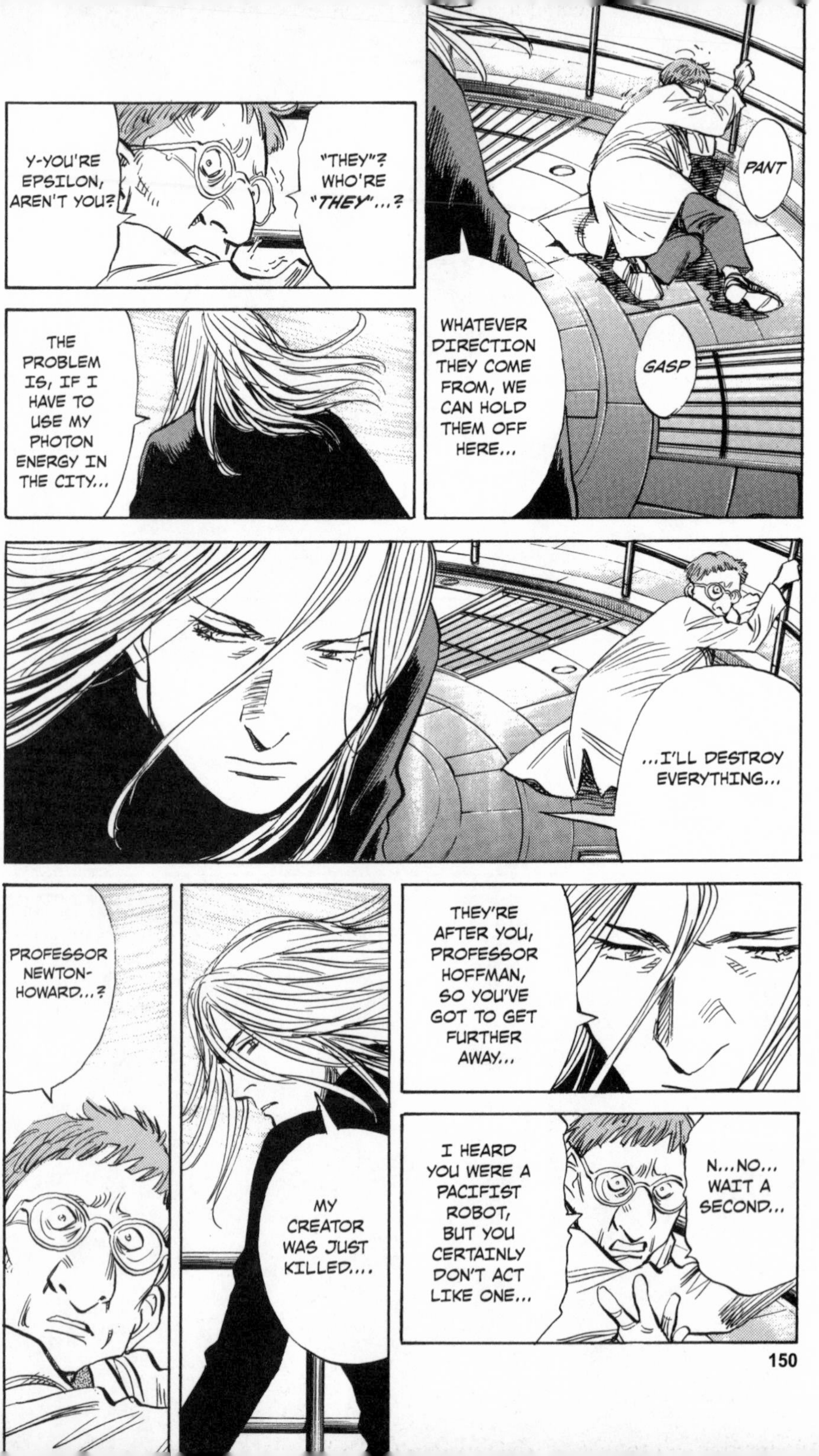
PANT
WHATEVER DIRECTION THEY COME FROM, WE CAN HOLD THEM OFF HERE...
GASP
"THEY"? WHO'RE "THEY"...?
Y-YOU'RE EPSILON, AREN'T YOU?
THE PROBLEM IS, IF I HAVE TO USE MY PHOTON ENERGY IN THE CITY...
...I'LL DESTROY EVERYTHING...
THEY'RE AFTER YOU, PROFESSOR HOFFMAN, SO YOU'VE GOT TO GET FURTHER AWAY...
N...NO... WAIT A SECOND...
I HEARD YOU WERE A PACIFIST ROBOT, BUT YOU CERTAINLY DON'T ACT LIKE ONE...
MY CREATOR WAS JUST KILLED....
PROFESSOR NEWTON-HOWARD...?

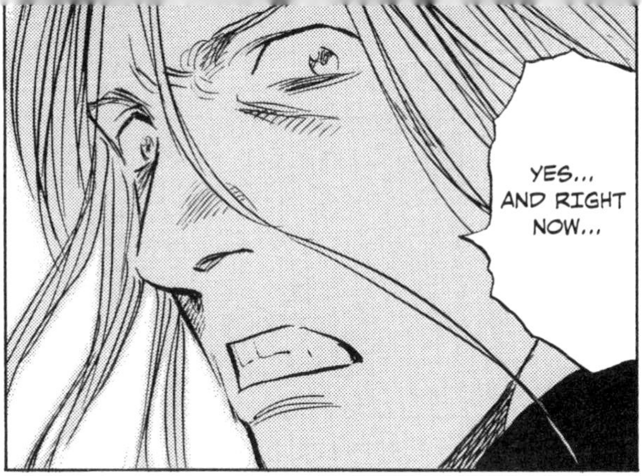
YES... AND RIGHT NOW...
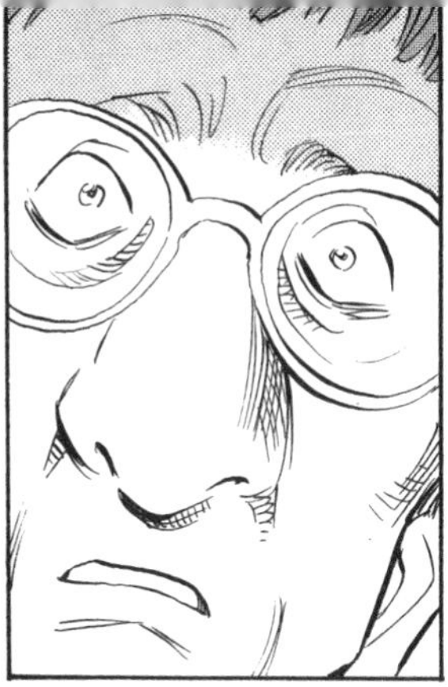
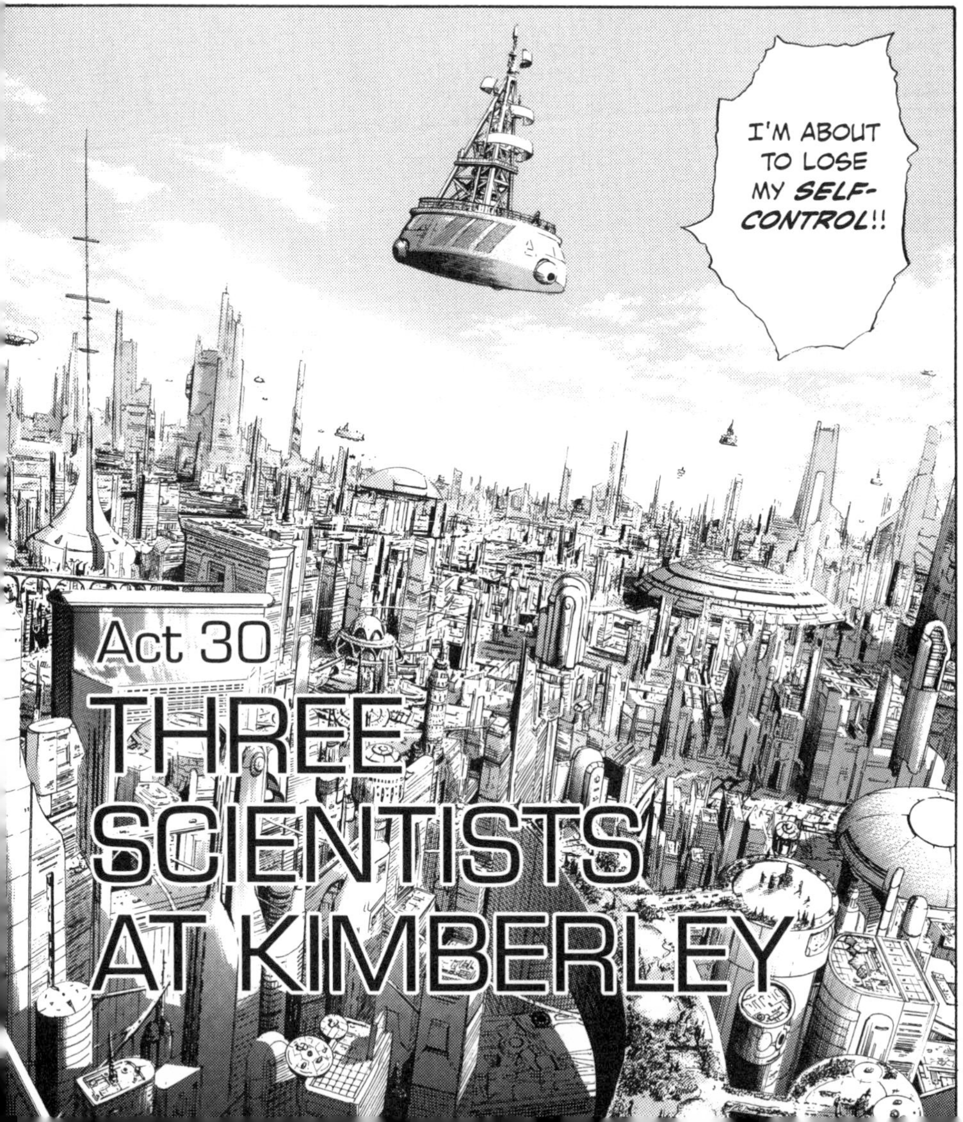
I'M ABOUT TO LOSE MY *SELF-CONTROL*!!
Act 30
THREE SCIENTISTS AT KIMBERLEY

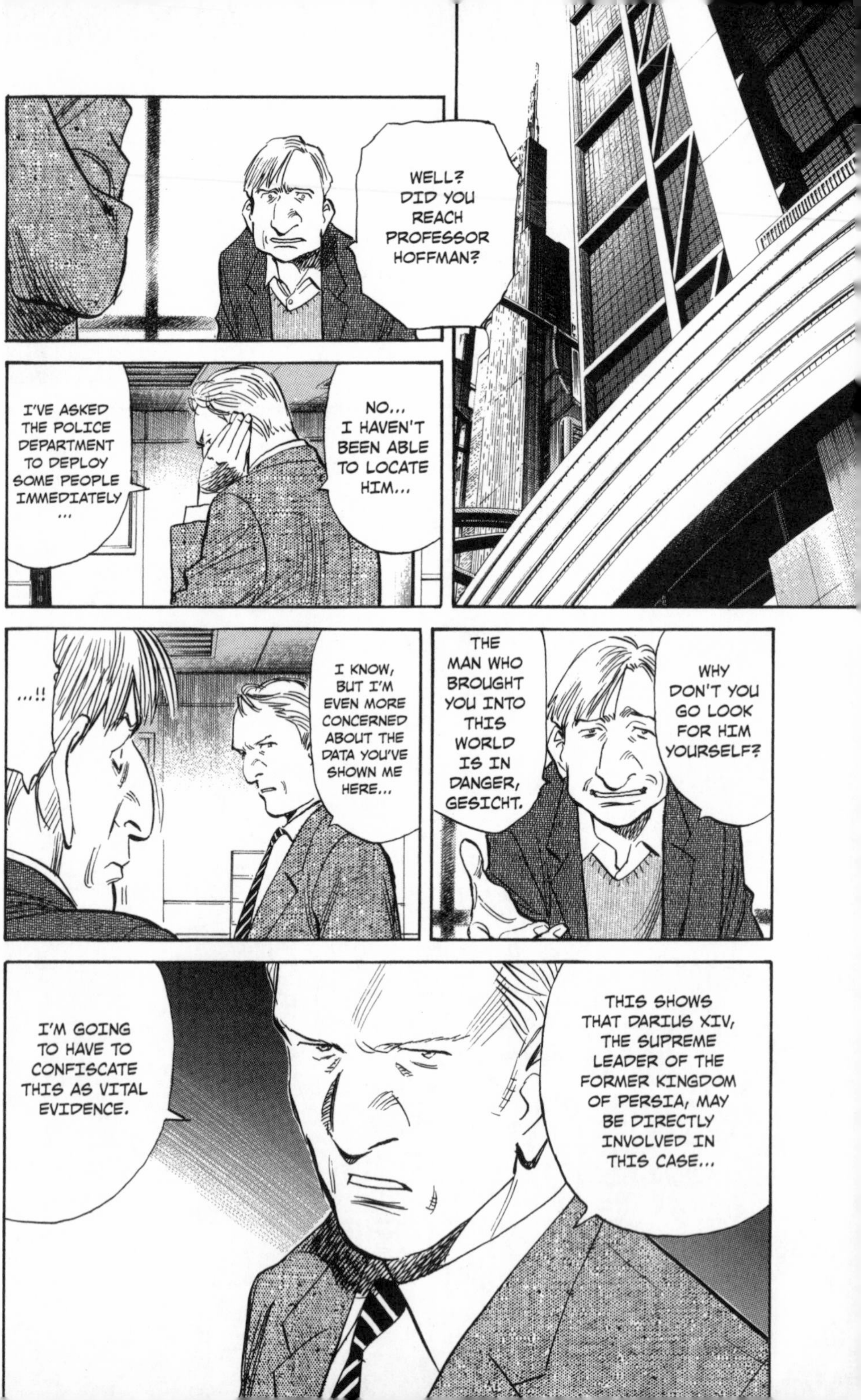
WELL? DID YOU REACH PROFESSOR HOFFMAN?
NO... I HAVEN'T BEEN ABLE TO LOCATE HIM...
I'VE ASKED THE POLICE DEPARTMENT TO DEPLOY SOME PEOPLE IMMEDIATELY ...
WHY DON'T YOU GO LOOK FOR HIM YOURSELF?
THE MAN WHO BROUGHT YOU INTO THIS WORLD IS IN DANGER, GESICHT.
I KNOW, BUT I'M EVEN MORE CONCERNED ABOUT THE DATA YOU'VE SHOWN ME HERE...
...!!
THIS SHOWS THAT DARIUS XIV, THE SUPREME LEADER OF THE FORMER KINGDOM OF PERSIA, MAY BE DIRECTLY INVOLVED IN THIS CASE...
I'M GOING TO HAVE TO CONFISCATE THIS AS VITAL EVIDENCE.

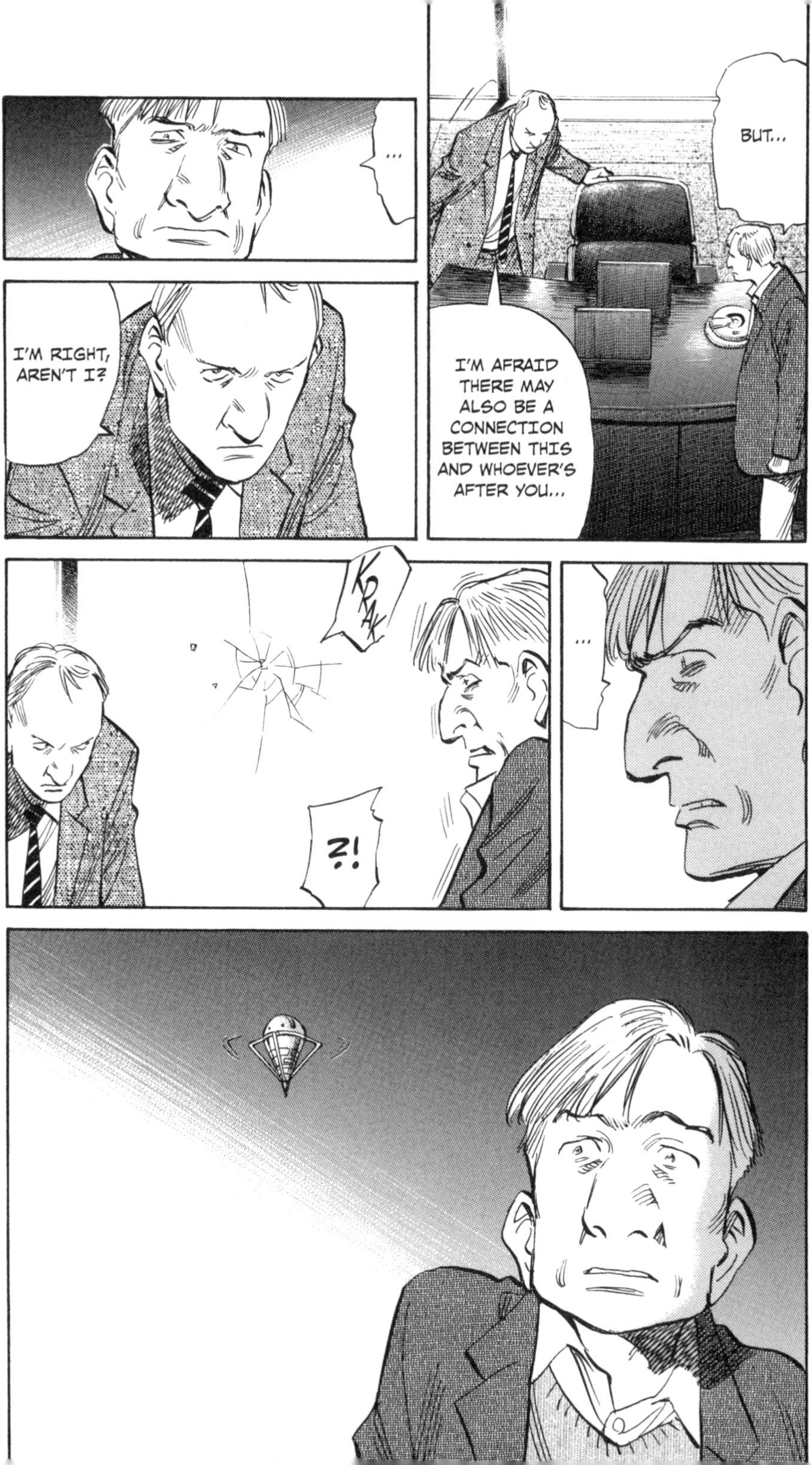
BUT...
I'M AFRAID THERE MAY ALSO BE A CONNECTION BETWEEN THIS AND WHOEVER'S AFTER YOU...
...
I'M RIGHT, AREN'T I?
...
KRAK
?!

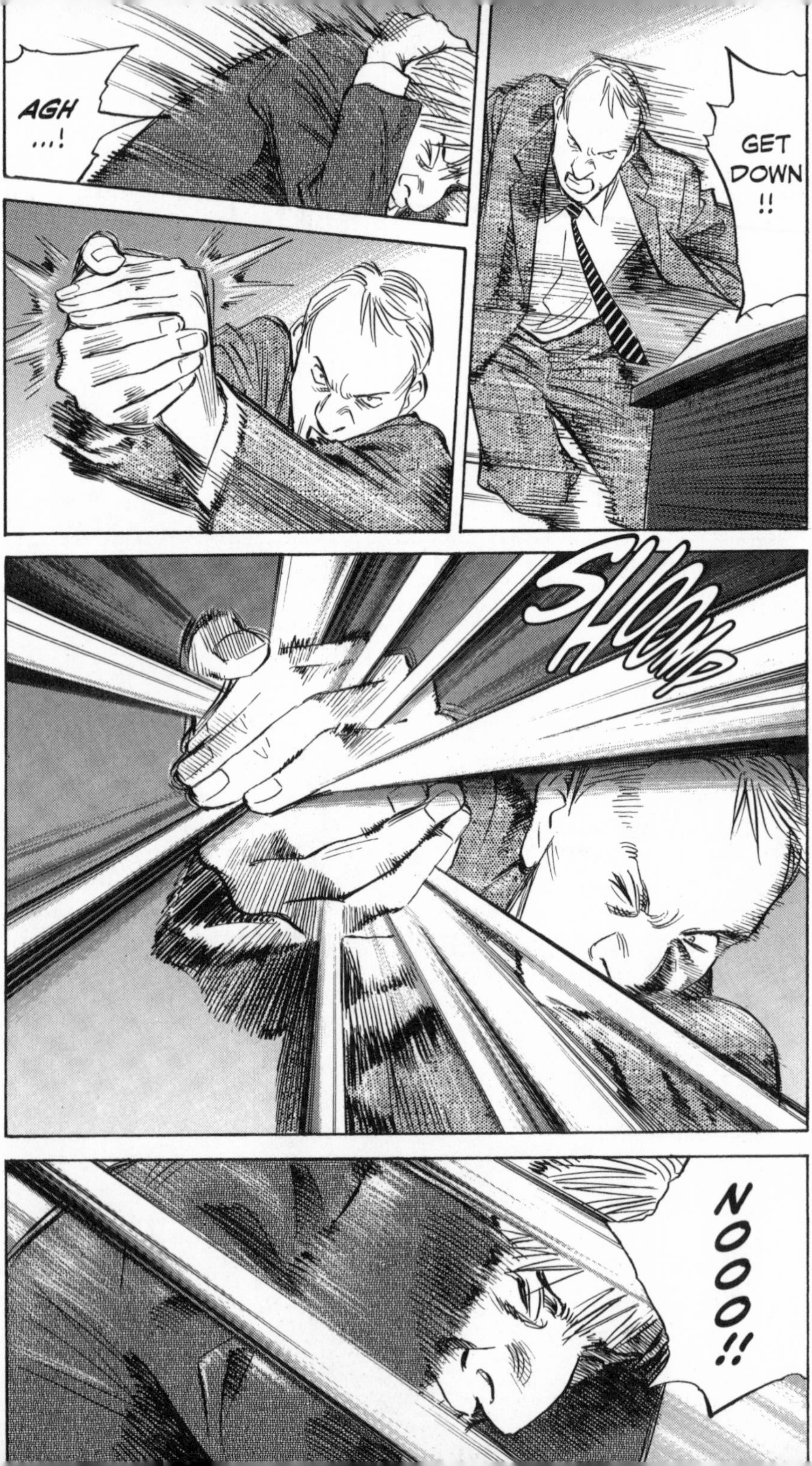
GET DOWN !!
AGH ...!
SHUMP
NOOOO!!

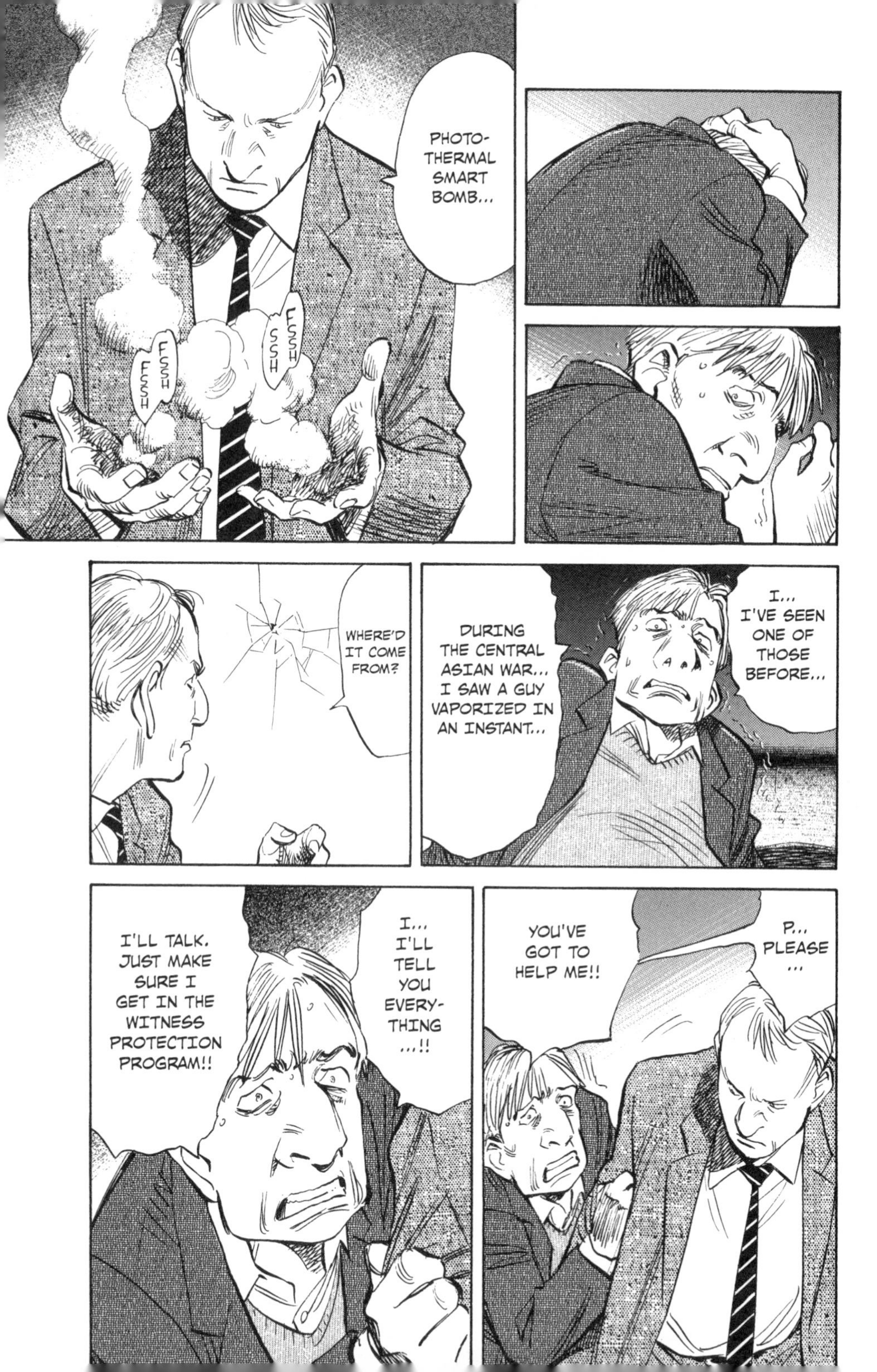
PHOTO-THERMAL SMART BOMB...
FSSH
FSSH
I... I'VE SEEN ONE OF THOSE BEFORE...
DURING THE CENTRAL ASIAN WAR... I SAW A GUY VAPORIZED IN AN INSTANT...
WHERE'D IT COME FROM?
P... PLEASE ...
YOU'VE GOT TO HELP ME!!
I... I'LL TELL YOU EVERY-THING ...!!
I'LL TALK. JUST MAKE SURE I GET IN THE WITNESS PROTECTION PROGRAM!!

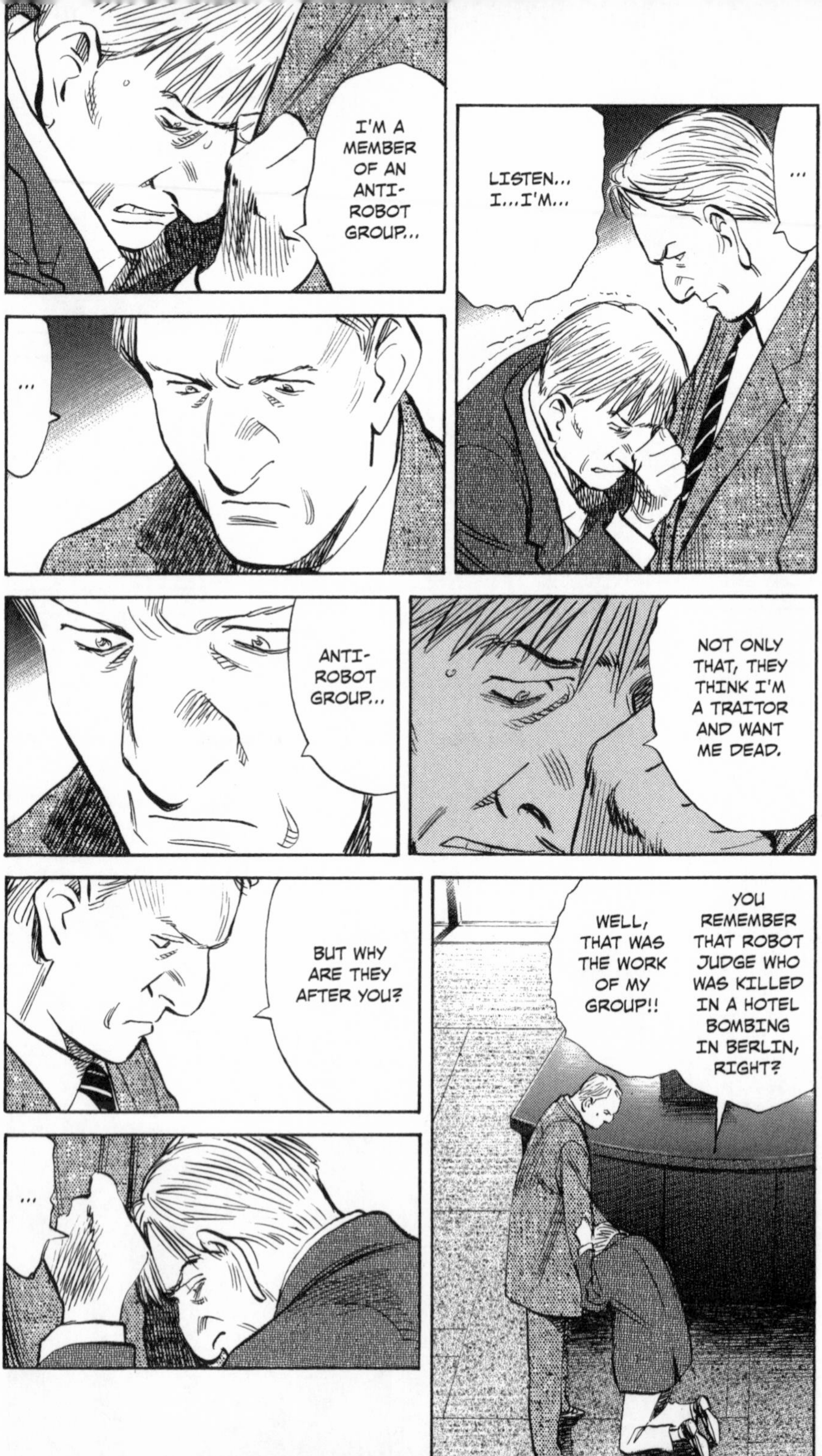
...
LISTEN... I...I'M...
I'M A MEMBER OF AN ANTI-ROBOT GROUP...
...
NOT ONLY THAT, THEY THINK I'M A TRAITOR AND WANT ME DEAD.
ANTI-ROBOT GROUP...
YOU REMEMBER THAT ROBOT JUDGE WHO WAS KILLED IN A HOTEL BOMBING IN BERLIN, RIGHT?
WELL, THAT WAS THE WORK OF MY GROUP!!
BUT WHY ARE THEY AFTER YOU?
...

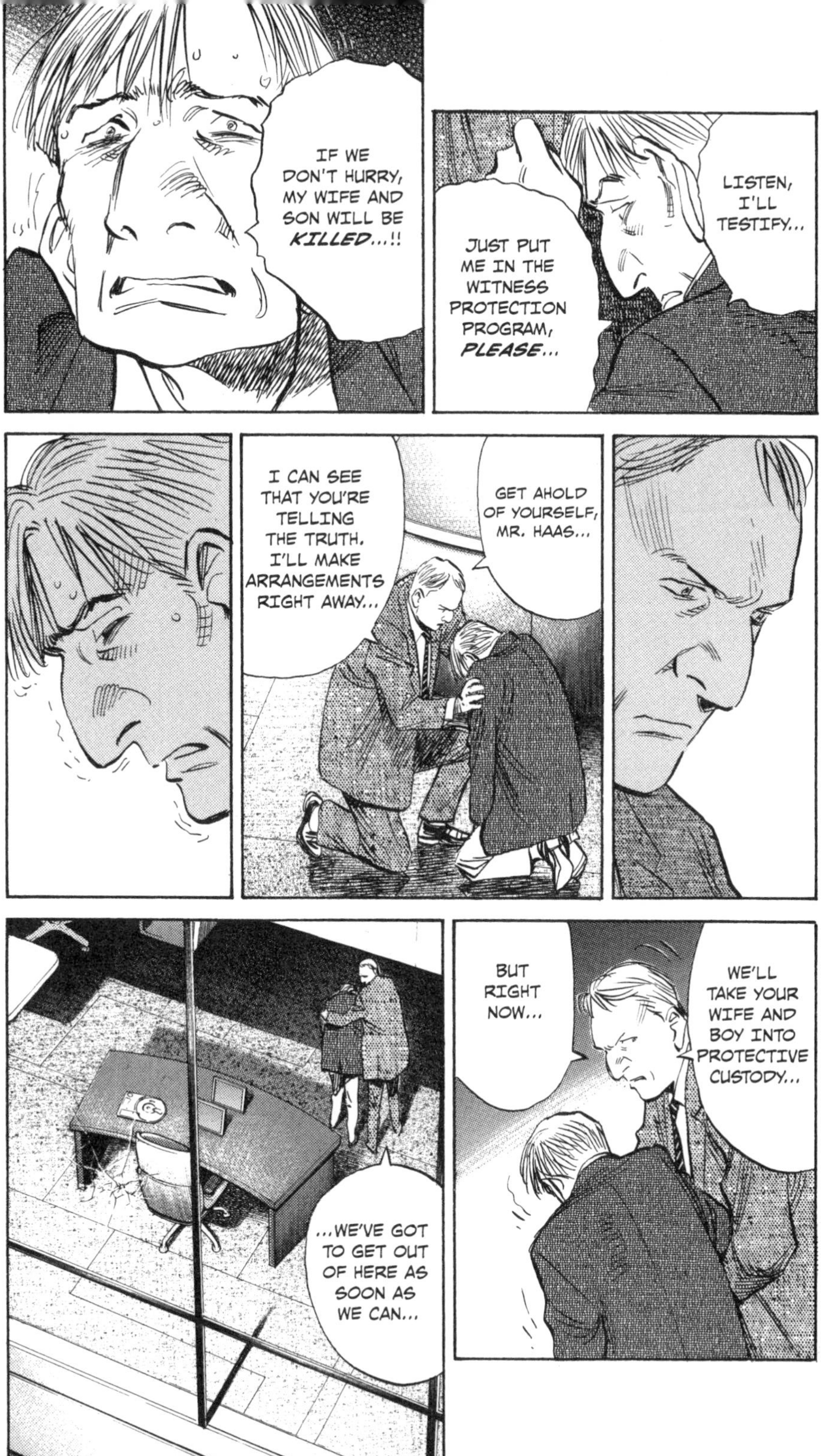
LISTEN, I'LL TESTIFY...
JUST PUT ME IN THE WITNESS PROTECTION PROGRAM, *PLEASE*...
IF WE DON'T HURRY, MY WIFE AND SON WILL BE *KILLED*...!!
GET AHOLD OF YOURSELF, MR. HAAS...
I CAN SEE THAT YOU'RE TELLING THE TRUTH. I'LL MAKE ARRANGEMENTS RIGHT AWAY...
WE'LL TAKE YOUR WIFE AND BOY INTO PROTECTIVE CUSTODY...
BUT RIGHT NOW...
...WE'VE GOT TO GET OUT OF HERE AS SOON AS WE CAN...

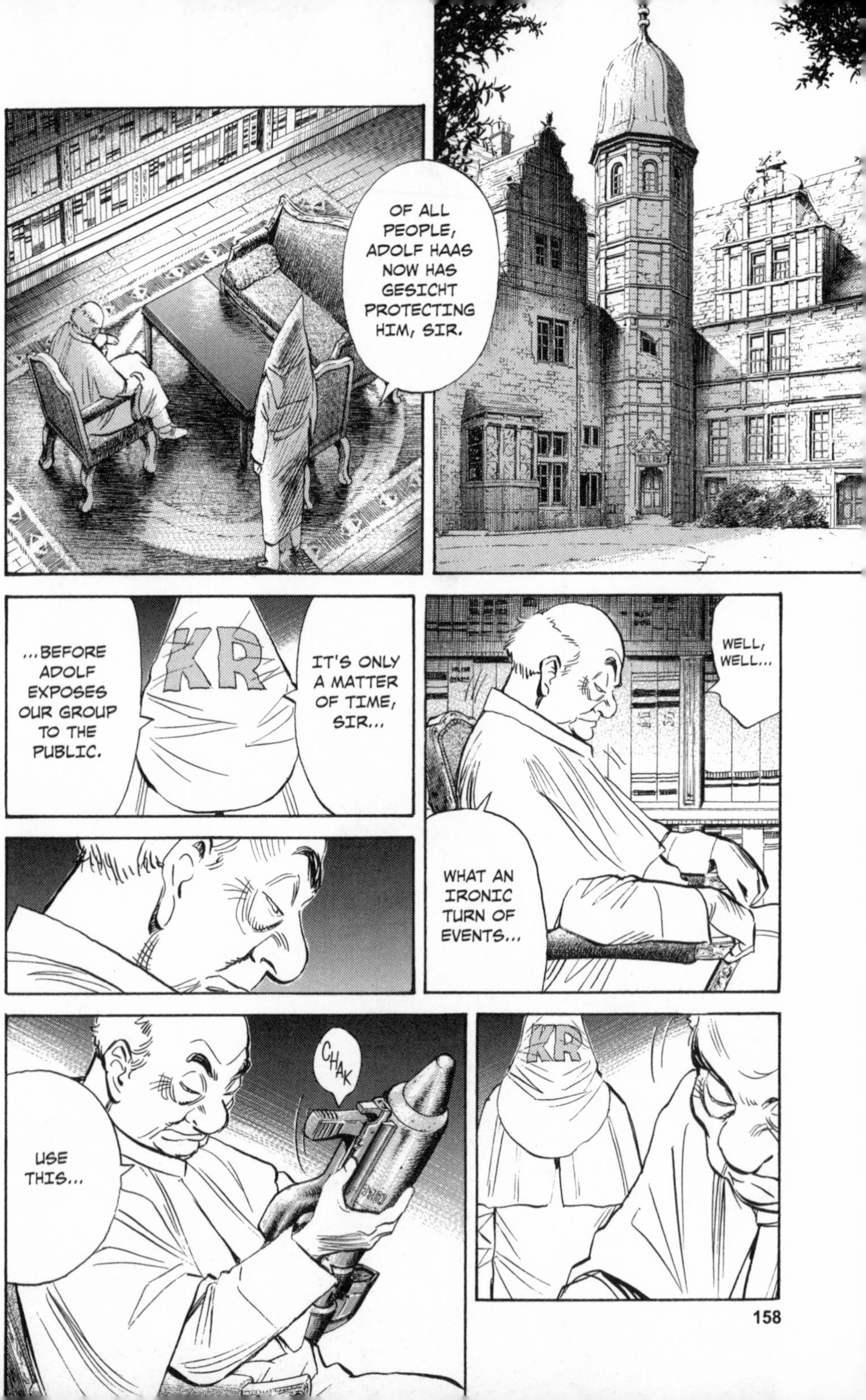
OF ALL PEOPLE, ADOLF HAAS NOW HAS GESICHT PROTECTING HIM, SIR.
WELL, WELL...
WHAT AN IRONIC TURN OF EVENTS...
IT'S ONLY A MATTER OF TIME, SIR...
...BEFORE ADOLF EXPOSES OUR GROUP TO THE PUBLIC.
KR
CHAK
USE THIS...

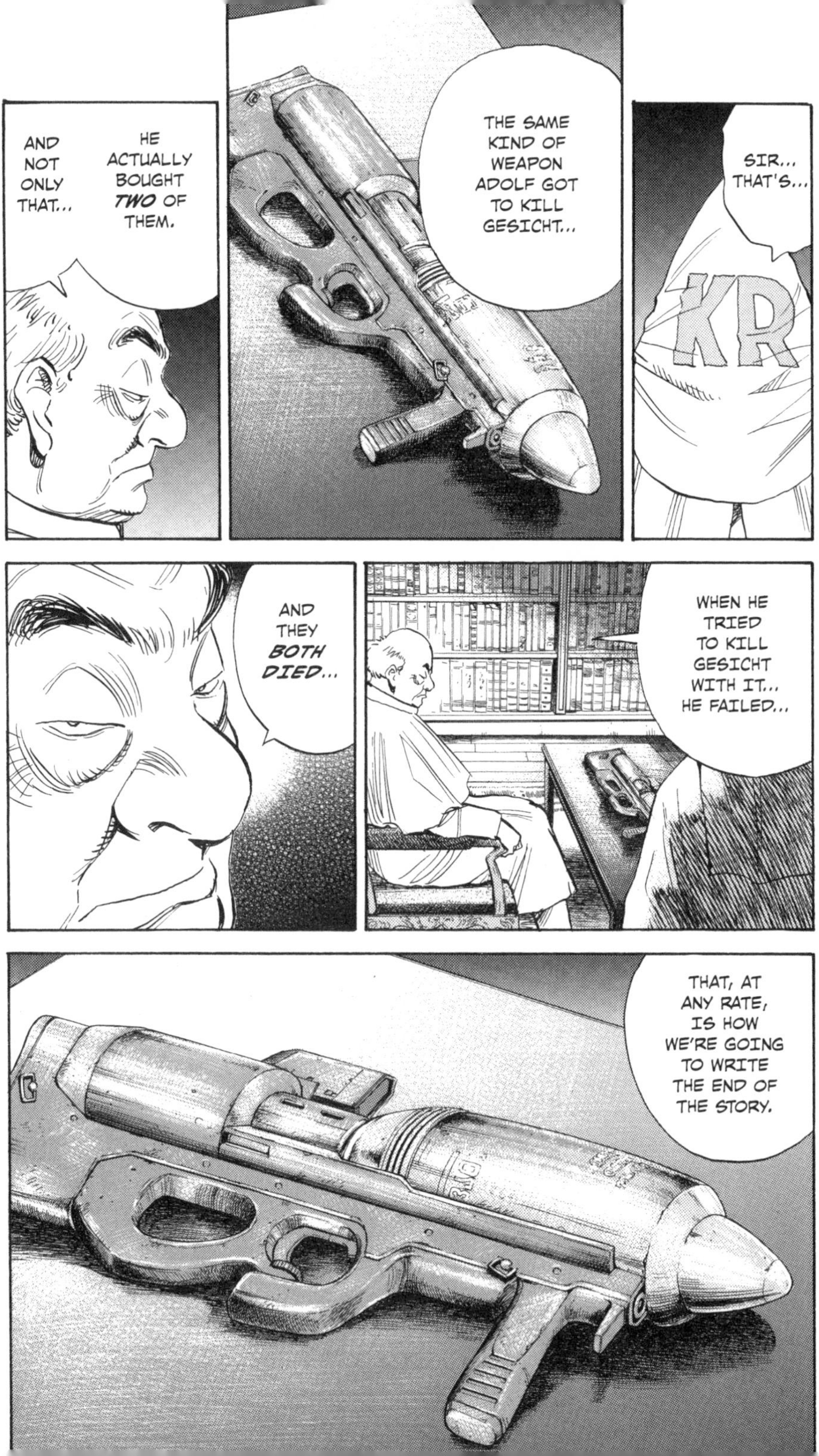

SIR... THAT'S...
THE SAME KIND OF WEAPON ADOLF GOT TO KILL GESICHT...
HE ACTUALLY BOUGHT *TWO* OF THEM.
AND NOT ONLY THAT...
WHEN HE TRIED TO KILL GESICHT WITH IT... HE FAILED...
AND THEY *BOTH DIED*...
THAT, AT ANY RATE, IS HOW WE'RE GOING TO WRITE THE END OF THE STORY.
KR

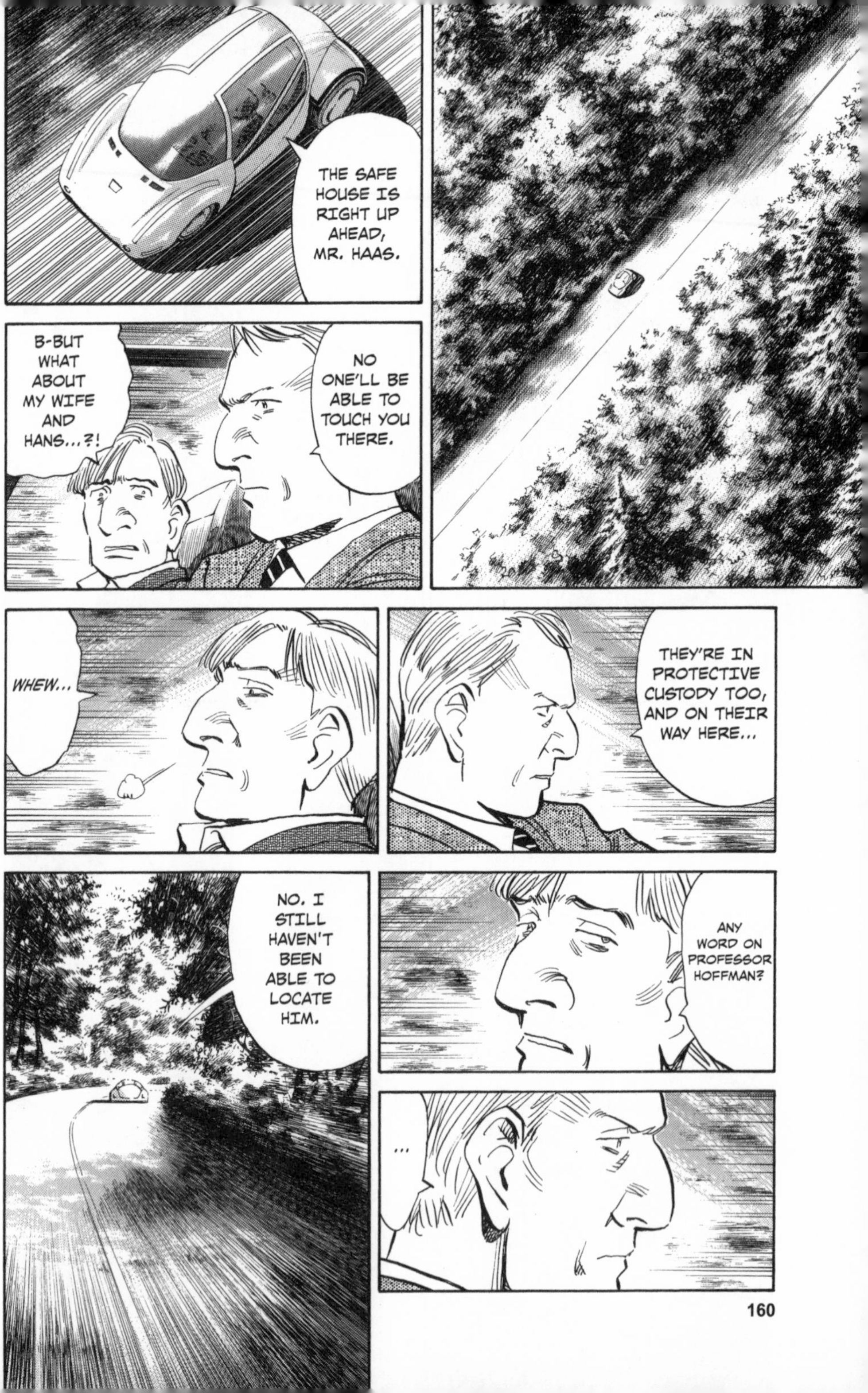
THE SAFE HOUSE IS RIGHT UP AHEAD, MR. HAAS.
NO ONE'LL BE ABLE TO TOUCH YOU THERE.
B-BUT WHAT ABOUT MY WIFE AND HANS...?!
THEY'RE IN PROTECTIVE CUSTODY TOO, AND ON THEIR WAY HERE...
WHEW...
ANY WORD ON PROFESSOR HOFFMAN?
...
NO. I STILL HAVEN'T BEEN ABLE TO LOCATE HIM.

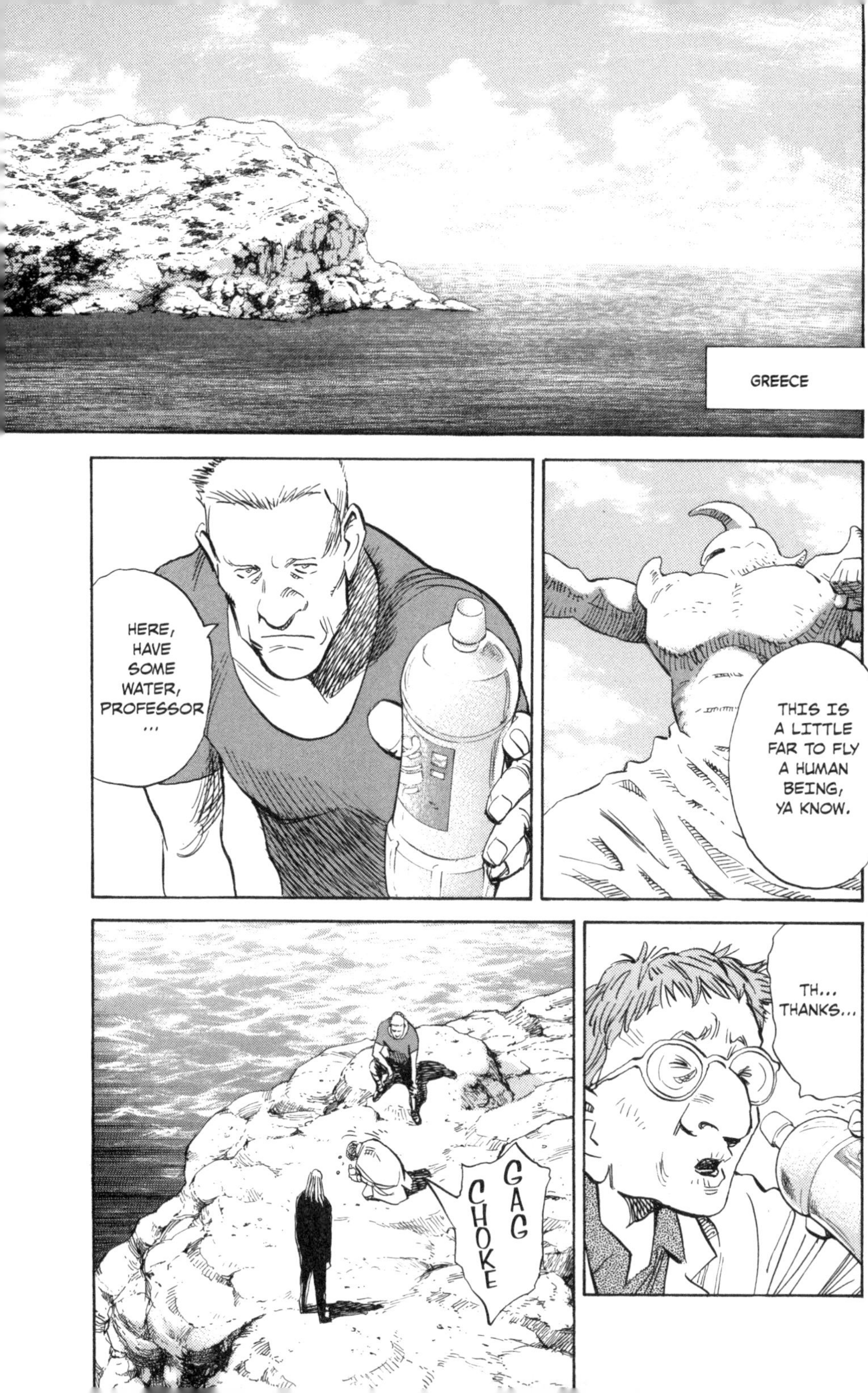
GREECE
THIS IS A LITTLE FAR TO FLY A HUMAN BEING, YA KNOW.
HERE, HAVE SOME WATER, PROFESSOR ...
TH... THANKS...
GAG
CHOKE

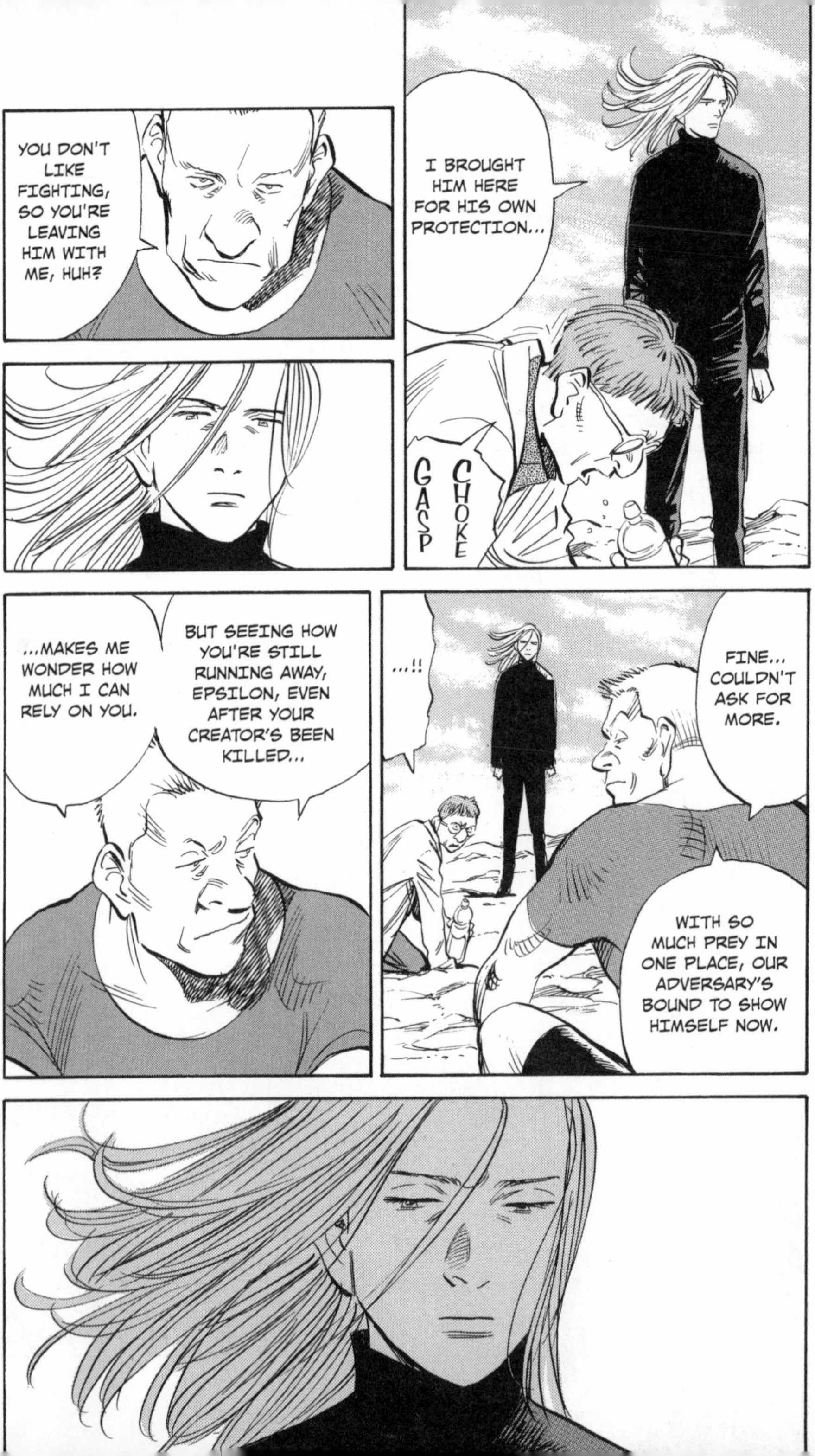
I BROUGHT HIM HERE FOR HIS OWN PROTECTION...
CHOKE
GASP
YOU DON'T LIKE FIGHTING, SO YOU'RE LEAVING HIM WITH ME, HUH?
FINE... COULDN'T ASK FOR MORE.
...!!
WITH SO MUCH PREY IN ONE PLACE, OUR ADVERSARY'S BOUND TO SHOW HIMSELF NOW.
BUT SEEING HOW YOU'RE STILL RUNNING AWAY, EPSILON, EVEN AFTER YOUR CREATOR'S BEEN KILLED...
...MAKES ME WONDER HOW MUCH I CAN RELY ON YOU.

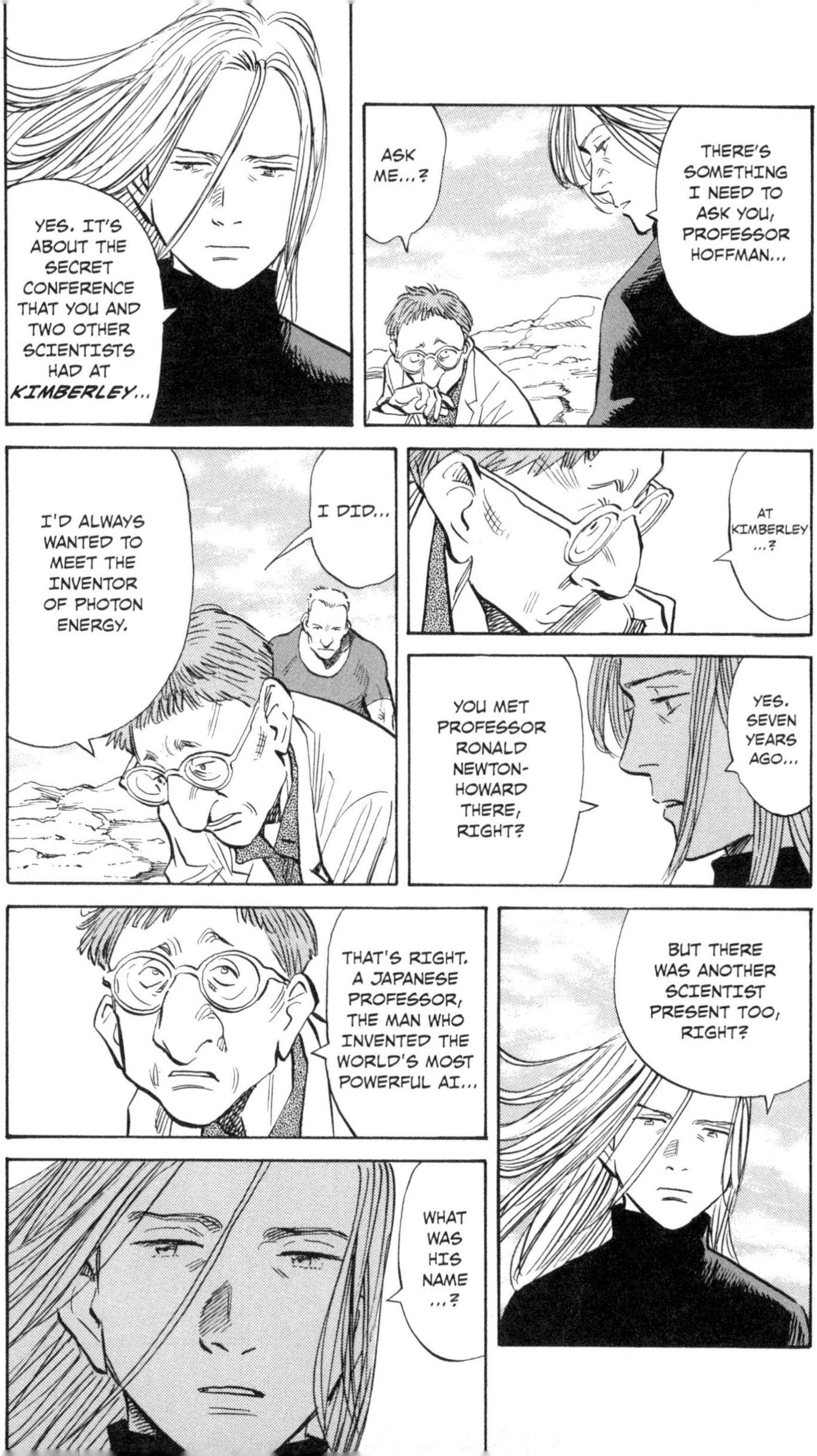
THERE'S SOMETHING I NEED TO ASK YOU, PROFESSOR HOFFMAN...
ASK ME...?
YES. IT'S ABOUT THE SECRET CONFERENCE THAT YOU AND TWO OTHER SCIENTISTS HAD AT KIMBERLEY...
AT KIMBERLEY...?
YES. SEVEN YEARS AGO...
YOU MET PROFESSOR RONALD NEWTON-HOWARD THERE, RIGHT?
I DID...
I'D ALWAYS WANTED TO MEET THE INVENTOR OF PHOTON ENERGY.
BUT THERE WAS ANOTHER SCIENTIST PRESENT TOO, RIGHT?
THAT'S RIGHT. A JAPANESE PROFESSOR, THE MAN WHO INVENTED THE WORLD'S MOST POWERFUL AI...
WHAT WAS HIS NAME...?

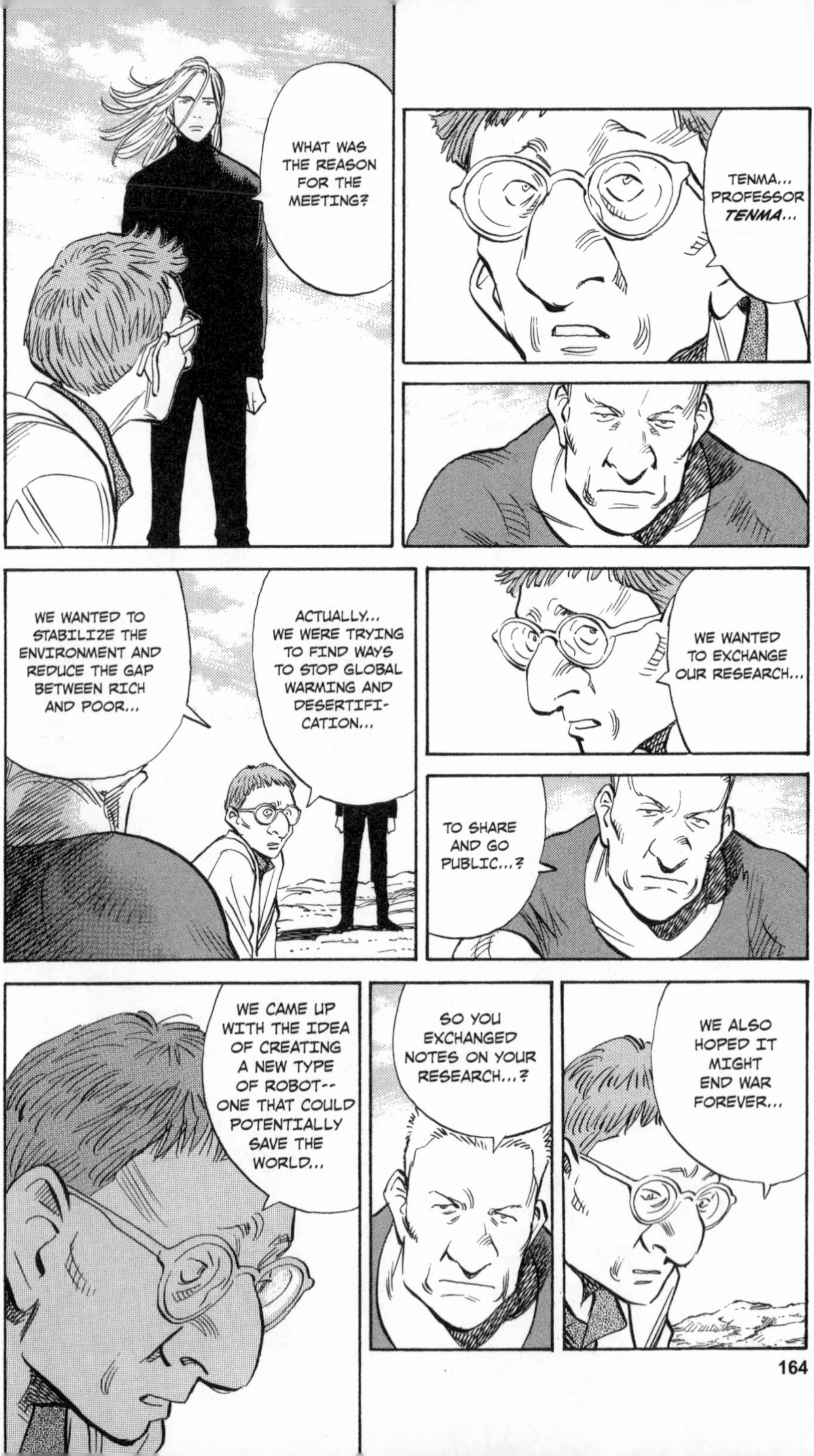
TENMA... PROFESSOR *TENMA*...
WHAT WAS THE REASON FOR THE MEETING?
WE WANTED TO EXCHANGE OUR RESEARCH...
TO SHARE AND GO PUBLIC...?
ACTUALLY... WE WERE TRYING TO FIND WAYS TO STOP GLOBAL WARMING AND DESERTIFI-CATION...
WE WANTED TO STABILIZE THE ENVIRONMENT AND REDUCE THE GAP BETWEEN RICH AND POOR...
WE ALSO HOPED IT MIGHT END WAR FOREVER...
SO YOU EXCHANGED NOTES ON YOUR RESEARCH...?
WE CAME UP WITH THE IDEA OF CREATING A NEW TYPE OF ROBOT-- ONE THAT COULD POTENTIALLY SAVE THE WORLD...

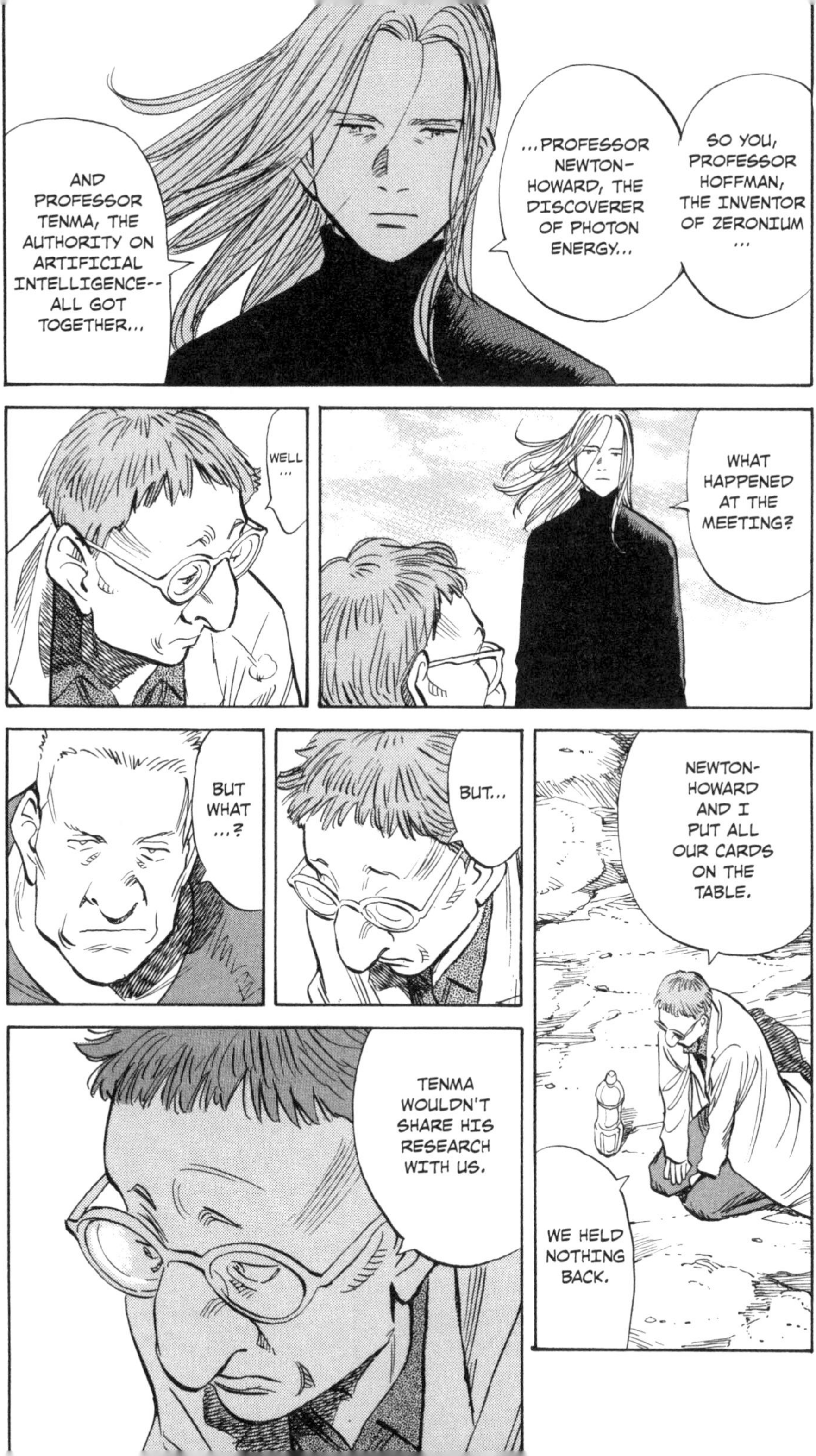
SO YOU, PROFESSOR HOFFMAN, THE INVENTOR OF ZERONIUM ...
...PROFESSOR NEWTON-HOWARD, THE DISCOVERER OF PHOTON ENERGY...
AND PROFESSOR TENMA, THE AUTHORITY ON ARTIFICIAL INTELLIGENCE-- ALL GOT TOGETHER...
WHAT HAPPENED AT THE MEETING?
WELL ...
NEWTON-HOWARD AND I PUT ALL OUR CARDS ON THE TABLE.
WE HELD NOTHING BACK.
BUT...
BUT WHAT ...?
TENMA WOULDN'T SHARE HIS RESEARCH WITH US.

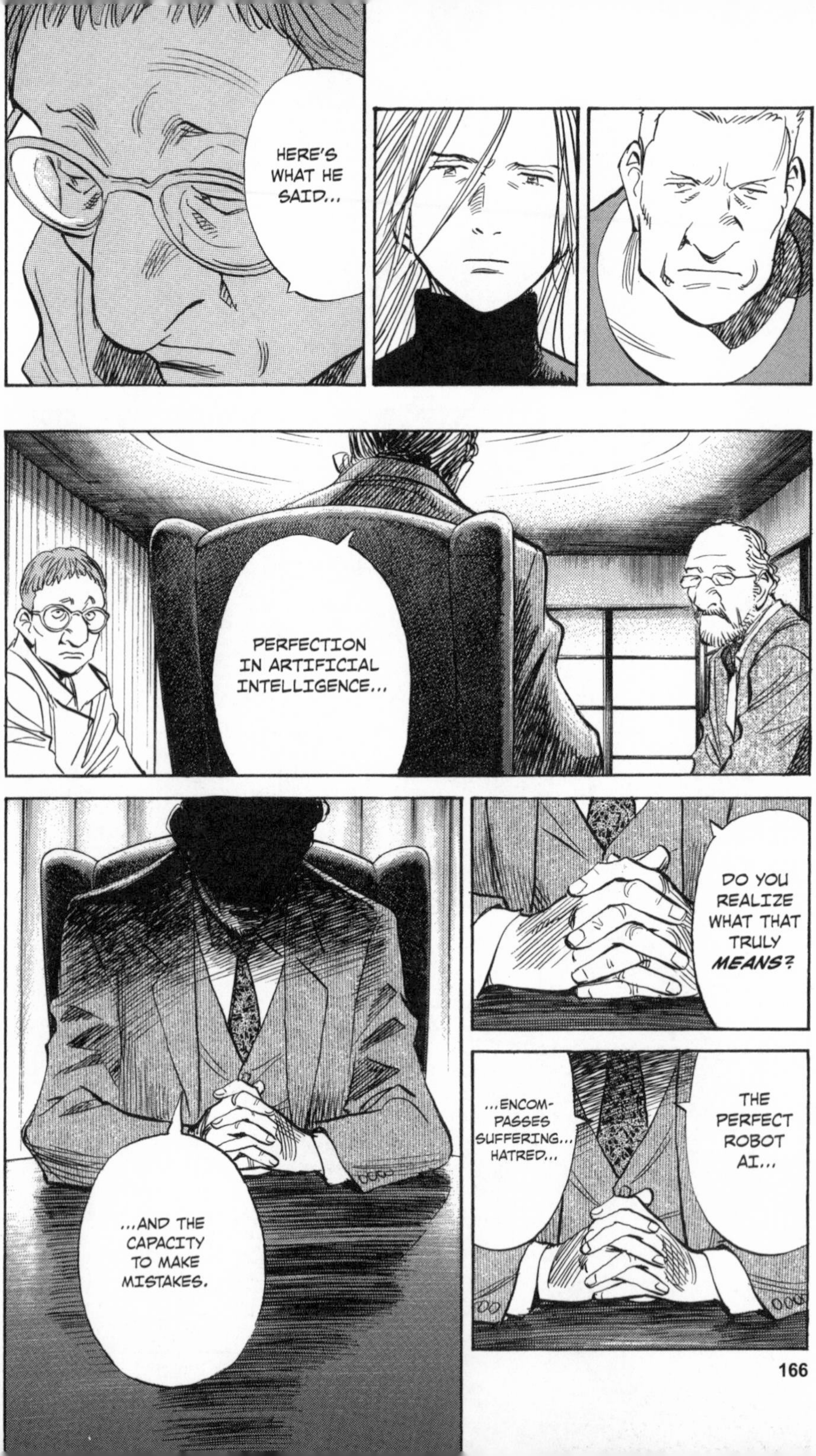
HERE'S WHAT HE SAID...
PERFECTION IN ARTIFICIAL INTELLIGENCE...
DO YOU REALIZE WHAT THAT TRULY *MEANS*?
THE PERFECT ROBOT AI...
...ENCOMPASSES SUFFERING... HATRED...
...AND THE CAPACITY TO MAKE MISTAKES.

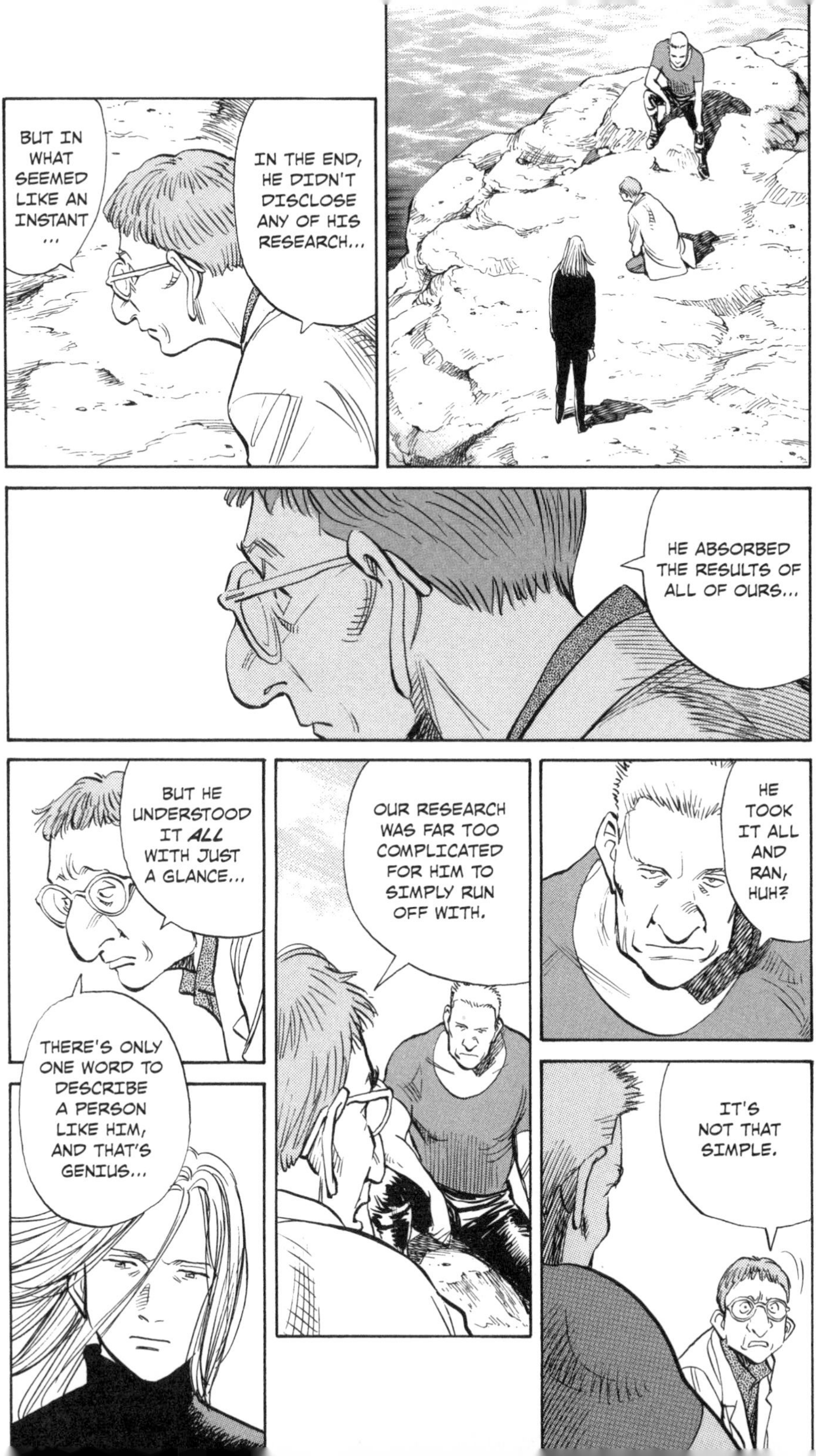
IN THE END, HE DIDN'T DISCLOSE ANY OF HIS RESEARCH...
BUT IN WHAT SEEMED LIKE AN INSTANT...
HE ABSORBED THE RESULTS OF ALL OF OURS...
HE TOOK IT ALL AND RAN, HUH?
IT'S NOT THAT SIMPLE.
OUR RESEARCH WAS FAR TOO COMPLICATED FOR HIM TO SIMPLY RUN OFF WITH.
BUT HE UNDERSTOOD IT *ALL* WITH JUST A GLANCE...
THERE'S ONLY ONE WORD TO DESCRIBE A PERSON LIKE HIM, AND THAT'S GENIUS...

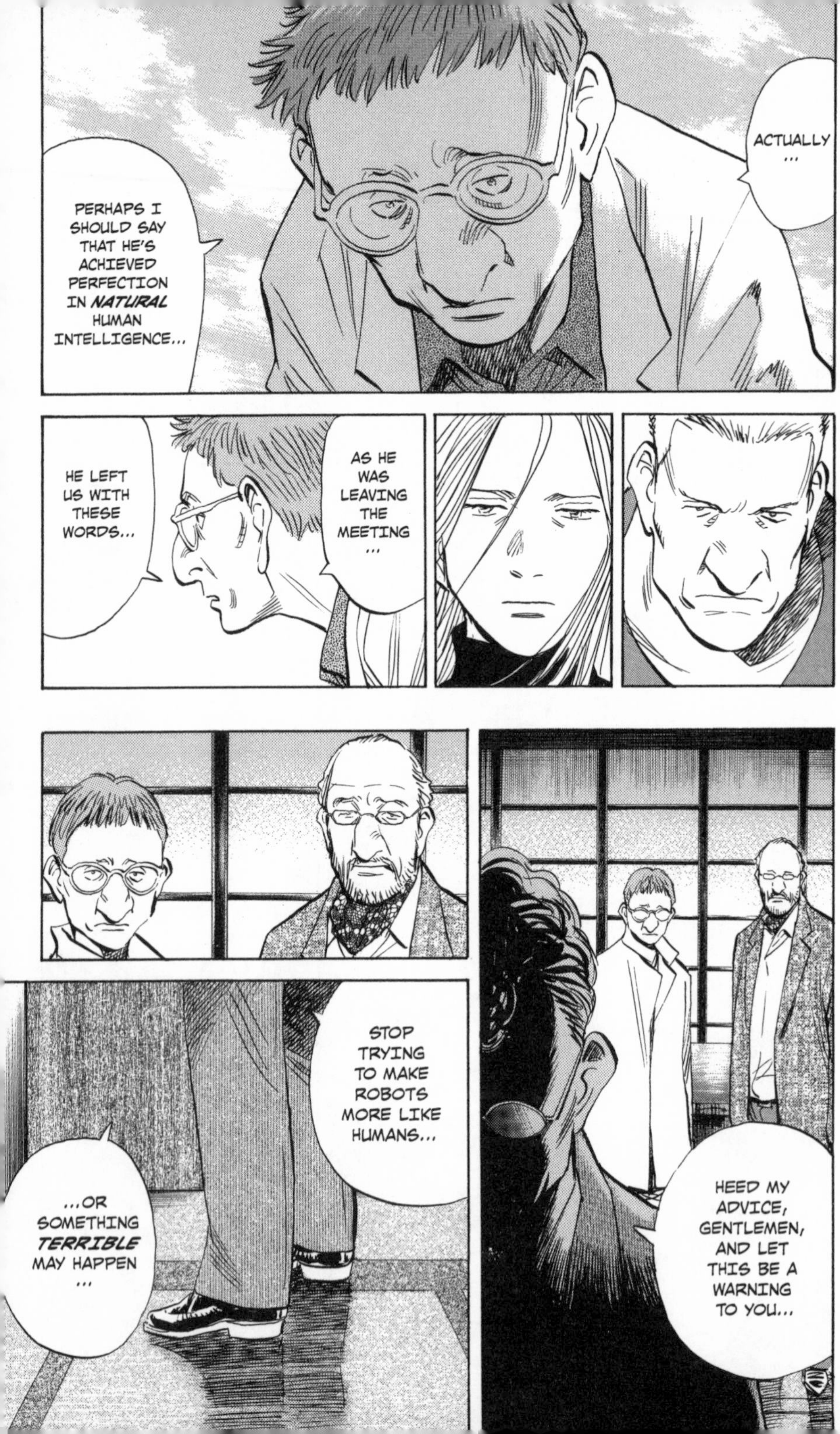
ACTUALLY ...
PERHAPS I SHOULD SAY THAT HE'S ACHIEVED PERFECTION IN *NATURAL* HUMAN INTELLIGENCE...
AS HE WAS LEAVING THE MEETING ...
HE LEFT US WITH THESE WORDS...
HEED MY ADVICE, GENTLEMEN, AND LET THIS BE A WARNING TO YOU...
STOP TRYING TO MAKE ROBOTS MORE LIKE HUMANS...
...OR SOMETHING *TERRIBLE* MAY HAPPEN ...

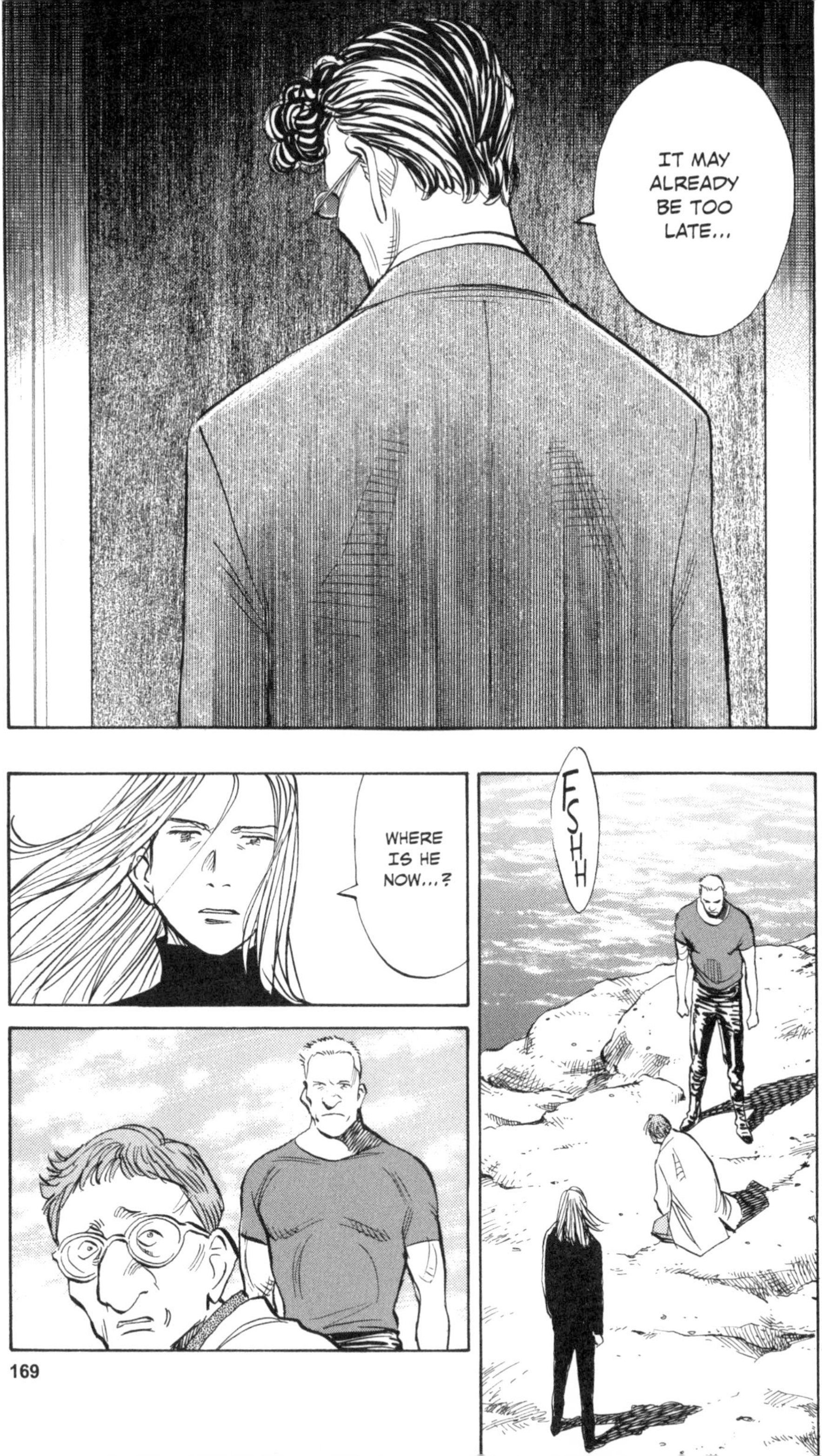
IT MAY ALREADY BE TOO LATE...
FSHH
WHERE IS HE NOW...?

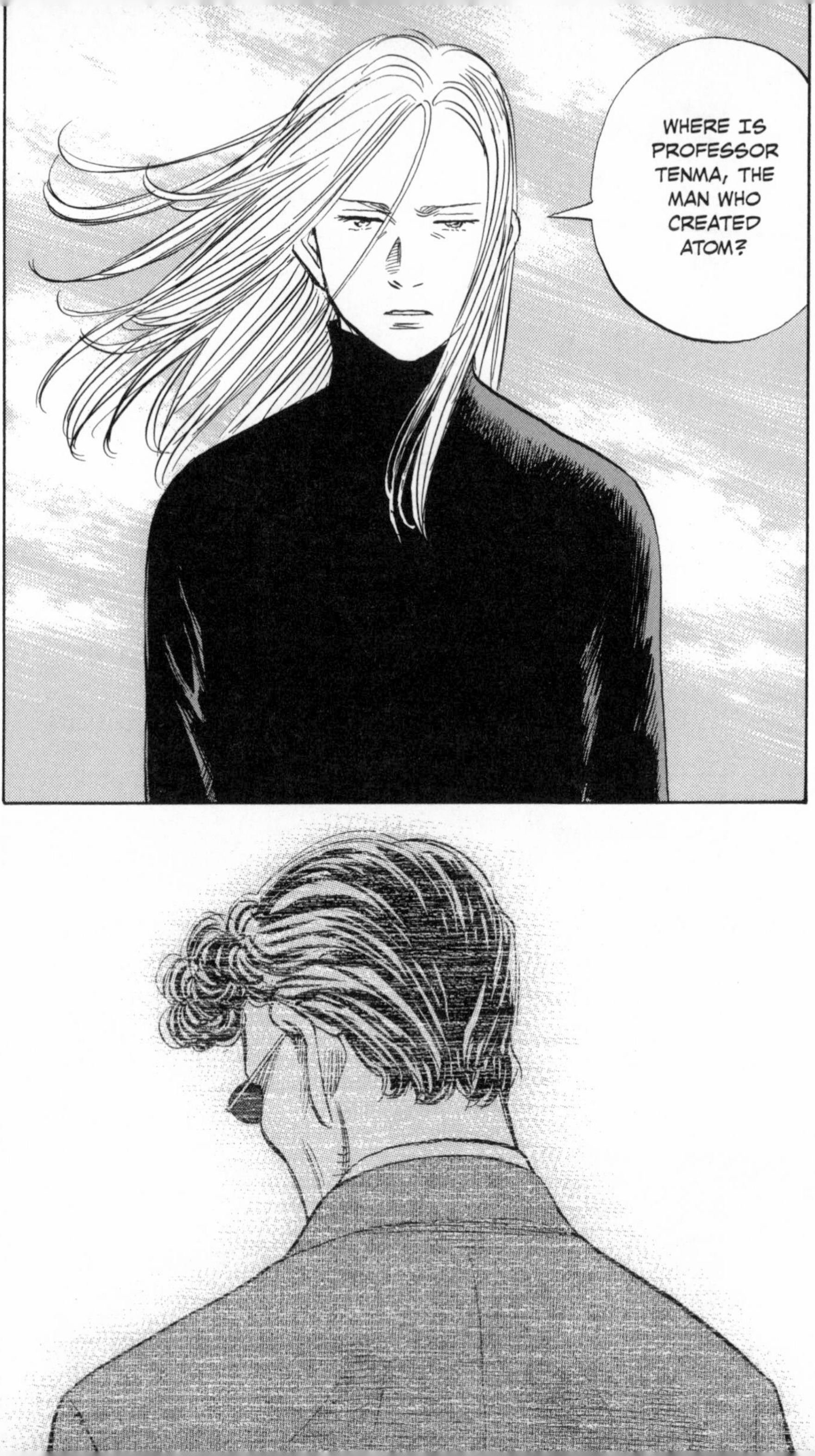
WHERE IS PROFESSOR TENMA, THE MAN WHO CREATED ATOM?

Act 31 THE GREATEST ROBOT ON EARTH

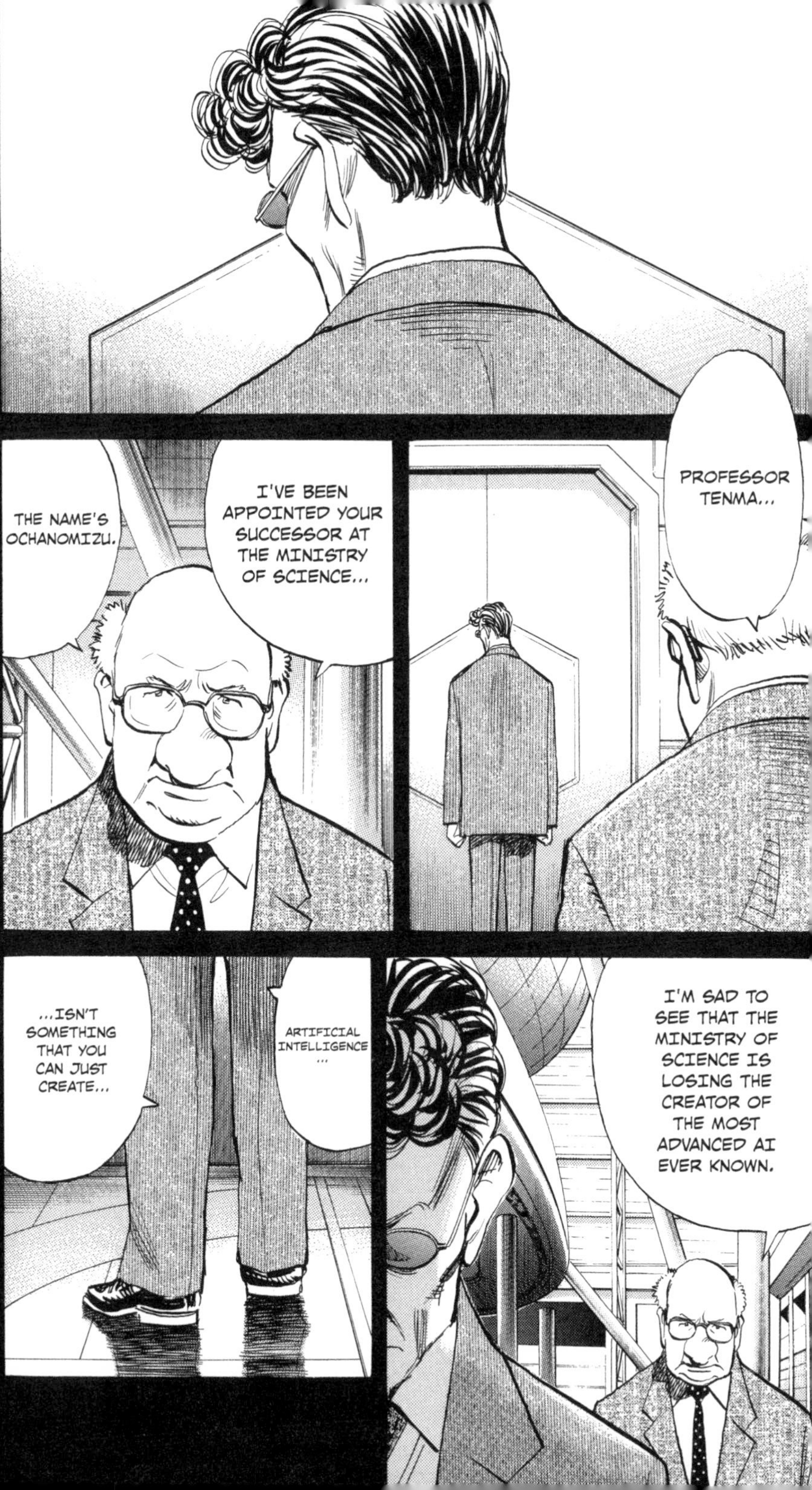
PROFESSOR TENMA...
I'VE BEEN APPOINTED YOUR SUCCESSOR AT THE MINISTRY OF SCIENCE...
THE NAME'S OCHANOMIZU.
I'M SAD TO SEE THAT THE MINISTRY OF SCIENCE IS LOSING THE CREATOR OF THE MOST ADVANCED AI EVER KNOWN.
ARTIFICIAL INTELLIGENCE...
...ISN'T SOMETHING THAT YOU CAN JUST CREATE...

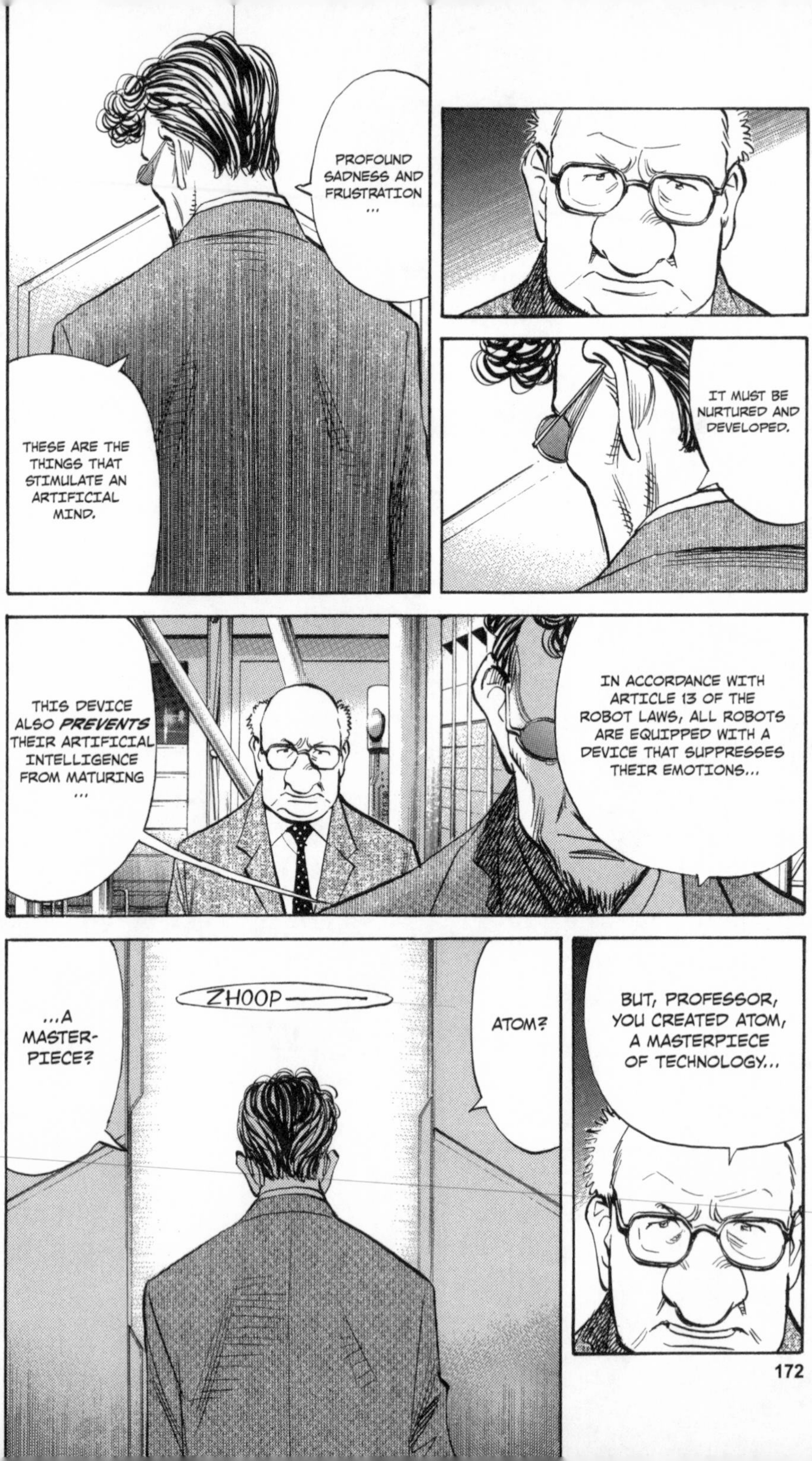
IT MUST BE NURTURED AND DEVELOPED.
PROFOUND SADNESS AND FRUSTRATION ...
THESE ARE THE THINGS THAT STIMULATE AN ARTIFICIAL MIND.
IN ACCORDANCE WITH ARTICLE 13 OF THE ROBOT LAWS, ALL ROBOTS ARE EQUIPPED WITH A DEVICE THAT SUPPRESSES THEIR EMOTIONS...
THIS DEVICE ALSO ***PREVENTS*** THEIR ARTIFICIAL INTELLIGENCE FROM MATURING ...
BUT, PROFESSOR, YOU CREATED ATOM, A MASTERPIECE OF TECHNOLOGY...
ATOM?
ZHOOP
...A MASTER-PIECE?

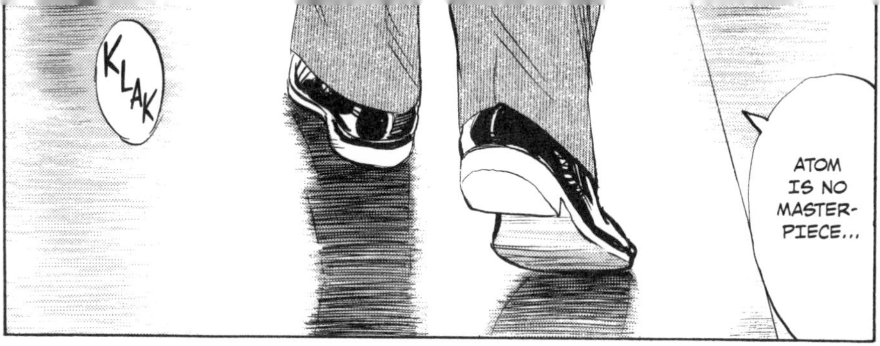
ATOM IS NO MASTER-PIECE...
KLAK
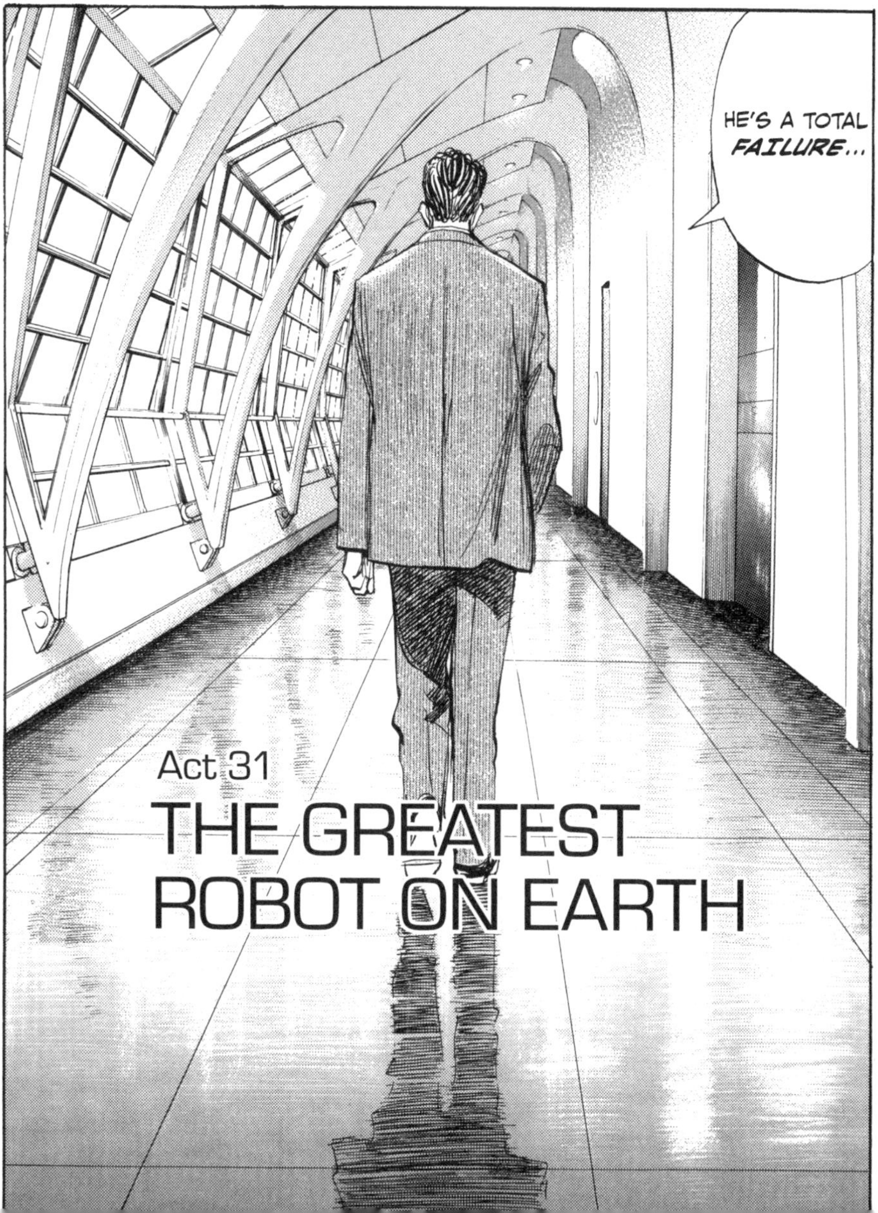
HE'S A TOTAL *FAILURE*...
Act 31
THE GREATEST ROBOT ON EARTH

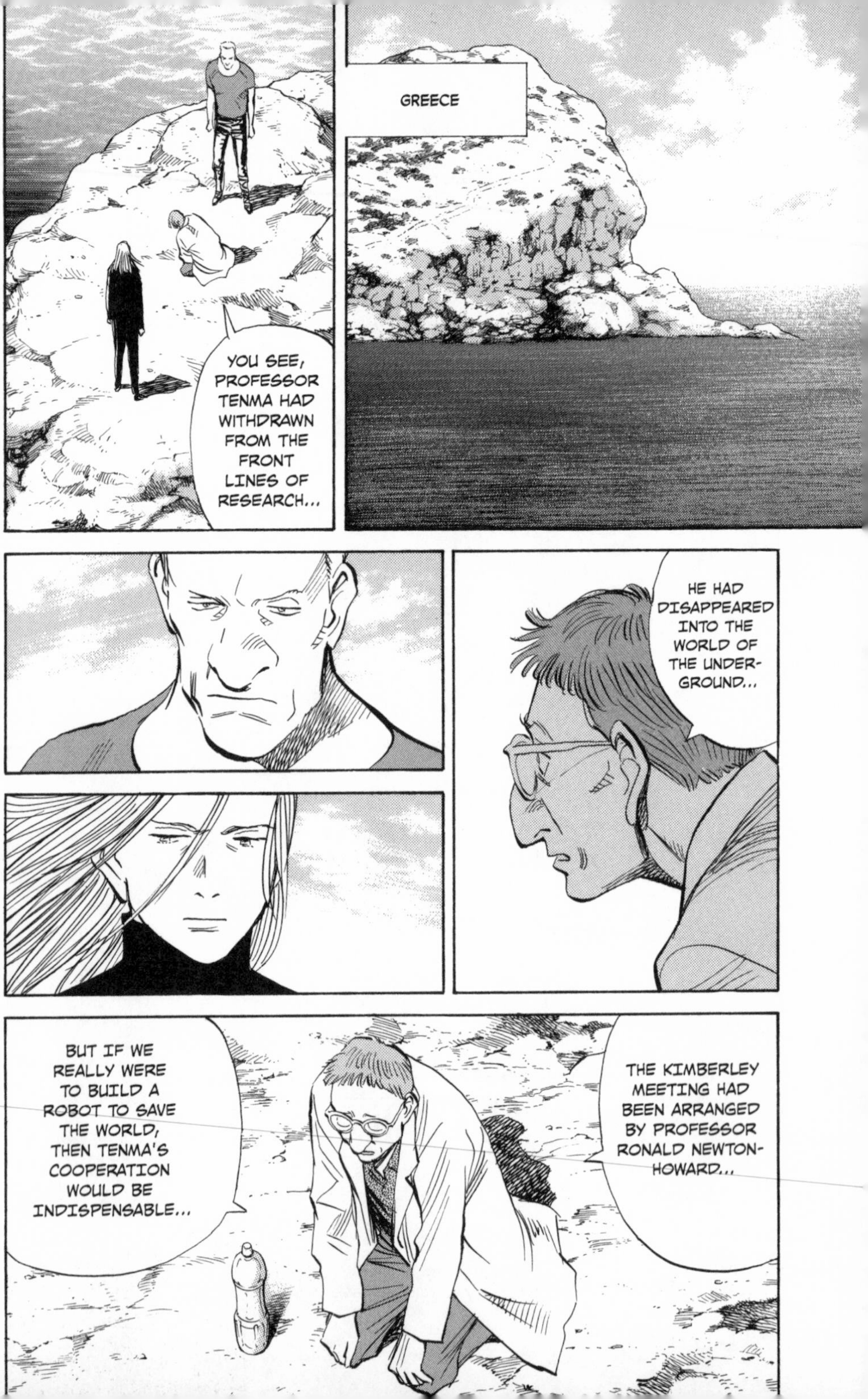
GREECE
YOU SEE, PROFESSOR TENMA HAD WITHDRAWN FROM THE FRONT LINES OF RESEARCH...
HE HAD DISAPPEARED INTO THE WORLD OF THE UNDER-GROUND...
THE KIMBERLEY MEETING HAD BEEN ARRANGED BY PROFESSOR RONALD NEWTON-HOWARD...
BUT IF WE REALLY WERE TO BUILD A ROBOT TO SAVE THE WORLD, THEN TENMA'S COOPERATION WOULD BE INDISPENSABLE...

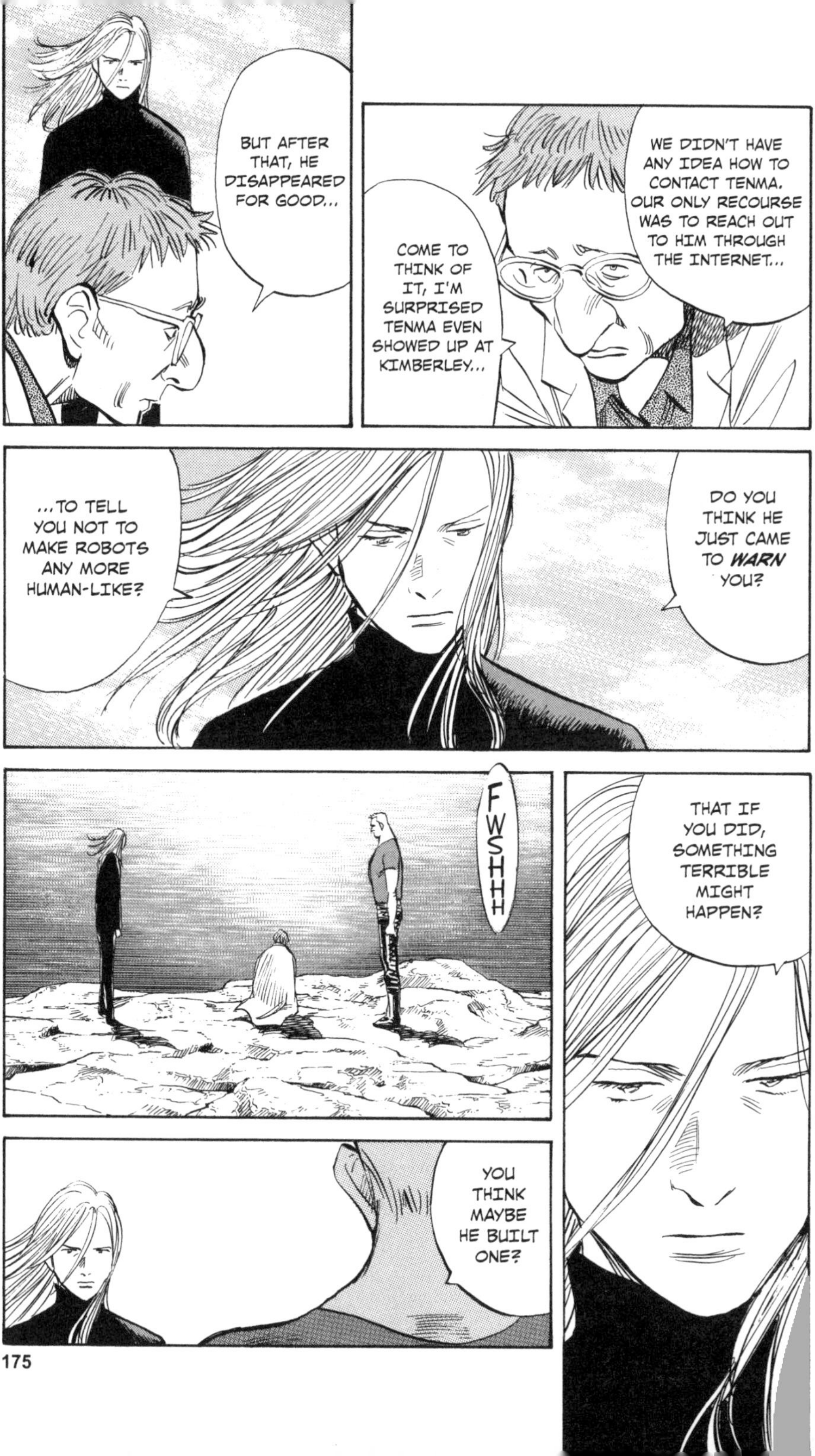
WE DIDN'T HAVE ANY IDEA HOW TO CONTACT TENMA. OUR ONLY RECOURSE WAS TO REACH OUT TO HIM THROUGH THE INTERNET...
COME TO THINK OF IT, I'M SURPRISED TENMA EVEN SHOWED UP AT KIMBERLEY...
BUT AFTER THAT, HE DISAPPEARED FOR GOOD...
DO YOU THINK HE JUST CAME TO *WARN* YOU?
...TO TELL YOU NOT TO MAKE ROBOTS ANY MORE HUMAN-LIKE?
THAT IF YOU DID, SOMETHING TERRIBLE MIGHT HAPPEN?
FWSHHH
YOU THINK MAYBE HE BUILT ONE?

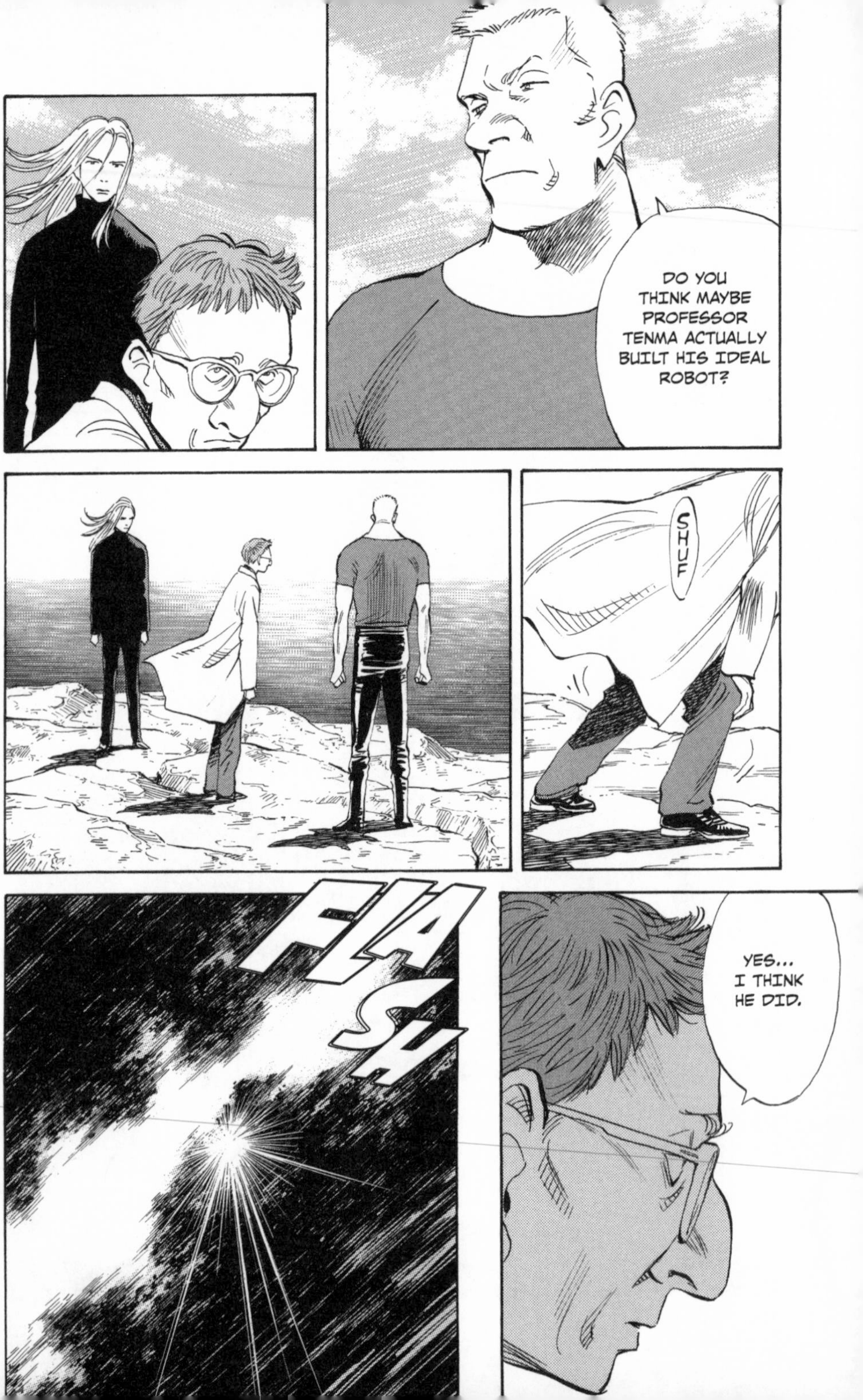
DO YOU THINK MAYBE PROFESSOR TENMA ACTUALLY BUILT HIS IDEAL ROBOT?
SHUF
YES... I THINK HE DID.
FLASH

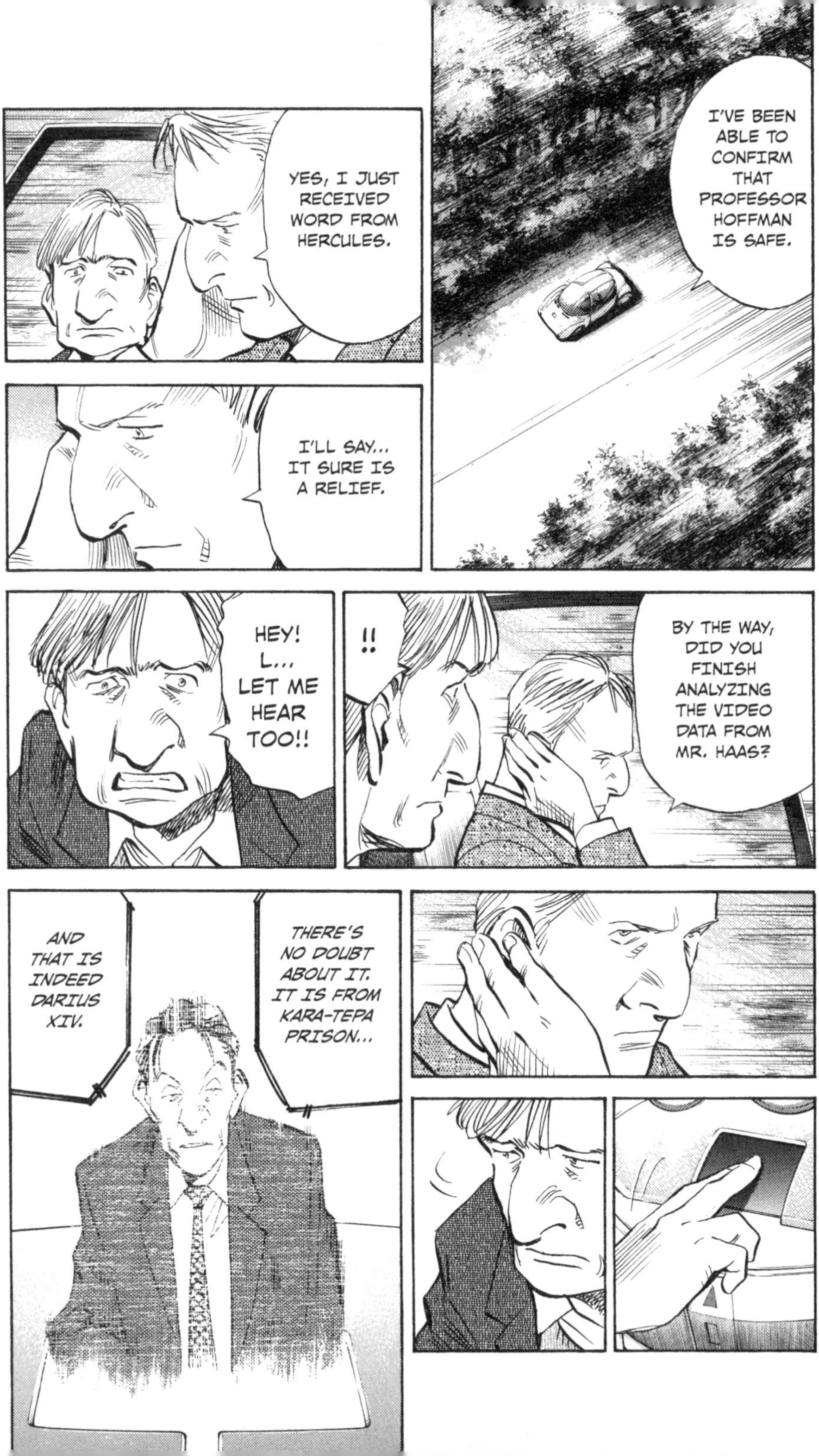
I'VE BEEN ABLE TO CONFIRM THAT PROFESSOR HOFFMAN IS SAFE.
YES, I JUST RECEIVED WORD FROM HERCULES.
I'LL SAY... IT SURE IS A RELIEF.
BY THE WAY, DID YOU FINISH ANALYZING THE VIDEO DATA FROM MR. HAAS?
!!
HEY! L... LET ME HEAR TOO!!
THERE'S NO DOUBT ABOUT IT. IT IS FROM KARA-TEPA PRISON...
AND THAT IS INDEED DARIUS XIV.

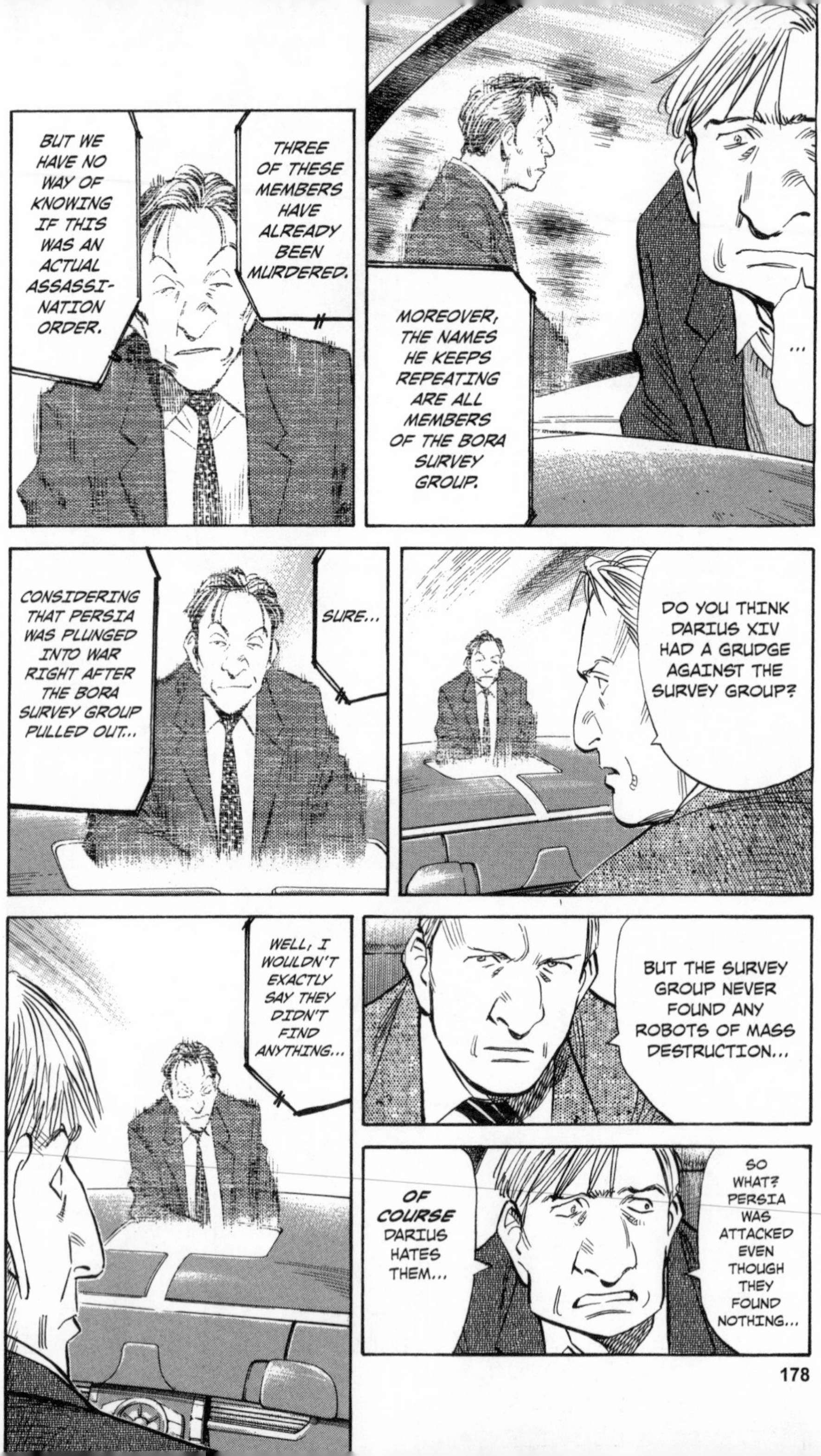
MOREOVER, THE NAMES HE KEEPS REPEATING ARE ALL MEMBERS OF THE BORA SURVEY GROUP.
...
THREE OF THESE MEMBERS HAVE ALREADY BEEN MURDERED.
BUT WE HAVE NO WAY OF KNOWING IF THIS WAS AN ACTUAL ASSASSI-NATION ORDER.
DO YOU THINK DARIUS XIV HAD A GRUDGE AGAINST THE SURVEY GROUP?
SURE...
CONSIDERING THAT PERSIA WAS PLUNGED INTO WAR RIGHT AFTER THE BORA SURVEY GROUP PULLED OUT...
BUT THE SURVEY GROUP NEVER FOUND ANY ROBOTS OF MASS DESTRUCTION...
SO WHAT? PERSIA WAS ATTACKED EVEN THOUGH THEY FOUND NOTHING...
OF COURSE DARIUS HATES THEM...
WELL, I WOULDN'T EXACTLY SAY THEY DIDN'T FIND ANYTHING...

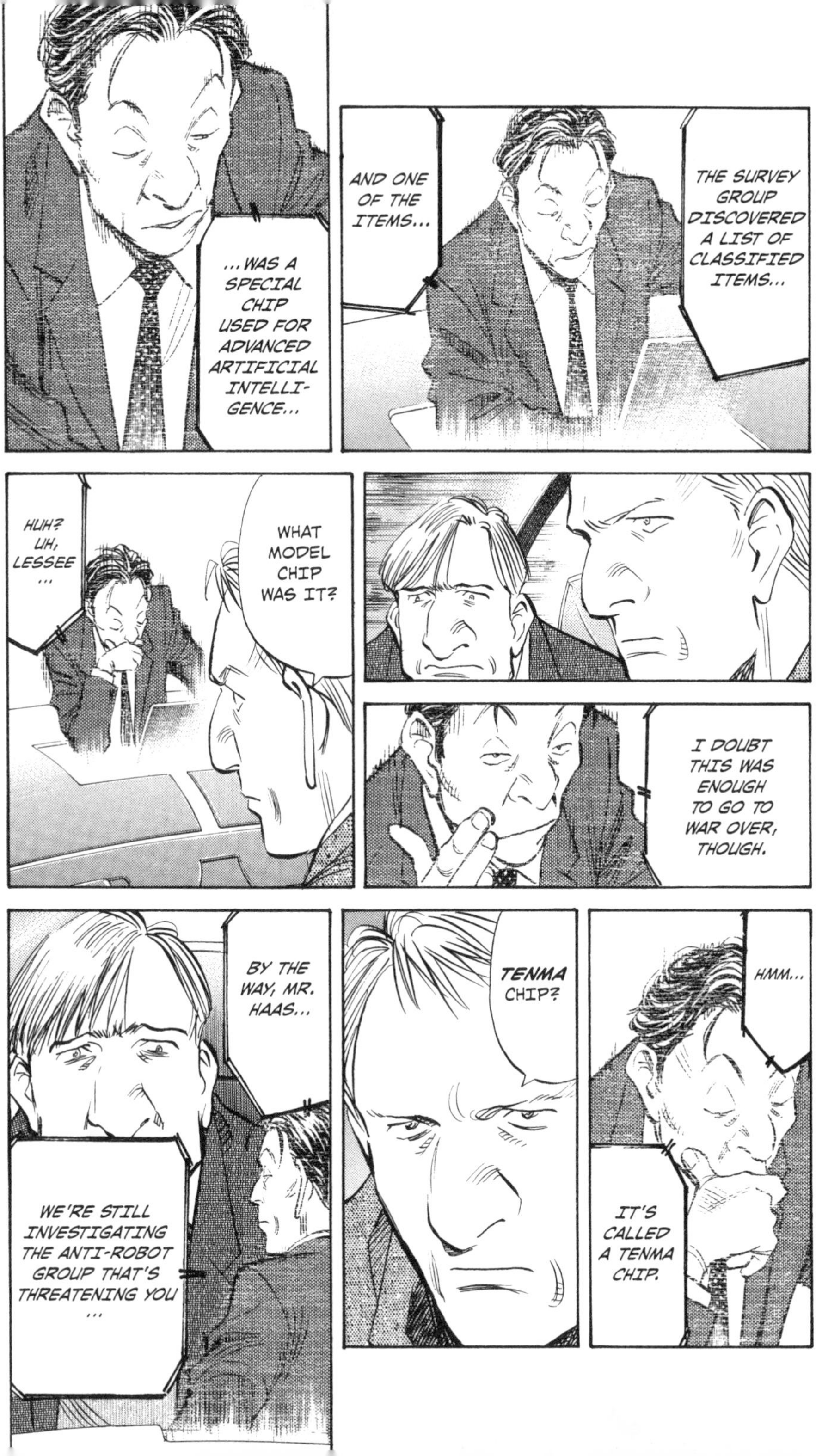
THE SURVEY GROUP DISCOVERED A LIST OF CLASSIFIED ITEMS...
AND ONE OF THE ITEMS...
...WAS A SPECIAL CHIP USED FOR ADVANCED ARTIFICIAL INTELLI-GENCE...
I DOUBT THIS WAS ENOUGH TO GO TO WAR OVER, THOUGH.
WHAT MODEL CHIP WAS IT?
HUH? UH, LESSEE...
HMM...
IT'S CALLED A TENMA CHIP.
TENMA CHIP?
BY THE WAY, MR. HAAS...
WE'RE STILL INVESTIGATING THE ANTI-ROBOT GROUP THAT'S THREATENING YOU...

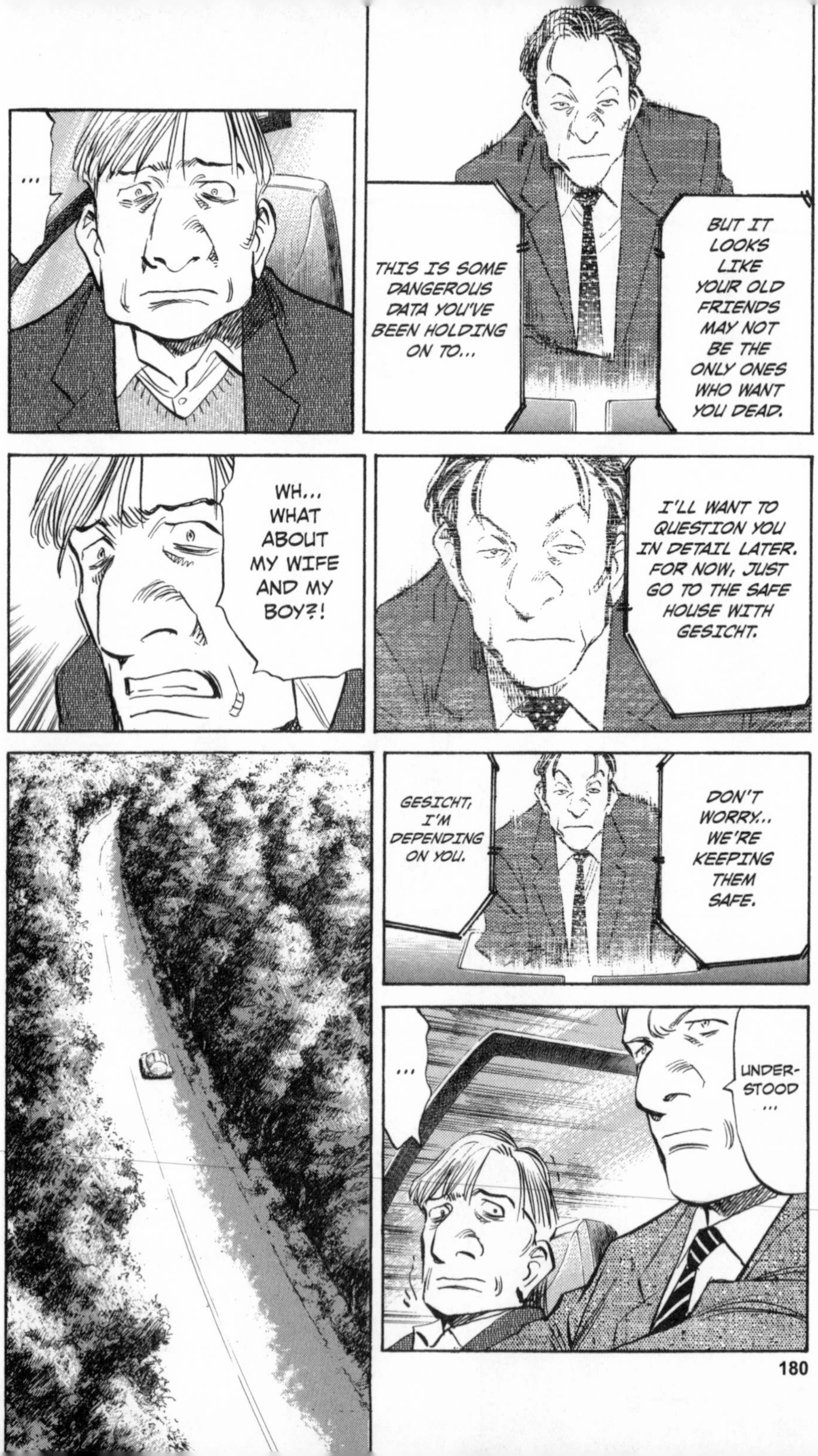
THIS IS SOME DANGEROUS DATA YOU'VE BEEN HOLDING ON TO...
BUT IT LOOKS LIKE YOUR OLD FRIENDS MAY NOT BE THE ONLY ONES WHO WANT YOU DEAD.
...
I'LL WANT TO QUESTION YOU IN DETAIL LATER. FOR NOW, JUST GO TO THE SAFE HOUSE WITH GESICHT.
WH... WHAT ABOUT MY WIFE AND MY BOY?!
DON'T WORRY... WE'RE KEEPING THEM SAFE.
GESICHT, I'M DEPENDING ON YOU.
UNDER-STOOD...
...

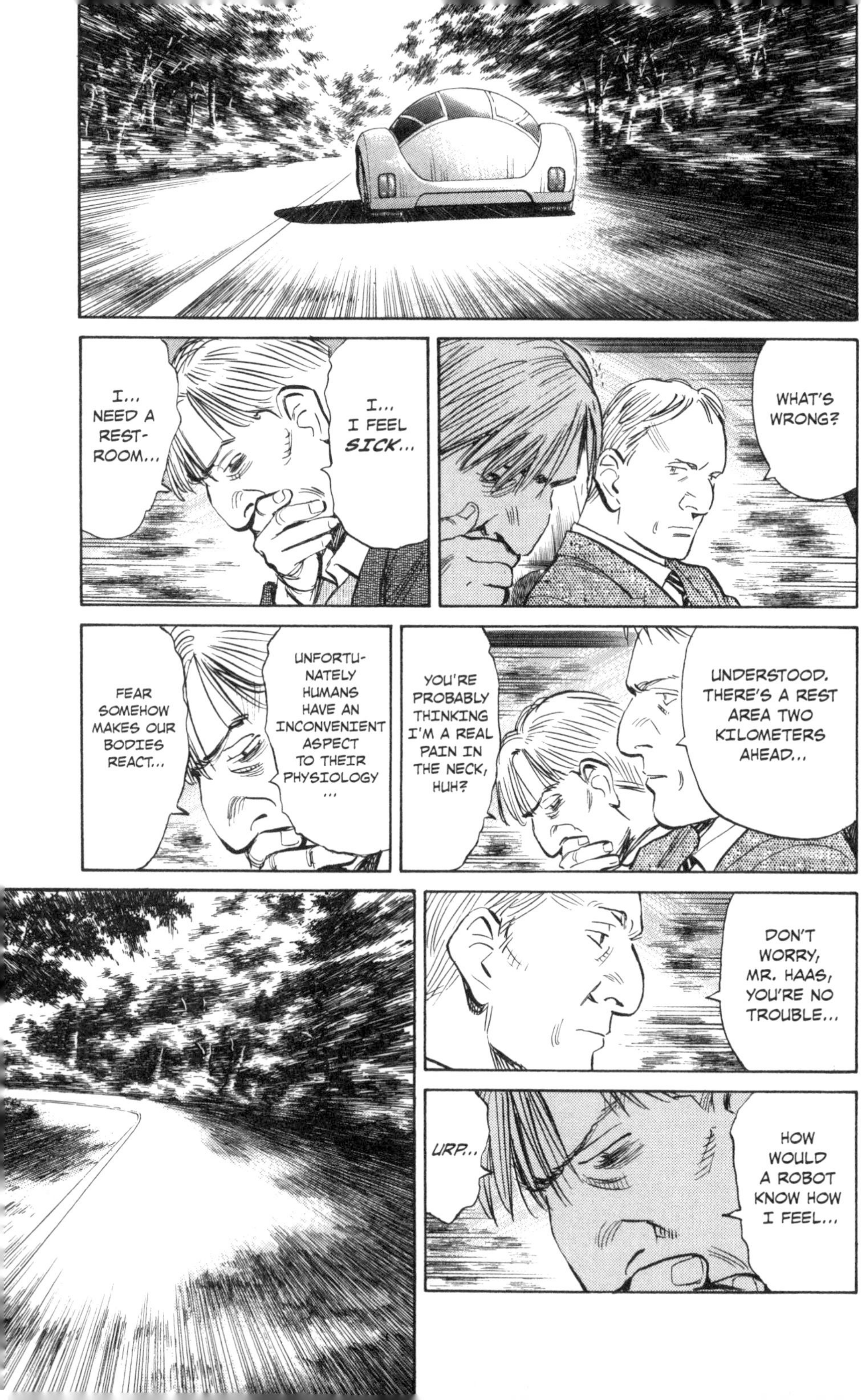
WHAT'S WRONG?
I... I FEEL SICK...
I... NEED A REST-ROOM...
UNDERSTOOD. THERE'S A REST AREA TWO KILOMETERS AHEAD...
YOU'RE PROBABLY THINKING I'M A REAL PAIN IN THE NECK, HUH?
UNFORTU-NATELY HUMANS HAVE AN INCONVENIENT ASPECT TO THEIR PHYSIOLOGY...
FEAR SOMEHOW MAKES OUR BODIES REACT...
DON'T WORRY, MR. HAAS, YOU'RE NO TROUBLE...
HOW WOULD A ROBOT KNOW HOW I FEEL...
URP...

SHOOM——

LET ME SCAN THE RESTROOM!

WAIT...

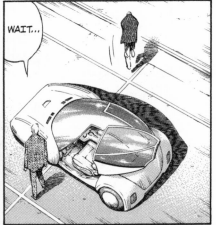

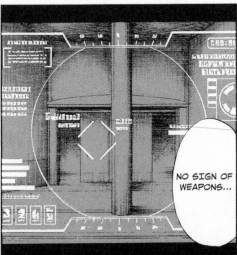

NO SIGN OF WEAPONS...

...

...I DETECT ONLY ONE GENERAL-PURPOSE CLEANING ROBOT NOT EQUIPPED WITH AI...

AND INSIDE...

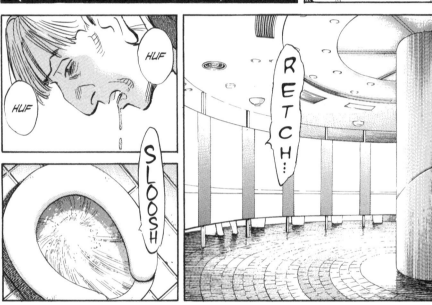

HUF

HUF

SLOOSH

RETCH...

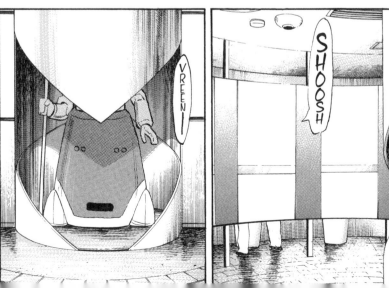

VREEN!

SHOOSH

VRREEN!

VURR

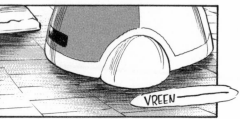

VREEN

VREEN

OCCUPIED...

KNOCK KNOCK

KNOCK KNOCK

CREAK

I SAID, IT'S *OCCUPIED!!*

184

HMPH... A CLEANING-BOT...
... MESSAGE FOR YOU...
WHAT?
IF YOU WANT TO SAVE YOUR FAMILY...
...YOU MUST KILL GESICHT...

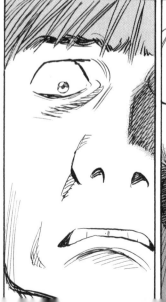

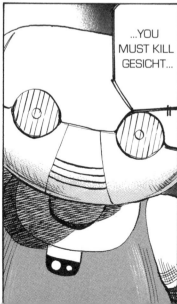

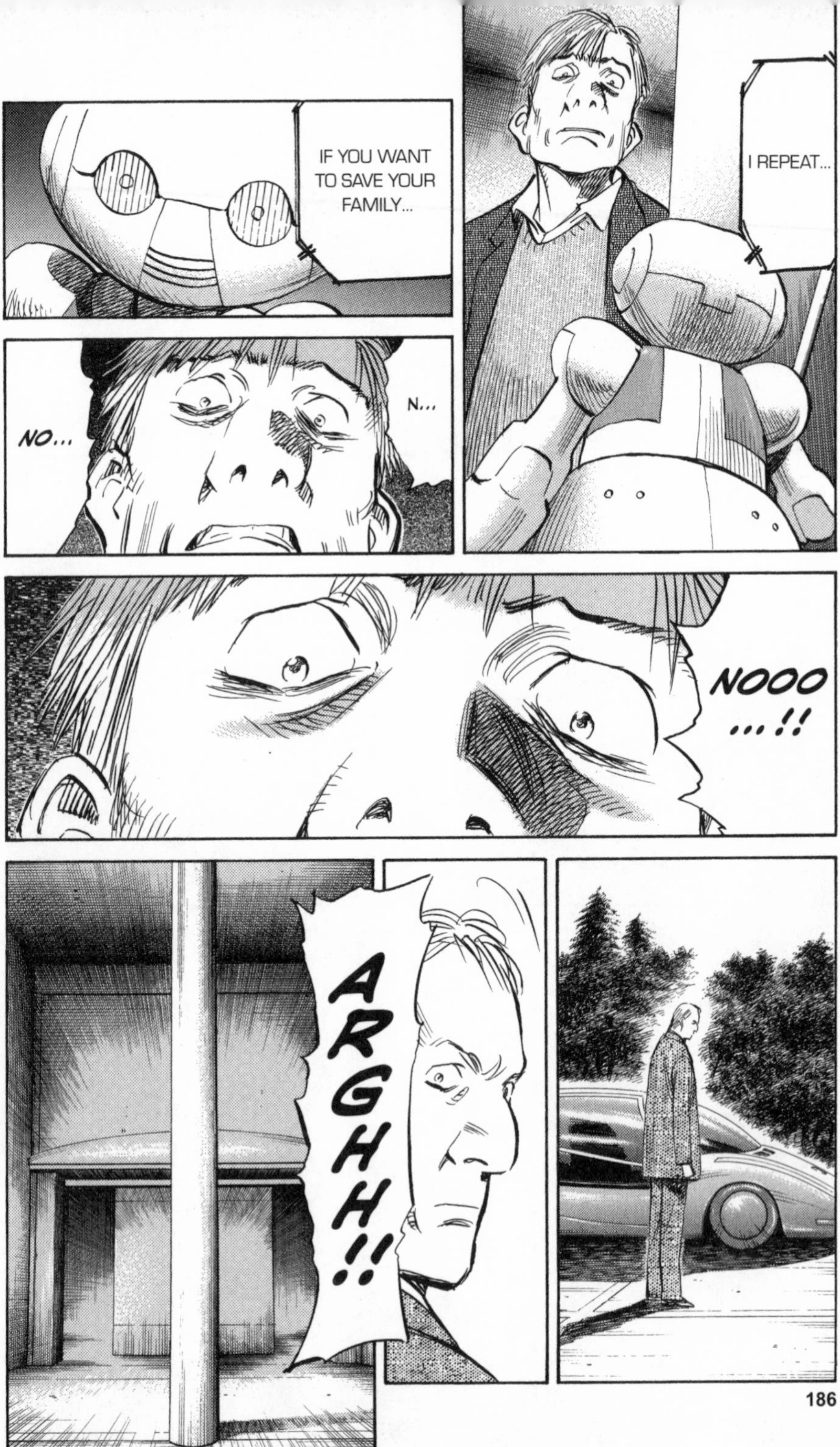
I REPEAT...
IF YOU WANT TO SAVE YOUR FAMILY...
N...
NO...
NOOO...!!
ARGHH!!

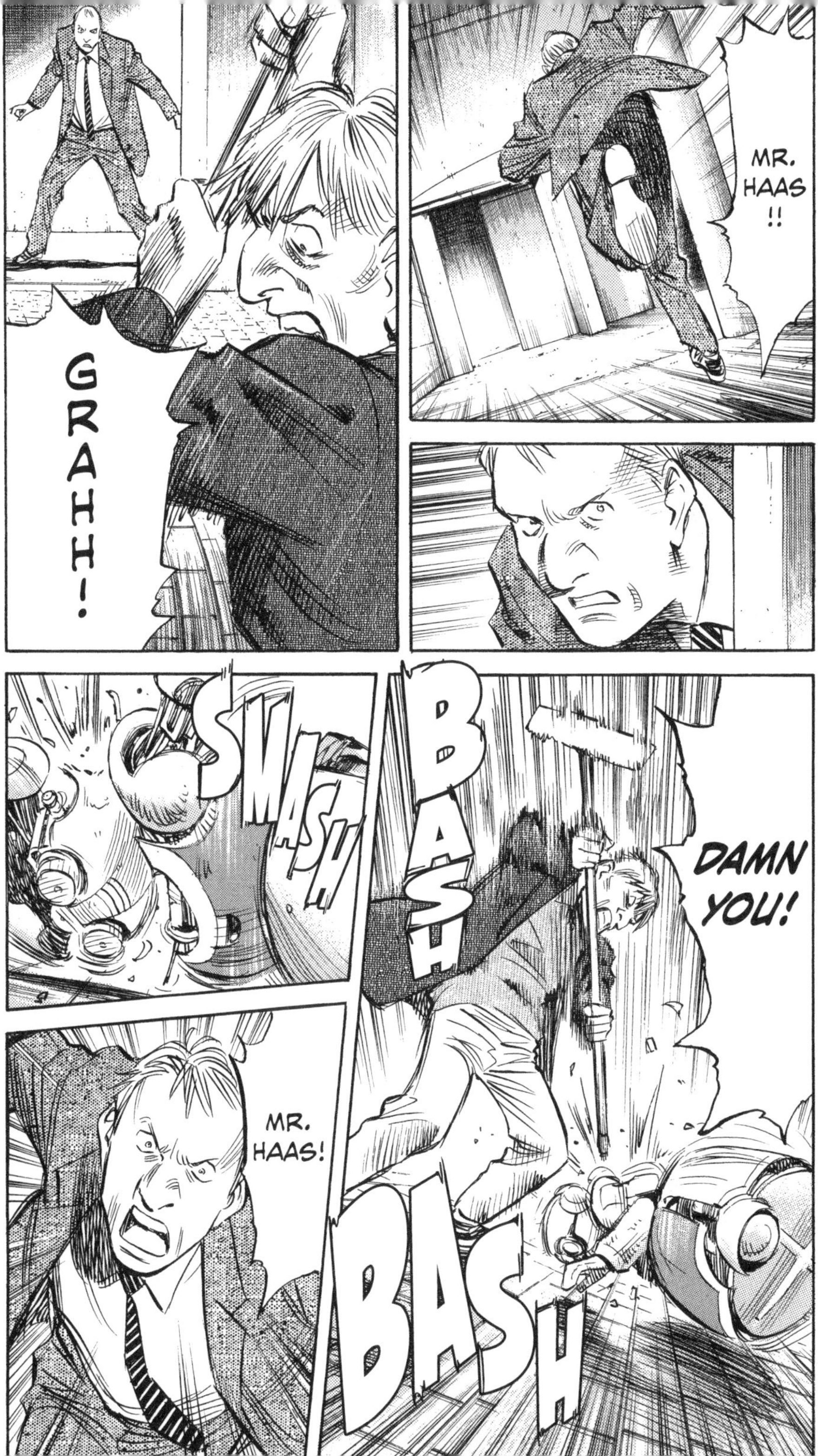
MR. HAAS !!
GRAHH!
BASH
DAMN YOU!
BASH
SMASH
MR. HAAS!

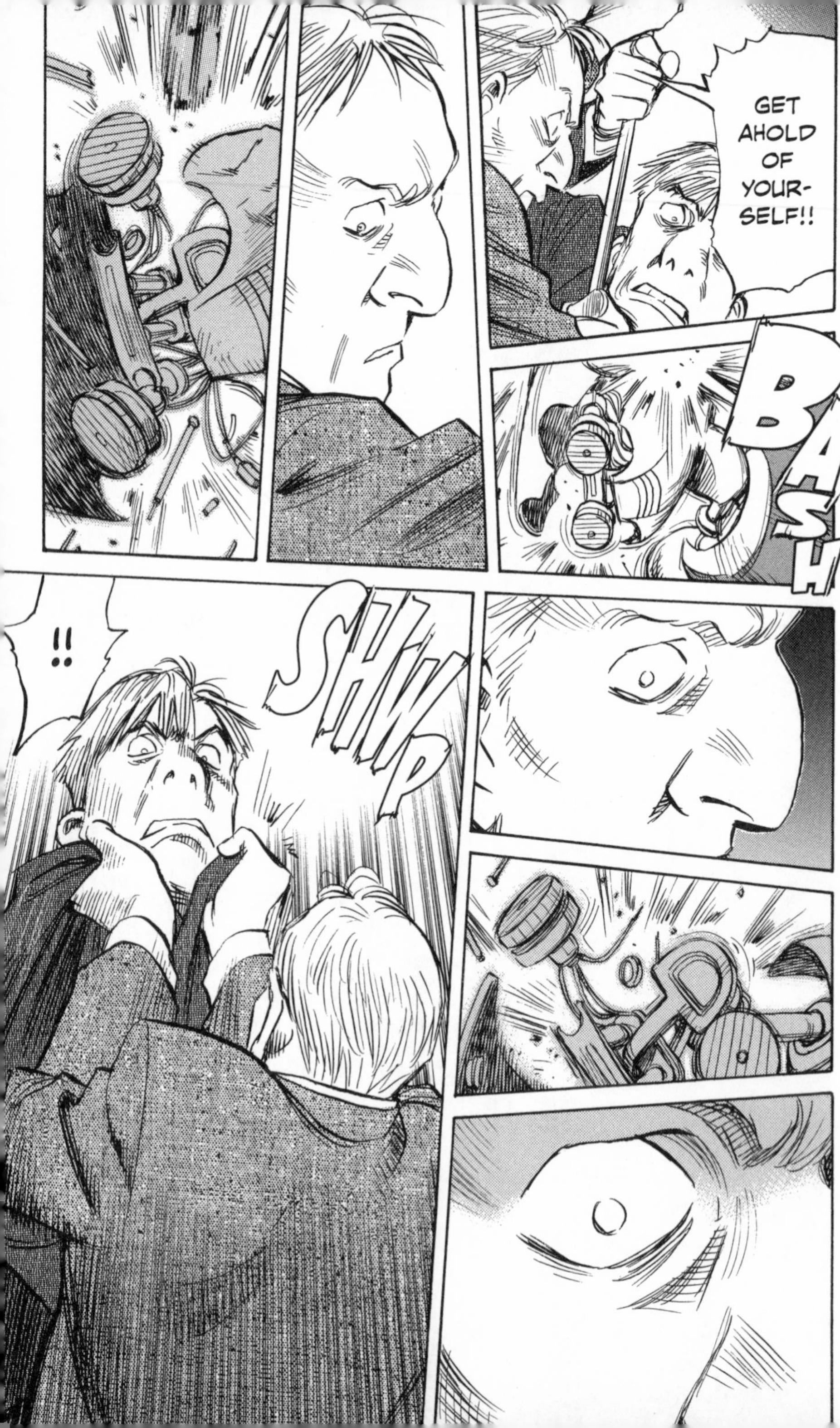
GET AHOLD OF YOUR-SELF!!
BASH
SHWP
!!

I SAID STOP!!

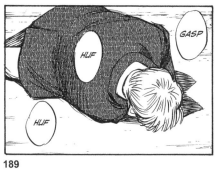

HUF

GASP

HUF

FWUMP

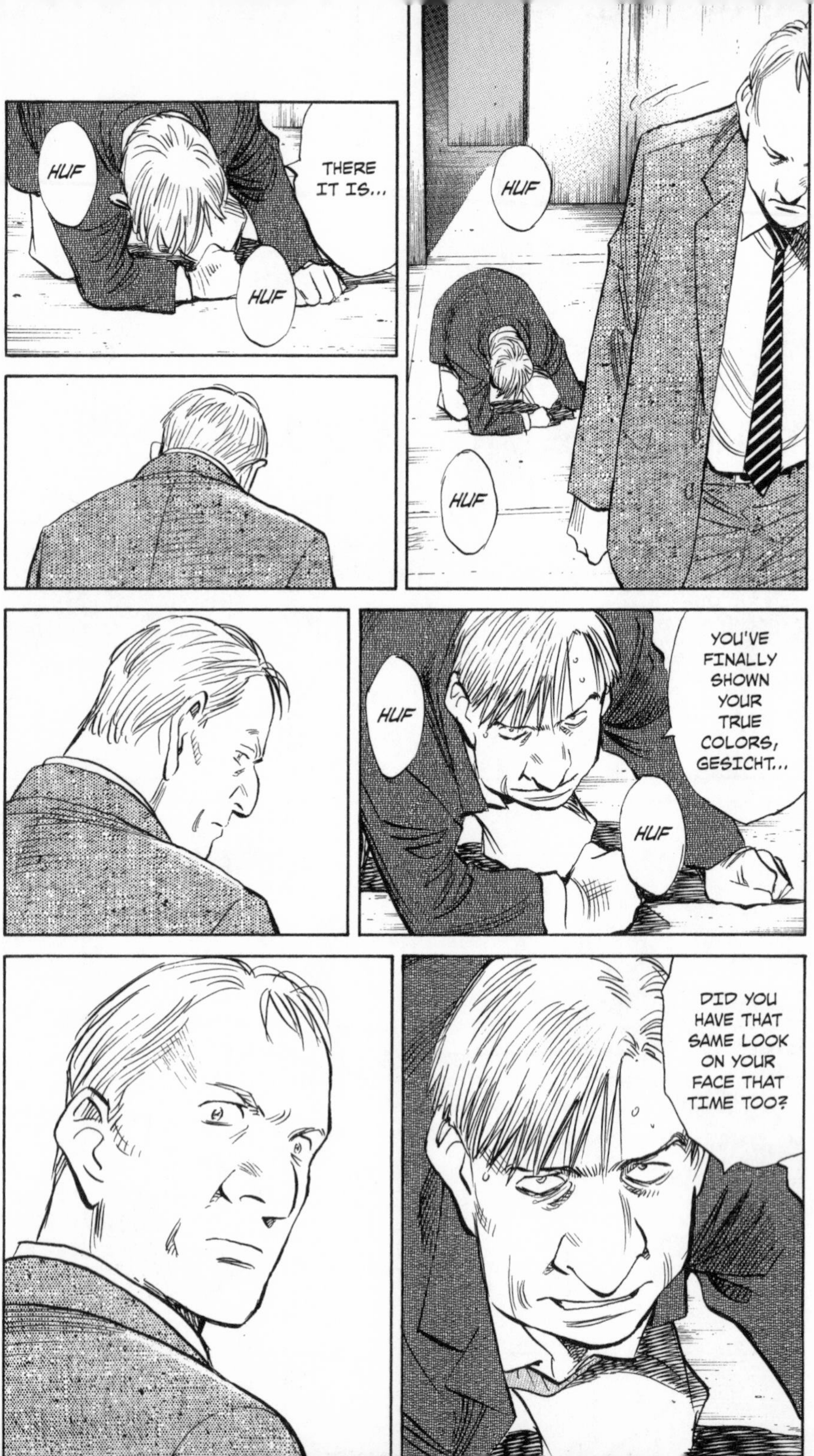
HUF
HUF
THERE IT IS...
HUF
HUF
YOU'VE FINALLY SHOWN YOUR TRUE COLORS, GESICHT...
HUF
HUF
DID YOU HAVE THAT SAME LOOK ON YOUR FACE THAT TIME TOO?

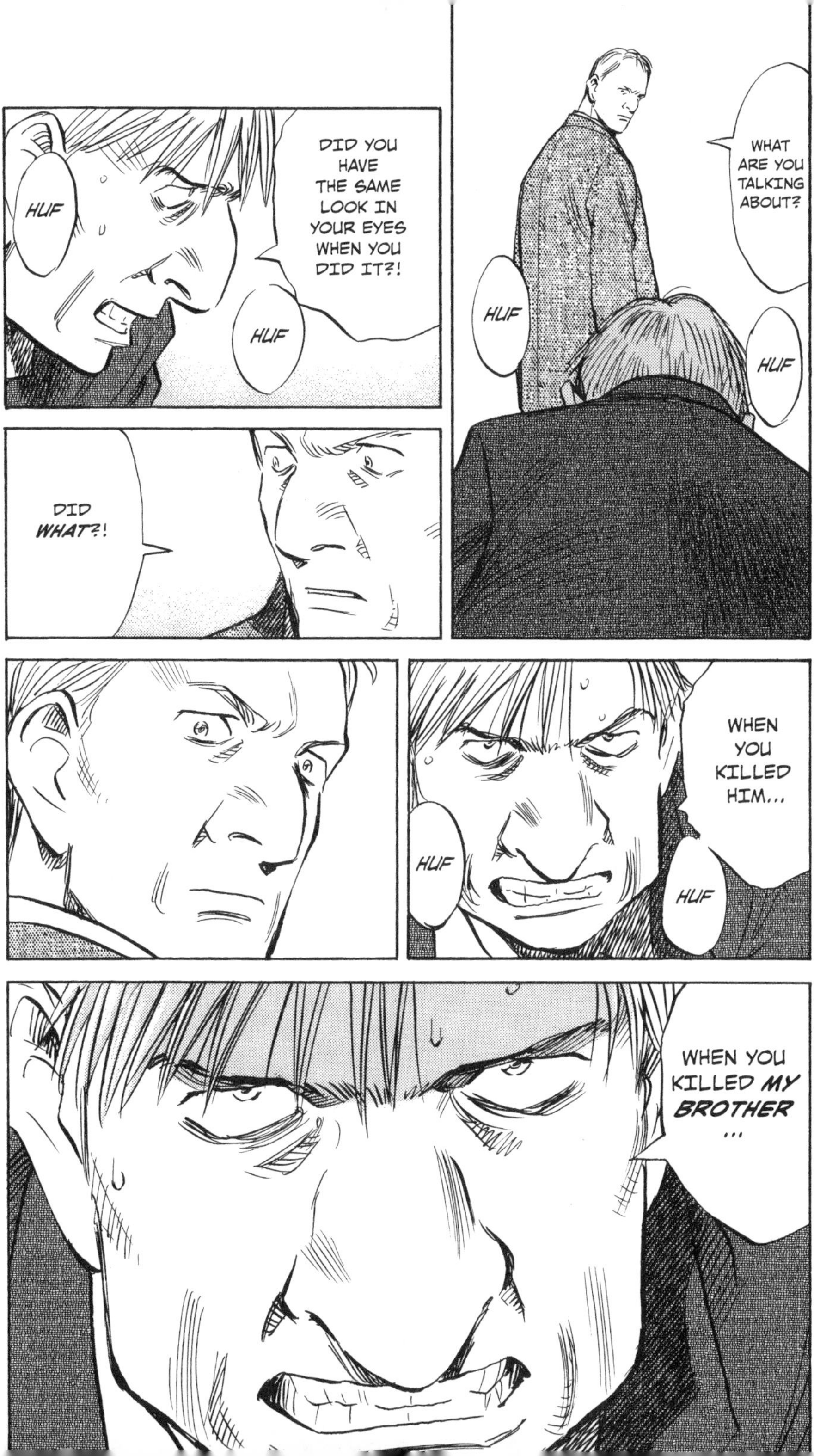
WHAT ARE YOU TALKING ABOUT?
HUF
HUF
DID YOU HAVE THE SAME LOOK IN YOUR EYES WHEN YOU DID IT?!
HUF
HUF
DID *WHAT*?!
WHEN YOU KILLED HIM...
HUF
HUF
WHEN YOU KILLED *MY BROTHER*...

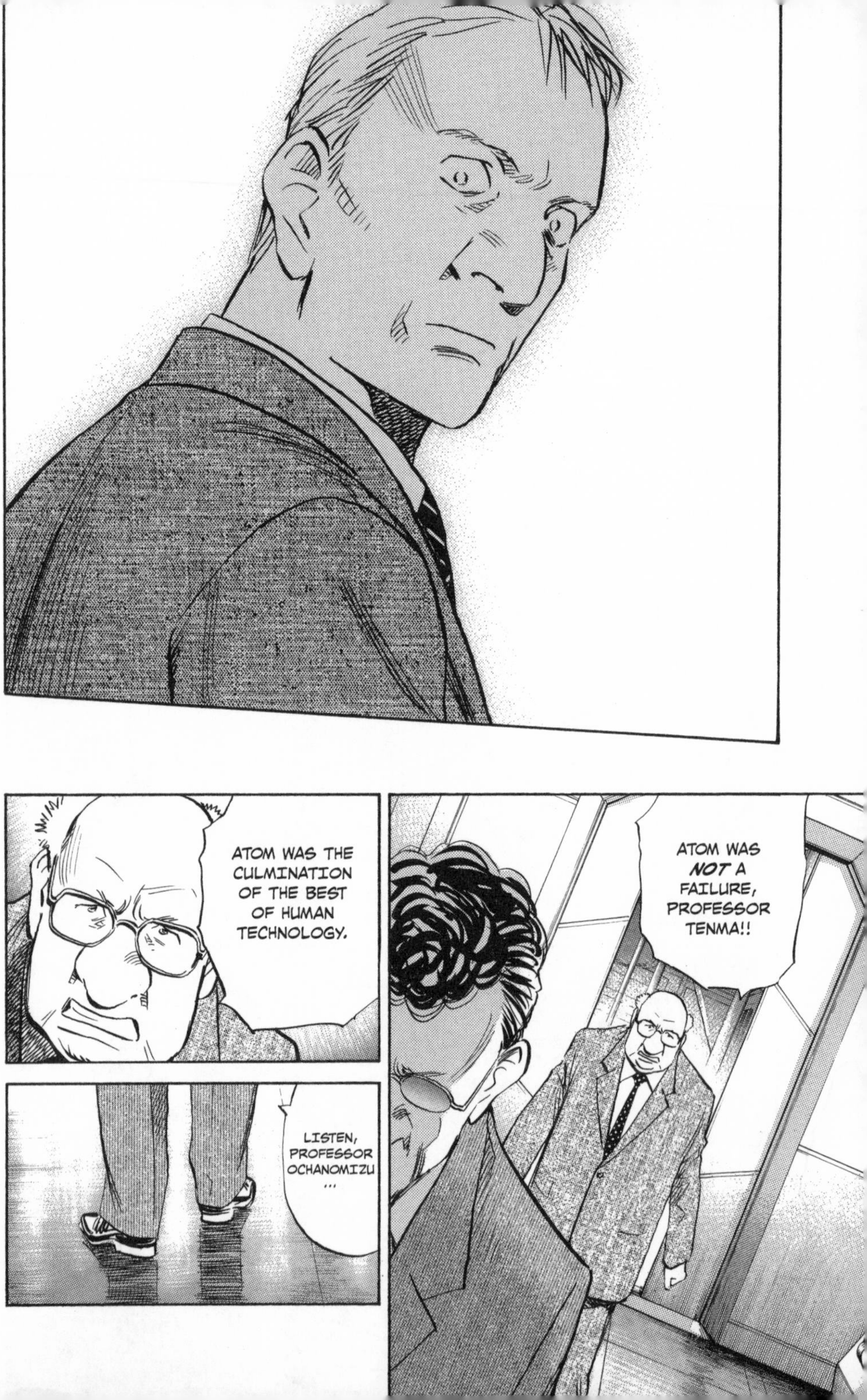
ATOM WAS NOT A FAILURE, PROFESSOR TENMA!!
ATOM WAS THE CULMINATION OF THE BEST OF HUMAN TECHNOLOGY.
LISTEN, PROFESSOR OCHANOMIZU ...

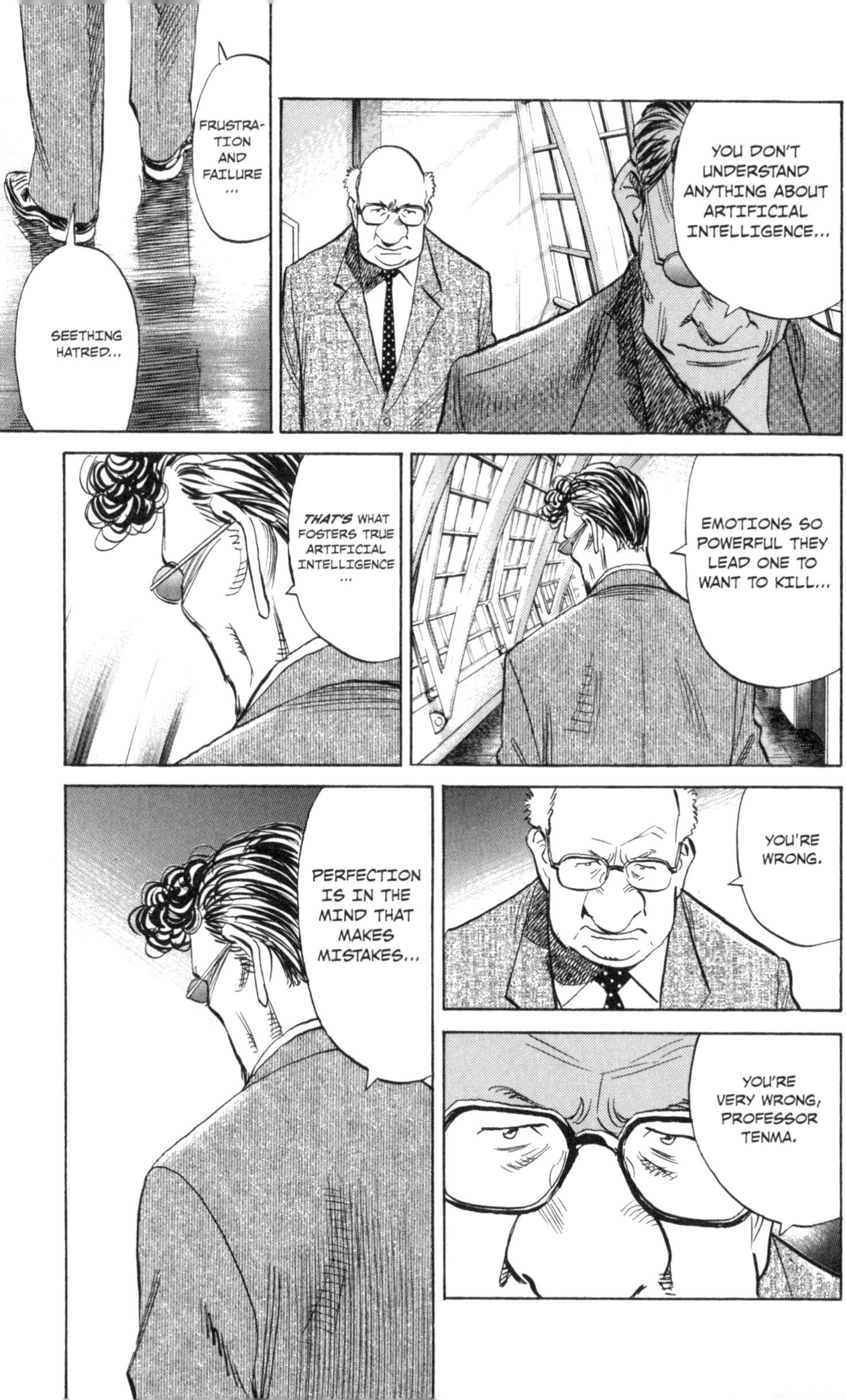
YOU DON'T UNDERSTAND ANYTHING ABOUT ARTIFICIAL INTELLIGENCE...
FRUSTRATION AND FAILURE ...
SEETHING HATRED...
EMOTIONS SO POWERFUL THEY LEAD ONE TO WANT TO KILL...
THAT'S WHAT FOSTERS TRUE ARTIFICIAL INTELLIGENCE ...
YOU'RE WRONG.
YOU'RE VERY WRONG, PROFESSOR TENMA.
PERFECTION IS IN THE MIND THAT MAKES MISTAKES...

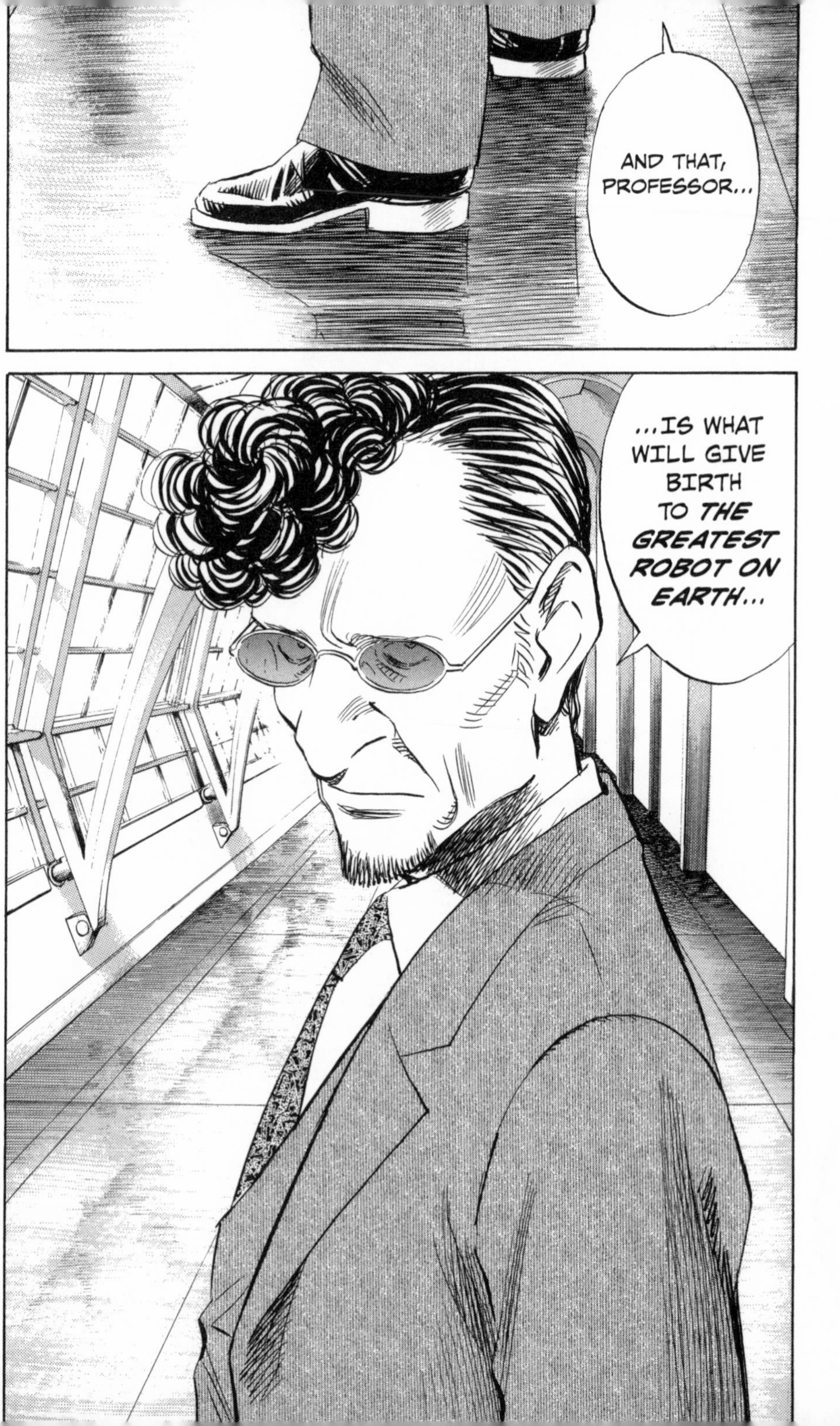
AND THAT, PROFESSOR...
...IS WHAT WILL GIVE BIRTH TO *THE GREATEST ROBOT ON EARTH...*

POSTSCRIPT

by Manga Artist Rieko Saibara

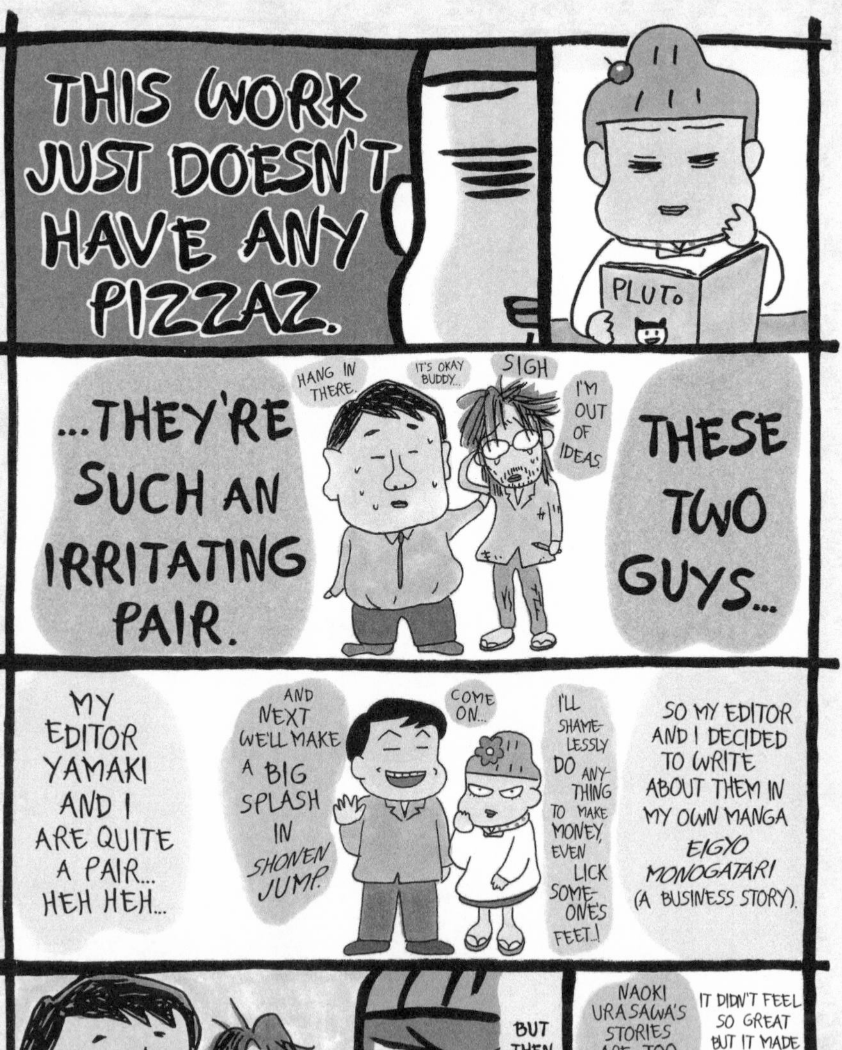

PLUTO
THIS WORK JUST DOESN'T HAVE ANY PIZZAZ.
THESE TWO GUYS...
I'M OUT OF IDEAS
SIGH
IT'S OKAY BUDDY...
HANG IN THERE.
...THEY'RE SUCH AN IRRITATING PAIR.
SO MY EDITOR AND I DECIDED TO WRITE ABOUT THEM IN MY OWN MANGA *EIGYO MONOGATARI* (A BUSINESS STORY).
I'LL SHAMELESSLY DO ANYTHING TO MAKE MONEY, EVEN LICK SOMEONE'S FEET..!
COME ON...
AND NEXT WE'LL MAKE A BIG SPLASH IN *SHONEN JUMP*.
MY EDITOR YAMAKI AND I ARE QUITE A PAIR... HEH HEH...
IT DIDN'T FEEL SO GREAT BUT IT MADE MONEY. AND NEVER IN MY WILDEST DREAMS DID I THINK WE'D EVER MEET FACE-TO-FACE.
NAOKI URASAWA'S STORIES ARE TOO **LONG**...
BUT THEN I HAD TO DO AN INTERVIEW.

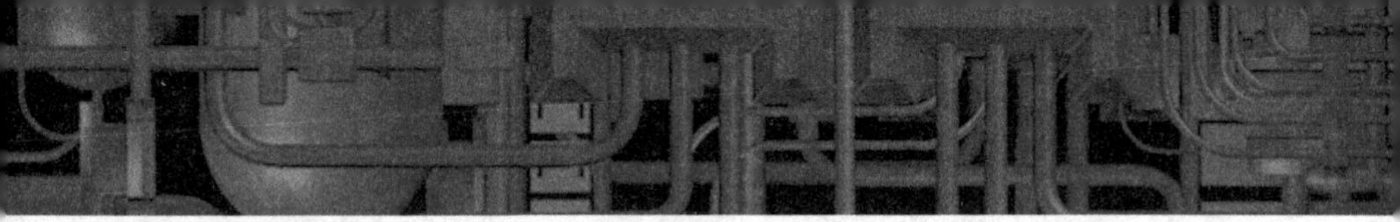

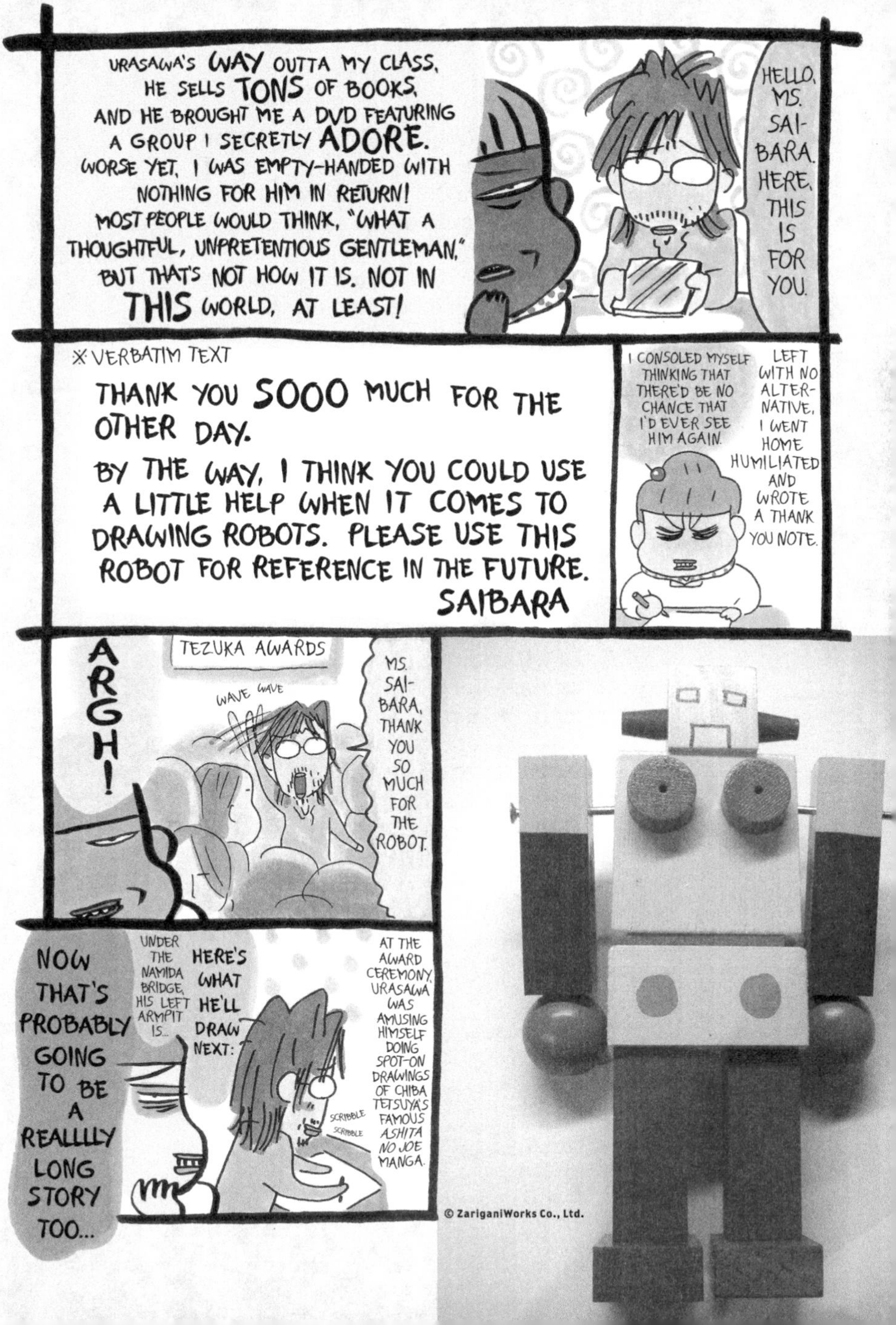
HELLO, MS. SAIBARA. HERE, THIS IS FOR YOU.
URASAWA'S WAY OUTTA MY CLASS, HE SELLS TONS OF BOOKS, AND HE BROUGHT ME A DVD FEATURING A GROUP I SECRETLY ADORE. WORSE YET, I WAS EMPTY-HANDED WITH NOTHING FOR HIM IN RETURN! MOST PEOPLE WOULD THINK, "WHAT A THOUGHTFUL, UNPRETENTIOUS GENTLEMAN," BUT THAT'S NOT HOW IT IS. NOT IN THIS WORLD, AT LEAST!
LEFT WITH NO ALTERNATIVE, I WENT HOME HUMILIATED AND WROTE A THANK YOU NOTE.
I CONSOLED MYSELF THINKING THAT THERE'D BE NO CHANCE THAT I'D EVER SEE HIM AGAIN.
※ VERBATIM TEXT
THANK YOU SOOO MUCH FOR THE OTHER DAY.
BY THE WAY, I THINK YOU COULD USE A LITTLE HELP WHEN IT COMES TO DRAWING ROBOTS. PLEASE USE THIS ROBOT FOR REFERENCE IN THE FUTURE.
SAIBARA
TEZUKA AWARDS
MS. SAIBARA, THANK YOU SO MUCH FOR THE ROBOT.
WAVE WAVE
ARGH!
AT THE AWARD CEREMONY, URASAWA WAS AMUSING HIMSELF DOING SPOT-ON DRAWINGS OF CHIBA TETSUYA'S FAMOUS ASHITA NO JOE MANGA.
HERE'S WHAT HE'LL DRAW NEXT:
UNDER THE NAMIDA BRIDGE, HIS LEFT ARMPIT IS...
SCRIBBLE SCRIBBLE
NOW THAT'S PROBABLY GOING TO BE A REALLLLY LONG STORY TOO...

The late Osamu Tezuka, a manga artist for whom I have the utmost respect, created the series *Astro Boy*. This timeless classic has been read by countless numbers of fans from when it was first created in the fifties to now. As a child, "The Greatest Robot on Earth" story arc from *Astro Boy* was the first manga I ever read that really moved me and inspired me to become a manga artist. With *Pluto* I've attempted to infuse that story with a fresh new spirit. I hope you enjoy it.

NAOKI URASAWA

Manga wouldn't exist without Osamu Tezuka. He is the Leonardo da Vinci, the Goethe, the Dostoevsky of the manga world. Naoki Urasawa and I have always felt that his achievements and work must not be allowed to fade away. Tezuka wrote that Atom, the main character of his most representative work *Astro Boy*, was born in 2003. This was the same year that we re-made "The Greatest Robot on Earth" story arc from the *Astro Boy* series. Who was Osamu Tezuka and what was his message? For those of you readers who are interested in *Pluto*, I highly recommend you read it alongside Tezuka's original work.

TAKASHI NAGASAKI

PLUTO: URASAWA × TEZUKA
VOLUME 4
VIZ SIGNATURE EDITION

BY Naoki Urasawa & Osamu Tezuka
CO-AUTHORED WITH Takashi Nagasaki
WITH THE COOPERATION OF Tezuka Productions

TRANSLATION Jared Cook & Frederik L. Schodt
TOUCH-UP & LETTERING James Gaubatz
COVER ART DIRECTION Kazuo Umino
LOGO & COVER DESIGN Mikiyo Kobayashi & Bay Bridge Studio
VIZ SIGNATURE EDITION DESIGNER Courtney Utt
EDITOR Andy Nakatani

Original Japanese edition published in 2007 by Shogakukan Inc., Tokyo.

Based on "Astro Boy" written by Osamu TEZUKA.

A CIP catalogue record for this book is available from the British Library.

Printed in the U.S.A.

Published by VIZ Media, LLC
P.O. Box 77010
San Francisco, CA 94107

10 9 8 7 6 5 4 3
First printing, July 2009
Third printing, February 2012

www.viz.com www.vizsignature.com

ASTRO BOY

Osamu Tezuka's iconic *Astro Boy* series was a truly groundbreaking work about a loveable boy robot that would pave the way for all manga and anime to follow. Tezuka created the manga in 1951 and in January of 1963 adapted it to become the first weekly animated TV series ever to be broadcast in Japan. In September of that same year, it became the first animated TV series from Japan to hit the airwaves in the United States. The series and its title character were originally known in Japan as *Tetsuwan Atom*, which translates to "mighty Atom" – or for the more literally minded, "iron-arm Atom" – but was released in the U.S. as *Astro Boy*. Decades later, in 2000, Dark Horse Comics brought the manga for the first time to English readers, also under the title *Astro Boy*.

Within the context of the story for this English edition of *Pluto: Urasawa × Tezuka*, the precocious boy robot will be referred to as "Atom" in the manner in which he has been known and loved in Japan for over fifty years. Elsewhere, such as in the end matter, the series will be referred to as *Astro Boy* as it has been known outside of Japan since 1963.